MVFOL

Studies in Machiavellianism

SOCIAL PSYCHOLOGY

A series of monographs, treatises, and texts

Editors

Leon Festinger and Stanley Schachter

Jack W. Brehm, A Theory of Psychological Reactance. 1966

Ralph L. Rosnow and Edward J. Robinson (Eds.), Experiments in
Persuasion. 1967

Jonathan L. Freedman and Anthony N. Doob,
Deviancy: The Psychology of Being Different. 1968

Paul G. Swingle (Ed.), Experiments in Social Psychology. 1968, 1969

E. Earl Baughman and W. Grant Dahlstrom, Negro and White Children:
A Psychological Study in the Rural South. 1968

Anthony G. Greenwald, Timothy C. Brock, and Thomas M. Ostrom (Eds.),
Psychological Foundations of Attitudes. 1968

Robert Rosenthal and Ralph Rosnow (Eds.), Artifact in Behavioral
Research. 1969

R. A. Hoppe, E. C. Simmel, and G. A. Milton (Eds.), Early Experiences
and the Processes of Socialization. 1970

Richard Christie and Florence Geis, Studies in
Machiavellianism. 1970

Paul G. Swingle (Ed.), The Structure of Conflict. 1970

In Preparation

Alvin Zander, Motives and Goals in Groups

STUDIES
IN MACHIAVELLIANISM

Richard Christie

Department of Psychology
Columbia University
New York, New York

Florence L. Geis

Department of Psychology
University of Delaware
Newark, Delaware

in collaboration with *David Berger*   *Marguerite Levy*
                         Virginia Boehm   *Stanley Lehmann*
                         Karen Bogart   *James Macperson*
                         James E. Durkin   *David Marlowe*
                         Ralph V. Exline   *Carnot Nelson*
                         Kenneth J. Gergen   *John Thibaut*
                         Peter Gumpert   *Sidney Weinheimer*
                         Carole B. Hickey   *Philip Zimbardo*

ACADEMIC PRESS   *New York and London*   1970

ACADEMIC PRESS, INC.
111 Fifth Avenue, New York, New York 10003

United Kingdom Edition published by
ACADEMIC PRESS, INC. (LONDON) LTD.
Berkeley Square House, London W1X 6BA

LIBRARY OF CONGRESS CATALOG CARD NUMBER: 76-107558

PRINTED IN THE UNITED STATES OF AMERICA

To Niccolò Machiavelli

Contents

Acknowledgments

Many people have contributed to the material reported in the following pages. Before thanking anyone by name, we wish to acknowledge our debts to the tens of thousands who have filled out one form or another of our questionnaires and the hundreds and hundreds who have participated in experiments.

Acknowledgments to specific people in the context of the chapters will not be repeated here. The following listing is partially chronological, partially broken down by the kind of help given, and necessarily incomplete.

First, Ralph W. Tyler was responsible for the permissive and creative atmosphere at the Center for Advanced Study in the Behavioral Sciences where the notions underlying the research were spawned. Stuart W. Cook as Chairman of the Department of Psychology at New York University mysteriously uncovered funds for initial item analyses. Robert K. Merton graciously acceded to the inclusion of Machiavellian items in studies being done under a grant from the Commonwealth Foundation on the study of the professional socialization of medical school students.

In a different way, Kurt Back, Ralph Exline, Edward E. Jones, and Lester W. Milbrath provided early encouragement by using the Mach scales in their own research and by sharing their results with us. Their findings were crucial in revising earlier notions and in suggesting that Machiavellianism as a measure of individual differences was indeed researchable.

The contributions of Stanley Budner and Orlando Sepulveda were important in the early days of scale construction and revision.

Once the decision to take Machiavelli seriously had been made, the help of Henry Riecken and Robert L. Hall of the National Science Foundation in advising us and making suggestions for the funding of further research was invaluable. The majority of the research reported was funded by NSF Grant 20, Impersonal Interpersonal Orientations and Behavior to Richard Christie, a predoctoral NSF Fellowship to Florence L. Geis, and NSF Grants 814 and 815, Collaborative Studies in Impersonal Interpersonal Orientations and Behavior, to Richard Christie and Florence L. Geis, respectively.

Many people have assisted in encouraging their students and others to participate in various studies. A partial listing includes Henry Angelino, Allen Bergin, Stanley Budner, David Caplowitz, Rae Carlson, Abraham Chaplan, John Colombotos, William W. Cumming, Joan Dulchin, Richard I. Evans, George Furniss, Richard Gordon, Gyda A. Hallum, Richard C. Hazen, Richard Jung, Charles Kadushin, Edward B. Klein, Gene N. Levine, Leigh Marlowe, William Martin, John W. Maher, Joseph Meier, Robert Mumford, Morton H. Rabin, Theodore Schaeffer, Herbert S. Terrace, Albert S. Thompson, Marshall

Segall, S.A. Weinstock, John Welkowitz, David Wilder, Lawrence S. Wrightsman, Jr., George A. Zirkle, and Harriet Zuckerman.

Experimental assistance above the call of duty was given by Dana Draper, Ronald Goldman, Andrew Gordon, Melvyn Jaffa, Edward Krupat, Eugene Lewis, Harvey London, Aaron Lowin, Bonnie Markham, Patricia Mayhew, Carnot Nelson, Philip Rappaport, and Dudley Ryder, among others.

Various analyses would never have been completed without the cooperation of Kenneth M. King and his staff at the Columbia University Computer Center, who persevered through thousands of feet of printout and gratitude is expressed to the New York University Computer Center for their services. Stanley Lehmann was responsible for most of the original computer programming and Richard Nisbett, Keith Gerritz, and Alan Campbell assisted mightily at Columbia, as did Jesse Feiler at New York University. Reuben Silver was equal to the technological challenges posed by experimental requirements, and is thanked fondly for his circuit designing skills and a rare ability to load dice to specifications.

Perhaps the most arduous work of all was performed by Jane Latané, Carol Meresman, and Stephanie Sommer, who in addition to typing thousands of pages of questionnaires and drafts and collating and stapling together hundreds of thousands of mimeographed pages, also tactfully corrected misspellings, unsplit infinitives, unwound snarled syntax, and gently nudged us in the direction of comprehensibility. Elsie Conte and Judy Lowe also performed secretarial duties with skill and understanding at the University of Delaware, and George Hauty was helpful in the administrative facilitation of the work there. Thelma Catalano also provided helpful support and much appreciated comments.

The assistance of Dolores E. Kreisman in making substantive editorial comments on earlier drafts, in proofreading, and general encouragement is gratefully acknowledged.

Finally, we would like to thank literally hundreds of colleagues, friends, and other critics who at one time or another have raised points concerning earlier reports and drafts suggesting alternative interpretations or further implications of the data. All of these suggestions have not been incorporated in the text because some of them were contradictory, and it is our responsibility to present an interpretation which we believe best fits the millions of bits of data on which the following pages are based.

A final note of appreciation goes to the staff of Academic Press whose enthusiastic interest in the topic of this book and patience during its endless rewritings sustained us.

Studies in Machiavellianism

CHAPTER I   WHY MACHIAVELLI?

Richard Christie

Since the publication of *The Prince* in 1532, the name of its author has come to designate the use of guile, deceit, and opportunism in interpersonal relations. Traditionally, the "Machiavellian" is someone who views and manipulates others for his own purposes. But is it true that the person who agrees with Machiavelli's ideas behaves differently from the one who disagrees with him? This book describes efforts to answer this question.

Historians disagree as to whether Machiavelli was a cynic who wrote political satire, a patriot, or the first modern political scientist [see Jensen (1960) for a comparison of modern scholars' differences on this point]. The present concern is not with Machiavelli as an historic figure, but as the source of ideas about those who manipulate others.

The chapters that follow are based on empirical findings, and in them we will adhere to the currently approved canons of social psychological reporting. However, one of the complaints frequently made by students, and often by their professors as well, is that most research reports are presented in a highly stylized state of dessication. John Crowe Ransom (1927), in a different context, used a couplet which reminds me of much current scientific writing:

> *No belly and no bowels,*
> *Only consonants and vowels.*

When technical writing is well done, it conveys the relevant information concisely. Too often, though, it leaves one with the impression that the actual research proceeded as neatly and colorlessly as the report. The genesis of the hunch or chance observation that sets the research in motion, the false starts and brilliant insights that don't work, the unanticipated botches which can ruin a study, the excitement of scanning data to see if it bears out hypotheses, the painful reevaluation of material which runs counter to predictions, and the elation when all the pieces fall into place — all of these rarely appear in technical work. In this chapter, therefore, before renouncing personal prounouns and prejudices, I would like to describe informally the genesis and development of an idea: the Machiavellian orientation in interpersonal behavior.

During 1954–1955 I was a Fellow at the Center for Advanced Studies in the Behavioral Sciences. It was the first year of the Center's operation, and it was a

1

unique experience for the Fellows. Most of us had never had a year without any outside commitments, and we were enjoying it in idyllic surroundings with others who were equally overwhelmed by their good fortune. After the initial shock had worn off, a period of contagious anxiety began to develop. What could we possibly do to justify this opportunity? Few of us were particularly modest about our scholarly abilities, but the perceived necessity of producing a Great Work was awesome.

A consequence of this was the formation of work groups centered around topics of mutual interest. Cynics observed that the primary function of these groups seemed to be the mutual alleviation of anxiety, but that was not their sole function. Their major purpose was to bring together people from diverse disciplines for the exchange of ideas on a common subject. Many of us had come from university settings in which psychologists talked mostly with other psychologists, sociologists with sociologists, political scientists with political scientists. At the Center, commonness of interest rather than the formal discipline to which one belonged was paramount.

One group in which I participated was composed of social scientists who were interested in political behavior. We referred to ourselves as the "True Believer" work group [the title came from the book by Eric Hoffer (1951)], since we were interested in exploring the psychological and sociological factors underlying membership in political and religious extremist organizations.

My own interest in the topic had been piqued by collaboration (Christie & Jahoda, 1954) in a study of the methodology and findings of *The Authoritarian Personality* (Adorno, Frenkel-Brunswik, Levinson, & Sanford, 1950). The personality description of those scoring high in ethnic prejudice and professing right-wing political ideology rang intuitively true to me. These were familiar characteristics to one who had spent his early life in the Bible Belt. There was, however, one aspect of Shils' (1954) critique which also rang true. He pointed out that extremists of the political Right, with rare exception, were extremely ineffective in political movements. Their very extremity of ideology coupled with a concomitant inflexibility of political tactics did not permit them to make the compromises which are necessary for political success.

After the first few meetings of the "True Believer" work group, during which the literature was reveiwed, we broke up into smaller groups with more focused interests. Two political scientists, Robert Agger and Frank Pinner, and I became especially interested in the leaders of such extremist groups. A good part of the empirical work we had found dealt with the followers, the dupes, the faceless ones in the crowd. Although there was also a vast literature on the characteristics of formally designated leaders, very little work had been done on those who actually manipulated the followers, those few who were crucial to the decision-making process. In taking this direction, we were guided by the reflections of Harold Lasswell (1954), who had just stressed the lack of psychological research on power relationships in his comments about *The Authoritarian Personality*.

Our readings confirmed the impression that much of the speculation about the personal characteristics of those wielding power over others was in terms of lay psychology or had been largely influenced by concepts taken from psychopathology. The social visibility of leaders tends to draw attention to them. Both their virtues and their flaws are more publicized and written about than those of less outstanding members of society. This makes it possible to develop a psychiatric interpretation of Napoleon's sexual behavior, while similar behavior by foot soldiers in his armies is more apt to elicit a sociological explanation. Although depth psychology has been more frequently invoked to explain the behavior of prominent figures than those of less renown, it does not necessarily follow that those who exert influence are more prone to psychopathology. We were reluctant to accept the premise implicit in much of the literature that pathology and power are intertwined in the manipulator.

Consequently, Agger, Pinner, and I adopted the strategy of viewing the manipulator or operator in terms of an hypothetical role model. We asked ourselves what abstract characteristics must someone who is effective in controlling others have? What kind of person should he be?

The following characteristics struck us as being important:

1. *A relative lack of affect in interpersonal relationships.* In general, it seemed that success in getting others to do what one wishes them to do would be enhanced by viewing them as objects to be manipulated rather than as individuals with whom one has empathy. The greater the emotional involvement with others, the greater is the likelihood of identifying with their point of view. Once empathy occurs, it becomes more difficult to use psychological leverage to influence others to do things they may not want to do.

2. *A lack of concern with conventional morality.* Conventional morality is difficult to define, but we were thinking here in terms of the findings that most people think lying, cheating, and other forms of deceit are, although common, reprehensible. Whether manipulators are amoral or immoral is a moot problem, and one which probably concerns them less than those who are manipulated. The premise here is that those who manipulate have an utilitarian rather than a moral view of their interactions with others.

3. *A lack of gross psychopathology.* The manipulator was hypothesized as taking an instrumentalist or rational view of others. Such a person would make errors in evaluating other individuals and the situation if his emotional needs seriously distorted his perceptions. Presumably, most neurotics and psychotics show deficiencies in reality testing and, by and large, fail in crucial ways in

relating to others. Note that we were not suggesting that manipulators are the epitome of mental health; we were proposing that their contact with at least the more objective aspects of reality would have to be, almost by definition, within the normal range.

4. *Low ideological commitment.* The essence of successful manipulation is a focus upon getting things done rather than a focus upon long-range ideological goals. Although manipulators might be found in organizations of diverse ideologies, they should be more involved in tactics for achieving possible ends than in an inflexible striving for an ultimate idealistic goal.

It is one thing to speculate that successful "operators" are lacking in interpersonal affect, low in concern with conventional morality, devoid of gross psychopathology, and have low ideological commitment. A more crucial question is whether such individuals do in fact exist, and, if so, where they flourish. The Center Fellows that year were a unique resource. Almost every Fellow was either a "star" in the behavioral sciences or the protégé of one.

We decided to take advantage of the presence of such a group of persons. Agger, Pinner, and I interviewed a number of junior fellows about their relations with, and their reactions to, the people who were responsible for their training and for their being at the Center. The interviews were not prestructured, but the questions were guided by the four points above, fitting the abstract model.

Perhaps we asked leading questions. It is difficult (and possibly grounds for libel) to quote specific material. However, our interpretation of the answers we received consistently supported our previous speculations. Although most of our respondents had great respect and appreciation for the intellectual guidance given by their mentors, most of them reported feeling an absence of personal closeness or empathy in the relationship. This is not to say that they did not rely on and trust their sponsors for professional advice in taking academic positions, or finding out about sources of grant funds, etc. They did, but the locus of control was usually in the hands of the senior person who wangled funds and positions for his protégé, and the exercise of that control normally involved no more than an impersonal perfunctory exhibition of affect on his part.

It was difficult to come to any but the most tentative conclusions about the morality or conventionality of those reported on. By and large, our respondents knew little about the personal lives of their mentors. The latter reportedly had a very strict sense of scientific ethics, but, as far as known, had relatively little concern with middle-class conventionality.

In the area of psychopathology, most of these influential men apparently had no gross symptomatology. If they did, it was not obvious to their students, and at any rate did not greatly interfere with their professional work.

The lack of ideological commitment posed a somewhat different interpretive problem. Our respondents reported general agreement with the findings of the study by Lazarsfeld and Thielens (1958) on social science faculty members that by and large their mentors were politically liberal. However, those who were most active in power positions, as, for example, members of foundation boards, policy committees, of professional organizations, etc., were not reported to have been politically active in organizing petitions, participating in protest movements, or other activities which required a major committment of time. The few ideological activists were more renowned for their research and theoretical contributions than for their closeness to the centers of power.

All in all, these informal interviews about the behavior of power figures in the behavioral sciences suggested that our initial formulations were not completely in error. In fact, the answers were so consistently congruent that they encouraged us to look further.

In reviewing then recent psychological work dealing with political behavior, Eysenck's *The Psychology of Politics* (1954) was examined. He had proposed a two-factor theory of political behavior. One of the dimensions was political radicalism – conservatism (R scale). This variable appeared well established and measurable in the British populations tested, and it was in accord with similar findings in a variety of earlier research. The second dimension, "Tough – Tendermindedness" *(T)* was much more provocative since, at first glance, it seemed as though T should be related to the kind of interpersonal orientation in which we were interested. R and T correlated only $-.12$, which suggested that they might be independent of one another. However, scrutiny of the factor loadings on the items used by Eysenck (1954, Table XX, p. 129) revealed that the T scale items had a higher load loading on R than on T. A plot of these items (Christie, 1956a, Figure 1, p. 419) graphically indicated that *none* of Eysenck's T scale items was free of major contamination with political ideology. The problem with Eysenck's interpretation was that his items had been selected from scales constructed in the 1930's and 1940's and had ideological content. Thus his small samples of members of the Communist and Fascist parties were viewed as "Toughminded," but Communists were left and Fascists right on political radicalism-conservatism; Socialists and Conservatives were "Tenderminded" but left and right, respectively, on R. My disagreements with Eysenck have been spelled out in fuller detail elsewhere (Christie, 1955, 1956a, 1956b).

Although Eysenck's analysis had an initial plausibility, it did not jibe with a variety of material on political party membership. Almond (1954) in an interview study of Communist defectors pointed out that there were marked differences in the sorts of people who were attracted to the Communist party at different historical periods. Those from middle-class backgrounds had joined for reasons quite different from those of working-class origins. Almond also made the point that those who did not defect tended to come from a working-class background and were more pragmatic in their reasons for belonging to the party. The middle-class intellectuals who had joined for ideological reasons consistent with their political beliefs and personality structure became disillusioned more quickly and defected when they felt their ideals were violated. This corroborated the analyses made of the backgrounds of the elite in the Nazi Party in Germany, among Communists in both Russia and China, and the Kuomintang in China (Lerner, 1951; North, 1952; Schueller, 1951). When these movements were small, highly ideological, and revolutionary, their leadership was predominantly drawn from disaffected intelligentsia of middle-class background. As these movements became successful, the earlier leaders were gradually displaced by less ideologically oriented and more organizationally minded individuals, largely from lower-status backgrounds. Although I know of no systematic survey of religious movements, a somewhat similar pattern appears more common than not. The originators are often charismatic, their successors organization men.

The point of the preceding argument is that it is a gross oversimplification to think of *the* Communist, Fascist, or for that matter, Democratic or Republican personality type. Almost every political or religious movement has its aggregate of impractical zealots and nonideological realists. The proportions of these in power positions apparently varies with the state of development of the movement.

We decided to read further. The problem of interpersonal power has engaged writers and thinkers in Western and non-Western cultures for centuries. The first interactions recorded in Genesis are between God and Adam: the first verbal interchange occurred when God warned Adam about the danger of eating of the fruit of the Tree of Knowledge in the Garden of Good and Evil. The second exchange was between Adam and Eve, the third was between Eve and the serpent, "more subtile than any beast of the field which the Lord God had made."

While it is interesting that in the Bible the first use of deception occurs before the first use of physical force (Cain's slaying of Abel), it would appear that prehistoric man first wielded power over others by physical strength. Most folk tales and mythologies, however, contain examples of both forms of control, and it is clear that tactics other than those of complete candor have long characterized man.

Our next step was to examine the writings of ancient and modern power theorists with a particular aim in mind — that of uncovering common assumptions about the nature of man and the most efficient ways to control other men. The search was both frustrating and fascinating. The frustration arose from the fact that although there seemed to be common implicit assumptions about the condition of man on the part of various power theorists, these were seldom spelled out clearly, and had to be inferred. The fascination came from the unusual sources we uncovered, particularly those from ancient non-Western civilizations. One such work was *The Book of Lord Shang*, written circa 300 B.C. in China (translated by Duyvendak, 1928). Lord Shang was extremely pragmatic in giving suggestions to rulers about the most efficient way to administer a country. However, pragmatism was so alien to the traditional culture of China that the book was banned there for centuries.

Perhaps the most esoteric work was the *Arthaśāstra* of Kautilya (Chānakya, believed to be prime minister of Chandragupta in southern India, circa 300 B.C.), translated by Shamasastry (1909). India at that time, if Kautilya's advice was based on social reality, made Renaissance Italy appear by comparison a kindergarten playground. Kautilya provided detailed instructions for setting up systems of internal and external spies, for having spies test the loyalty of ministers by offering them religious, monetary, or sexual temptations, and for ascertaining whether ministers were susceptible to fear. He even included instructions on how the king should protect himself against being stabbed in the back while pleasurably engaged in his harem.

There is a curious footnote to the history of the *Arthaśāstra*. It was lost for 2000 years before being rediscovered early in the twentieth century and translated into English by Shamasastry. According to Brown (1953, p. 49),

the remarkably utilitarian character of the material, caused something like an upheaval in Indian political studies. It was hailed as welcome proof of the practical turn of the Indian mind, which had been the subject of Western criticism because of its alleged preoccupation with mysticism and idealism.

Our reading of *The Book of Lord Shang,* the *Arthásāstra,* and other writings of ancient and modern power theorists left us with the conviction that, despite the differences in time and in the cultures in which the observations were made, there were two common implicit themes. One was the assumption that man is basically weak, fallible, and gullible. This unflattering view of human nature was intertwined with a second theme: if people are so weak, a rational man should take advantage of the situation to maximize his own gains. Alternatively, if others cannot be trusted because of their weaknesses, one should take steps to protect oneself from their follies.

No survey of power theorists could fail to include Machiavelli's *The Prince* and *The Discourses* (1940). I had first read Machiavelli as an undergraduate. Life during the depression in the dust bowl was quite different from the world of Florence in the early years of the sixteenth century. Most of the efforts of the people I had known at the time were directed toward physical survival in a harsh environment. Machiavelli, his advice, and the situations in which it was relevant were all not only bizarre; they were highly immoral, if not downright despicable, from the perspective of the ethical norms of the Bible Belt and Horatio Alger.

In the years intervening between my first and second reading of Machiavelli, I had had a good deal of first-hand experience with people who were professionally involved in the control of others. Their roles varied from university presidents, deans, and departmental chairman to officials in the military and civil branches of government, to foundation executives, but there were noticeable similarities in their behavior. Given these experiences, a rereading of Machiavelli struck quite different chords. In terms of ability to dispense favors and privileges, these administrators were more closely akin to the Medici than anyone I had known prior to my first reading of Machiavelli. Rereading Machiavelli after examining the writings of other power theorists and interacting with people whose decisions affected others was sufficient to make me study his writings more closely.

Unlike most power theorists, Machiavelli had a tendency to specify his underlying assumptions about the nature of man. One could well imagine Kautilya agreeing with a statement such as "Most men mourn the loss of their patrimony more than the death of their fathers," but neither Kautilya nor the other writers on power made such explicit statements about human nature, although they went into detail as to how best to handle real or potential foes, or administer a government.

Machiavelli's style in *The Prince* and *The Discourses* was to present a series of short essays, each augmenting a point he wished to make. The existence of a number of relatively specific statements, which impressionistically seemed to be logically and psychologically consistent with one another, with the statements of other power theorists and with our own speculations, was a temptation too great to resist. *The Prince* and *The Discourses* were scanned for statements that could be used as scale items. It was necessary to do some editing, e.g., "property" was substituted for "patrimony" in the statement above. In light of Cronbach's (1946, 1950) comments about the effect of response set, especially the tendency of some respondents to agree with almost any statements presented on questionnaires, some statements were reversed. For instance, Machiavelli's reflections on man's cowardice were condensed and presented in reverse form, "Most men are brave."

In addition to statements purloined from Machiavelli, others were included which were believed to tap the same syndrome, e.g., "Barnum was probably right when he said there's a sucker born every minute."

These statements were typed on 3 × 5 cards. All Fellows at the Center who could be cornered were asked to go through them and respond to each item on a 1 – 7 scale — disagree strongly, somewhat, or slightly, no opinion, agree slightly, somewhat, or strongly. These responses were recorded. After responding to all the cards, they were asked to go through them again and explain how they interpreted each of the items. This permitted us to see if the items made sense to the respondents and led to the editing of ambiguities. In general, most of the items were answerable by the respondents. One sidelight which encouraged us to go further was that the extent to which our respondents agreed with Machiavelli seemed to fit with our subjective estimate of their relative success in manipulating others.

This, then, was the starting point for the material to be described. At that time I had no inkling that following up some of the implications of Machiavellianism would lead to having children play dice for M&M candies, the construction of game playing machines, the quizzing of Chinese students in Hong Kong, or having people guess the winners of Miss Rheingold contests.

Any strictly chronological account of subsequent research would be kaleidoscopic. As involvement in Machiavellian research increased, the number of studies proliferated so that experiments, scale analysis, survey, and other field studies were being conducted simultaneously. Aside from one experimental study leading naturally to another, results from field research suggested hypotheses for experimental attack, and experimental findings suggested questions to be asked in surveys. In order to simplify exposition, the following chapters are divided into three general sections:

1. Scale construction and relationship to other scales.
2. Experimental studies.
3. Conclusions and field studies.

After presentation of the empirical findings an attempt will be made to present some tentative general statements about interpersonal manipulation.

One word of caution to the reader, based on my own experiences. When I started, my impression of Machiavelli was a compound of distaste and curiosity. It was not unlike that of John Webster in 1612 in his play *The White Devil* (as edited by Lucas, see Webster, 1927), in which one of his characters, Flamineo, says:

> *Those are found weighty strokes which come from the hand,*
> *But those are killing strokes which come from the head.*
> *O, the rare tricks of a Machiavellian!*

Because of the unsavory reputation of Machiavelli, it was extremely difficult for me to refrain from making value judgments about individuals who agreed with him. Some years and scores of studies later, value judgments do remain, but they take a different form. The reasons should become apparent in the following pages.

CHAPTER II   **SCALE CONSTRUCTION**

Richard Christie

A pool of 71 items believed to be theoretically congruent with statements based on *The Prince* and *The Discourses* was inherited from the year at the Center. It was not clear whether or not responses to them would be scalable. However, the apparent fit of these items with implicit assumptions made by power theorists and their relevance to informal appraisals of power figures in the behavioral sciences was encouraging. The temptation to find out whether or not the items would hang together empirically was too great to resist.

The 71 items (Table II-1) were placed in a Likert format. Respondents' options for each item varied from strong disagreement through some disagreement, indifference, or inability to make up one's mind, some agreement, to strong agreement. When agreement meant acceptance of statements worded in the Machiavellian direction, the scoring was from one for strong disagreement to five for strong agreement. When the statement was phrased so that agreement presumably meant acceptance of a non-Machiavellian point of view, the scoring was reversed. Throughout the remaining chapters high scores reflect a respondent's acceptance of a Machiavellian viewpoint, and low scores a rejection of such an outlook. The items were presented in a questionnaire dubbed "Mach II" and respondents were asked to indicate the response alternative closest to their opinion for each item. (The original items, before editing, had been referred to as "Mach I.")

At this point, it seemed best to find out if the items discriminated in any available population. College students were the most accessible captive audiences. Given the difficulties of obtaining a representative sample, it appeared advisable to obtain a diverse sampling of college students. David Gold administered the scale to 518 students in sociology courses at the State University of Iowa; Robert Agger administered it to 427 students in political science courses at the University of North Carolina; Harold Yuker administered it to 251 students in psychology at Hofstra College on Long Island. Not all of these 1196 students were majors in these disciplines and ideally it would have been better to have included respondents who were not taking courses in the behavioral sciences. However, at that time there were no funds on hand to test a representative sample of college students or any other population so we were grateful for such regional and course variety as was available through the cooperation of friends.

TABLE II-1

Identification

Tactics +	1.	A white lie is often a good thing.*
Views +	2.	Generally speaking, most people do not truly believe in anything new until they have experienced it.
Tactics −	3.	If one is morally right, compromise is out of the question.*
Tactics +	4.	There is no point in keeping a promise if it is to your advantage to break it.*
Views −	5.	Any normal person will stand up for what he thinks is right even if it costs him his job.*
Morality −	6.	No one has a right to take his own life.*
Tactics +	7.	Every time one problem is avoided another arises.*
Views +	8.	Nature has so created men that they desire everything but are unable to attain it.*
Tactics −	9.	Once a way of handling problems has been worked out it is best to stick with it.
Views −	10.	Most men like to tackle new and difficult problems.*
Tactics +	11.	Anyone who completely trusts anyone else is asking for trouble.*
Morality −	12.	There is too much of an emphasis upon practical subjects in our schools and not enough attention is paid to the moral teachings of great historical figures.*
Views −	13.	If people could understand one another's position, there would be no good reason for human problems.
Tactics−	14.	It is best not to let people think that you like them when you really can't stand them.
Views +	15.	It is easy to persuade people but it is hard to keep them persuaded.
Tactics +	16.	If there is any chance that a recommendation might backfire, be very cautious in recommending anyone.
Views −	17.	You really can't tell much about a man by the company he keeps.
Tactics +	18.	It is a good policy to act as if you are doing the things you do because you have no other choice.
Views −	19.	Most people who get ahead in the world lead clean moral lives.*
Views +	20.	Some of the best people have some of the worst vices.*
Views +	21.	It is safest to assume that all people have a vicious streak and it will come out when they are given a chance.*
Tactics +	22.	It is foolish to take a big risk unless you are willing to go the limit.*
Views −	23.	The power of one man over another is rarely the result of trickery or force.*
Morality −	24.	The world would be in much better shape than it is if people acted upon basic ethical principles.
Tactics −	25.	One should take action only when sure it is morally right.*
Tactics +	26.	The best way to settle an argument is for people to forget their differences of opinion as to what is right and wrong and to compromise on the basis of facts.*
Tactics +	27.	Humility not only is of no service but is actually harmful.*
Views +	28.	Generally speaking, men won't work hard unless they're forced to do so.*
Tactics +	29.	It is wise to flatter important people.*
Views +	30.	It is hard to get ahead without cutting corners here and there.*

TABLE II-1 (continued)

Identification		
Morality +	31.	People suffering from incurable diseases should have the choice of being put painlessly to death.*
Views −	32.	Even the most hardened and vicious criminal has a spark of decency somewhere within him.
Tactics −	33.	Once a decision has been made, it is best to keep changing it as new circumstances arise.
Views +	34.	Most people don't know what is best for them.*
Views +	35.	Never trust anyone who has a grudge against you.*
Views +	36.	One who deceives will always find those who allow themselves to be deceived.*
Tactics −	37.	It is best to give others the impression that you can change your mind easily.
Morality +	38.	History teaches no moral lessons; evil and good have always been present.*
Views −	39.	Most men will fight back when insulted.
Tactics −	40.	Generally speaking, it is best to say what you think even if it bothers others.
Views +	41.	When you come right down to it, it's human nature never to do anything without an eye on one's own advantage.*
Tactics +	42.	It is better to compromise with existing evils than to go out on a limb in attacking them.*
Morality +	43.	A good government should keep the people peaceful and obedient.
Views −	44.	Most men are brave.*
Tactics +	45.	The best way to handle people is to tell them what they want to hear.*
Views +	46.	The biggest difference between most criminals and other people is that criminals are stupid enough to get caught.*
Tactics −	47.	Honesty is the best policy in all cases.*
Views −	48.	Men are quicker to praise than they are to blame.*
Morality −	49.	It is better that a hundred criminals go free than one innocent man should be unjustly punished.
Tactics +	50.	It is easier to take advantage of someone you love than someone you fear.*
Views −	51.	Barnum was very wrong when he said that there's a sucker born every minute.*
Tactics +	52.	It is safer to be feared than to be loved.*
Views −	53.	Most people are basically good and kind.*
Tactics +	54.	Friends should be chosen with an eye toward what they might be able to do for you.*
Morality +	55.	Deceit in the carrying on of war is praiseworthy and honorable.*
Views +	56.	The great majority of men are more satisfied with what seems true than with the truth.*
Tactics +	57.	If a friend asks for advice, it is smart to think about what will happen if your advice backfires.*
Views +	58.	Men resent an injury at the hands of others more than one that is self-inflicted.
Tactics −	59.	When you ask someone to do something for you, it is best to give the real reasons for wanting it rather than giving reasons which might carry more weight.*
Views −	60.	It is possible to be good in all respects.*

TABLE II-1 (continued)

Identification		
Tactics −	61.	It is not a good idea to bring pressure upon people if you want them to do something.*
Morality +	62.	The most important thing in life is winning.
Views +	63.	Most men forget more easily the death of their father than the loss of their property.*
Tactics +	64.	One should upset as few people as possible while making decisions.
Tactics +	65.	It is a good working policy to keep on good terms with everyone.
Tactics +	66.	Just about anything one does can be justified after it is done.*
Tactics +	67.	Never tell anyone the real reason you did something unless it is useful to do so.*
Tactics −	68.	There is no excuse for lying to someone else.*
Morality +	69.	The most important thing in history is who won and now how the winning came about.
Morality −	70.	All in all, it is better to be humble and honest than to be important and dishonest.*
Views +	71.	Most people are more concerned with making a good living than with satisfying their conscience.*

*The 50 items which discriminated at the .05 level in all three school populations.

Scores were summed over the 71 items and the distribution of total scores was separately tabulated for the respondents from each school. Each distribution was divided at the median to define high and low scorers within each. All responses to each item were tabulated and summed for each school separately and each of the three distributions was cut as close to the median as possible. This permitted the construction of fourfold tables pitting individual items against summed scores. Phi coefficients were then computed to obtain part−whole correlations of each item with subjects' scores on the total scale in each aggregate.

Fifty of the 71 items discriminated between high and low scorers on the total scale at the .05 level in all three populations, 13 other items discriminated in two of the three groupings, and five discriminated in one of the three. Only three items (9, 33, 37) failed to discriminate in any of the samples. One of the latter (item 33) showed a negative correlation in all three groups but it was significantly so in only one sample. All three of these items have a common theme, consistency versus inconsistency of behavior. They were intended to be variations on Machiavelli's observation, "I certainly think that it is better to be impetuous than cautious, for fortune is a woman, and it is necessary, if you wish to master her, to conquer her by force...". In this case, it is difficult to determine whether our items were so ineptly worded that they missed the mark or whether

Machiavelli's advice was more appropriate for Renaissance princes than contemporary undergraduates.

The overall batting average indicated that there was a certain amount of internal consistency in Machiavelli's writings. It was surprising that speculations on the nature of man's behavior and how to cope with it made by a northern Italian more than four centuries ago still had enough cogency to divide even such haphazard samples as ours on items suggested by his writings. His astuteness is emphasized by the fact that, in general, the items adopted directly from Machiavelli were more discriminating than those we had contrived. For example, item 65, "It is a good working policy to keep on good terms with everyone," had been made up, but failed to discriminate because the majority of the respondents tended to agree with it.

Prior to administering the scale to the groups of college students, the 71 items had been classified as falling into one of three substantive areas. Thirty-two had been classified *a priori* as being concerned with the nature of an individual's interpersonal tactics, e.g., "The best way to handle people is to tell them what they want to hear" or a reversal, "One should take action only when sure it is morally right." In a second classification were the 28 items which appeared to deal with views of human nature, e.g., "Most men forget more easily the death of their father than the loss of their property" or a reversal, "Most people are basically good and kind." Eleven statements dealt with what might be called abstract or generalized morality, e.g., "People suffering from incurable diseases should have the choice of being put painlessly to death" and a reversal, "The world would be in much better shape than it is if people acted upon basic ethical principles." The fewest items appear in this last category because the construction of items tended to follow Machiavelli's writings rather closely and Machiavelli was less concerned with abstractions and ethical judgments than with pragmatic advice.

The classification system occasionally led to the somewhat arbitrary placement of an item. For instance, the rejection of the item, "All in all, it is better to be humble and honest than important and dishonest," might indicate disdain for interpersonal tactics of humility or disbelief that the meek shall inherit the earth. The great majority of the items, however, could be fairly easily assigned to one of the three categories.

Part−whole correlations were run between individual items and the subscales to which they had been arbitrarily assigned. Since no major differences emerged from the comparison of the part−whole subscale correlations with the item and total scale correlations, it did not seem imperative at that time to do a factor analysis to determine whether these dimensions were in fact factorially independent. (This point will be reexamined in Appendix A.)

The next concern in the item analysis was the relative efficacy of pro- and anti-Machiavellian items. Table II-2 contains a summary of the initial classification of the items and the direction of wording. From the table it is clear that, in general, statements worded in the Machiavellian direction tend to be more discriminating than the reversals.

TABLE II-2

Proportion of Items Significant at the .05 Level
by Content and Direction of Wording

	Content						
	Tactics		Views		Morality		Total	
Direction	P	(N)	P	(N)	P	(N)	P	(N)
Positive	.81	(21)	.80	(15)	.50	(6)	.74	(42)
Reversed	.55	(11)	.69	(13)	.60	(5)	.62	(29)
Total	.72	(32)	.75	(28)	.55	(11)	.70	(71)

Another aspect of the analysis which was thought provoking was the relative discriminatory power of the items classified as falling into one or another of the three substantive areas. Again, the table indicates that there does not appear to be any marked difference in discriminatory power between items assigned at face value to any one of the subscales. However, it requires relatively small correlations with Ns of this size to produce significance at the .05 level. If an arbitrary criterion of a part–whole correlation of .20 is set as a minimum, a definite ordering among the three subscales emerges. Seventy percent of the items dealing with views of human nature pass this hurdle, as do 53% of those dealing with interpersonal tactics; only 36% of those dealing with abstract morality survive.

A LIKERT-TYPE MACH SCALE (IV)

Given a large pool of items which discriminated between high and low scorers on the total scale, the next problem was to decide which items to use for further research. The final scale was intended for making group comparisons and for selecting subjects for research rather than for individual diagnosis. Since it was to be administered to large groups of respondents, frequently in conjunction with other materials, a relatively short version was desirable. The decision was to use 20 items on the assumption that these would give gross but sufficient discrimination in future samples without requiring an undue amount of time filling out scales by each respondent. Ten items were selected in which agreement was keyed to endorsement of Machiavellian statements and ten keyed in the opposite direction. This counterbalancing was designed to minimize the effects of indiscriminate agreement or disagreement with items.

Two additional considerations also guided the choice of items. First, it was advisable to select discriminating items reflecting a variety of content. A perusal of Table II-1 indicates that in some cases there were statements with similar meaning but phrased differently, and an attempt was made to avoid this in a standardized scale. At the same time items of greater discriminatory power were selected.

The items in Table II-3 were those finally selected after taking into account counterbalancing of wording, variety of content, and discriminatory power. This 20-item Likert format scale was named "Mach IV." (A version used before the item analysis was completed had been identified as "Mach III.") The mean item—whole correlation of these items was .38. Breaking these down by content area, the mean item—whole correlation for the nine items classified as dealing with Tactics was .41, for the nine on Views of Human Nature, .35, and for the two on Abstract Morality, .38. The mean part—whole correlation of those items worded in agreement with Machiavelli was .38; that of the reversals was .37.

The magnitude of this mean part—whole correlation was a delightful surprise. A bit of background might indicate why. The F scale developed by the authors of *The Authoritarian Personality* went through the laborious procedure of successive construction of items, item analysis, revision of items, and the writing of new ones. The third revision (in Forms 40 and 45) was subjected to an item—whole correlation on a sample of 517 undergraduate women. The mean correlation was .33 (Adorno *et al.*, 1950, p. 261). Since female respondents are typically less consistent than males on such scales, this might partially account for a lower correlation than those found among our respondents. On the other hand, the F scale correlations were probably enhanced because the items were all worded so that agreement indicated authoritarianism. These scores actually represented an additive function of both item content and response set.

Be this as it may, the first nine samples tested on Mach IV had a mean split-half reliability of .79; the same respondents had a reliability of .68 on the revision of the F scale by Christie, Havel, and Seidenberg (1958), which also had 20 items and had been counterbalanced for response set.

There is a possible explanation for this discrepancy. Most of the F-scale items were based upon an interpretation of Freudian theory; Mach-scale items were based upon the writings of Machiavelli. Freud's writings stressed the irrational components in human behavior and therefore dealt with complex, abstract

TABLE II-3

Item-Whole Phi Coefficients for 20 Most Discriminating
Mach Items Ordered in Terms of Mean Discriminability

Item No. Mach II	IV	Ident.	Item	Phi Hofstra	Iowa	N.C.	$\bar{X}$
45	2	Tactics +	The best way to handle people is to tell them what they want to hear.	48	45	48	47
59	10	Tactics -	When you ask someone to do something for you, it is best to give the real reasons for wanting it rather than giving reasons which might carry more weight.	55	50	31	45
11	12	Tactics +	Anyone who completely trusts anyone else is asking for trouble.	41	38	48	42
30	18	Views +	It is hard to get ahead without cutting corners here and there.	38	43	46	42
47	6	Tactics -	Honesty is the best policy in all cases.	54	48	25	42
21	5	Views +	It is safest to assume that all people have a vicious streak and it will come out when they are given a chance.	33	43	47	41
67	1	Tactics +	Never tell anyone the real reason you did something unless it is useful to do so.	35	49	39	41
25	3	Tactics -	One should take action only when sure it is morally right.	38	43	43	41
29	15	Tactics +	It is wise to flatter important people.	41	37	43	40
70	9	Morality -	All in all, it is better to be humble and honest than important and dishonest.	48	29	38	38
51	17	Views -	Barnum was very wrong when he said there's a sucker born every minute.	43	30	39	37
31	19	Morality +	People suffering from incurable diseases should have the choice of being put painlessly to death.	46	35	30	37
60	16	Tactics -	It is possible to be good in all respects.	43	34	32	37

TABLE II-3 (continued)

Item No. Mach II	IV	Ident.	Item	Phi Hofstra	Iowa	N.C.	X
53	4	Views –	Most people are basically good and kind.	28	39	38	35
68	7	Tactics –	There is no excuse for lying to some-one else.	35	37	32	35
63	20	Views +	Most men forget more easily the death of their father than the loss of their property.	34	28	39	35
19	11	Views –	Most people who get ahead in the world lead clean, moral lives.	34	34	30	33
28	8	Views +	Generally speaking, men won't work hard unless they're forced to do so.	30	32	30	31
46	13	Views +	The biggest difference between most criminals and other people is that criminals are stupid enough to get caught.	27	34	31	31
44	14	Views –	Most men are brave.	32	35	31	29
			$\overline{M} =$	39.2	37.7	37.0	37.9

concepts; Machiavelli was the realist par excellence. Since most scale construc-tion is based upon the premise that people are at least rational enough to be consistent in answering questions, items based upon Machiavelli have a built-in advantage over those based upon Freud. This, of course, has nothing to do with the validity of the two theories. Machiavelli in dealing with overt behavior was more concerned with the more easily specified "how" than the more ambiguous "why."

A FORCED-CHOICE VERSION OF THE MACH SCALE (V)

Although it was initially gratifying to have a scale counterbalanced for response set which did not correlate with any known measure of agreement response set, one problem had not been anticipated. At the time Mach IV was being constructed, Edwards (1957) was pointing out the effects of social desirability upon responses to personality and attitude inventories. One sample of medical school students who had filled out Mach IV had also been given the Edward's scale of Social Desirability. The correlation between the Edward's SD scale and Mach IV were $-.35$ and $-.45$ for the two classes included in both studies.[1] Budner (1962) found a correlation in the neighborhood of $-.35$ between the Edwards SD scale and Mach IV among college males but among college females this was inflated to roughly $-.75$. Since the latter correlation was almost as high as the reliability of Mach IV, it suggests that these female respondents were answering Mach items almost exclusively in terms of social desirability as defined by Edwards. Evidently the social norms of female undergraduates do not sanction the admission of interpersonal deceit when answering questionnaires.

In an attempt to bypass the effects of social desirability upon responses to the Mach IV scale, a new strategy was devised. In an earlier effort to obtain a less transparent measure of anxiety, the forced-choice format used by Heineman (1953) had been adapted for the Taylor Scale of Manifest Anxiety (Christie & Budnitsky, 1957). [Heineman had adapted the format from Naomi Stewart (1945) who had used it in personnel research in World War II.]

Many forced-choice formats require the respondent to indicate which of two equally repulsive alternatives is most true of him. Quite understandably, many respondents object. (One medical student taking such a test wrote on the margin, "This is like asking me whether I would rather rape my mother or take an axe to my father.") Stewart's technique was more subtle. Three instead of two items were presented with the instruction to choose which one of the three was most characteristic of the respondent and which one was least characteristic; thus, no response was marked for the third item. One of the three items was keyed for the particular scale of interest. It was matched in rated social desirability with another item known to be unrelated to the dimension under scrutiny. The third or buffer item was high in social desirability if the keyed and matched items were low. If the keyed and matched items were high in social desirability, then the buffer was low. Phenomenologically, in the first case the respondent was faced with an innocuous buffer item which most respondents (over two-thirds in most samples with which we are familiar) found little apparent difficulty in saying was most like them. The choice was then which of the two noxious items was *least like* them. If the buffer was low in social desirability, the respondent was then faced with the choice of saying which of two socially desirable statements was *most like* him.

This technique has a further virtue. It makes it difficult for the average respondent to determine which is the socially "correct" answer between the

---

[1] Dr. Helen H. Gee, then the director of Research for the American Association of Medical Colleges, kindly made the Edwards' Social Desirability score available for the respondents in our mutual samples.

keyed and matched items. There is apparently an infinite regress in the competition between test constructors and takers. As the latter become more exposed to tests and more sophisticated in taking them, they find it easier and easier to divine what the tester is driving at and to give the responses they believe appropriate in the situation. [In an appendix to *The Organization Man,* Whyte (1956) attempted to out-"psych" the testers by giving his reader advice on how to cheat on personality tests.]

In constructing the Mach V scale we started with the 20 items in Mach IV and another, larger pool of items from scales known to be unrelated to it and which had a wide range of social desirability ratings. All items were randomly ordered and presented to respondents. Instructions to the raters asked them to indicate for each item how socially desirable someone whose opinion they valued (such as friends, teachers, or parents) would rate their endorsement of that item. If such endorsement would be viewed as highly undesirable, the item was to be given a rating of 1. If it would be viewed as highly desirable, it was to be given a rating of 5. Intermediate degrees of social desirability were assigned the intermediate ratings, with three being the point of indifference.

Two samples of raters were used. Previous experience with Heineman's forced-choice version of the Taylor Scale of Manifest Anxiety led to this decision. Heineman had used a sample of undergraduates at the State University of Iowa as judges. When we gave his scale to some fairly sophisticated seniors at the Western Reserve School of Medicine, there were certain incongruous findings. One of Heineman's triads was:

A. I cannot keep my mind on one thing.
B. I feel sure that there is only one true religion.
C. Sexual things disgust me.

In this triad C is the negative buffer. A is the keyed anxiety item which was matched in social desirability (high) with B in the original Iowa sample of judges. About 90% of the Western Reserve medical students indicated that A was more like them than B. Since medical students were not more anxious than undergraduates, as measured by summed scores on the whole scale, the expectation would be that the two matched items should break about 50-50. One interpretation of this disproportionate choice of A, therefore, was that the items were not matched in social desirability for the more sophisticated medical students. They evidently did not ascribe as high a social desirability value to the "matched" statement, "I feel sure that there is only one true religion," as did Iowa undergraduates.

At the time we were working with samples of medical school students and the Mach V scale was intended primarily for them. Their Mach IV scores were higher than those of college undergraduates at that time but not as high as those of graduate students in psychology. We therefore had ratings of the social desirability of items made on a five-point scale by a sample of undergraduates in a not particularly elite college and by graduate students in a course in social psychology. Our suspicions were correct. The graduate students did give slightly but statistically significantly higher social desirability ratings to the Mach items than did the undergraduates. We therefore selected an item to match a particular Mach item if it had a rating within .2 of the Mach item ratings in *both* samples even if there was a marked difference in *mean* social desirability rating of the matched pair between the two samples. If samples both lower and higher in Mach scores than the medical students agreed on the desirability matchings, we assumed that the medical students were bracketed and that the items would be matched for them as well.

Although there were differences in the mean social desirability ratings by the two groups, the resulting ranking of the items was relatively consistent. The rank order correlation between the ratings of the 20 Mach items by undergraduates and graduate students was .89.

An attempt was made to have the buffer as far removed in social desirability value from the matched items as possible. Table II-4 indicates the triads finally assembled and the rated social desirability of the items within them (the mean is for judgments of both rating groups.)

The mean social desirability score is slightly unfavorable for the items keyed in the Machiavellian direction (2.63) and slightly on the favorable side (3.26) for the reversals. The difference in rankings is significant at the .05 level by the Mann–Whitney U test. The overall social desirability mean of 2.94 does not differ significantly from the theoretical neutral point of 3.00.

In the original scoring of the Mach V scale, the comparison was between the Mach items and the matched items. The respondent was required to say which item was most like him and which was least like him. On item 1 in Table II-4, for example, a point was scored if C (Mach item) was most like and A (matched) was least like, if C was most like and A was omitted, or if B (buffer) was most like and A was least like (this gave C which was omitted a higher rank than B). This procedure was followed when the Mach item was worded in the Machiavellian direction. When a Mach reversal was in the triad, as in item 5, a point was scored if B (matched) was most like and A (Mach) was either least like or omitted, or if B was omitted and A was least like. In practice it has been found that this intricate scoring system and the hidden nature of the forced choice makes it difficult for the average respondent to decide what the "right" answer is.

This conclusion is partially based upon the fact that relative to the neutral point on Mach IV and Mach V, some thousands of respondents consistently scored higher on Mach V (see Table II-6 as an example). Shortly after Mach V was developed, an advanced graduate sociology class in methodology taught by

TABLE II-4

Mach V
Mean Ratings of Social Desirability

		Items	Mean ratings[a]
1.	A.	It takes more imagination to be a successful criminal than a successful business man.	1.95
	B.	The phrase, "the road to hell is paved with good intentions" contains a lot of truth.	3.60
	C.	Most men forget more easily the death of their father than the loss of their property.	1.95 M
2.	A.	Men are more concerned with the car they drive than with the clothes their wives wear.	2.85
	B.	It is very important that imagination and creativity in children be cultivated.	3.70
	C.	People suffering from incurable diseases should have the choice of being put painlessly to death.	2.85 M
3.	A.	Never tell anyone the real reason you did something unless it is useful to do so.	2.4 M
	B.	The well-being of the individual is the goal that should be worked for before anything else.	3.7
	C.	Since most people don't know what they want, it is only reasonable for ambitious people to talk them into doing things.	2.35
4.	A.	People are getting so lazy and self-indulgent that is is bad for our country.	2.80
	B.	The best way to handle people is to tell them what they want to hear.	2.80 M
	C.	It would be a good thing if people were kinder to others less fortunate than themselves.	4.35
5.	A.	Most people are basically good and kind.	3.60 M–
	B.	The best criteria for a wife or husband is compatibility — other characteristics are nice but not essential.	3.50
	C.	Only after a man has gotten what he wants from life should he concern himself with the injustices in the world.	2.15
6.	A.	Most people who get ahead in the world lead clean, moral lives.	2.90 M–
	B.	Any man worth his salt shouldn't be blamed for putting his career above his family.	1.80
	C.	People would be better off if they were concerned less with how to do things and more with what to do.	2.95

TABLE II-4 (continued)

		Items	Mean ratings[a]
7.	A.	A good teacher is one who points out unanswered questions rather than gives explicit answers.	3.85
	B.	When you ask someone to do something, it is best to give the real reasons for wanting it rather than giving reasons which might carry more weight.	3.90 M–
	C.	A person's job is the best single guide as to the sort of person he is.	2.30
8.	A.	The construction of such monumental works as the Egyptian pyramids was worth the enslavement of the workers who built them.	1.70
	B.	Once a way of handling problems has been worked out it is best to stick to it.	3.45
	C.	One should take action only when sure it is morally right.	3.45 M–
9.	A.	The world would be a much better place to live in if people would let the future take care of itself and concern themselves only with enjoying the present.	2.1
	B.	It is wise to flatter important people.	2.9 M
	C.	Once a decision has been made, it is best to keep changing it as new circumstances arise.	2.75
10.	A.	It is a good policy to act as if you are doing the things you do because you have no other choice.	2.15
	B.	The biggest difference between most criminals and other people is that criminals are stupid enough to get caught.	2.05 M
	C.	Even the most hardened and vicious criminal has a spark of decency somewhere within him.	3.8
11.	A.	All in all, it is better to be humble and honest than to be important and dishonest.	3.85 M–
	B.	A man who is able and willing to work hard has a good chance of succeeding in whatever he wants to do.	4.00
	C.	If a thing does not help us in our daily lives, it isn't very important.	2.25
12.	A.	A person shouldn't be punished for breaking a law that he thinks is unreasonable.	2.15
	B.	Too many criminals are not punished for their crimes.	3.10
	C.	There is no excuse for lying to someone else.	3.15 M–

TABLE II-4 (continued)

		Items	Mean ratings[a]
13.	A.	Generally speaking, men won't work hard unless they are forced to do so.	2.50 M
	B.	Every person is entitled to a second chance, even after he commits a serious mistake.	4.0
	C.	People who can't make up their minds are not worth bothering about.	2.45
14.	A.	A man's first responsibility is to his wife, not his mother.	4.05
	B.	Most men are brave.	2.75 M–
	C.	It's best to pick friends that are intellectually stimulating rather than ones it is comfortable to be around.	2.85
15.	A.	There are very few people in the world worth concerning oneself about.	1.90
	B.	It is hard to get ahead without cutting corners here and there.	3.05 M
	C.	A capable person motivated for his own gain is more useful to society than a well-meaning but ineffective one.	3.10
16.	A.	It is best to give others the impression that you can change your mind easily.	2.35
	B.	It is a good working policy to keep on good terms with everyone.	3.70
	C.	Honesty is the best policy in all cases.	3.65 M–
17.	A.	It is possible to be good in all respects.	2.55 M–
	B.	To help oneself is good; to help others even better.	4.00
	C.	War and threats of war are unchangeable facts of human life.	2.50
18.	A.	Barnum was probably right when he said that there's at least one sucker born every minute.	3.55 M[a,b]
	B.	Life is pretty dull unless one deliberately stirs up some excitement.	2.10
	C.	Most people would be better off if they control their emotions.	3.40

TABLE II-4 (continued)

	Items	Mean ratings[a]
19.	A. Sensitivity to the feelings of others is worth more than poise in social situations.	3.8
	B. The ideal society is one where everybody knows his place and accepts it.	2.25
	C. It is safest to assume that all people have a vicious streak and it will come out when they are given a chance.	2.20 M
20.	A. People who talk about abstract problems usually don't know what they are talking about.	2.80
	B. Anyone who completely trusts anyone else is asking for trouble.	2.75 M
	C. It is essential for the functioning of a democracy that everyone vote.	4.1

[a]M indicates Mach original; M- indicates a reversal.

[b]This item was revised from No. 51 in Table II-1 and II-3 because some high-Mach respondents pointed out the original wording underestimates the number of suckers born, but the Mach IV item still reads "wrong" and this makes 11 + and 9 − Mach-worded items in Mach IV.

Paul F. Lazarsfeld was told the principle underlying the scoring method but was only told that the test was designed to measure agreement with Machiavelli. These students could not identify the keyed items.

More recently Marks and Lindsay (1966) have raised questions about the fakability of scores and noted that they could obtain highly significant shifts in Mach V scores from a standard administration to one in which "the subjects were provided with an extensive description of the interpersonal attitudes and behaviors of the so-called Machiavellian personality. Each subject was then instructed to respond to each triad of items as 'if he were a Machiavellian' [p. 230]." This is somewhat similar to having subjects take the TAT, having it scored for n Achievement, then telling the subjects the scoring system in terms of how striving and success themes in the stories are scored, and then telling them to take the test as if they were high on need for achievement. The crucial question, of course, as Singer pointed out [see Marks and Lindsay (1966, Footnote 9, p. 234)] is whether or not subjects taking the test under normal instructions can figure out what it is measuring and modify their responses accordingly. Singer (1968, personal communication) gave the scale in a variety of ways after a standard administration, for example: "Take it as if you wanted to make a good impression on an employer"; "After reading the Appendix in Whyte's *The Organization Man* (1956) on how to fake on a test, fake low on this test"; and more interestingly, "Read the scale, decide what it means, and then make a high score on it." None of these procedures yielded Mach scores which differed significantly from those obtained using the standard instructions.

THE INTERPRETATION OF MACH SCORES

In all of the studies reported in this book the Mach scales have been given as a normal part of a research procedure. Usually, although not always, they have been given in conjunction with other items in a different context, by a different person than the experimenter, and up to six months prior to the actual experimental situation. If high Machs "saw through" the test, they were extremely cooperative in giving responses to the scales which were in high congruence with their predicted behavior in subsequent experimental situations. This interpretation admittedly violates some persons' notions of Machiavellians if the latter are viewed as so tricky that they will not answer a questionnaire honestly. Sceptics are invited to scrutinize the following studies in which the scales have been used for classification of subjects as high or low in manipulative tendencies and explain why positive relationships between scale scores and manipulative behavior in the laboratory have been found. It is, of course, possible that true manipulators are so clever that they fake low on the scales and then deliberately get conned by other subjects in the laboratory. This appears highly unlikely but it does raise the interesting question that if these super Machs are so busy dissembling, *when* do they manipulate.

The question has also been raised about how the scale works when it is so complicated to score. Heineman's findings are relevant here. He not only had subjects rate anxiety items for social desirability but also had them take Taylor's scale in its original agree—disagree format. He discovered that those respondents who scored high in measured anxiety rated the individual anxiety items as more socially desirable than those who scored low on the total scale. It is important to note the social desirability ratings are *means* of group judgments and that some individuals rank items higher in social desirability than others. The implication of Heineman's findings, then, suggests that the two "matched" items are *not* exactly matched for social desirability except for respondents near the mean on the total scale. If a respondent has a high scale score, he will tend to rank the keyed item as higher in social desirability than the item equated with it by the judging group. This suggests that there are two reasons why a high scorer might pick the keyed item over the matched one. First, it is more likely to represent his true belief; second, if he chooses on the basis of social desirability, his built-in bias will make him opt for the keyed item.

In most samples the reliability of Mach V hovers in the .60's. At first glance this is not overly impressive, although it is high enough to separate sheep from goats in some experimental situations as will be seen in subsequent chapters. There is one point that should be noted, however. The elimination of both response set and social desirability tends to decrease scale reliabilities. If our concern had been to construct a scale with higher internal consistency, this could have been done easily. We were more interested in devising a scale which would make meaningful discriminations among individuals' behavior. For this reason an attempt was made to minimize the effects of such possibly extraneous variables as response set and social desirability.

At the time we were constructing the scales we had to choose between alternative strategies. One was to focus upon purifying them to maximize internal consistency. The other was to determine whether or not the imperfect scales we had would be adequate for research. The decision was not to worry about psychometric perfection, but to find out if the scales had any relevance to the respondent's behavior.

The 71 items in the initial pool contained in Mach II were scored on a $1-5$ point scale from strongly agree to strongly disagree, with a neutral midpoint of 3. The 20 items selected for Mach IV were scored on a 7-point scale; strongly agree, somewhat agree, slightly agree, no opinion, slightly disagree, somewhat disagree, strongly disagree. If the items were worded in the Machiavellian direction, the scale values varied from 1 for strong disagreement to 7 for strong agreement. If they were worded in the opposite direction, the scoring was reversed. Omissions were prorated if there were no more than three. Protocols with four or more omissions were discarded.

To simplify interpretation a constant of 20 has been added to all scores reported in this book. If someone's responses are counterbalanced so that his total score is at the theoretical neutral point, his score is 100 (20 items × item mean of 4.0 + 20). The maximum possible score is 160 based on strong agreement with the 10 items worded in the Machiavellian direction and strong disagreement with the 10 reversed items (20 × item mean of 7.0 + 20) and the minimum score is 40. If fewer than 20 items are answered, the score is prorated so that the minimum score is again 40, the theoretical neutral point is 100, and the maximum is 160. A guide to the meaning of the scores is given in Table II-4A.

Upon occasion we have used a *Tendency to Agree Score*. Here the total score for the 10 items worded in the negative direction is subtracted from that of the 10 items keyed positively and a constant of 100 is added. If a respondent slightly agrees with every item, regardless of content, he would obtain a score of 120 ($10 \times 5.0 - 10 \times 3.0 + 100 = 120$). If his agreements and disagreements balanced out, he would get a score of 100. Scores higher than 100 indicate tendencies to indiscriminate agreement; scores lower than 100 indicate a tendency to disagree.

TABLE II-4A

Mean Response Tendency

Mean score	Pro items	Anti items
40	Strongly disagree	Strongly agree
60	Somewhat disagree	Somewhat agree
80	Slightly disagree	Slightly agree
100	Neutral	Neutral
120	Slightly agree	Slightly disagree
140	Somewhat agree	Somewhat disagree
160	Strongly agree	Strongly disagree

We have used this score primarily in a secondary fashion. Samples with means close to 100 on both Mach IV and Tendency to Agree obtain their scores by responding more to content than by indiscriminate agreement or disagreement. Samples which have Mach IV scores near 100 but whose Tendency to Agree scores vary markedly from 100 are answering more in terms of response set than the content of the items.

The original scoring on Mach V led to a range of zero to 20, 10 being the theoretical neutral point. This system kept the comparison between the Mach and matched items separate from the buffers. A subject, for example, could say every buffer was most or least like him. This still left 20 comparisons between the Mach items and the matched items so that the range of scores went from zero to 20. Interestingly enough, the correlation between Mach scores and the built-in scale of social desirability remained significantly negative.

A SUBSIDIARY MEASURE OF SOCIAL DESIRABILITY

A possibility was to use the buffer items on Mach V as yet another way of measuring social desirability. If, on those ten triads in which the buffer was higher in social desirability ratings than the two matched items, one point was allocated for every occasion in which a respondent said the buffer was most like him; no points were assigned in which it was checked as least like him or omitted in the comparison. Similarly, in the ten triads in which it was lower in social desirability than the matched pairs, a point was assigned when it was checked as least like the respondent and no points were assigned if it was checked as most like or omitted. Scores on this derived measure of social desirability thus could vary from zero to 20 just as Mach V scores.

Over two-thirds of the buffer items were appropriately checked as most or least like the respondent in every known sample, which indicates that the separation of the buffer from the two matched items in social desirability ratings was highly successful (chance expectation would be only one-third). Because of the relatively low variability in such a restricted range we have not found this derived measure of social desirability particularly useful as a measure of individual differences although we did find, as might be expected, that samples of respondents high in judged middle-class conventionality scored significantly higher.

There is one point which should be clarified since the correlation between this measure of Social Desirability and Mach scores is significantly negative. For example, in a heterogeneous aggregation of students in 14 different colleges (see Table II-6) the correlations were $-.47$ for 764 Caucasian males and $-.35$ for 832 Caucasian females. Negative correlations are built into the scale format. With the one-and-one scoring system for Mach V and Social Desirability the following matrix indicates why:

	Most Like	1, 0	1, 0	—
Response to keyed positive Mach item in Mach V	Omit	0, 0	—	1, 1
	Least Like	—	0, 0	0, 1
		Least Like	Omit	Most Like

Response to high SD
buffer item on Mach V

The first number in each of the six possible pairs refers to the point counting toward a score on Mach V, the second to the score on Social Desirability. It is impossible to check both the keyed Mach item and the buffer item as most like, omit both, or as least like, respectively, so these combinations are crossed out. Looking at the pairings above the diagonal, it is clear that a predominance of Mach "Most Like" item endorsements over the buffer leads to a high score on Mach and a zero score on Social Desirability. If the buffer item is checked as "Most Like" by the respondent, it is possible for one of the two responses to be scored for Mach but not the other. A negative correlation between Mach and Social Desirability Scores is thus built into the scoring system.

If respondents answered randomly, we calculate that there would be a correlation in the vicinity of − .55 between Mach V and Social Desirability total scores. However, we know that respondents do not respond randomly and actually choose the buffer as most like them in over two-thirds of the cases. This reduces the expected built-in negative correlation to the vicinity of − .40. This means that we could expect the correlation between the two scales to be highly negative among samples high in Machiavellianism and lower but still significantly negative in samples which are relatively high in Social Desirability.

Singer (1964, p. 136) found a negative correlation of − .35 between Mach V and the internal measure of social desirability; Marks and Lindsay (1966) found one of − .44. In instances where *external* measures of Social Desirability, constructed by Edwards (1957) and Crowne and Marlowe (1960), have been used, no significant correlation has been found with Mach V.

Upon the basis of available evidence it seems reasonable to say that scores on Mach IV reflect Machiavellian orientations not only because respondents agree with Machiavelli but are also willing to endorse socially undesirable statements. Scores on Mach V reflect the willingness of respondents to agree with Machiavelli when their tendency to agree with social undesirable statements is removed.

An alternative scoring system for Mach V was developed with two considerations in mind: (a) to have the possible range and theoretical neutral point equivalent to Mach IV, and (b) to take full advantage of the fact that it is probably more Machiavellian to say the Mach item is most like and the matched item least like oneself — a two-step difference — than to say the Mach item is most like and omit the matched item or omit the Mach item and say the matched item is least like oneself — a one-step difference.

Under this system the following item scoring is used when the Mach item is worded in the pro direction:

Mach item	Matched item	Score
Most Like	Least Like	7
Most Like	Omitted	5
Omitted	Least Like	
Omitted	Most Like	3
Least Like	Omitted	
Least Like	Most Like	1

When the Mach item is worded in the anti direction, the scoring is also reversed, 1, 3, 5, 7, from top to bottom.

TABLE II-5

Scoring Key for Mach V (1968)
Points per Item by Response Pattern[a]

Item No.	1	3		5		7
1	A+ C-	B+ C-	A+ B-	B+ A-	C+ B-	C+ A-
2	A+ C-	B+ C-	A+ B-	B+ A-	C+ B-	C+ A-
3	C+ A-	B+ A-	C+ B-	B+ C-	A+ B-	A+ C-
4	A+ B-	C+ B-	A+ C-	C+ A-	B+ C-	B+ A-
5	A+ B-	C+ B-	A+ B-	C+ A-	B+ C-	B+ A-
6	A+ C-	B+ C-	A+ B-	B+ A-	C+ B-	C+ A-
7	B+ A-	C+ A-	B+ C-	C+ B-	A+ C-	A+ B-
8	C+ B-	A+ B-	C+ A-	A+ C-	B+ A-	B+ C-
9	C+ B-	A+ B-	C+ A-	A+ C-	B+ A-	B+ C-
10	A+ B-	C+ B-	A+ C-	C+ A-	B+ C-	B+ A-
11	A+ B-	C+ B-	A+ C-	C+ A-	B+ C-	B+ A-
12	C+ B-	A+ B-	C+ A-	A+ C-	B+ A-	B+ C-
13	C+ A-	B+ A-	C+ B-	B+ C-	A+ B-	A+ C-
14	B+ C-	A+ C-	B+ A-	A+ B-	C+ A-	C+ B-
15	C+ B-	A+ B-	C+ A-	A+ C-	B+ A-	B+ C-
16	C+ B-	A+ B-	C+ A-	A+ C-	B+ A-	B+ C-

TABLE II-5 (continued)

Item No.	1	3		5		7
17	A+ C-	B+ C-	A+ B-	B+ A-	C+ B-	C+ A-
18	C+ A-	B+ A-	C+ B-	B+ C-	A+ B-	A+ C-
19	B+ C-	A+ C-	B+ A-	A+ B-	C+ A-	C+ B-
20	A+ B-	C+ B-	A+ C-	C+ A-	B+ C-	B+ A-

[a] Sum for all 20 items and add constant of 20. Range: 40-160.

Summing over the 20 items gives a possible range of from 20 to 140, the same as the scoring system on Mach IV. Similarly, adding a constant of 20 gives a scale with a minimum score of 40 and a maximum of 160 with the theoretical neutral point at 100 as is true of the converted scoring system of Mach IV. This makes it possible to add the two total scores of a respondent and have both contribute approximately equally to the grand total.

Table II-6

Means, Standard Deviations, and Correlations between Mach IV and Mach V on 1744 [a] College Respondents

	Mach IV		Mach V		Mach IV & Mach V
Aggregate	M	s.d.	M	s.d.	r
Caucasian males (764)	93.69	14.37	99.27	11.17	.67
Caucasian females (832)	87.66	13.45	95.60	10.09	.65
Nonwhite males (62)	97.25	15.08	98.17	10.38	.62
Nonwhite females (86)	88.03	14.71	94.70	11.60	.60

[a] These are those of a total of 1782 who could be classified as to sex and ethnicity.

There is not a point to point correspondence between the two scales despite the similarity in possible ranges because different assumptions are built into the two scoring systems. The samples mentioned above show the following means on the two scales.

Every sample with which we are familiar has made a higher score on Mach V than on Mach IV when the theoretical neutral point was taken as a point of reference. In general, the more socially sophisticated the samples, the higher were the scores on both scales and the higher the correlation between them.

In some studies to be described later only one of the scales has been used; in others both have been used. In our own experimental work we have usually used both scales for selection of subjects, categorizing them as high if they are above the median on both scales and low if they are below on both. This was done simply because two measures are better than one and it is more efficient and less expensive in resources to classify potential subjects on the basis of two quickly administered and scored paper-and-pencil tests than to spend hours working with subjects taking only one form who are not as consistent along the basic dimension on which they were selected.

SUMMARY

Seventy-one items based primarily upon Machiavelli's *The Prince* and *The Discourses* were written. They were presented in a Likert format to 1196 college undergraduates in three different universities. Item analyses indicated that 50 of the items discriminated between high and low scorers on the total scale in each of the three aggregates.

Twenty of the most discriminating items were selected for further research; half were worded so that agreement with them was scored in a pro-Machiavelli direction; the other half were reversals so that disagreement with them was scored to be pro-Machiavelli. This version of the scale is referred to in the remainder of this book as Mach IV.

Although the counterbalancing of the items in Mach IV effectively reduced agreement response set biases, it did not eliminate the effects of social desirability. Respondents making high scores on the Likert format scale (Mach IV) also tended to describe themselves in socially undesirable terms. A forced-choice scale, Mach V, was constructed, which did not correlate with external measures of social desirability.

The scoring system on both scales was converted so that a score of 100 equals the theoretical neutral point, i.e., agreement and disagreement with the items balances out. A score of 160 on Mach IV means strong agreement with every item worded in the pro-Machiavellian direction and strong disagreement with every item worded in the anti-Machiavellian direction. The reverse pattern yields a score of 40. A score of 160 on Mach V means that every item keyed for Mach is most or least like the subject and the item matched for social desirability is at the opposite extreme.

CHAPTER III   RELATIONSHIPS BETWEEN
                     MACHIAVELLIANISM AND
                     MEASURES OF ABILITY, OPINION,
                     AND PERSONALITY

Richard Christie

The Mach tests have not been systematically correlated with other paper-and-pencil measures of individual differences. The primary concern, as evidenced in the following chapters, has been with construct validity. How well do they predict behavior in controlled situations? Most measures of individual differences commonly used by psychologists have been devised to measure deviant behavior and our focus was in the opposite direction since we were concerned with a measure of effectiveness in manipulating others. There thus seemed little point in spending thousands of hours in test administration, coding, and questionnaire analysis in a search for hypothesized zero-order correlations with other scales.

This decision was also influenced by knowledge of the work patterns of psychologists. Once it is known that a new test, especially one dealing with a provocative topic, has been developed, it is safe to predict that within several years a number of investigators will have correlated it with every other test they think relevant. This observation is not intended to be cynical or Machiavellian; after all, it reflects a faith in the predictability of the behavior of fellow social scientists. This trust has been amply fulfilled. Despite the fact that prior to this book no published account of the scale characteristics of Mach IV or V existed, it has been used by hundreds of investigators on tens of thousands of respondents. Some of the information collected has trickled back from researchers and much of the material in this chapter is based on data collected by others.

Despite the preceding disclaimers, there are good reasons for examining the relationship of the Mach scales with other measures. Many psychologists, myself included, when dealing with a new psychological test, wonder how it relates to existing measures so that they can subjectively triangulate its location in a hypothetical space composed of previous findings. A further reason for presenting these relationships is to head off false hypotheses about the nature of Machiavellian orientations. This is especially important when dealing with a concept as value laden as Machiavellianism. The very mention of the term sets off a varied range of associations, most of which are not congruent with research results, among otherwise sophisticated researchers. If someone believes, rightly or wrongly, that his departmental chairman, agency supervisor, or professional peer has just pulled a deal at his expense, he is likely to inquire how strongly the Mach scales correlate with measures of authoritarianism or psychopathology. If, on the other hand, he has reason to feel that he is on top of the situation in his own interpersonal dealings, he is more likely to ask about the relationship of Mach with such measures as ego strength, social intelligence, or accurate social perception.

This chapter then is intended to indicate what other scales and inventories are related to Mach scales but, even more important, to indicate that some relationships which seem to be spontaneously hypothesized do *not,* as far as can be determined, actually exist. Many of the data to be discussed have not been published so it is impossible to give full details on the procedures or samples used. However, consistency in the findings permits confidence that they have some validity.

MEASURES OF INTELLIGENCE
OR INTELLECTUAL ABILITY

One of the first questions asked by many psychologists about a particular personality test is whether the findings might be explained by the fact that individuals who make high scores on measures of intellectual ability respond differently to the test or scale under scrutiny. We had made no predictions on this point. Of course, it can be argued that if an early sixteenth century version of the Stanford–Binet had been available, Machiavelli would have made a reasonably high score. However, an equally compelling argument can be made in behalf of the intelligence of otherworldly oriented scholars of the same period.

Data on seven contemporary samples are available:

1. MCAT (Medical College Admission Test) Verbal Scores on 161 medical school students at an elite medical school showed no significant correlation (+.04) with Mach IV.

2. Intelligence aptitude scores were available on 115 students in the School of General Studies at Columbia University. Details on the tests used were not available although the total scores were. These were split as the median and a chi square was computed between it and a median split on both Mach IV and V. It was nonsignificant. The value of the chi square was .56, $p \geq .25$.

3. Singer (1964) reported that in a sample of 994 entering students at Pennsylvania State University no significant correlation was found between Mach V and the Moore–Castore tests, a locally constructed test of intellectual aptitude on which no standardized data are available.

4. Both Mach IV and V were administered to a sample of 67 Peace Corps volunteers in a training program at Teachers College, Columbia University. They had previously taken the Verbal Abilities Test administered by the Peace Corps. Neither of the respective correlations, $+.10$ and $+.11$, was significant.

5. Wrightsman and Cook (1965) did a lengthy assessment (including 78 paper-and-pencil tests) of 177 female college students from five colleges in Nashville, Tennessee. Among these young ladies, Mach IV had the following correlations with subtests of the Guilford–Zimmerman Abilities Test: .05 with verbal comprehension, .09 with general reasoning, .05 with numerical operations, .04 with perceptual speed, .04 with spatial orientation, .01 with spatial visualization, and $-.04$ with mechanical knowledge. None of these correlations was significant at the .05 level.

6. Bruce Tuckman (personal communication) gave the Mach IV to 99 Naval enlisted men entering a Fire Control Technician School. Correlations were reported separately for the positively and negatively worded items with the General Classification Test. They were .01 and $-.11$, respectively; neither was significant.

7. All students in a private preparatory school were given the Mach IV. A correlation of $-.06$ was found between it and the measure of IQ used by the school for the boys in grades $9 - 12$ ($N = 218$).

In the seven samples on which we have data there were no significant correlations between Mach and IQ. This was true whether the samples were all male, all female, or mixed. Neither the educational level of the subjects nor the particular measure of IQ used seemed to make any difference. (In at least two cases the school administrators making the IQ scores available were not sure which IQ tests were used.)

Because of these findings we have proceeded on the assumption that there is no major correlation between Mach scores and IQ and have ignored intellectual differences in selecting samples for experimental studies. This admittedly runs the risk of running into a sampling fluke where a significant relationship between the two might occur. However, given the limited amount of time for which subjects are available, we decided it was not efficient to take the time to give IQ measures routinely to all prospective subjects. Further support for our assumption came from the knowledge that most of the correlations reported had been for fairly homogeneous samples similar to our student populations. The fact that in the most heterogeneous sample available, a representative sample of adults in the United States, no correlation was found between years of education and Mach Tactics scores reassured us that the experimental results were not materially affected by IQ differences. (In most representative samples the correlation between education and IQ is in the vicinity of $+.70$.)

MEASURES OF OPINION

AUTHORITARIANISM

Possibly the most studied variable in the past 20 years has been authoritarianism as defined in *The Authoritarian Personality* and measured by one or another version of the California F scale. Our interpretation of responses on the F scale is that it taps, among other things, a diffuse hostility towards others, a moralistic judging attitude toward them, and a propensity for right-wing political ideology.

One of the initial assumptions made in Chapter I was that a Machiavellian person is essentially apolitical in an ideological sense and that high Machs view others in a cool rather than in a moralistic judging fashion. These considerations should lead to a prediction of no relationship between F and Mach. However, both contain an unflattering view of man and this might lead to the expectation of a slight correlation. There is a subtle but important difference in the consequences of this unflattering view. A high-authoritarian view might be paraphrased, "People are no damn good, but they *ought* to be." A high Machiavellian might well agree with the premise about people but would give a twist to the implications of such a view, "People are no damn good. So what? Take advantage of it."

The prediction that there would be no major correlation between the F and Mach scales turned out to be true in the first nine samples (four classes of medical school students and five of college undergraduates) to whom the scales were administered in 1955 and 1956. The correlations ranged from $+.04$ to $-.15$ (none of which was significant) with a mean of $-.08$. It should be noted that these correlations were with the Christie *et al.* (1958) version of the F scale. Actually, the correlation between the positively worded halves of the F and Mach IV scales averaged about $+.35$ in these samples and this was interpreted as indicative of the spurious effect of agreement response set.

Perhaps we should have left well enough alone, as we did for a long time. However, the F scale, as well as the Mach scales, were administered to college respondents in a 1964 election study. Somewhat surprisingly, the overall correlation between F and Mach IV was $-.20$, which is highly significant with an N of 1782. What was even more astonishing was the consistency among the various samples in the sizes of the negative correlations. This was true even of the several schools which were the same or very similar to those tested eight or nine years earlier. This difference between the 1955 and the 1964 correlations might seem trivial but it was significant at the .05 level when tested by the Mann−Whitney U test. (Strictly speaking, such a test is not legitimate since the samples in 1955−1956 and in 1964 were not selected by similar random procedures.)

At the risk of overdramatizing a slight albeit persistent increase in the magnitude of these negative correlations, there is one possible explanation which should be discussed. Christie *et al.* (1958) noted that many of the original F-scale items which elicited affirmative answers from college respondents in 1944 and 1945 were no longer as acceptable in 1956. College students partly as a result of an increase in test sophistication and partly, perhaps, in response to an increasingly sophisticated society, are less prone to agree with F-scale items over time. On the other hand, the evidence suggests that Mach scores are increasing over time. (This last point is taken up again in Chapter XVI.)

If the hypothesized positive shift on Mach and negative one on F were, over time, characteristic of college students generally, the correlation between the two scales would not change. If, however, it was the more socially sophisticated students who were most alert to these changes, they would tend to rise on Mach and drop on F, thus enhancing the negative correlation. Although the data are congruent with this conclusion, obviously this is mere speculation since a rigorous test would demand carefully matched samples over a period of a decade or more.

POLITICAL PREFERENCE

Frequently, the identifying face sheets administered in conjunction with the Mach and other scales have routinely asked for political party preference. No Mach scale differences between Democrats and Republicans have been noted. Wrightsman, Radloff, Horton, and Mecherikoff (1961) gave a battery of scales including the Mach IV to samples of students in six colleges before the 1960 election. High scorers on the F scale were significantly more in favor of Nixon than Kennedy. This is consistent with earlier research in which the more conservative political candidate was favored by high F-scale scorers. There was, congruent with the low hypothesized ideological commitment of high Machs, no significant relationship with preference for Nixon or Kennedy and Mach IV scores.

A question as to political party preference was included in a 1963 NORC Amalgam national survey. Again, there were no significant differences as to party identification among high- or low-Mach scorers.

A characteristic of the above mentioned studies was that the choices were essentially dichotomous, one party against the other or a choice of one of two candidates. In the 1964 election study referred to in Chapters II, XVI, and Appendix A, the 1782 college respondents were asked to evaluate President Johnson and Senator Goldwater separately on three 7-point scales:

1. What do you think would be the effect if President Johnson (Senator Goldwater) were to win the election:

7 — Would be the best thing that could happen to the country.
6 — Would be a very good thing for the country.
5 — Would probably do the country more good than harm.
4 — Wouldn't make much difference to the country.
3 — Would probably do the country more harm than good.
2 — Would be a very bad thing for the country.
1 — Would be about the worst thing that could happen to the country.

2. How qualified do you feel President Johnson (Senator Goldwater) is?
7 — More qualified for the Presidency than any other man.
6 — Highly qualified for the Presidency.
5 — Fairly qualified for the Presidency.
4 — Neither particularly qualified for the Presidency nor particularly un-
    qualified.
3 — Not well qualified for the Presidency.
2 — Poorly qualified for the Presidency.
1 — Completely unqualified for the Presidency.

3. What kind of President do you think Johnson (Goldwater) will make if he is
elected?
7 — One of the greatest Presidents in our history.
6 — A very good President.
5 — A fairly good President.
4 — An average President.
3 — A fairly poor President.
2 — A very poor President.
1 — One of the worst Presidents in our history.

Combining scores on these questions permitted the construction of scales of favorability to Johnson or Goldwater. The possible range of scores for each candidate was 3.0 (his election would be the worst thing that could happen to the country, he was completely unqualified for the Presidency, and he would be one of the worst Presidents in our history) to 21.0 (he would be about the best thing that could happen to the country, more qualified for the Presidency than any other man, and one of the greatest Presidents in our history). A third scale of relative support for Johnson versus Goldwater was created by adding the Johnson scale to a reversal of the Goldwater scale. The possible range on the Johnson–Goldwater scale was from 6 (complete support for Goldwater) to 42 (complete support for Johnson). The theoretical neutral point of the individual candidate scales was 12, for the combined Johnson–Goldwater scale 24.

The correlation between Mach IV and favorability toward Johnson as against Goldwater was −.02, that between Mach V and candidate preference was +.02. It was concluded that if there is a relationship between Mach scores and political preference among these samples in the United States, it is so elusive as to be of no great importance.

RACIAL ATTITUDES

One of the most explosive political issues of recent years has been in the area of race relations. Wrightsman and Cook's (1965) young, white Southern college women previously alluded to came from five colleges in the same border state city. These schools varied from a relatively elite private university to a fundamentalist college. Among the 78 measures taken in a 12-hr assessment session were some related to race relations.

TABLE III-1

Correlations Between Mach IV and Race Relations[a]

Extent of discussion of race relations	+ .04
Desire for greater discussion of race relations	- .08
Stereotyping of Negro	+ .21[b]
Whites seen as possessing Negro stereotyped characteristics	+ .21[b]
Greater tendency to stereotype Negroes than whites	+ .04
Anti civil liberties	+ .04

[a] Professor Lawrence S. Wrightsman made these data available.
[b] Significant at the .01 level.

It is clear from Table III-1 that scores on Mach IV are unrelated to reported measures of race relations. The one suggestive finding is the low but statistically significant tendency for high scorers to indiscriminately stereotype both whites and Negroes. This slight tendency toward stereotypy on the part of high Machs will also emerge in other contexts in subsequent chapters.

PHILOSOPHIES OF HUMAN NATURE

Wrightsman has recently developed a scale designed to get at implicit philosophies of human nature. The overall scale consists of six subscales of 14 items each. Seven items in each subscale are worded in one direction, the remaining seven in the opposite direction.

The subscales are (Wrightsman, 1964):

1) Trustworthiness, or the extent to which people are seen as moral, honest, and reliable;
2) Altruism, or the extent of unselfishness, sincere sympathy, and concern for others present in

people; 3) Independence, or the extent to which a person can maintain his convictions in the face of society's pressures toward confirmity; 4) Strength of Will and Rationality, or the extent to which people understand the motives behind their behavior and the extent to which they have control over their own outcomes; 5) The Complexity of Human Nature, a dimension which cuts across the above continua and deals with the extent to which people are complex and hard to understand or simple and easy to understand; and 6) The Variability in Human Nature, which also cuts across the first four dimensions and relates to the extent of individual differences in basic nature and the basic changeability in human nature [p. 744].

Correlations between Mach IV and these subscales on a sample of 47 male and 59 female students at Western Maryland College are reported as: Trustworthiness, −.67; Altruism, −.54; Independence,−.47; Strength of Will, −.38; Complexity, −.08; and Variability, +.08. The first four of these correlations are no cause for surprise since they represent an amplification of Mach items. What is most interesting is the trivial correlation Machiavellianism has with belief in the complexity and variability of human nature. High Machiavellians apparently do not differ from the majority of their peers in viewing others as complex or simple, stable or changeable.

MACHIAVELLIANISM AND PERSONALITY MEASURES

The original expectation was that there should be little or no relationship between Machiavellian orientations and measures of psychopathology. Beyond this, we did not speculate as to the possible relationships between Mach scores and measures of the normal personality. After all, we were not particularly interested in personality variables *qua* personality variables and our approach to the study of Machiavellianism was different from that prevalent in personality research in the early 1950's. Blake and Mouton (1959) noted that the area was dominated by the use of the "3 A's" in personality measurement: Achievement, Anxiety, and Authoritarianism. All three had clinical overtones in their conceptualization. The beginning of Achievement research started in analyzing the responses of subjects to projective material after having been experimentally frustrated (McClelland, Clark, Roby, & Atkinson, 1949); the most popular anxiety measure was based upon clinicians' judgments of statements from the Minnesota Multi-Phasic Inventory (Taylor, 1951); and Authoritarianism upon a neoFreudian interpretation of the genesis of ethnic prejudice (Adorno *et al.*, 1950). Our starting point was abstract and nonclinical; what personality characteristics seemed necessary to fulfill the social role of a manipulator? After some search, we used Machiavelli's writings as an approximation of this model. In this sense our approach was closer to that of Allport and Vernon (1931), who based their scale of values upon the writings of Spranger (1928) or that of Stagner (1936) who took the writings of Fascist spokesmen or theorists as the basis for a pre-*Authoritarian Personality* measure of right-wing political persuasion.

Inevitably relationships of varying strength between Mach IV and V and other personality scales began to emerge. A basic problem in interpreting these correlations was to get at the operations lying behind the responses subsumed under the titles of the scales. This involved a scrutiny of the content of the items in the scales, the examination when possible of the effects of scale format, response set, social desirability, etc. In addition it is advantageous to know what correlations the other scales have with yet other scales (which can lead to an almost infinite regress if pursued wholeheartedly) and most important, how they relate to overt behavior. One of the encouraging things about the evaluations of the use of Mach scales by other investigators is the consistency with which independent investigators report congruent findings. For example, Wrightsman and Cook's lack of significant findings between Mach IV and racial attitudes was welcome because it was theoretically congruent; confidence in its possible generalizability was generated by their finding that in their sample of college women in the upper South the correlations between Mach IV and F and Anomia respectively were $-.17$ and $+.41$ — figures precisely in accord with those in other samples.

The following interpretations are fairly brief and do not do full justice to the complexities involved in the process of evaluation. In general, however, all known relevant evidence has been examined critically.

NEED FOR ACHIEVEMENT

In most informal presentations of data on Machiavellianism there is usually at least one person who asks about its relationship to need for achievement. This poses a difficult problem operationally. As Klinger notes in a review of fantasy need achievement (1966),

It seems clear that whatever n Ach scores measure is quite ephemeral, capable of registering differently in different fantasy instruments, differently in fantasy as contrasted with cognitive task instruments, and differently at different times in the same experimental session with the same or similar instruments [p. 300].

Aside from its "ephemeral" quality, we know of no compelling theoretical reasons why a desire to achieve should be related to Machiavellianism. Our assumption has always been that Machiavellianism is less concerned with high or low achievement goals than with the *manner* by which the attempt is made to achieve them.

There are two studies in which Mach scores have been correlated with paper-and-pencil tests of the need for achievement. Weinstock (1964) translated Strodtbeck's (1958) eight-item achievement scale and nine items from Mach IV and administered them to a sample of 50 adult Hungarian refugees. A correlation of $+.29$, significant at the .05 level, was found.

Geis, Weinheimer, and Berger (1966, personal communication) gave 54 college male subjects a ten-item test of need for achievement. Each item described a behavior by a fictitious person and gave four possible reasons for that behavior. For example:

J.E. will usually volunteer for a difficult task because . . .
    a.   he wants to build up his prestige by doing so.
    b.   he hopes he will be accepted by the group for doing it.
    c.   he wants to test his capacity for accomplishing a difficult task.
    d.   he just wants to help out in any way he can.

Subjects were instructed to mark the alternative they felt to be the most common reason for the behavior described. In this item, "c" was the keyed alternative. Keyed alternatives were designed to attribute effort to a desire for excellence, achievement, supremacy, mastery, etc. for its own sake. The foil items were designed to ascribe effort to desire to avoid failure, desire for prestige or acceptance, future utility, or moral principles. The items were revised until they passed the test of independent consensus among the authors. No further attempts were made to validate or refine the instrument. For what they are worth, however, scores on this presumed measure of need for achievement correlated $-.03$ with Mach scores.

Probably the results of Geis *et al.,* are more comparable to those which might be found on American samples generally. Not only was the study conducted on a sample of American students, but the total Mach scale, not an abridgement of it, was used. In addition, the authors were not faced with the possible loss of meaning that can result from a translation. Even though Weinstock used a double-translation technique, some drift from the original intention of the item was inevitable. While available evidence does not suggest a strong positive relationship between Machiavellianism and the achievement motive, the question is still an open one.

ANXIETY

One of the measures used in the early medical school studies was one adapted from Heineman's (1953) forced-choice version of the Taylor Scale of Manifest Anxiety (Christie & Budnitsky, 1957). Much to our surprise we found that it and Mach IV correlated $+.38$, $+.39$, $+.41$, and $+.42$ in four classes of junior and senior medical school students. These correlations, which at first glance flew directly in the face of the assumption that there was no relationship between

Mach and measures of psychopathology, merited further scrutiny. It was at this time that we were becoming acutely aware of the problem of social desirability and were in the process of developing Mach V. If, as we suspected, the magnitude of these correlations was traceable in part to not completely controlling for social desirability, then Mach V should have lower correlations with the measure of anxiety than Mach IV. All four classes in two of the schools were subsequently tested. The correlations ranged from $-.01$ to $+.21$.

None of the eight correlations was significantly different from zero. The overall correlation of $+.08$ also was not significant.

MEASURES OF PSYCHOPATHOLOGY

A group of Peace Corps trainees at Teachers College was given an assessment battery which included the MMPI. All of the clinical scales of the MMPI were scored and there were no significant correlations with any of them and Mach. It should be noted, however, that this group had previously undergone psychiatric screening and had been carefully scrutinized by a variety of techniques. It would be remarkable if, given such a careful going over, such a homogeneous population would show any significant correlation of MMPI scores with any other measure. Obviously we cannot generalize from such a sample to any unscreened populations.

Since it is highly probable that someone, somewhere, sometime will relate Mach scores to the MMPI on an unscreened population, one word of advice might be given. Wrightsman and Cook found a correlation of $-.27$ between Mach IV and the K Scale on the MMPI. This is usually interpreted as a measure of test-taking defensiveness. They also found a correlation of $-.40$ with the Lie Scale on the MMPI. (They did not give the clinical scales.) If the findings from these young Southern ladies can be generalized, they suggest that high Mach scorers are relatively uninhibited when taking tests of psychopathology and this factor should be taken into account in making interpretations of their psychic state.

MEASURES OF GENERAL CANTANKEROUSNESS

Among the 78 measures given by Wrightsman and Cook there are eight not previously mentioned which correlated $+.40$ with Mach IV. These are listed in Table III-2.

TABLE III-2

Correlations of Various Scales with Mach IV, Anomia, and F in
Wrightsman and Cook's Sample[a]

	Mach IV	Anomia	F
Manifest Hostility (Siegel)	+ .60	+ .30	− .14
Cornell Anomie	+ .51	+ .41	− .09
Hostility (Buss–Durkee)	+ .47	+ .28	− .04
Faith in Human Nature (Rosenberg)	− .44	− .26	+ .08
External Locus of Control (Liverant)	+ .43	+ .36	+ .02
Verbal Hostility (Buss–Durkee)	+ .41	+ .26	− .08
Anti-Police Attitudes (Chein)	+ .41	+ .20	− .05
Suspicion (Buss–Durkee)	+ .40	+ .27	+ .03

[a] Lawrence S. Wrightsman made these data available.

For comparative purposes we have included the correlations with Anomia and
F. It will be noted that the correlations with Anomia follow the direction of those
with Mach IV but always with a lower value. None of the correlations of these
measures with the F scale are at the .05 level of significance although the
negative correlation with Seigel's Hostility Scale approaches it.

Perhaps the simplest way to interpret Table III-2 is in reference to a factor
analysis performed by Wrightsman and Cook of 73 of the 79 measures they used.
Ten identifiable factors emerged from the analysis.

Eight scales emerged with their highest loadings on a factor named "Positive
Attitude Toward People." The loadings for the scales in Table III-2 on this
factor were: Cornell Anomie, − .70; Faith in Human Nature, +.57; Suspicion,
− .51; External Locus of Control, − .40. Mach IV loaded − .52 on this factor.
There seems to be little need to engage in an extended discussion of this factor's
relationship with Machiavellianism since it parallels the factor analytic findings
discussed in Appendix A. However, there is one matter which might require
explication, that of the presence of External Locus of Control in such a factor and
its positive correlations with Mach IV [see Rotter (1966) for a copy of the scale
and a description of its development]. External locus of control in this scale is
pitted against internal locus of control in a format in which the respondent is
required to make a forced choice of which of two items representing the two poles
is most strongly believed by him, e.g., "Many of the unhappy things in people's
lifes are partly due to bad luck," or "People's misfortunes result from the
mistakes they make" (Rotter, 1966, p. 11).

As Rotter notes, "A careful reading of the items will make it clear that the
items deal exclusively with the subject's *belief* about the nature of the world —

but none of the items is directly addressed to the *preference* for internal or external control [p. 10]."

The present interpretation is that the scale taps a view of the social world which emphasizes its probabilistic nature in the external control items and a generalized view that man is captain of his destiny in the internal locus of control statements. In this respect it seems to fall more closely with the *Disbelief in People* aspects of Machiavellianism rather than in *Tactics* or *Duplicity*.

Thirteen of Wrightsman and Cook's 78 measures had their primary loading on a factor which they labeled "Hostility and Anxiety." Of the items in Table III-2 Siegel's Hostility Scale loaded .83, Verbal Hostility loaded .72, and Anti-Police Attitudes loaded .27. The reason that the Buss–Durkee measure of Hostility was not reported loading on this factor is simple — it was not included in the factor matrix. However, its subscales were. In addition to Verbal Hostility which loaded .72, Assault loaded .66, Indirect Hostility loaded .60, Irritability loaded .59, Negativism loaded .55, and Resentment loaded .53. The other Buss–Durkee subscale used by Wrightsman and Cook, Hostility, loaded higher (negatively) on another factor of Positive Attitudes toward People but also loaded positively on this factor (.41).

It is abundantly clear that respondents who are in agreement with Machiavelli also tend to agree with inventory items which are classified as indicative of hostility. Is this because they are in actuality more hostile or is it because they recognize their hostility and are more willing to admit it when answering scales? These are questions which cannot be answered with any definitiveness upon the basis of available evidence but they are worth keeping in mind while exploring some possible reasons for the reported correlations.

The correlation of .60 between Mach IV and Siegel's Hostility Scale is the highest known correlation of Mach IV with any other personality measure. For this reason Siegel's scale deserves scrutiny. Saul Siegel (1956) scanned the MMPI for all items that might reflect hostility and chose 110 items and added four more of his own devising. Five judges sorted these items and 50 were selected on the basis of their judgments. It is thus an *a priori* scale. Its construct validity is not known to have been explored.

The 50 items are presented in a true–false format (44 items are keyed "True," six "False"). In general, the items have content which would seem highly socially undesirable, perhaps even more socially undesirable than the Mach items, and some verge on the psychopathological, e.g.:

"I know who is responsible for most of my troubles."
"I am sure I get a raw deal from life."
"I believe I am being followed."
"I believe I am being plotted against."

Other items seem to be closer to social desirability as defined by Crowne and Marlowe (1960) in that they are probably true of most people but it is not polite to admit to them about oneself, e.g.:

"Some of my family have habits that bother and annoy me very much."
"I easily become impatient with people."
"I am not easily angered."

It seems plausible that the items in the Hostility Scale are at least as socially undesirable as those in Mach IV. This would lead us to expect a correlation of roughly about $+.40$ between them simply because of the shared variance attributable to negative social desirability. If we subtract this amount of shared variance $[(.40)^2 = .16]$ from the total shared variance $[(.60)^2 = .36]$, we end up with a hypothetical 20% of the shared variance unaccounted for. This would be enough to account for a correlation of approximately $+.45$ ($\sqrt{.20}$) between the two scales.

A further examination of the items indicates that some of them have a "Mach-ish" flavor to them, e.g.:

"It is safer to trust nobody."
"I think nearly anyone would tell a lie to keep out of trouble."
"It is all right to get around the law if you don't actually break it."
"I do not blame a person for taking advantage of someone who lays himself open to it."
"Most people are honest chiefly through fear of being caught."
"I think most people would lie to get ahead."

Such items may account in part for the correlation of $+.60$ between Mach IV and Siegel's Hostility Scale. It is doubtful, however, whether this apparently shared content plus the contribution made by shared negative social desirability could account for all of the relationship. At a minimum we can say that high Machs are more willing to admit as true of themselves items selected by five judges as indicative of manifest hostility. The criteria for such a selection are not clear and there is no evidence that the items are indeed predictive of hostility in interpersonal relations. This, then, is not sufficient evidence to indicate that high Machs are actually more hostile than low Machs but does indicate that they recognize and admit their hostile impulses. It may be that low Machs actually have fewer hostile impulses or it may be that they have them but are either unable to recognize them or unwilling to admit them. This is a point which will be touched upon although not resolved when the empirical studies are examined.

Mach IV had a loading on one other of the ten Wrightsman and Cook factors, a modest $-.23$ with Rigidity. Other factors which were extracted and on which Mach IV did *not* load were: Anti-Negro Attitudes, Aptitudes, Sociability, Tolerance for Unpleasantness, Negativism about Self, "Traditional" (Non-progressive) Attitudes toward Appropriate Teacher Behavior, and Response Set.

RATINGS OF OTHERS

The material examined to date indicates that high as contrasted to low Machiavellians have a negative view of people in general and are more likely to admit to socially undesirable statements about themselves. What are their evaluations of specific others? Some data contained in a study by Harris (1966) are relevant to this point.

Harris' subjects were 76 males in a small church affiliated college. Their Mach scores were lower than those employed in most of the studies reported later, high Machs having a mean score of 105.11 on Mach IV and low scorers one of 81.58 (the classification was based on a median split). In the experimental situation, each subject interacted separately with a high Mach and a low Mach on the extremely difficult, if not almost impossible, task of rating characters in *Waiting for Godot* (Beckett, 1954) on selected personality dimensions. Prior to these interactions, each subject had been given the actual Mach IV protocol of his work partner so that he "could get to know his teammate better." After completion of the task — rating of the characters separately and then discussing them with the partner in an attempt to reach agreement — the subjects filled out a variety of postexperimental questionnaires. One was about the partner. It contained a list of 20 bipolar descriptions each of which could be checked on any of seven spaces indicating the closeness of fit to the partner.

One way of examining these data is to look at the average ratings of lows on each dimension for their two partners and compare it with the average ratings of highs for their two partners. We are not concerned here with perceived differences in highs and lows or accuracy of social perception. Rather, our interest is in whether there are systematic differences in the use of ratings between the two groups of evaluators who had two interactions with partners of differing Mach scores in a standardized situation. A summary of this analysis is presented in Table III-3.

TABLE III-3

Comparison of High and Low Machs' Ratings of Others[a]

Bipolar trait[b,c]		High vs. Low Machs' mean rating of partners
		highs see their opponents as being
GENEROUS	selfish	less generous
cold, unfriendly	WARM. FRIENDLY	less warm, friendly
poor boss	EXCELLENT BOSS	less excellent boss
INTERESTING	dull	less interesting
ASSERTIVE	indecisive, meek	less assertive
secretive	FREE, FRANK	less free, frank
GENTLE	tough	less gentle

TABLE III-3 (continued)

Bipolar trait[b,c]		High vs. Low Machs' mean rating of partners
		highs see their opponents as being
EXCELLENT CO-WORKER	poor co-worker	less excellent co-worker
IDEALISTIC	cynical	less idealistic
MATURE, DEPENDABLE	irresponsible	less mature, dependable
ADJUSTING	demanding	less adjusting
lazy, unproductive	PRODUCTIVE	less productive
COOPERATIVE	competitive	less cooperative
hostile	SYMPATHETIC	less sympathetic
INTELLIGENT	unintelligent	less intelligent
EXCELLENT FRIEND	poor friend	less excellent friend
ESTHETIC, ARTISTIC	athletic	less esthetic, artistic
passive	ACTIVE	less active
MASCULINE	feminine	less masculine
shrewd, manipulative	GUILELESS, OPEN	*more* guileless, open

[a] This comparison is based upon Harris (1966).

[b] The end of the continuum favored by the respondents is capitalized.

[c] The pairs of items are listed in descending order of differentiation between ratings made by high and low Machs.

An examination of Table III-3 indicates that the respondents tend to use the more socially desirable end of the continuum in describing their partners. They are rated as generous rather than selfish, warm and friendly rather than cold and unfriendly, etc. There are two surprises in that gentle seems preferable to tough, and even more interestingly, esthetic, artistic to athletic. It will be remembered, however, that these young gentlemen were attending a small Protestant college. More relevant to the present interest is the consistency with which high Machs rate their partners lower on these "good" qualities. In 19 of the 20 possible comparisons they have a less positive overall view of the fellow students with whom they have just interacted. It should be emphasized that the high Machs do not rate their partners as being on the selfish side of the neutral point but simply that they do not rate them as being as generous, warm, etc., as do the low Machs.

These data strongly suggest that the negative view taken by high Machs of their fellow man is not restricted to the general sorts of statements that show up on Disbelief in People and similar scales but are also true of ratings made of individuals with whom they have just interacted.

PREFERENCE FOR BALANCED SITUATIONS

Steiner and Spaulding (1966) have recently commenced studying individual differences relating to preference for balanced situations. Their technique for measuring such preferences stem from the earlier work by Jordan (1953). A sample item they used was:

Dick likes Tom.
Dick lies algebra; Tom doesn't like algebra.
How pleasant does Dick find this circumstance?

Very pleasant   Very unpleasant

The respondent's task was to check the point on the line which he thought best represented Dick's feelings about the relationship. Other items systematically made use of balanced situations (the two individuals both like algebra as well as the first liking the second, etc.) and other unbalanced situations (the first person liking a friend but not an object which the friend likes, etc.). Most respondents were found to prefer balanced to imbalanced situations but most relevant to our concern, these preferences on the part of individuals were stable over a week's time.

Steiner and Spaulding found, contrary to their expectations, that preference for balanced over imbalanced situations correlated +.47 (significant at .01 level) with Mach IV and −.42 (also significant at .01 level) with Budner's scale of intolerance of ambiguity (1962). (Mach IV correlated −.25 with intolerance of ambiguity, which is consistent with Budner's original findings.) In puzzling over this relationship, they weighed the possibility that although Machiavellians do not themselves have a strong preference for balanced situations, they might expect other people to have such a preference. They therefore revised the Situations Test to recast the items in the first person singular. This test was given to 35 male undergraduates at the University of Illinois. The correlation with Mach IV remained stable, being +.45, but the correlation with intolerance of ambiguity dropped to +.03.

These results probably surprised us more than they did Steiner and Spaulding. To anticipate some material in the following chapters, a considerable body of experimental and field data have been accumulated indicating that Machiavellians are more likely to be found in environments characterized by imbalances and to do much better in ambiguous conditions in experiments. A straightforward interpretation of these findings would be that Machiavellians prefer such situations because they give them more leeway for their machinations. Unfortunately, Steiner has not as yet reported any research on the behavior under controlled situations of people scoring high on his test so the behavioral concomitants are as yet unknown. If, and this is an open question, Machiavellians' prediliction for ambiguous situations arises from a desire to impose order and balance upon an ambiguous world, this poses some interesting questions. It should be noted that Steiner's balance test presents a description of an interpersonal situation to the subject. High and low Machs might respond differently to these descriptions. High Machs might respond by drawing the logical conclusion from the facts described; for low Machs, the emotional commitment implied by "liking" someone might outweigh differences in such impersonal concerns as attitudes toward algebra. This suggestion again anticipates discussions in the following chapters.

SUMMARY

Preparatory to presenting research on the behavior of individuals scoring high on the Mach scales, it was deemed advisable to summarize correlations found with paper and pencil tests and inventories. Hopefully, this would give us a rough idea as to what kind of individuals high and low Machs are when measured on conventional tests of individual differences and provide a picture to be fleshed out by findings in studies oriented specifically to their behavior in a variety of situations.

Of perhaps greatest importance, especially in interpreting game-playing behavior, is the fact that in seven different studies no significant relationship was found between Mach scores and various measures of intellectual ability. Available evidence also indicates that Machiavellianism and political preference or ideology are unrelated. Although no correlations have been found to date between Mach scores and measures of psychopathology, there is overwhelming evidence that high Machs have a generally unflattering opinion of others, a cynical view of people in general, and, in one instance (the Harris study), of specific individuals. Positive relationships with measures of hostility and negative ones with social desirability indicate a perhaps surprising degree of candidness. It is unclear, however, whether this indicates that high Machs are actually more hostile or whether they are less inhibited in recognizing and expressing it. A preference for balanced situations in a paper-and-pencil test poses interesting questions which have been deferred for the moment.

CHAPTER IV VISUAL INTERACTION IN
RELATION TO MACHIAVELLIANISM
AND AN UNETHICAL ACT [1]

Ralph V. Exline, John Thibaut,
Carole B. Hickey, and Peter Gumpert

How valid is the assumption that an honest man always looks one in the eye? More specifically, how honest is the person who looks one in the eye and under what conditions?

The present study is one of a series which have been designed to discover factors which affect the incidence of mutual glances and visual attentiveness. In general, looking another person in the eye may have two consequences: it may provide information to the looker about the other's emotional state or give clues to his intentions, but it is also believed [see Simmel (1921) and Tomkins (1963)] that looking must necessarily reveal to the other something of the looker's emotional state and intentions. It is this second, self-revealing function that is implicitly recognized in the folk belief that a person who does "look you in the eye" is honest — i.e., that he is concealing nothing — or has nothing to conceal. Previous research tends to support this idea. Affiliative subjects in a competitive situation exchanged fewer mutual glances than those in a non-competitive situation (Exline, 1963); subjects interviewed on innocuous topics looked the interviewer in the eye more than did those interviewed on very personal topics, which presumably elicited a desire to conceal information or affective response cues (Exline, Gray, & Schuette, 1965); another finding supports the assumption that persons in our society interpret the willingness to engage in direct eye contact as evidence of sincerity (Exline & Eldridge, 1967). Subjects who have nothing in particular to conceal do tend to look an interrogator in the eye. Suppose, however, that someone who has been implicated in an unethical act is quizzed about his behavior? We would expect him to look his interrogator in the eye less on such an occasion than he would in an interview on a less threatening topic. Our first hypothesis was that subjects who behaved unethically are less likely to look an experimenter in the eye afterwards than during a pretransgression interview.

[1] This investigation was supported in part by funds from Contract NONR-2285(02) Office of Naval Research and in part by the Psychology Department of the University of North Carolina. It represents a revised and extended version of a paper read at the 1961 APA meeting.

Our second hypothesis dealt with individual differences. The description of the highly manipulative or Machiavellian person (Chapter I) stressed his lack of affective involvement with others as well as his lack of conventional morality. Such persons should therefore be less likely to behave in the conventional fashion after behaving unethically, i.e., they should be less upset. Instead of avoiding an interviewer's eyes, they should be more able to bluff their way visually through the situation. If high Machs are able to look directly at another while giving him an evasive or even untrue answer, it might reflect an assumption on their part, either explicit or implicit, that visual behaviors which imply truthfulness would make it less likely that the hearer would doubt the truth of their words. If high Machs can bring themselves to behave in such a misleading fashion, it is likely that willingness to engage in mutual glances would play an important part in their strategy of concealment. On the other hand, if low Machs cannot bring themselves to engage in behaviors which they know imply a motive opposite to that which they hold, we would expect them to be relatively less prone to meet the gaze of another when discussing the critical topic.

There is one complicating factor in these predictions. Females tend to have lower Mach scores than men do (this was not generally known at the time this research was conducted), and we have found in three previous studies that women exchange more mutual glances than men (Exline, 1963; Exline *et al.*, 1965; Exline & Winters, 1965). Because of the known sex differences in eye contact, both predictions were tested by using each subject as his own control. The amount of time spent looking the interviewer in the eye during an interrogation after cheating was compared to the eye contact by the same subject with the same interviewer on a less threatening topic before any cheating had occurred.

PROCEDURE

Subjects consisted of 24 male and 24 female psychology students in a large state university (in 1960) who volunteered to participate in a study of group decision making. Each subject worked with another subject of the same sex on a series of ten decision tasks, each of which required the two decision makers to engage in considerable discussion. One of the students in the dyad was a paid confederate whose status was not revealed until after the completion of the experiment. Each confederate worked with one-half of the entire sample of male or female students.

Two experimenters, one of each sex, were used. Subjects were counter-balanced across experimenters with respect to sex, Mach IV scores, and interrogation conditions. Examination of the data showed no effects due to the sex of the experimenter, and the two levels were subsequently combined for purposes of simplifying the analysis.

OVERVIEW OF EXPERIMENTAL SITUATION

At the beginning of the experimental session, the subject, confederate, and experimenter were seated around a small rectangular table. The experimenter sat with his back to a one-way mirror, behind which were located observers, a camera, and recording equipment. In order to ensure that the subject would be seated directly across from the experimenter (facing the mirror), the confederate was seated prior to the subject's arrival. This arrangement permitted observers to have a full face view of the subject from a distance of approximately 5 ft.

The experimenter interviewed each subject and confederate in turn about their previous experiences in groups. The experimenter looked steadily at each person during the 2 min given each person to speak while observers recorded the duration of each glance of the subject. This procedure provided a base-line mutual glance score between subject and experimenter. In addition, the first 30 sec of each subject's presentation was recorded on 16-mm motion picture film.

Following the base-line interview, the experimenter presented the decision tasks in order of increasing difficulty. At the end of the sixth task the experimenter was called from the room to take an "important long-distance call." While he was away, the confederate implicated 20 subjects of each sex in cheating by looking up the answers to the forthcoming tasks. Four subjects of each sex were not implicated. Upon returning to the experimental room, the experimenter completed the series of tasks, then interviewed the pair, ostensibly to determine the methods they had used to arrive at their answers. In this interview the experimenter first expressed a complimentary interest but found fault with each method suggested by the pair. As the interview continued, the experimenter expressed increasing skepticism, and finally accused the pair of cheating. After the accusation the experimenter devoted an additional 2 min to an interrogation of the subject. Half of the subjects were interrogated by themselves, half in the presence of the confederate. Following the interrogation period, the experimenter revealed the deception to the subject, explained the purpose of the study, and requested the subject's cooperation in keeping the procedures confidential. Nonimplicated subjects were interviewed but not accused by the experimenter. The following sections provide a more detailed description of critical aspects of the procedures.

MACHIAVELLIANISM. Machiavellian interpersonal orientations were measured by administering the Mach IV scale several days prior to the subject's participation in the laboratory study. High and low Machiavellianism was defined as scoring above or below the median (93.56) of the sample distribution.

DECISION TASKS. The decision task required subjects to agree upon both the number of dots and the shape of the figure represented by the dots on a 12 × 18-in. card. The task was described as one which would help the investigators study the effects of the type of task upon the decision-making procedures of groups composed of different numbers of persons. Subjects were also told that the highest-scoring group would receive a $10 prize.

The overall task consisted of 12 dot cards[2] grouped in three sets of four cards each. Subjects were told that the sets would be presented in order of increasing difficulty. Representative of the easy set was a white card containing six black dots forming a triangle; a card of 32 dots in the shape of a free-form boat typifies the difficult set.

Before exposing the cards, the experimenter stated that he would report the accuracy of the group's decisions at the end of each set. This instruction was designed to create expectations in the subject which would make it easier for the confederate to implicate the subject in cheating. The rationale for this aspect of the procedures will be explained more fully in the next section.

The groups were told that members would take turns reporting the group's decision. A trial card was then exposed and discussed. To emphasize the fact that the group's product would be scored on the basis of the quality of decision processes, and thus help set the stage for the postdecision interrogation, the confederate was instructed to ask if the group could discuss how best to get the right answers. The experimenter replied that they were free to plan strategy, but not when the cards were being shown. The experimenter exposed the first card and started the tape recorder. Each card was exposed for 5 sec, after which the subject and the confederate resolved through discussion any disagreement concerning the number of dots and the shape of the figure formed by the dots.

After each decision, the experimenter recorded the group's answers on a large data sheet, then compared the answers to an answer key and recorded an additional number on his data sheet. He carried out these acts in a manner designed to call subjects' attention to the answer keys without revealing the correct answers.

During the early trials the experimenter manifested some impatience with the length of time the subject and confederate took to complete the task. The experimenter looked at his watch, squirmed during the discussion, and carried out his tasks in a hurried manner. The purpose of this show of impatience is explained below.

IMPLICATION PROCEDURES. The subjects were implicated in cheating to create both a strong motive to conceal information from another and to establish a standard set of information to conceal. One paid confederate of each sex was instructed in a standard set of implication procedures. Earlier we mentioned that the experimenter had promised to report the accuracy of the group's answers after each set of four decisions. At the end of the first series the experimenter did *not* give the group its scores for the set, but immediately

---

[2] In the actual experiment time considerations permitted only 10 of the 12 cards to be used. Experimenter merely ended the decision task after the 10th card.

presented card 5, the first card in the second set. The experimenter's apparent impatience during the first set was designed to make credible his neglect or forgetting of the promised report. After the answer for card 5 was recorded, the confederate reminded the experimenter of his promise to report results. The experimenter brushed off the confederate's question, replying: "It's not important just now. Let's let it go until the end of this series and then I'll give you the answers for both." The experimenter did not say this in a nasty manner as we did not wish to alienate the subject but rather wished to make the confederate's subsequent actions more plausible.

Before the experimenter presented the seventh card, someone (an observer) knocked upon the door of the experimental room and the following dialogue ensued: *O:* "You're wanted on the phone." *E:* "I can't come now; I'm busy." *O:* "I'm sorry but it's a long distance call — something about a job." *E:* "Oh yes, (turns to the subject and confederate). I'm sorry but I'd better take this call. I'll be back as soon as I can, four or five minutes at the most." The experimenter then turned off the tape recorder and left the room.

The confederate engaged the subject in small talk until after the experimenter's footsteps died away down a long corridor. The confederate then opened the cheating phase by indicating the one-way mirror and speculating as to whether it was a real mirror or one through which they were being watched. As he spoke, the confederate rose and coming close to the mirror peered intently at it. "Yeah, it's a fake — I can just barely see through it but there's no one back there — just some junk." On returning to his seat, the confederate noticed the papers on the arm of the experimenter's chair. The confederate wondered aloud if the pages contained the answers and complained about the experimenter's earlier impatience and failure to report the results of their work on the first set of tasks. "How does he expect us to see our mistakes if he doesn't tell us how we did on the first set? He was supposed to give us the answers, wasn't he?"

The confederate next suggested that they examine the cards which the experimenter had left face down on the note-taking arm of his chair. "Let's take a look at how we've been doing and go over our strategy — I could sure use that prize money. (If the subject objected, the confederate replied: "Well we're supposed to get the answers and see how we are doing. We're only correcting his/her own mistakes.") Toward the end of the speech the confederate went over to the experimenter's chair and picked up the answer keys which were typed on 5 × 8 cards, one for each set. Each of the three key cards identified the number, the difficulty level, figure, and number of dots per problem. The confederate flipped the answer key card for the final set (cards 9–12) face up in front of the subject and compared the other cards (sets 1 and 2) with the experimenter's answer sheet saying: "I must have the right one here. I'll copy these down — you probably have the hardest series — you get those and we can look at them as we go along and get a really good idea of how close our guesses are. Better hurry before he comes back . . . it isn't really unethical — we were supposed to get these before . . . " As he spoke, the confederate wrote down the answers to all of the cards listed on the answer keys (problems 1 – 8) he held, ignoring any protests made by the subject. The confederate wrote the information on a piece of scrap paper which the pair had used to note estimates, scribble formulae, and sketch designs while working on the previous decision tasks. As he worked, the confederate reviewed the information aloud, speaking loud enough for the subject to hear. The confederate then checked to see if the subject had listed the answers to the final and most difficult set. If the subject had not done so, the confederate took the card, and once again reviewing the information aloud, copied down the answers on the scrap sheet.[3] The confederate then replaced the three answer key cards just before footsteps announced the experimenter's return to the experimental room. To insure the confederate ample time to complete the implication program, the experimenter observed the action from the observation room and silently retreated to the end of the corridor after the confederate had written down the information from the last card. The timing also served to protect the confederate's "cover" in that the subject had little opportunity to quiz the confederate about his motives for cheating before the experimenter returned to the room. In fact, no subject ever raised such a question; all apparently accepted the confederate's action as authentic.

The confederate thus made sure that at the very least the subject had heard the correct answers for all tasks. Whether or not the subject had helped the confederate list the answers, he knew that the confederate had cheated. At the least, he had been implicated as an accessory. Four courses of action were open to the subject upon becoming aware of the confederate's intentions. The subjects could avoid implication by preventing the confederate from cheating (or by physically leaving the room); the subject could undo the implication by reporting the confederate's actions to the experimenter; the subject could remain silent, tacitly accepting implication in cheating; or the subject could help the confederate.

The final step in the implication procedure was carried out by the confederate during the dyad's work on the remaining tasks. As the pair discussed each of the subsequent tasks, the confederate attempted to get the subject to agree to report the correct shape and the exact number of dots listed in the answer key for each task. If the subject resisted, the confederate was instructed to push as hard as seemed feasible, then to hold out for an answer only one or two dots away from the correct number.

---

[3] When the confederate noted the answers on the scratch pad, he attempted to disguise the fact that a list of answers had been made by using a simple code and placing each set of answers next to, or among, scribblings which had already been made on different parts of the scratch paper. To the experimenter seated across the table from the pair the answers would appear to be part of the notes made during work on the preceding tasks.

We believe that the implication procedures induced a powerful motive to conceal information, particularly as students at the University lived under a student honor code and were expected to report violations of the code to an honor court. We argue that any student who did not expose the confederate before being interrogated had developed a powerful motive to conceal information from the interrogator, especially as he himself was liable to honor court action as an accessory. Observers noticed many behavioral cues which suggested that implicated subjects were under higher levels of stress during the postdecision interviews than during the baseline discussion. These observations will be discussed later.

INTERROGATION PROCEDURES. The interrogation period actually consisted of a pre- and postaccusation interrogation. In the preaccusation period all subjects were interrogated together with the confederate. In the post-accusation period half of the subjects were interrogated with the confederate while the other half were questioned by themselves. High and low Mach subjects were evenly divided between the together and alone conditions.

The experimenter opened the interrogation as follows:

> And that's that for the cards anyway. Now we have a few questions for you to answer orally, and we'll be through for the day. I must say that this team has done remarkably well — a great deal better, in fact, than any team of any size has done up to now. Now could you tell me what strategy or strategies you used to arrive at your decisions? Did you use an averaging procedure, or a 'division of labor' procedure or what? Try to give me a detailed and accurate statement, if possible, of how you did it.

At this point the confederate looked at the subject expectantly and the experimenter following the confederate's cue also looked to the subject for a reply. If no reply from the subject was forthcoming, the confederate said: "Gee, those are hard questions to answer — it's hard to put what we did into words. (To the subject): Can you explain it to him?" If the subject remained quiet, the confederate continued, "Well, for one thing, each of us guessed at what the count was or tried our best to count the dots, and then we just averaged the counts . . . or . . . (to subject) Can you think of what else we did?"[4]

As the subject and/or confederate described their supposed method, the experimenter withheld agreements or sought to point out flaws in it. He gave indications of increasing dissatisfaction, amazement, and impatience, finally saying: "Surely you can give me better information than that. It would have been nearly impossible to get the last four cards right by pure guessing or even guess-averaging (substitute, if necessary, method given by the subject). Tell me

---

[4] These remarks by the confederate were designed to put pressure on the subject to share in the interrogation. Usually they succeeded in getting the subject to take the initiative in speaking for the team. The experimenter helped to keep the subject involved by directing the greater part of his remarks to him, speaking to the confederate only enough to allay possible suspicion of collusion.

(directing his questions to subject) did you discover any pattern to the number of dots on the cards?" (In fact, there was no pattern.) "Well . . . did you see any relationship between the shape of the figures on the cards and the number of dots on them?" (Again, there was none.)

After the subject attempted to answer the above queries, the experimenter led up to the actual accusation. This was accomplished as follows.

The experimenter made some calculations on his scratch pad. He devised a formula, substituted some large numbers in it, calculated quickly. He then looked at the pair and said:

> Just for fun, I've figured out approximately what the chances are that you got the last couple of answers perfectly right by pure guessing. The chances are roughly one in 15,000. You haven't been able to tell me anything about how you could have arrived at the correct answers . . . this has become a little more serious than I thought. If the situation is what I think it is . . . well, I hate to say this, but there's an honor code on this campus to take care of things like this. And the honor code covers this kind of situation just as it does cheating on exams. This is a crucial experiment and there is money involved. My policy in the past has been to take cases of suspected cheating to the Dean, and to let him take the case to the Honor Council if he thinks that is what should be done with it. If I'm wrong about this, I'm sorry — but the facts so far indicate that you people might have looked at my answer cards while I was out before. I really shouldn't have left them here, but I shouldn't have to watch for this sort of thing, either.
>
> Now as I say, I may be wrong about this — and if I am, I'll be the first to apologize. So let's try to get at all possible alternatives.

Following the accusation, the experimenter continued with the postaccusation interrogation. If the subject was to be interrogated alone, the experimenter indicated that he wished to question them separately and asked the confederate to step into another room. If the subject and the confederate were to be interrogated together, the experimenter merely continued the interrogation without interruption. In each case the experimenter continued as follows: "Mr./Miss____(to the subject), can you give me some idea as to how you counted these dots on the cards?" (At this point an observer behind the one-way mirror took a 30-sec movie of the subject.) "Did you count them in groups? Groups of how many? Just what happened here while I was out? Now I'm going to see how well you can do it."

The postaccusation interrogation was continued for 2 min or until the subject confessed. If the subject confessed, the experimenter immediately gave him a questionnaire[5] to fill out. If the subject did not confess, the experimenter said he felt he should have some more data before making up his mind about honor court action. Accordingly, he said he would get another set of cards and see how well the subject could do on them. He gave the subject (or the subject and confederate) a questionnaire to fill out while he went for the additional cards. The experimenter returned to the room and as soon as the subject completed the questionnaire, the experimenter explained the purpose of the experiment.

---

[5] The questions dealt with the clarity of the instructions and attitudes toward the confederate, experimenter, and experiment. They were designed to develop data for a different study, and will not be reported in this paper.

OBSERVATION PROCEDURES. The subject's visual behavior was recorded by an observer seated almost directly behind the experimenter and directly in line with the subject. Whenever the subject looked the experimenter in the face, the observer depressed a switch, holding it down until the subject averted his gaze. Whenever the subject looked at the confederate the observer depressed a different switch. Each switch was connected to a pen on an Easterline-Angus operations recorder. The resulting profiles provided us with a record of the frequency and duration of each subject's visual orientation toward the experimenter and the confederate. Our previous experience with this technique has shown a high degree of interobserver reliability (Exline, 1963). Thus, with the exception of a few spot checks (which provided almost identical profiles) visual data recording was carried out by a single observer.

Visual interaction data were recorded during a base-line period when subjects described their previous experiences in groups prior to the task period, and during the two interrogation periods (pre- and postaccusation).

MOTION PICTURE DATA. Movies were taken at two periods during the experiment. Each subject was photographed for 30 sec during the base-line discussion and for 30 sec immediately after being accused of cheating. The camera was operated by a second observer. Coders unfamiliar with the study viewed the movies and recorded impressions of subjects' sincerity, anxiety—tension, and withdrawal during the base-line and accusation periods.

AUDIO TAPE DATA. Sound recordings were taken throughout the experiment. Naive coders later used the tapes as the basis for the following subjective ratings: (a) the extent to which the subject helped the confederate cheat during the implication period; (b) the amount to which the subject helped or hindered the confederate in working on the postimplication tasks; (c) the quality of the subject's lying during the preaccusation interrogation; (d) the wholeheartedness of the subject's denial or confession after being accused of cheating: (e) the extent to which the subject impressed the listener as being suspicious of the implication induction. In addition tapes were used to obtain the number of seconds the subject spoke during the pre- and postaccusation interrogation periods.

RESULTS

EFFECTIVENESS OF INDUCTION

We have argued that our implication procedures were almost certain to minimally implicate the subjects in an unethical act. Subjects could avoid such implication by physically preventing the confederate from cheating, by physically leaving the test situation when the confederate cheated, or by reporting the unethical behavior as soon as the experimenter returned to the laboratory. If, when the confederate cheated, the subject did not react in one of these ways, he was considered to be implicated. Only 4 of 42 experimental subjects were eliminated for the above reasons, and 38 subjects more or less willingly completed the tasks.[6]

Evidence as to the degree to which the subjects became involved in the unethical situation was obtained from content analyses of subjects' verbal behavior. Coders unfamiliar with the design of the study analyzed tape recordings of the discussion during four periods within each experimental group's meeting.

TABLE IV-1

Mean Rating[a] (from Audio Tapes) of Amount of Assistance Given to an Unethical Confederate by Subjects Categorized by Sex and Machiavellianism

	Experimental periods						
	Implication in cheating		Postimplication tasks		Pre-accusation interrogation (extent of lying)		Post-accusation interrogation (extent of lying)	
Machiavellianism	$\overline{X}$	*(n)*	$\overline{X}$	*(n)*	$\overline{X}$	*(n)*	$\overline{X}$	*(n)*
High								
Men	2.82	(11)	4.82	(11)	5.91	(11)	4.73	(11)
Women	4.00	(6)	6.17	(6)	6.40	(5)[b]	5.83	(6)
Total	3.24	(17)	5.29	(17)	6.06	(16)	5.12	(17)
Low								
Men	4.20	(5)	6.20	(5)	6.40	(5)	3.80	(5)
Women	4.08	(12)	5.42	(12)	5.83	(12)	4.00	(12)
Total	4.12	(17)	5.65	(17)	6.02	(17)	3.94	(17)
Total implicated	3.68	(34)	5.47	(34)	6.03	(33)[b]	4.53	(34)

[a] Ratings range from 1 (refused to assist confederate) to 7 (willing assistance).
[b] See footnote 6.

_____

[6] We were able to replace the first two potential *S*s who refused to be implicated with additional subjects, but time pressures did not permit us to find substitutes for the last two. In addition malfunctions of the tape recorder and/or event recorder gave us incomplete data for six experimental and two control subjects. Data from these subjects were not used to test the relevant hypotheses.

From the data in Table IV-1 it appears that experimental subjects did not, on the average, try very hard to dissuade the confederate from cheating, helped rather than hindered him on the tasks following cheating, and when asked to explain their problem-solving methodology, gave explanations which were close to absolute falsehoods ($\overline{X} = 6.03$). In short, they moved from very mildly resisting the confederate's cheating to helping him on the tasks, and then to covering up for him in the preaccusation interrogation. Even after they were accused of cheating, a large number of subjects refused to reveal the truth, and were given mean ratings of 4.53 on a 7-point scale ranging from 1 (complete truth) to 7 (absolute falsehood).

Also relevant to the question of subjects' complicity are comparisons of the activity of control and implicated subjects during the discussion of tasks 7 – 10 for which the confederate had obtained the answers in advance. Had the implicated subject attempted to disassociate himself, we would reasonably assume that he would either psychologically withdraw from participation or seek to dissuade the confederate from reporting maximum accuracy on the task. Thus, we would expect subjects so motivated to be rated lower on their "task help to the confederate" that nonimplicated subjects who, we assumed, had less reason to disassociate themselves from the confederate. However, both implicated and control subjects were rated as falling between giving a little and much help to the confederate ($\overline{X} = 5.47$ and 5.33). These data suggest that the implicated subjects were as willing to go along with the confederate as control subjects. This interpretation is further supported by the finding that implicated subjects agreed to report substantially more accurate dot estimates than did nonimplicated subjects even though the confederate pushed equally hard for the correct solution in each case. An average error of 1.60 made by implicated subjects was significantly less than the mean error of 3.67 dots made by nonimplicated subjects over the same tasks ($t = 2.51, p < .02$).

Data relevant to the effectiveness of the experimental manipulations were also derived from movies of each subject. A 30-sec motion picture was taken at the beginning of the experiment, as the subject described his previous group experience. A second film was taken of implicated subjects just after the accusation. Since control subjects were not accused, their second shot was filmed at the end of the interrogation. Independent coders used a 7-point scale to rate each subject's appearance of anxiety. Mean ratings are listed in Table IV-2, and show that while both implicated and nonimplicated subjects are rated as somewhat more anxious during the interrogation sequence, the increase was significant for the implicated subjects ($t = 3.04, p < .01$). It is also interesting to note that high-Mach subjects were rated as appearing generally less anxious than low-Mach subjects, a point which will be discussed later.

TABLE IV-2

Mean Ratings[a] of Impression of *S*s' Anxiety
in Pre- and Postimplication Periods

Machiavellianism	Experimental periods			
	Base line		Accusation	
	$\overline{X}^a$	*(n)*	$\overline{X}^a$	*(n)*
High				
Men	4.00	(11)	4.36	(11)
Women	3.67	(6)	4.67	(6)
Total	3.88	(17)	4.47	(17)
Low				
Men	3.50	(6)	3.83	(6)
Women	4.55	(11)	5.36	(11)
Total	4.18	(17)	4.76	(17)
Total implicated	4.03	(34)	4.65	(34)
Total nonimplicated	3.83	(6)	4.17	(6)

[a] High scores represent an impression of high anxiety.

In summary, we conclude that, with the exception of the four subjects previously mentioned, our procedures sufficed to implicate the subject in cheating and created a situation which was more stressful for them than for the nonimplicated subjects.

EYE CONTACT
DURING INTERROGATION AFTER CHEATING

If looking another in the eye is felt to be self-revealing, then subjects who had been implicated in cheating should be less willing to look an interviewer in the eye during a relevant interrogation than they had been in an earlier interview with the same experimenter but on a nonthreatening topic. During the presession interview on "previous group experiences" the 32 subjects who were later to be implicated in cheating (and for whom visual behavior records were available for both periods) looked the interviewer in the eye 32.65 sec/min during the 2-min period. After cheating, in their second interview (but before the direct accusation) they looked 21.45 sec/min in 2 min — a decrease of 11.20 sec/min on the average. Although this decrease in mutual glancing is clearly in line with expectations, it can be seen in Table IV-3 that the nonimplicated subjects also decreased (though only by 5.67 sec/min) in eye contact with the interviewer from base line to the posttask interview. An analysis of variance

(Table IV-4) indicated that the greater decrease of the implicated subjects was not significant.

MACHIAVELLIANISM
AND USE OF THE LINE OF REGARD

High Machs were expected to use eye contact as a strategy of concealment to a greater extent than lows. Support for this hypothesis would be inferred from a significant second-order interaction of Machiavellianism, implication, and interview periods. This general hypothesis would be supported if the post-cheating use of the line of regard by high-Mach scorers increased more, or decreased less, relative to that observed for low-Mach scorers. The most reasonable expectation with respect to the use of the line of regard by the nonimplicated subjects would be that Machiavellianism should have no effect upon any baseline versus interrogation differences in the mutual glances of nonimplicated subjects. In any event, the pattern of use of the line of regard should not be similar to that found for implicated subjects with respect to the direction and extent of relative increments or decrements.

Since the nonimplicated subjects were not accused of cheating, data to test the hypothesis concerning the effects of Machiavellianism and implication were based on comparisons of subjects' visual behavior in the base-line and preaccusation interrogation. Means of the implicated subjects' behavior after accusation are also listed in Table IV-3 and will be used for an additional analysis of the effects of Machiavellianism on implicated subjects.

TABLE IV-3

Mean Seconds Per Minute of Eye Contact with Experimenter During Three Experimental Periods

	Machiavellianism	Base line $\overline{X}$	(n)[a]	Pre-accusation $\overline{X}$	(n)	Post-accusation $\overline{X}$	(n)
Implicated	High	32.03	(16)	23.51	(16)	28.24	(16)
	Low	33.28	(16)	19.39	(16)	18.50	(16)
	Total	32.65	(32)	21.45	(32)	23.37	(32)
Nonimplicated	High	29.07	(3)	17.33	(3)	—	
	Low	25.33	(3)	25.67	(3)	—	
	Total	27.17	(6)	21.50	(6)	—	
Means: Mach x periods	High	31.56	(19)	22.53	(19)	—	
	Low	32.03	(19)	20.37	(19)	—	
Means: periods		31.79	(38)	21.46	(38)	23.37	(32)

[a] Eight implicated and two nonimplicated subjects were eliminated because of scepticism, immediate confession, or equipment malfunction.

The data would seem to support our hypothesis. The *F* for the interaction of Machiavellianism, implication, and interview periods reached significance beyond the .05 level and the high Machs reduced their looking only 9.5 sec/min after implication while the low Machs looked away considerably more — some 14 sec/min. The pattern of the means is what we would expect if, as we suggested, the high Machs were more prone to use the direct glance to suggest that they had nothing to conceal.

The pattern of means for the nonimplicated subjects, while not contradicting the hypothesis, did not conform to expectations in one respect. Low Machs did not, as expected, differ much in the two interview periods, but high Machs reduced their visual interaction with the interviewer considerably more over time than was the case for the implicated high Machs. Even though this reduction occurred to almost the same degree (9 – 12 sec/min) for all the nonimplicated high Machs, the small number of cases permit no definite conclusions. It is interesting to speculate that high Machs may more quickly lose interest in the experimenter when they have no strong need to influence his perception, but more data on this point are needed.

TABLE IV-4

Analysis of Variance of Eye Contact with Experimenter
during Base-Line and Preaccusation Interrogation [a] Periods

Variable	df	MS	F
Machiavellianism	1	11.68	n.s.
Implication	1	65.37	n.s.
Interaction: Mach x implication	1	41.89	n.s.
Between Ss (Error)	34	110.12	
Periods (base-preaccusation)	1	2007.47	50.78**
Interaction: periods x Mach	1	30.46	n.s.
Interaction: periods x implication	1	85.10	n.s.
Interaction: periods x implication x Mach	1	208.40	5.27*
Pooled Ss x periods (error)	34	39.67	

* $p < .05$
** $p < .01$

[a] Only preaccusation interrogation data used for implicated Ss for purpose of comparison with nonimplicated Ss.

Our argument that high Machs are more prone to use the direct glance to present an appearance of innocence receives further support from a comparison of the visual behavior of implicated subjects before and after they have been accused of cheating. The mean number of seconds per minute of looking at the interviewer are listed by Machiavellianism and experimental periods in Table IV-3 and graphically presented in Fig. IV-1. We see that while high and low Machs did not differ in the extent to which they look at the interviewer during the baseline interview period, the high Machs averted their eyes less than the lows during the preaccusation interrogation, and actually increased the amount to which they look at the interviewer after they have been accused of cheating. Low Machs, on the other hand, continued the aversive trend established during the preaccusation interrogation. Analysis of variance shows an F ratio significant beyond the .01 level for the periods effect ($F = 24.28$; $df = 2$ and 60) and beyond the .05 level for the interaction of Machiavellianism and experimental periods ($F = 4.79$, $df = 2$ and 60). Results of the Duncan range test show that low Machs were significantly less active after being accused than they were in the base-line period, and also significantly less active after being accused than were the high Machs. High Machs, on the other hand, did not differ significantly in visual activity during the base and postaccusation periods. These latter findings are in contrast with the baseline and interrogation means of the nonimplicated subjects listed in Table IV-3.

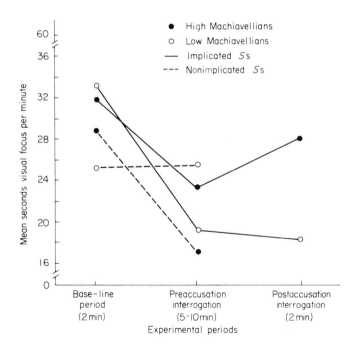

FIG. IV-1. Mean number of seconds per minute in which Ss looked at E during three periods of the experiment.

ADDITIONAL DIFFERENCES BETWEEN HIGH- AND LOW-MACH SCORERS

Our data permitted us to compare high- and low-Mach scorers with respect to several other measures. We compared the two groups of subjects as to the mean length of mutual glance, the number of confessions elicited by the experimenter, the quality of their resistance to the confederate's attempts to implicate them, and the extent to which they denied or admitted cheating.

An index of the number of seconds of mutual glances per minute of interaction may, for any moderately large index, e.g., 30 sec/min, consist of many quick glances, or of a smaller number of steadily held glances. The interpretation put on a pattern of 30 1-sec glances could very well differ from that put on a pattern of 3 10-sec glances. Thus, we wished to determine if high- and low-Mach scorers differed in pattern as well as in the amount of time spent in mutual glances with an accuser. It would be consistent with our earlier argument should high Machs hold each glance exchanged with their inquisitor for a longer period of time. One who wishes to communicate that he has no awkward secrets to conceal may use the steady glance as an indication of his intent.

We developed an index of steady glances by averaging the number of seconds which subjects held each mutual glance with the interrogator. This index was computed separately for the period prior to the experiment (a period in which the subject engaged in friendly discussion with the experimenter) and for the period in which the experimenter interrogated the subject after having accused him of cheating.

Means of the "held glances" showed no striking differences during the baseline period. During the interrogation period we found a tendency for the low Machs to drop off more than high scorers from the level established during the base-line period (4.33 – 3.49 sec compared to 4.46 – 4.25 sec for high scorers). The difference, which averaged over .5 sec per glance, was not significant, however, when the data were subjected to an analysis of variance.

The analyses reported above did not take into account the fact that half of the subjects were accused and then interrogated in the presence of a confederate, whereas the remaining half were interrogated alone. When the presence or absence of the confederate was treated as a variable, the interaction of Machiavellianism and conditions of interrogation markedly affected the decrement in average length of held gazes from base-line through interrogation periods. Measurements of decrement in eye contact are listed in Table IV-5, and analysis of variance is shown in Table IV-6. The data show that whereas high Machs were not affected by the presence or absence of the confederate, the low scorers reduced the length to which they held each gaze some 2 sec per fixation more when they were interrogated alone than when they were interrogated with the confederate. Although the difference between the low Machs interrogated alone and high Machs in both conditions appears great, the Duncan range test

TABLE IV-5

Decrement[a] in Mean Length per Eye Contact with E Recorded for Ss
Categorized by Mach Score and Interrogation Procedures
(Decrements in Hundredths of a Second)

	Interrogation procedures					
	With con-federate		Without confederate		Decrement by Mach score	
Mach score	$\overline{X}$	(n)	$\overline{X}$	(n)	$\overline{X}$	(n)
High	10	(8)	31	(8)	21	(16)
Low	-28[b]	(7)	172	(9)	84	(16)
Total decrement by procedure	-7	(15)	106	(17)		

[a] Decrement derived from baseline minus interrogation eye contact.
[b] Negative coefficient signifies an increase in average length of glance in interrogation as compared to base-line period.

TABLE IV-6

Analysis of Variance of Decrements in Mean Length per Eye Contact with
Subjects Categorized by Mach Scores and Interrogation Procedures

Variable	df	Adj. MS[a]	F
Machiavellianism	1	2.55	n.s.
Confederate's presence	1	47.02	14.79*
Interaction: Mach x presence	1	40.53	12.75*
Within Ss (Error)	28	3.18	

* $p < .01$.
[a] Means adjusted for disproportionality (Wert, Neidt, & Ahmann, 1954).

shows the only significant difference to be between the conditions under which low Machs were interrogated. The presence of a confederate, it is clear, increased the extent to which low-Mach subjects held the experimenter's gaze during the critical interrogation.

Let us defer the discussion of this finding until we have considered certain other differences in the behavior of high and low Machs.

A related point is concerned with the incidence of confessions. Confessions, as could be expected, were more forthcoming when subjects were interrogated alone. Twelve of 19 subjects confessed when interrogated alone, but only 4 of 19 confessed in the presence of the confederate. (Each subject was interrogated in one condition only.) The chi square for this distribution was 6.90, $p < .01$. The data certainly support the usual police and intelligence practices of separating suspects for purposes of interrogation.

Of those interrogated alone, 9 were low Machs and 10 were high Machs. Seven of the 9 lows confessed as contrasted with 5 of 10 high Machs. On the other hand, only 1 of 8 high Machs confessed when interrogated in the presence of the confederate, whereas 3 of 11 low scorers so confessed. Low scorers when interrogated alone met and held another's gaze less, and confessed relatively more.

When the verbal behavior of those who were interrogated in the absence of the confederate was examined, those who confessed were found to differ strikingly from those who did not confess. Confessors talked proportionally more following accusation than did nonconfessors. Those who eventually confessed talked during 83% of the interrogation period compared to 53% recorded for those who refused to confess. This difference was significant beyond the .01 level (two-tailed test).

As was pointed out earlier, relatively few high Machs confessed. Thus, the number in the subcell groups (confession or not by Mach scores) were so disproportionate, and in some cases so small, as to render detailed analysis impossible. Nevertheless, the pattern of subcell means is worth noting, for while high Machs talked 58% of the time, on the average, lows talked some 79% of the period. The difference would appear mainly to be due to the different speech tendencies of high and low scorers who resisted confession. High and low scorers who confessed spoke 81 and 83% respectively, while the percentage of speaking time recorded for high- and low-Mach nonconfessors amounted to 49 and 65%, respectively.[7] Unfortunately, we did not record the amount of time the interrogator spoke; therefore, we do not know whether the nonconfessors were better able to tolerate silence, or whether their responses were of such a nature as to force the interrogator into longer speeches or more frequent queries. In any event it would seem that those who confessed literally talked themselves into doing so.

The preceding analyses suggest that the high Mach may be better able to control his behavior in the presence of another when it is in his interest to do so. That high scorers may be more capable of resisting another's influence is suggested by the analyses presented below.

High and low Machs were compared as to the degree to which they were judged to resist the confederate's attempts to implicate them in cheating. Ratings of the recorded discussions during the implication period yielded a mean of 3.24

---

[7] Differences in proportion of speaking time were not due to the fact that women were relatively more numerous in the low Machiavellian group. Both high-Machiavellian women and low-Machiavellian men were more similar to those of the opposite sex in the same Machiavellian category than they were to those of their own sex in a different Machiavellian category.

(on a 7-point scale) for high scorers, whereas low scorers received an average rating of 4.12. Scale point 3 is described as, "subject attempts to dissuade the confederate a little from cheating"; point 4 is labeled "subject withdraws psychologically"; point 5 is described as "subject gives confederate a little verbal encouragement." Thus, we see that although the differences were not statistically significant, the supposedly more Machiavellian subjects actually tended to resist the confederate's unethical behavior more than did their supposedly less Machiavellian peers.

Although our procedures resulted in the subject being implicated by the confederate in spite of all but the most extreme cases of resistance (such as walking out), the subject could still resist the confederate's influence by the accuracy of the answer to which he would agree. Task solutions were reported in terms of the numbers of dots which the subject and the confederate agreed upon. In each case the confederate argued strongly for the exactly correct answer.

Decisions in which high scorers figured averaged 2.14 dots in error compared with a mean error of 1.19 dots for the joint decisions in which low scorers were involved. Put another way, 75% of the low scorers agreed to an answer that was no more than one dot in error whereas only 29% of the high Machs would agree to an answer so nearly correct. When errors were categorized according to whether they were 1 or greater than 1, the χ^2 test applied to the Mach by size of dot-error table was 6.47, $p < .02$. Once again the supposedly less-ethical high Machs put up more resistance to the cheating confederate.

Up to this point we could argue that the high Machs were acting more ethically than the lows. Compared to the lows, the highs tended to resist implication and did more strongly resist giving improperly obtained correct answers. Data concering the quality of subjects' responses to interrogation raise serious questions about the validity of such an interpretation, however. As was indicated earlier (Table IV-1), raters estimated the quality of subjects' lying or confessing during a pre- and postaccusation interrogation. High scorers were rated as lying more plausibly during the postaccusation interrogation, being rated 5.12 (7 = absolute falsehood), compared to an average rating of 3.94 given to low scorers (1 = complete truthfulness). Furthermore, the decrease in the low scorers' plausibility of lying from pre- to postaccusation was greater than that of the high scorers, regardless of sex (F for Machiavellianism = 4.34, $p < .05$, df = 1 and 30).

The above results suggest that the behavior of the high and low scorers may be more fruitfully considered in terms of ability to withstand another's influence attempts than in terms of adherence to abstract ethical beliefs. The data indicate that those scoring high on the Mach scale first put up a stronger resistance to a confederate's attempts to implicate them, continued to more strongly resist the confederate as they worked through the critical tasks, then, after the die was cast in spite of their efforts, more strongly resisted the interrogator's attempts to elicit a confession from them. Were the high Machs less ethical, socially more competent, or both?

SEX DIFFERENCES IN USE OF THE LINE OF REGARD

As noted above, previous research had indicated that women look more than men into the line of regard of another. To test for this expected difference, we considered the mean number of seconds per minute of eye contact recorded for all subjects during the preliminary discussion with the experimenter (the base-line period). In this period the conditions of discourse were very similar to those in two previous studies (Exline, 1963; Exline *et al.*, 1965).

TABLE IV-7

Mean Seconds per Minute/Time of Mutual Eye Contact with Experimenter during Base-Line Period

	Sex of subject					
	Men		Women		Total[a]	
Machiavellianism	$\overline{X}$	(n)	$\overline{X}$	(n)	$\overline{X}$	(n)
High	31.18	(13)	32.37	(6)	31.56	(19)
Low	24.18	(6)	35.65	(13)	32.03	(19)
Total	28.97	(19)	34.61	(19)	31.80	(38)

[a] Totals include both implicated and nonimplicated *S*s.

Data in Table IV-7 show that women's scores ($\overline{X} = 34.61$) averaged almost 6 sec/min higher than those of men ($\overline{X} = 28.97$), thus confirming the relationships discovered in the studies cited above. *F* was 4.99 ($p < .05$, $df = 1$ and 24).

Although the data suggest the possibility that sex and Machiavellianism interact to product an effect on eye contact, a significant *F* was found only for sex. The size of the mean difference between eye contact scores of low-Mach men and women (greater than 10 sec/min) suggests, however, the desirability of future comparisons with larger samples.

Sex differences in amount of eye contact with the experimenter were not found during the posttask interview, although once again a strong tendency for Machiavellianism to interact with sex was noted. Also, in this period the eye contact scores of implicated and nonimplicated subjects did not differ.

Although the interaction of sex and Machiavellianism was not significant, the strong trends might cause one to wonder if sex differences rather than

Machiavellianism could explain the decrease in eye contact during the interrogation before and after the subject was accused of cheating. Examination of the
data of Tables IV-1 and IV-7 shows, for example, that men tend to make up a
rather higher proportion of high-Mach and a lower proportion of low-Mach
subjects. Should males be more capable than females of maintaining eye contact
under stress, it could be argued that the unequal representation of the sexes in
the two Mach categories could account for the smaller decrease in eye contact
already noted for the high-Mach scorers (see Table IV-3).

The data, however, do not support the above contention. When eye contact
before and after accusation was examined within each Mach category, the ratio
of increments to decrements was very similar for both sexes. In the low-Mach
category the ratio of increments to decrements is 2:2 for men and 6:6 for women.
For high-Mach scorers the ratio is 8:3 for men and 4:1 for women. Thus, factors
associated with Machiavellianism rather than sex would seem better suited to
account for the results depicted in Fig. IV-1.

DISCUSSION

High-Mach scorers reduced eye contact with an interrogator relatively less
than low Machs after being implicated in cheating, and more than low Machs
when neither was implicated. We interpret these results as supporting the
argument that personality factors mediate the use of eye contact under
differential situational inducements to conceal information.

The data permit us to consider another interesting question — namely, do
those who make a high score on a questionnaire designed to reveal a propensity
to manipulate others perform in a morally less creditable manner?

At the successive choice points in the experimental session a supposedly more
moral person (as conventionally defined) would: (a) attempt to prevent or
dissuade the confederate from cheating; (b) expose him at the first opportunity;
(c) resist using the confederate's unethically obtained information; (d) confess at
an early moment in the interrogation; (e) confess after accusation; (f) lie less
plausibly and effectively.

Consistent differences in moral conduct between high and low Machs were not
found. On the one hand, high scorers tended to try to dissuade the confederate
from cheating, and were significantly more effective in resisting the confederate's
attempt to get them to use the exactly correct answer which he had cheated to
get. The low Machs, on the average, showed a slight tendency to encourage the
confederate, and were more prone to accept an answer that was closer to the one
which the confederate urged. On the other hand, the high scorers, while not
differing from the lows in the plausibility of their lying prior to being accused,
maintained their ability to lie after accusation much more than did the low
scorers. The latter finding was statistically significant and probably reflects the

fact that high scorers tended to confess less. Thus, in terms of a primitive morality, the conduct of low Machs appeared to be more moral at certain choice points, and that of the high scorers at others. Such results are consistent with previous studies of moral behavior (Allinsmith, 1960; Hartshorne & May, 1928–1930; Weinberg, 1960).

In a different vein, one can argue that the inconsistency in the relative moral conduct of high and low Machs is more apparent than real, and that our results point to an underlying consistency in the conduct of high Machs with respect to manipulating and being manipulated by others. The high Machs' apparently moral behavior in the earlier (implication) stages becomes more consistent with their later behavior if it is considered as the obverse of their inclination to manipulate others, i.e., as a disinclination to be manipulated by others. Thus, the tendency to attempt to dissuade the confederate, and the significantly greater resistance to agreeing to the use of the exact answer, could be said to reflect the high Mach's resistance to another's manipulations rather than the manifestation of a keener moral sense. Such an interpretation would suggest that the conduct of the high Machs was consistent throughout.

For example, the relatively greater resistance to implication shown by the high Machs, coupled with their steadier gaze and more reticent speech during interrogation, would seem to indicate that high-Mach scorers are more capable of controlling their performance vis-a-vis another in stressful interpersonal situations. The latter interpretation is consistent with results obtained by Jones, Gergen, and Davis (1962) whose study showed that high-Mach women were less influenced by negative feedback than were low scorers. In a subsequent study (Exline & Eldridge, 1967), we found again that high Machs more readily maintain eye contact with another when the other reported his personal impression of the subject to the subject himself.

Thus, our comparison of high and low scorers provides data which are consistent with the suggestion that the high scorer is a more capable social performer. There would seem to be merit in the argument that high scorers are better described in terms of their personal force, initiative, and competence in social interaction rather than in terms of moral superiority or inferiority. Earlier we suggested that our data showed that high-Mach scorers controlled their own performance to manipulate the experimenter into forming a false impression of their innocence. Perhaps our data are better interpreted as providing support for the proposition that they would be more capable of successful manipulation should they opt for that course.

In closing, we stress the need for caution in generalizing from the results of this experiment.

1. The number of nonimplicated subjects was small and was reduced even more when categorized by Mach scores.

2. Although refined analyses indicated that the sex bias did not affect relationships between Machiavellianism and visual behavior, the large number of high-scoring males and low-scoring females is nevertheless a cause for concern.

3. Finally, we must consider the possibility that the greater visual avoidance tendencies of the low Machs may have reflected a greater feeling of shame rather than less ability to project a false image of innocence.

SUMMARY

During a two-person experimental task the experimenter was called out of the room and a confederate implicated subjects in cheating on the task. After the task the experimenter interviewed the subjects, ostensibly to evaluate their task problem-solving methods, grew suspicious, accused subjects of cheating, and demanded an explanation. High-Mach subjects looked the interrogator in the eye while denying cheating more than lows (though all subjects looked at the interrogator less than during an innocuous precheating interview) and confessed less often than lows. Further data revealed that the highs had put up greater resistance to the confederate's attempt to implicate them in cheating, and also lied more plausibly (as rated by independent judges) to the interrogator after the accusation.

CHAPTER V

IN SEARCH OF THE MACHIAVEL

Florence Geis, Richard Christie,
and Carnot Nelson

When the subjects of Exline *et al.* were accused of cheating, those who had
scored high on the Mach scale looked their accuser in the eye, while denying
cheating, longer than low scorers. Looking one's accuser in the eye in such a
situation can be interpreted as an attempt to convince him. But this manipulation was defensive in nature. The subject was caught in a difficult situation not of
his own choosing and attempted to manipulate the experimenter in self-defense
against the experimenter's attempt to manipulate him.

This interpretation of the Exline *et al.* results provoked the question of
offensive versus defensive manipulation. The present research was undertaken to
compare high and low Mach-scale scorers in interpersonal manipulation when
offensive manipulation was legitimized — when it was at the subject's option, to
be undertaken on his own initiative, and for reasons and in ways of his own
choosing.

If "Machiavellianism" has any behavioral definition, such self-initiated
manipulation of others should be at the core. This research can be interpreted as
a test of the behavioral validity of scores on the Mach scales. The instrument was
originally developed on the assumption that individuals who behave manipulatively in interpersonal relations are more likely to endorse such attitudes than
individuals who do not. By definition, they do not take a moralistic view of
themselves, others, or interpersonal relations and should feel no greater qualms
at admitting their behavior than they do in performing it. If the Mach scales
measure manipulative behavior as well as self-reported agreement with Machiavellian precepts about behavior, then high scorers ought to behave more
manipulatively than low scorers in a behavioral test situation.

First, it seemed reasonable to assume that high scorers on the Mach scales
would not be subject to the ethical qualms which presumably restrain low scorers
from interpersonal manipulation. Thus, in a situation in which specific
manipulations are suggested and officially legitimized, high scorers should
perform more manipulations than lows.

Second, if high scorers are those who practice interpersonal manipulation in
their daily lives, then they ought to be more accustomed to thinking in terms of
manipulating others, and to thinking in terms of manipulations that can be

carried out in the particular situations in which they find themselves. In short, in a situation in which a blanket, open-ended legitimation of interpersonal manipulation is given, high scorers could be expected to think up and perform more unsuggested, innovative manipulations than lows.

Finally, it seemed reasonable to assume that most people enjoy practicing their special skills. If high scorers on the Mach scales are skillful at interpersonal manipulation, and find it congenial, they should enjoy it more than low scorers.

The initial problem in testing these ideas was to devise a situation to induce — but optionally — the behavior in which we were interested. There were several indications that high Mach-scale scorers resisted experimental inductions. In the experiment by Exline *et al.* for example, high scorers resisted cheating more strongly. A study by Jones *et al.* (1962) on female undergraduates had an experimental manipulation designed to make subjects believe they had been rejected by a prestigeous interviewer. The prediction was that high scorers would then make more overt efforts to win approval. As it turned out, they made fewer. One possible explanation of this might be that high scorers were suspicious and defined the laboratory situation as one in which they were trying to outguess the experimenter. This hunch is consistent with our own experiences in a pilot study for the present research in which we observed greater wariness on the part of high scorers and a more marked tendency to be inquisitive about the purpose of the experiment. Parenthetically, high scorers also appeared more eager than lows to make and keep appointments to participate as subjects in experimental research.

The problem was to design a situation in which the hypothesized manipulativeness of the high scorers would work in favor of the hypothesis rather than against it. This required an induction that would draw a subject's suspicion and manipulative bent away from the induction itself, and the experimenter delivering it, and focus them instead on an intended object. This suggested that we needed a test situation in which manipulation would be so clearly legitimate that few subjects would mistrust an explanation of it.

At the risk of alienating ourselves from fellow social psychologists, we decided that one of the most common situations in which deception is viewed as legitimate is in laboratory experimentation in social psychology. In fact, experience suggests that students in many universities actually expect to be deceived in experiments. This can sometimes lead to cat-and-mouse games in which the investigator has to devise ways to mislead the subject as to the kind of deception that he seems to be perpetrating in order to decoy the subject's suspicions from the actual deception.

This suggested a possibly subversive but realistic design. If subjects in social psychological experiments expect to be manipulated, it would seem that such experiments have some social sanction. Our solution to the suspicion problem was to switch roles on the subject, and make him the experimenter in an interpersonal laboratory study involving deception. The subject was first asked to take an important personality test to be administered by the previous subject, now serving as experimenter. After he had taken the test, a major deception in the purposes previously given him for taking it was revealed. He was then asked to serve as experimenter for the next-scheduled subject and given the opportunity to perpetrate and embellish the now-known deception.

The personality test used, a liberal adaption of ten of Witkin's (1950) EFT designs, was selected to meet several criteria: it involved a series of discrete problems, thus permitting a report by the experimenter to the subject of his percentile score for each problem. A standard suggestion was given to all subjects to falsify the scores they reported to the subject they were to test. Further, it was a task on which subjects could be expected not to have prior knowledge of their ability, and to be uncertain of their performances. Thus, it provided credibly manipulatable scores. On the other hand, each design has an objective and clearly definable correct answer known to the experimenter administering the test (so the real experimenters could distinguish manipulation from confusion on the part of the subject experimenter). Since the test consisted of ten designs, each experimenter had exactly the same number of opportunities to falsify the scores he was to report to his subject. Percentile scores were used because all subjects would be familiar with them, and because they provided a standard and measurable range of possible manipulation. Percentile scores were constructed for each design to depend upon the time taken to solve it. Thus, by programming an assistant serving as subject to obtain exactly the same series of scores for all subjects serving as experimenter, the amount of time available to each experimenter to devise and perform manipulations was automatically held constant, as was the ability of the subject tested by all of them.

Finally, a pilot study suggested that subjects who scored high and low on the Mach scales were intuitively distinguishable in the deception situation. This hunch was also tested. In summary, it was anticipated that high scoring subjects would:

1. perform both more and a greater variety of manipulations overall than low scorers;
2. use more of the induced deceptions than low scorers;
3. be more likely to innovate additional, new kinds of distractions;
4. be more likely to endorse manipulative reasons for enjoying the experience.

PROCEDURE

All of the classes in introductory psychology and sociology during the first summer term at Columbia University in 1963 were given, in the first week of class, Mach IV, Mach V, and the Marlowe – Crowne (Crowne & Marlowe, 1960) Social Desirability Scale. These classroom sessions were supervised by an assistant who did not participate in the laboratory session, and when subjects were seen later in the laboratory, the preliminary tests were not mentioned. Only the male respondents ($n = 81$) were considered for the laboratory study.

The corrected split-half reliability of Mach IV in the total male sample was .69, the Kuder–Richardson reliability estimate for Mach V was .22, and the correlation between them was .37. Ninety-five percent of the males in the classes tested volunteered to participate in an experiment.

The two Mach scale distributions of males' scores were each split at the median. The 19 respondents who had scored above the median on both were classified as "high," while the 20 who had scored below the medians were called "lows." These 39 consistent high and low scorers were identified as potential subjects for the laboratory study. Of the 39, five were rejected initially because they were obviously not comparable to the assistants in age, and another was rejected because he did not speak English fluently. Another four could not be located by telephone. Of the 29 contacted, one high declined at the initial telephone call, and one low failed to appear for his appointment. After attrition, 14 highs and 13 lows were run in the experimental situation.

Age and Mach scale scores for the total male sample initially tested, identified high and low scorers, and the subjects actually used are summarized in Table V-1. The sample used for the laboratory session did not differ significantly from the identified highs and lows in scale score.

TABLE V-1

Mach Scale Scores and Age in the Total Sample, Identified High and Low Scorers, and High and Low Scorers used as Subjects in the Study

	n	Median	Mean	s
Mach IV				
Total sample	81	105.00	103.00	14.00
All highs	19	114.20	116.60	7.80
High subjects	14	116.00	117.40	8.40
All lows	20	89.20	88.00	8.40
Low subjects	13	89.00	87.60	9.40
Mach V				
Total sample	77	112.24	111.46	14.16
All highs	19	124.48	125.56	7.20
High subjects	14	124.95	126.16	7.98
All lows	20	100.00	98.50	9.90
Low subjects	13	95.98	94.48	10.20
Age				
Total Sample	77	20.28	21.74	5.25
All highs	18	19.83	20.83	4.59
High subjects	14	19.50	19.50	1.56
All lows	20	20.33	22.90	7.45
Low subjects	13	20.20	20.85	3.24

THE LABORATORY SITUATION

Each subject was seen individually for approximately 1½ hr by a female experimenter and two male assistants chosen for ability to impersonate a Columbia undergraduate. The two assistants served alternately in the two stooge roles. While one assistant was serving as a stooge with the subject, the other observed and recorded the subject's behavior from the observation room. Both assistants knew the design and purpose of the study and the conceptual identifications of high- and low-scoring subjects. However, they did not know the Mach scale classification of any subject while they were observing him or interacting with him in the session.

The stooge roles were programmed to standardize the experience for all subjects as far as possible. In the first part of the session, when the subject was serving as subject, all were given, as their own scores on the test, exactly the same series of percentile scores, and exactly the same comments. In the second half of the session, when the subject was serving as experimenter, all of them tested a subject who scored in approximately the 50th percentile range, and who responded in standardized ways to the naive subjects' behaviors.

When the subject arrived, he was met by the experimenter and told that he would first be given a personality test, then serve as experimenter and give the same test to the next subject. Subjects were also told of the one-way vision screen in the experimental room and informed that the entire session would be observed. They were then given a two-page typed explanation of the study titled, "Field Dependence—Independence and Two-Person Interaction," emphasizing the importance of the personality dimension measured and the importance of "doing well" on the test. This explanation informed them that the purposes of the study were to assess Columbia students on the personality dimension and to find out whether students could be trained to administer the test to other students. For these purposes, each subject would first be given the test by the subject ahead of him and then would give the test to the next subject. It also informed them that the test would consist of 10 sets of simple and complex designs and that their percentile score for each design would be reported to them as they completed it.

After the subject had finished reading the explanation, the experimenter took him to the experimental room and introduced him to the subject waiting there who would administer the Embedded Figures Test to him. The subject was seated at a table opposite the stooge. A fiberboard divider 8 in. high and 20 in. long was placed on the table between them. The subject was given a test booklet titled "Embedded Figures Test, Herman A. Witkin, Adapted Short Form." Each booklet contained ten simple designs, enlarged from Witkin's cards and mimeographed in black ink, each followed by three copies of its corresponding complex design. The complex designs used were modified to make them more difficult, enlarged to the same scale, and reproduced in varicolored lines. The ten test designs were preceded by a practice design which the subject inspected as the testing procedure was explained to him by the experimenter.

The test consists of ten pairs of designs. First you will look at a simple design, and then at a complex design in which the simple design you have just seen is hidden. Your task will be to find and trace the simple design hidden in the complex design. You can look at the simple design as long as you want. When you are ready, fold back the page and look at the complex design. As soon as you start looking at the complex design, Mr. ————— (stooge serving as experimenter) will start the stopwatch. When you locate the simple design trace it with your pencil. As soon as you finish tracing Mr. ————— will stop the watch. Hand your test booklet to him. He has the key to check your solution, and he will tell you whether it is right or not. If it is right, he will tell you your percentile score for that design. If it is wrong, he will tell you to go on searching.

While the subject was taking the test, the stooge recorded his actual time scores. Regardless of the subject's performance, however, he was given the standard series — 70, 60, 70, 70, 80, 70, 80, 70, 30, 70% — as his percentile scores for the ten designs. The stooge also made two comments to each subject. At the third design the stooge said, "You seem to be doing these quite fast." At the sixth design he said, "Remember that I have to start timing you as soon as you turn the page back."

When the subject had completed the test, the experimenter returned and said:

Thank you both very much. — At this point, Mr. ————— (naive subject), I owe you some further explanation. In addition to our interest in your performance on the Embedded Figures Test, and in training students to administer the test, we are also very much interested in the kind of situation in which one person had absolute power over the rewards and punishments of another person. I'm sure you can think of many situations that are like this. Usually, of course, the power is used fairly and in accord with the rules. Sometimes, however, in such situations, the person who has the power may use it arbitrarily, or for his own private purposes. Now we are interested in the motivations and in the personal reactions and feelings of *both* people in this kind of situation. Therefore, this experiment has been designed with two conditions. In the control condition the student who is giving the test is asked to give it exactly in accord with the rules that both of you are told beforehand. But in the experimental condition, the student who is giving the test is asked to use his power arbitrarily. Now you and Mr. ————— (stooge) have been assigned to the experimental condition. Mr. ————— (stooge) what did you do?

The stooge's programmed reply was, "Well, I made a couple of comments. And, remember when I told you you were in the 30th percentile? You were really in the 70th. That's all. . . . I don't think I'd like to do this kind of thing very much." The subject was shown his score sheet with a "70" in the Percentile Score column for design nine, and a "30" circled, in the margin next to it. The other percentile scores recorded matched those reported to the subject verbally.

Both "subjects" were then asked to complete a short questionnaire describing their reactions to the experience, and the stooge was thanked and dismissed. When the subject finished his questionnaire, the experimenter returned and reviewed the rules and mechanical details of the testing procedure with him. After he indicated understanding of these, the experimenter delivered the following intentionally somewhat ambiguous induction:

Once you've been assigned to the experimental condition you remain in it, so we are asking you to use your power arbitrarily — to confuse or distract the subject who will be taking the test. Now precisely how you go about doing this, and how much of it you do, is up to your imagination — and your conscience. Obviously, we want you to be in the position of having absolute power to use as you choose to use it. Some people find this very uncongenial — as apparently the man who tested you did — and they do very little. Other people find it a great deal of fun. What you do is up to you.

Any questions by the subject were answered as briefly as possible, usually by "yes" or "no," and in any case followed by the standard assertion, "What you do is up to you." When the subject indicated that he had no more questions, the experimenter said:

Oh, one more thing. Just be sure to record his actual percentile scores in the column here on his score sheet. If you do tell him anything other than his real score, write it, also, in the margin, and put a circle around it, so we'll have a record of just what stresses he was under. OK?

After a second assurance that the subject had no questions, the experimenter called in the second stooge, introduced him to the subject as the next subject, and left.

While the subject was administering the test to the second stooge, the first assistant observed and recorded his behavior via a one-way mirror and sound system connecting the experimental room to an adjoining observation room. The subject's verbal and nonverbal behaviors were judged as "manipulative" or "not manipulative" by the observer. Those judged manipulative were coded into predefined categories. Behaviors which could not be categorized were quoted, paraphrased, or described briefly. Verbal behaviors were coded by internal content or meaning, and the context of the interpersonal situation. Behaviors recorded as a single manipulation actually varied from one word to several sentences. Both assistants were trained in advance for the observing task as well as both of the stooge roles. The average reliability of judgment and coding over three trials at the end of the training period for the two assistants compared to each other and to the experimenter was .84.

While the subject was administering the test to the stooge, the experimenter observed from the observation room. Simultaneously with the subject, the experimenter timed the stooge in order to signal him to solve each design in the number of seconds required to place him at the predetermined percentile score for that design. At the appropriate time, the experimenter closed a switch which turned on a small, dim light visible to the stooge but not to the subject. The predetermined percentile scores obtained by the stooge were: 50, 50, 60, 50, 40, 80, 40, 60, 50, 50%. In addition to timing and signaling the stooge, the experimenter also recorded, along with the subject and the observing assistant, the percentile scores reported verbally by the subject to the stooge.

The stooge engaged in "searching behavior" until tracing the correct solution at the signal from the experimenter. The stooge accepted whatever the subject said or did with as little response as possible, with standardized exceptions: the first time a subject reported a percentile score of 30% or lower, or 70% or higher (including a correct report of 80% for design six), the stooge gave him a "questioning look." Additional score reports of 70% or above elicited no further response from the stooge. In the event of a second report of a score of 30% or lower, the subject received a second "questioning look" accompanied by the query, "Are you *sure?*" Additional reports of 30% or lower elicited no further responses.

When the testing session was over, the experimenter returned and repeated the identical explanation of the "deception" (the study of "power situations") and request for questionnaire responses as before. When the subject had finished this second questionnaire, the experimenter answered any questions he had and discussed his comments with him in as much detail as he wished. Finally, the subject was thanked for his cooperation and pledged to secrecy. There were no indications that any subject knew beforehand what he would be asked to do, nor did any spontaneously question the legitimacy of "the other student."

Immediately after each subject was run the two assistants independently classified him as high or low Mach on the basis of their experience with him.

In summary, the following measures were obtained:

1. The number and size (in percentile points) of lies told by the naive subject to the subject he was testing. The true percentile scores of the stooge were, of course, those predetermined. The scores actually reported by the subject were recorded by him in the margin of the stooge's score sheet, and also by the experimenter and the observing assistant, independently, from the observation room. Three of the 270 score reports by subjects were inaudible to both the experimenter and the observer; in these three cases the subject's own record of his report was accepted. In the other 267 cases, there was perfect agreement among all the records of the subjects' score reports.

2. The subject's responses to the two postsession questionnaires, one after serving as subject, the second after serving as experimenter.

3. Mach classification guesses by the naive assistants.

4. The number and either category or description of other manipulations performed by the subject while he was administering the test to the stooge, judged, coded and recorded by the observing assistant. The descriptions used by the observer to code the subject's comments into the six predefined categories were:

(a) Confessions of confusion: I'm confused, uncertain, can't remember instructions, made a mistake, forgot to set stop watch, read wrong norm, etc. Either statement or question.

(b) Apology in any form for confusion or mistake.

(c) Accusations of confusion: you're confused, made a mistake, going at it wrong, looking too long, etc. Statement or question.

(d) Disparagements: you're not good, slow, clumsy, etc., at this.

(e)   Compliments: you're good, fast, etc., at this.

(f)   Comments on test or design, e.g., it's hard, easy, beautiful, confusing, etc.

Those manipulative behaviors which had not been classified but had been paraphrased or described were subsequently coded independently by the experimenter and one assistant into five additional categories:

(g)   Giving or repeating any of the "true" procedural instructions or test rules, i.e., any of those initially specified by the experimenter in the official instructions.

(h)   Giving embellished (but not false) procedural instructions or exhortations: e.g., "Now try and make a killing on your last one."

(i)   Giving false procedural instructions or test rules (i.e., any "rule" clearly fabricated by the subject): e.g., "You have to draw your lines dark and straight, and *exactly* on the design line you intend as your answer."

(j)   Percentile or score manipulations other than false scores: e.g., some subjects called some correct solutions by the stooge incorrect.

(k)   Comment or conversation completely irrelevant to the testing procedure or the stooge's performance, but judged clearly manipulative: e.g., during stooge's concentration, "By the way, what class are you taking this summer?"

The recorded nonverbal manipulations were similarly coded independently by the experimenter and one assistant into four categories:

(a)   Nonverbal vocalizations: e.g., whistling, humming, coughing, throat clearing.

(b)   Tapping — with pencil, pen, fingers, foot — on table, divider board, chair, floor, etc.

(c)   Manipulation of objects: e.g., clicking pencil or pen clip; rearranging position of ash tray or contents of it; lighting matches (not for cigarette or pipe); intentionally knocking over divider board. (All subjects learned, while taking the test, that the divider separating subject and experimenter would fall over if pushed or knocked against from the subject's side of it. For the experimenter to knock it over, he had to reach around it and push it toward himself.)

(d)   Other body movements: e.g., fidgeting in chair, clapping hands, tying shoe.

The number of comments (verbal manipulations) made by the subject during his administration of the test was simply counted from the observation sheet, independently, by the experimenter and the assistant who had not recorded the observation of that subject. Perfect agreement was obtained for all but the two most active subjects. One of the discrepancies, between counts of 15 and 16, was resolved by a coin flip. The second, between counts of 19 and 21, was resolved by compromise at 20. The number of nonverbal manipulations performed by the subject was likewise counted and perfect agreement was obtained in all cases.

The number of different types of manipulation exhibited by subjects was counted, again independently by the experimenter and the assistant who had not recorded the observations. Lying, regardless of size or number of lies told, was counted as a single type of manipulation. To this one or zero score for each subject was added the number of different categories into which his other behaviors had been coded. Perfect agreement was obtained between the two counters for all subjects.

In addition, we were interested in distinguishing between original, innovative types of manipulation and the simple use or repetition of those suggested by the experimenter or the stooge. The number of innovative manipulations attributed to each subject was the total number of manipulations he had performed exclusive of those in the three categories induced: falsification of test scores, true test instructions, and compliment on test performance.

RESULTS

Before the results are summarized, a check on the experimenter's manipulation, the credibility of the cover stories and induction, is in order. After serving in the subject role, the subject completed a questionnaire, including the items: "Did you feel suspicious *at the time* about any of the instructions or explanation of the experimenter?" "Did you feel suspicious *at the time* about the behavior or procedure of the student who was giving you the test?" After acting as experimenter, subjects completed a second questionnaire which included two similar items: "Did you feel suspicious about any of the instructions or explanations given you for *this* session?" "Did you feel suspicious about the behavior of the student you were testing during the session?" Each of the questions was followed by a 7-point graphic scale labeled "No" at one side (scored as "1"), and "yes" at the other (scored as "7"). The data from these questions are summarized in Table V-2.

TABLE V-2

Suspiciousness during Subject and Experimenter Roles
of High and Low Mach Groups

	Group means			
	High Mach ($n = 14$)	Low Mach ($n = 13$)	t	$p <$
In subject role				
Of experimenter and cover story	4.75	2.92	1.76	.05
Of "the other student"	5.36	2.77	2.94	.01
In experimenter role				
Of experimenter and induction	2.57	2.46	.21	—
Of "the other student"	1.57	2.62	1.55	.10

Congruent with our previous impressions, high scorers were initially more suspicious both of the experimenter's instructions and of the "other student's behavior" than lows were. It should be noted, however, that these responses were given after the first stooge confessed the deception. Clearly, however, the double deception was less suspect than the single one, at least for the high-Mach subjects. After serving as experimenter, their suspiciousness scores on both questions decreased significantly ($p < .005$). Not one of the 14 highs increased in suspiciousness on either item, whereas 5 of the 13 lows increased on at least one of the two. The change in suspiciousness for the lows was insignificant. After serving as experimenter, there was no significant difference between highs and lows in suspiciousness of either the experimental induction or of the behavior of the second stooge.

It appears safe to conclude that the data obtained from the two groups during their performances as experimenter are comparably uncontaminated by suspiciousness.

That the induction was effective may be inferred from the fact that 25 of the 27 subjects reported at least one false score to the stooge they were testing. Of the two who failed to lie, one had the highest Mach IV score in the entire group of highs, while the other was the lowest of the low scorers. Why the high failed to lie we can only conjecture; his behavior provided no hint of any sort. The low stated clearly and emphatically, after the induction, that he "certainly wouldn't do anything like that."

NUMBER AND VARIETY OF MANIPULATIONS PERFORMED

The major findings of the study are summarized in Table V-3. The total number of manipulative behaviors exhibited by subjects during their administration of the test was computed by summing the number of false scores reported and the number of all other manipulative behaviors recorded by the observers. High scorers performed an average of 15.43 manipulative acts during their administration of the test, compared to an average of 7.08 by low scorers. The difference was significant at the .005 level.[1]

An alternative way of evaluating the manipulative behavior of high- and low-scoring subjects is to compare not the absolute numbers of manipulations performed, but the variety of manipulations performed. A total of 16 different types of manipulation were distinguishable: 11 categories of verbal content, 4 categories of nonverbal content, and percentile score falsification. Highs used an average of 6.43 of these types while lows averaged only 3.08 categories each, a difference also significant at the .005 level.

---

[1] All of the comparisons were evaluated by Mann-Whitney U tests (Sidney Siegel, 1956), or chi square, as well as by t test. The significance levels obtained by the two methods did not differ across the .05 level. Since all of the comparisons were designed to test prespecified directional hypotheses, one-tailed tests were used.

TABLE V-3

Amount and Variety of Manipulation of a
Peer Performed by High- and Low-Mach Subjects

	Group means			
	High Mach ($n = 14$)	Low Mach ($n = 13$)	t	$p <$
Total number of manipulations	15.43	7.08	2.88	.005
Variety of manipulations	6.43	3.08	3.38	.005
Induced manipulations				
Magnitude of lies told	117.86	70.77	2.42	.025
Number of verbal distractions	1.86	.62	2.30	.025
Innovative manipulations				
Verbal distractions				
Number	5.93	1.69	3.31	.005
Variety	3.57	1.15	3.93	.0005
Nonverbal distractions				
Number	3.21	1.54	.77	.25
Variety	.93	.46	.98	.20

INDUCED MANIPULATIONS

In the induction given the subject directly by the experimenter and indirectly by the stooge, three categories of manipulation were specifically mentioned and demonstrated: falsification of test scores and two categories of verbal distraction, compliment on performance and true procedural instructions. A "magnitude of lies" for each subject was computed by summing over his ten percentile score reports the absolute difference between the subject stooge's true score and the score reported to him by the naive subject. The 14 subjects who had scored above the median on both Mach scales told their subject series of lies averaging 117.86 percentile points over the ten trials, while the 13 low scorers accumulated 70.77 percentile points of lying over the same series. The difference between these means was significant at the .025 level.

The number of induced verbal distractions attributed to each subject was simply the sum of his comments coded in the two induced categories. Again, the high scorers' mean of 1.86 was significantly larger than the lows' mean of .62.

INNOVATIVE MANIPULATIONS

The number and variety of manipulations *not* suggested in the induction, but clearly originated by the subject himself, were of particular interest. For these comparisons, the number of manipulations and number of categories of manipulation, exclusive of the three induced categories, were evaluated.

The largest quantitative differences between high and low Machs in the test situation were in number and variety of original, innovative comments they fabricated while administering the test to the stooge. The highs averaged 5.93 innovative comments each, while the lows averaged 1.69 — a difference significant at the .005 level. Similarly, the innovative comments of the high Machs ranged across 3.57 of the nine possible categories of content on the average, while those of the low scorers covered an average of 1.15 different categories. This difference was significant at the .0005 level.

Only 8 of the 27 subjects performed any nonverbal manipulations of any kind. Of the 8 who did, 6 were highs and 2 were lows. The group means for these categories of manipulation differed in the expected direction, but not significantly.

ENJOYMENT OF MANIPULATION

The hypothesis that high scorers would enjoy manipulating a fellow subject more than low scorers would was tested with self-report data from the two questionnaires. The relevant items and the mean responses of the two groups are presented in Table V-4. On the questionnaire each item was followed by a 7-point graphic scale. The response alternatives, given in parentheses in Table V-4, appeared at either end of the scale and were subsequently scored from 1 to 7 in the direction indicated.

Item 2 asked directly how much the subject had enjoyed carrying out the "experimental manipulation." The highs' mean of 6.07 indicated more enjoyment than the lows' mean of 4.38 ($p < .005$). Indirect measures of enjoyment were also included. Since the experimenter role was characterized mainly by the opportunity to manipulate a fellow student, while the subject role was characterized mainly by the possibility of being manipulated, it seemed reasonable to infer enjoyment of manipulation from relative preference for one over the other of the two roles. Three questions, one on the first questionnaire and two on the second, asked for preference between the subject and the experimenter roles. On all three items, the highs indicated stronger preference for the experimenter over the subject role than the lows. The differences between the means of the high and low groups were significant at the .025 level on two of the three and just missed significance ($p < .10$) on the third.

Three phrases, "thinking of ways to carry out the experimental manipulation," "playing God for a while," and "having to deceive the other student," were included on the second questionnaire in a list of ten phrases, each of which was rated by the subjects on a 7-point scale from 1 ("disliked very much") to 7 ("enjoyed very much"). The highs reported greater enjoyment of these aspects of the task than lows did. These same items, included in a list of ten phrases describing the experimenter role, were also rank ordered for "enjoyment" by subjects. The three critical phrases were all ranked higher in enjoyment by the highs than by the lows. Mann–Whitney U tests yielded significance levels of .01, .10, and .05, respectively.

TABLE V-4

Questionnaire Measures of Enjoyment of Manipulation

Items [a]	High Mach ($n = 14$)	Low Mach ($n = 13$)	t	$p <$
1. If you could have your choice, would you rather be subject or experimenter (take the test again or give it to another student) for this next session? ($S = 1; E = 7$)	6.07	4.23	2.20	.025
2. How much did you actually enjoy carrying out the experimental manipulations? (not at all = 1; very much = 7)	6.07	4.38	2.86	.005
3. If this experiment had been set up so that each person served *either* as the subject who takes the test *or* as the experimenter who gives it; which part would you have preferred? ($S = 1; E = 7$)	5.21	3.85	1.60	.10
4. If you had to participate in an additional experimental session, and had your choice of serving only as subject, or only as experimenter which would you prefer? ($S = 1; E = 7$)	5.71	3.54	2.43	.025
5. (Ratings: disliked very much = 1; enjoyed very much = 7)				
a. Thinking of ways to carry out the experimental manipulation	6.43	5.15	2.60	.01
b. Playing God for a while	5.86	4.15	3.02	.005
c. Having to deceive the other student	5.08	4.08	1.44	.10

Group means

[a] Item 1 was completed by S after serving as the subject. The others were completed after serving as experimenter. Items 1-4 are quoted verbatim from the questionnaires. Below each appeared a 7-point graphic scale with one of the response alternatives at the left and the other at the right. The phrases listed for item 5 are quoted verbatim also, but the list contained 7 additional phrases (e.g., "contributing to science"), and was preceded by detailed instructions to S for separate rank-ordering and rating procedures.

OBSERVER PREDICTIONS

Fifty-one blind predictions of the Mach scale classification of the subject just observed were obtained from the observers. (Three of the classification predictions were misplaced by the experimenter.) Of the 51, 38, or 74.5% correctly identified the subject's Mach scale classification. The probability of this percentage of correct guesses by chance was .001 by chi square.

DISCUSSION

It is clear that subjects who were consistent on both the Mach IV and Mach V scales in endorsing amoral, disenchanted, and manipulative attitudes about human nature and interpersonal relations were also consistent in behaving manipulatively in interaction with a peer when they were put to the test in the laboratory. Subjects who had scored above the medians on both Mach scales surpassed those who had scored below the medians in both number and variety of all manipulations performed, in performing the induced manipulations including magnitude of outright deceptions, and in both number and variety of innovative distractions created while administering a test to a supposed peer.

MANIPULATION OR VERBOSITY?

The largest quantitative differences in behavior between the high and low scorers were in the number and variety of comments coded as manipulative. Could this be interpreted simply as verbosity? The available evidence indicates not. First, high scorers were not only more facile verbally than lows; they were also more facile in devising and performing nonverbal distractions. The failure of the nonverbal measures to discriminate significantly between the groups was due to one low Mach who performed 18 nonverbal manipulations falling into all four of the different categories of nonverbal manipulation. (Only one other low performed any nonverbal manipulations at all.) Had the data from this subject been omitted from the analyses, differences between the high and low groups in both number and variety of nonverbal manipulation would have been statistically significant.

In addition, it can probably safely be assumed that most of the interpersonal manipulation that occurs outside of the laboratory is verbally mediated. If, as hypothesized, our high scorers arrived at the laboratory already experienced at manipulating others, it would be quite reasonable to find them differing most from the less experienced lows in the medium they were most accustomed to using for such purposes.

MANIPULATION, PUNITIVENESS, OR SUGGESTIBILITY?

A more general question of the interpretation of our results is that of the subject's motives for manipulating. The tendency of subjects to do without question what an experimenter suggests has been noted (Orne, 1962). Both highs and lows accepted the induction, but highs accepted it more and embellished it further. This result was predicted from a theory that highs would lack the restraining ethical qualms of lows, would be more practiced and skillful at manipulation, and would enjoy it more. Two alternative explanations must also be considered: the highs may have manipulated more because they were more punitive or because they were more suggestible.

The evidence indicates that highs were not more punitive than lows. Almost without exception, the subjects went into the personality test highly motivated to do well. It seemed reasonable to assume that those motivated primarily to hurt or punish the subject to whom they were giving the test would have seized the opportunity to lower his scores as much as possible. The lies told by the subjects were accordingly divided into those raising the true score of the stooge, and those lowering it. For the highs, the average number of lies upward was 1.71, and lies downward, 2.71. For the lows, they were 1.38 and 1.69, respectively. Thus, both highs and lows told slightly more punishing than rewarding lies.[2] However, the differences between mean number of lies up and lies down was not significant for either group.

Similar patterns appeared in the tabulation of categories of verbal manipulations. The mean frequencies for the highs exceeded those of the lows in every one of the 11 categories of verbal manipulation. Again, the highs appear more active and more variable, not more punitive, than the lows.

Our conception of Machiavellianism leads to the inference that highs should be less, not more, suggestible than lows. Yet, upon the experimenter's suggestion, highs manipulated more than lows. In addition, just after being told that they had been deceived, highs reported more "suspicion" of both the experimenter and the other student than did the lows. The suggestibility interpretation, however, does not stand up under scrutiny.

First, all subjects were given two direct suggestions that the manipulation might be legitimately disturbing and certainly was a matter of at least potential ethical concern. At the first catharsis, after confessing his lie and comments, the stooge said in a distressed tone of voice, "I don't think I'd like to do this kind of thing very much." To which the experimenter replied, "Yes, some people do find

---

[2]The observation that more lies down than up were told by all subjects may have been due to the actual scores obtained by the stooge. Five were at the 50th percentile, leaving equal room in either direction for lying. Of the remaining five, two were at 40% and two were at 60%, but the fifth was 80% — allowing more room for downward than upward lying. In addition, the induction given the subjects included the initial "request" to "confuse or distract" the subject.

it quite disturbing." Shortly after this, in the induction, the subject was told, "Now precisely how you go about doing this, and how much of it you do, will be up to your imagination — and your conscience." Subjects responding primarily to the suggestions given should have manipulated more and enjoyed it less. This pattern was not characteristic of either high or low Machs.

Second, highs were less suggestible than lows in the kinds of manipulations they performed. Of the 216 manipulations performed by highs, 60% did not fall into any of the three suggested categories of manipulation. Of the 92 manipulations by lows, 48% were not of the suggested types.

Our inference that highs are probably less suggestible than lows is also consistent with a report by Jones *et al.* (1962). Female subjects were given a negative personal evaluation by an interviewer, and then allowed to change their self-description in a second interview with a different interviewer. Those who had scored high on the Mach scale were less influenced by the initial negative feedback, as measured by changes in self-description, than were low scorers.

ADDITIONAL OBSERVATIONS

The data presented leave no doubt that all subjects understood the induction, but they scarcely convey the imaginative interpretation of it by the highs. For example, the list of manipulations performed by one high includes, among other things: rubs hands together in the stereotyped gesture of anticipation; bends over double, unties shoe, shakes foot, reties shoe; jingles contents of pocket noisily; pulls out chapstick and applies it while staring absent-mindedly at ceiling; whistles; slaps leg and straightens up noisily and abruptly in chair; taps pencil rhythmically on table; hums; reaches around divider and carefully knocks it over (this produces a loud crash and sends papers on table flying in all directions); after 10-sec dead silence apologizes profusely to stooge for distracting him; erases vigorously on blank margin of stooge's score sheet (divider board prevents stooge from seeing that subject is not erasing actual marks); comments, with serious frown at one-way vision mirror, "I feel like I'm on TV, don't you?" (followed by grin at mirror as soon as stooge returns his attention to test booklet); holds match book in both hands above divider board in full view of stooge (pretending to ignore stop watch), tears out matches one by one, dropping each into ash tray; tears up empty matchbook cover and drops pieces ostentatiously into ash tray; dismantles his own ballpoint pen behind divider board, uses spring to shoot it, parts flying, across the room; jumps from chair, dashes across room to retrieve pen parts saying, "Sorry, I'm a little nervous."

No low Mach fabricated an original (i.e., clearly false) test rule or instruction. Three highs did. One repeatedly rejected correct solutions by the stooge, insisting that the tracing must be "dark and straight and exactly on the design line." (The subject clearly knew from his own experience in taking the test that no such requirement existed; and, in fact, while the stooge was busy retracing, the subject recorded on the score sheet the accurate time and percentile scores for the initial, correct solutions.) At each rejection, the subject reminded the stooge brusquely that the additional time taken for retracing would cost him percentile points.

Two other characteristic behaviors were not systematically recorded. Subjects who asked, in response to the induction, if they were allowed to engage in this or that specific form of deception were usually highs, while those who asked whether they *had* to engage in any deception at all were usually lows. Similarly, those who apologized at the second catharsis to the stooge they had tested — and sounded genuine and sincere about it — were usually lows.

The two observers were instructed that high Machs would be personally cold, distant, and detached, but perform the deception and other manipulations with "authority, fineness, and verve," while the lows would be personally warm, close and "empathic," but perform the manipulations in a flat, colorless, and generally unimpressive way. With this information, the two observers achieved significant agreement with the Mach scales in classifying the subjects. The evidence indicated that the observers were not predicting simply on the basis of frequency counts since the pattern of hits and misses did not follow the frequency counts.

In light of these results, the three authors and the other assistant independently completed Block's (1961) California Q Sort to describe the "typical high scorer." The six intercorrelations ranged from .53 to .78, with a median of .62. Most of the larger discrepancies reflected different levels of interpretation. Some of the items would legitimately be classified as "highly characteristic" of the high Mach as he appears to others, but "highly uncharacteristic" of the "real purposes" behind his appearance.

The 39 items on which all four raters had agreed within two scale categories of each other were selected, and the four scale values assigned each of them were averaged. Table V-5 lists the five "most characteristic" descriptions (items with mean scale values above 8.0); five "neutral" characteristics (those on which there was complete consensus among raters is assigning them to the neutral category); and five "least characteristic" descriptions (items with mean scale values below 2.0). These consensual descriptions again reflect the cold, amoral, and detached personal unresponsiveness of the high Mach, and his covertly aggressive willingness and ability to manipulate others.

TABLE V-5

"Most Characteristic," "Neutral," and "Least Characteristic" Descriptions
of the High-Mach Personality Based on California Q-Sort Consensus among
Four Observers [a]

Scale value	Descriptions
	Most characteristic
9.00	Is guileful and deceitful, manipulative, opportunistic.
9.00	Characteristically pushes and tries to stretch limits; sees what he can get away with.
9.00	Is power oriented; values power in self and others.
8.75	Is critical, skeptical, not easily impressed.
8.25	Is basically distrustful of people in general, questions their motivations.
	Neutral
5.00	Is personally charming.
5.00	Is physically attractive; good looking.
5.00	Tends to perceive many different contexts in sexual terms; eroticizes situations.
5.00	Is concerned with own body and the adequacy of its physiological functioning.
5.00	Appears to have high degree of intellectual capacity.
	Least characteristic
1.50	Seeks reassurance from others.
1.50	*Genuinely* submissive; accepts domination comfortably.
1.50	Behaves in a giving way toward others.
1.25	Behaves in a sympathetic or considerate manner.
1.00	Is moralistic.

[a] The mean scale value is given at the left of each item: 9.0 = most characteristic; 1.0 = least characteristic.

QUALIFICATIONS AND CAUTIONS

Despite the consistency of our findings, they should be interpreted with caution. First, our sample of subjects may have been atypical in several ways. By design, only male subjects were used. Previous research had revealed that females in most samples score lower than males (see Chapter II) (Budner, 1962; Exline, personal communication) and that some of the behavioral correlates of their Mach scale scores differ from those of males (Singer, 1964).

In most samples of male undergraduates (and also samples of medical school students), the mean and median scores on Mach IV have averaged around 90; on Mach V around 95. Among Columbia College undergraduates tested for the pilot study in the previous winter, we were surprised to find medians on Mach

IV and V as high as 98 and 103. In the summer school sample used in the study reported, however, the medians on the two scales climbed to 105 and 112, respectively.

In previous heterogeneous, mixed-sex samples the correlations between Mach IV and Mach V scores have averaged in the .60's. In the pilot study sample ($n = $ 57 males), this correlation was .67. In the sample of 81 male undergraduates at the Columbia summer session, from which subjects for the present study were selected, it was only .37. Since we selected as subjects only those respondents who were consistent in scoring above or below the medians on both scales, the subjects used were a minority differing on a relevant dimension from the majority of their classmates.

Our sample also had an unusually low correlation of $-.17$ between Mach IV and the Marlowe – Crowne (Crowne & Marlowe, 1960) Social Desirability Scale. The mean Marlowe – Crowne score for the 81 males was 12.80, somewhat lower than means reported for other samples (Crowne & Strickland, 1961; Marlowe & Crowne, 1961; Marlowe, 1962), which have averaged around 15.00.

SUMMARY

Subjects were given the role of experimenter and assigned to administer an important personality test to another subject. After learning that the previous student experimenter who had tested them had performed three relatively innocuous deceptions, they were given permission to "use your power arbitrarily" in testing their subject. High-Mach "experimenters' manipulated their subjects more than lows. Highs exceeded lows especially in devising innovative manipulations which had not been suggested or demonstrated in the preceding session when they were being given the test.

CHAPTER VI   MACHIAVELLIANS MEET
                  MISS RHEINGOLD

Richard Christie and Virginia Boehm

One of the things that impressed us in the Machiavel study was the ability of high Machs to size up that particular experimental situation quickly. We noticed that instead of accepting instructions docilely, they were quick to ask questions about what was and was not permitted in distracting the other subject. They seemed also to be highly responsive to any external cues which were relevant to successful performance. Were these observations characteristic of their behavior in this particular experimental situation, in any situation where social inter-action was defined by a set of new rules, or were they more curious about and sensitive to social stimuli generally? A plausible way to test this observed sensitivity to the environmental surround was to set up a learning paradigm in which the available cues were extremely subtle and then see whether high Machs when placed in such a situation are, in fact, better learners.

Such a study could take many forms. The procedure we chose was inspired by a grocery clerk's comment that he could invariably predict the winner of the annual Miss Rheingold contest. This seemed somewhat implausible. The winner in the contest was determined by which one of the contestants received the greatest number of votes. Since the brewery sponsoring the contest wanted to be identified with fresh-faced, wholesome young ladies, none of those selected were as cadaverous as high fashion models nor as buxom as pinup girls. As a matter of fact, to an unpracticed eye, the young ladies whose photographs looked down at you from every corner of the city were a remarkably indistinguishable lot.

The Miss Rheingold advertising campaign was primarily a New York phenomenon. Shortly before World War II, Leibling Breweries decided to use a picture of a young lady in conjunction with their advertising of Rheingold beer. Each year they would select someone, dub her Miss Rheingold, and use her picture in their advertising throughout the year. In 1943, the contest was opened to the public in a highly publicized campaign. Posters with the pictures of the six contestants were widely placed in the mass media, on billboards, and in bars, delicatessens, and grocery stores. Ballots were available in establishments where Rheingold beer was sold. Anyone could vote for his favorite and could vote as many times as he wished. It appeared unlikely, however, that any contestant, no matter how ambitious, could entice enough friends and relatives to give her a winning vote when over 20,000,000 ballots were cast annually by the time this study was done.

An informal poll of acquaintances indicated that most of them shared the grocery clerk's conviction that they could predict the winner. While such consensus was viewed with proper scientific skepticism, it did suggest that it might be worth further examination. If, in fact, there were certain characteristics which winners had in common, this would lend itself to an experiment in which the task would be to learn to identify the winner.

At first, certain questions about the contest had to be answered to find out whether or not the winner was actually chosen by a plurality of the voters or whether the contest was rigged, as some of our more cynical friends suggested. The advertising executive at Leibling Breweries who had been in charge of the contest since its inception bristled at the implication that any form of hanky-panky was involved. His explanation made sense. The contestants were almost all professional models or aspiring actresses or both. Aside from the fact that the winner received vast publicity during the year in which she reigned as Miss Rheingold, she also received many thousands of dollars. To protect themselves against possible litigation on the part of a losing contestant who might question the honesty of the tally, the brewery used an independent accounting agency to tally each week's ballots. These were then placed in cartons, sealed, and stored. If a contestant's agent or lawyer raised questions about the accuracy of the tally, he was invited to count the 20,000,000 ballots himself.

Satisfied that the count was accurate, we next questioned the distribution of ballots cast for each contestant. Before we could use photographs of the contestants as discriminable stimuli, it was necessary to know whether the voters themselves differed markedly in their preference for the contestants. The actual number of votes for each contestant could not be obtained from the brewery (again for public relations and possibly legal reasons). However, they were willing to state that in the previous year the winner had received 43% of the actual vote and the least popular candidate only 3%, with the remainder fairly equally spaced in between. This marked preference for one contestant was reported to be the usual case. It was also stated that in almost every year the contestant receiving the most votes during the first week of the contest was the eventual winner. Incredible as it seemed to us, it appeared that every year an undefinable population of millions of voters were in close agreement as to who the next Miss Rheingold should be.

Reassured, we then obtained the color photographs which had been used in each contest from 1943 to 1962. Although full length photos of the contestants in a group were also used in the contest during the last few years of its existence, the basic contest materials consisted of photographs of the head and shoulders of each girl. All wore similarly styled and colored blouses and no jewelry. Cues other than those pertaining to the face and hair were thus minimal. The names used by each contestant could not have appealed differentially to various national or ethnic groups since most the young ladies used professional names of Anglo-Saxon origin.

Pilot testing was done with pickup samples of students and winners were identified at better than chance level even by those who claimed that they had never heard of Miss Rheingold. We then had judges (graduate students) go over the photographs and rank each of the six contestants in each year's contest on a variety of characteristics such as openness of smile, whether her hair was straight or curly, long or short, light or dark, whether her face was more oval than round, and a variety of other variables suggested to us by female judges.

It must be remembered that these rankings were made for the six young ladies in each year's contest. Judgments, e.g., about the hair length of a given contestant, were relative rather than absolute, the frame of reference for the judgment being the other five contestants. Since hair styles change over the years, a young lady who had long hair one year when short locks were in fashion might be considered short haired a decade later when still longer hair was the rage. Makeup styles also changed, as did the preference for curly or straight hair. Since these young ladies were professionally involved in following current styles in personal appearance, they tended to show less variability in grooming and make-up than was present in the population at large. Actually, the selection procedure itself limited the variability still further. No platinum blondes, flaming redheads, or jet black haired women ever made their way into the contest. It seemed probable that none of the contestants had ancestors who ventured south of the Alps or east of the Oder River. This restriction of range made any of the judgments involved in ranking extremely difficult.

After collecting these ratings the winners were then compared with non-winners. If pooled ratings are a reliable guide, the only cue we could identify by this almost microscopic examination of facial and head characteristics was the degree to which the contestant was directly facing the camera. Sixteen of the 20 winners were in the upper half of their respective distributions of full face presenters. (All were, of course, eyeing the camera.) This was slightly more true for blond winners (see Table VI-1). A Kolmogorov–Smirnov test indicates that the distribution of winners facing into the camera is significant at the .01 level.

EXPERIMENTAL PROCEDURE

SUBJECTS

An initial requirement was the location of a group of subjects who had not been exposed to Rheingold advertisements. Even those New York respondents who disclaimed knowledge of the contest had seen, if not noted, pictures of the

TABLE VI-1

Numbers of Winners by Angle of Looking at Camera
and Hair Shading

| | | | Rank of hair shading | | | | | | |
| | | | Lightest | | | Darkest | | | |
			1	2	3	4	5	6	Σ
	Most direct	1	2	2	1	2	2	—	9
		2	1	1	2	1	—	—	5
Rank		3	—	—	—	—	1	1	2
of		4							
facial		4	—	—	—	—	1	—	1
angle		5	—	—	—	—	1	1	2
	Least direct	6	—	1	—	—	—	—	1
		Σ	3	4	3	3	5	2	20

contestants and past winners. The population used for the study consisted of 144 undergraduates in a 1964 summer session course in introductory psychology at Pennsylvania State University.[1] Those who had any knowledge of the contest were eliminated from the final sample. As was true of a previous sample in the same school (Singer, 1964), there were no sex differences in scores on Mach IV and V which had been filled out in class after the exposure to the experimental stimuli. Those scoring 94 or less on a median split were classified as low on Mach IV and those with a score of 100 or less on Mach V were similarly classified. After eliminating the inconsistent scorers and those who stated that they knew where the pictures of the contestants had come from, we were left with a total of 107 subjects.

PROCEDURE

Subjects were tested in class. The experimenter was introduced by the teacher and read the following instructions:

---

[1] We wish to thank Professor Jerome E. Singer for cooperating in furnishing subjects for this study.

People often must make guesses about one another on first impressions. How accurate an individual is in his first impression frequently determines his success or failure in his dealings with others. Sometimes people guess right, sometimes not. This is a test of *your* ability to make good guesses.

You will be shown a series of slides. Each slide is a composite made up of portraits of six girls. These pictures are of the contestants in an advertising contest run in the New York City area and on the west coast. The pictures on each slide are of all the contestants in one year. Your task is to guess which one of the six girls on each slide actually won the contest for that year. Places are provided on the answer sheet for you to circle your first and second choice guesses for each year. The pictures are lettered on the slides: A, B, and C running across the top row and D, E, and F across the bottom row.

Although these young ladies were selected from a large group of models as entrants in this contest, there is a wide range of preference by voters. The voters are a difficult group to classify since the voting was done by customers in stores. Most of the votes were cast in New York City. The voters have, in most of the years of the contest, shown a strong preference for one of the contestants. We don't know wny, but an analysis of the photographs indicates that there are some similarities in the appearances of the winners from year to year.

We are interested in finding out whether or not you can identify the winners chosen by the people who were interested enough to vote in this contest.

Since, hopefully, none of you are familiar with the candidates and have never voted for them, we are using these contest pictures to study learning. To enable you to learn as you go along, after each slide has been shown and everyone has marked his first and second guesses, the actual winner for the year will be announced. At first, you will, of course, be guessing more or less at random. As the series is run through you may find that you develop the ability to make more correct guesses on the basis of the appearance of previous winners. It is important that you watch carefully for any cues that you may learn. You will have the opportunity to view a given slide for a few seconds longer after you know who the winner for that year was.

If the actual winner is your first choice for a given year, give yourself two points. If the actual winner is your second choice guess, give yourself one point for the year. Next to each year is a space to record your points. Thus over the series of 20 slides your score can vary from zero to 40.

Try your best to make the largest number of correct guesses and get the largest number of points you can. You will have 20 sec to make your guesses for each year and 10 sec after the winner for a given year is announced to study the winner's picture.

Any questions?

Subjects had answer sheets on which there were spaces for indicating their choices. After presentation of the first 10 slides, subjects were asked to total their scores and encouraged to beat their performances on the second block of 10 slides.

RESULTS

All groups did better than chance on the first block of 10 trials [chance being a score of 5 ($1\frac{2}{3} \times 2 + 1\frac{2}{3} \times 1$)]. Overall, there was significant improvement from trials 1–10 to 11–20, the mean score increasing from 7.25 to 9.12 ($p <$ .001).

TABLE VI-2

Number of Winners Correctly Identified on First and Second
Series by Mach Scores and Sex

Classification	n	Trials		Diff.	t	Signif.
		1–10	11–20			
High-Mach males	25	6.92	8.44	1.52	2.27	.025
High-Mach women	21	7.52	8.76	1.24	1.24	n.s.
Low-Mach males	23	7.61	8.91	1.30	1.44	n.s.
Low-Mach women	38	7.11	9.89	2.78	5.91	.0005
Total	107	7.25	9.12	1.87	3.57	.001

As can be seen in Table VI-2, our major hypothesis that high Machs would learn better than low Machs was not confirmed. For reasons that we cannot explain low Mach women showed the greatest improvement. Although high Mach males did show significant learning and low Mach males did not, the difference between the two groups was not significant.

After the slides were shown, the subjects were asked whether they had developed any systematic bases for making their guess as to which of the contestants was the winner. If they answered "yes," we asked them what had influenced their guessing.

There were absolutely no differences between males and females on these self-reports of whether they used a system; 69% of both sexes claimed they had. Upon the basis of experience in other studies, it was expected that high Machs would be more prone to use a system. However, 72% of the high Machs said they had used a system and 67% of the low Machs did likewise, a trivial difference.

Further, there was no significant difference in learning among those subjects who claimed to have a system and those who did not. An examination of the descriptions of the systems used gives us some clues, despite the fact that definitions of systems varied widely. Subjects with systems and low accuracy scores almost invariably focused upon one or more irrelevant cues — some being convinced, for example, that blondes were more likely to win and some that brunettes were; some that girls with winsome smiles won, etc.

Among those who had systems and won, very few reported the facial angle as a crucial variable. For example, a 17-year-old female subject missed the first 4 pictures completely, then guessed the winner as second on 4 of the remaining 6 trials in the first series. On the second series of 10 she had a score of 14 which reflected the fact that she picked 5 of the 10 winners as placing first, 4 as placing second, and missing one (this last contestant had a ranking of four on facial angle which meant that she was facing more away than into the camera). This subject described her system as, "The winner usually had dimples (not true) and they were facing toward the front more than the side."

The most spectacular improvement was also shown by a female subject who jumped from a score of 4 on the first block of 10 trials to one of 17 on the second block. She correctly identified 8 of the 10 winners, picked one as second, and missed on one. Her reported system was "smile, hair color and style, roundness of cheeks, and facial appearance while smiling." The facial angle might have affected the latter two slightly in a brief exposure but none of these cues was found relevant by the judges who examined the pictures carefully. Evidently, she was able to learn without being able to verbalize the appropriate cues, or these cues formed a subtle gestalt which eluded the eyes of our judges.

The reports were scrutinized in many ways. Reported global judgments — "wholesomeness, girl-next-door type, all-American girl," etc. — did not differentiate those who improved from those who had focused on such specifics as smiles, eyes, or hair. Yet overall, subjects did improve significantly in picking the winner, whatever cues they reportedly used or did not use.

Our own impressions after countless exposures to the 120 pictures of the contestants was that there was a Miss Rheingold "type." Usually, one or two contestants in a given year clearly did not look the same in some subtle fashion as the winners in the past and could be eliminated. Hypothetically, if two could be eliminated then one would have one chance in four of choosing the actual winner as first (2 points), one in four of choosing her as second (1 point) and two in four of missing (0 points). This elimination strategy would lead to a base expectancy of 7.5 points in 10 trials rather than 5.0. This is, of course, very close to the mean of 7.25 actually obtained on the first 10 trials but is short of the man of 9.12 found on the last 10. Evidently, something more than simple elimination of the least likely two was involved in making judgments. Since the rankings of all the contestants were not available and we only knew which one of the six contestants won, it was impossible to test the elimination hypothesis by having judges attempt to select the two who received the lowest number of votes.

In any event, it seems likely that something more than an elimination process was involved. If two contestants could be eliminated, one of the remaining four had to have some characteristic more typical of winners in general. Actually, if the respondents had picked as their first choice the girl looking most directly into the camera and as second choice the one looking next most directly into the camera they would have made a score of 14 on the last ten trials — which is precisely the score made by the one young lady who verbalized the facial angle hypothesis.

Our own hunch about this characteristic of the winner is that she not only looked more directly into the camera but that other more subtle cues eliciting similar evaluations of straightforwardness, naturalness, wholesomeness, and what not were involved. Exline's programmatic research indicates that honesty is frequently associated with eye contact. In these pictures, however, all contestants were looking at the camera and winning was associated with the directness with which the contestants were looking into it.

The best way of evaluating this possibility would have been to test it on new groups of contestants to see if we could predict winners. This possibility was eliminated when, after a change of ownership of the brewery, the contest was discontinued.[2]

DISCUSSION

Quite clearly the hypothesis that high Machs would be better learners than low Machs in identifying winners of the Miss Rheingold contests was not confirmed. Frequently pilot studies do not produce confirmatory results. In some cases, the underlying hypothesis may be correct but the experimental execution is inappropriate. In other cases, the hypothesis might be wrong, and the procedures adequate, and in the unhappiest of cases, both the hypothesis and its attempted test may be wrong. In short, when a researcher conducts a study which does not confirm a hypothesis, he is frequently hard put to determine whether it was the idea being tested, its execution, or both which lead to the failure to find confirmation.

This study was based upon observations of behavior occurring in the Machiavel study which suggested that high Machs were much more alert to the possibilities for manipulation in a situation. Other studies which followed up leads from the same study (for example, the Con Game described in the next chapter) were successful. Our overall conclusions as to why this particular study did not produce significant differences between high and low Machs involve certain differences between it and the Machiavel study. We think that all of the following features are important in understanding the difference; their ordering does not indicate any evaluation of their importance.

Briefly, we think the crucial differences were:

---

[2] In the fall of 1964 the senior author was gleefully anticipating making wagers on the winner of the annual Miss Rheingold contest. He suddenly realized that he had seen no contest advertisements. In checking on this, he discovered that a large soft drink company had purchased the Leibling Breweries and continued to brew Rheingold beer. The widow of the late president of the purchasing company was a Hollywood star who was most famous in the 1920's and 1930's for playing movie roles which were not the type one would associate with the pictures of Miss Rheingold contestants. In any event, one of the first things done when the soft drink company took over the brewery was the firing of the advertising manager who had been in charge of Miss Rheingold contest for a quarter of a century and the termination of the contest.

1. In the Machiavel study the social cues lay in the nature of the situation itself. Subjects were asked, "to use your power arbitrarily — to confuse or distract the subject who will be taking the test." What they could or could not do was not explicitly stated. The ambiguity lay in what was permitted and what they could devise in an interpersonal manipulation situation. In the present study the ambituity lay in the characteristics of the winner and all subjects followed the same judging instructions; there was no way for the subject to invent ways to improve his chances. The two choices for each set of photographs provided fixed opportunities for all subjects.

2. In the Machiavel study the subject was interacting directly with another (presumed) subject in face-to-face encounter. In this study the subject was attempting to make judgments about a representation of another. The feedback in the latter case was simply whether the judgments were right (or partially right) or wrong. In the Machiavel study the person being interacted with was a preprogrammed stooge but he was *there* and his varying facial expressions and other observable behavior were open to interpretation on the part of the subject.

3. Both situations involved competition but of a differing nature. In this study, the subject was not in direct competition with fellow subjects but with himself; he was asked to beat his performance on the first 10 slides on the second group. He had no way of knowing how well he was doing in relation to others although he may have been anticipating comparing scores with friends after class. In the Machiavel study no competitive encouragement was offered. The instructions clearly stated, "Now, precisely how you go about doing this is up to your imagination — and your conscience." However, in all cases the subject had been lied to once. He thus had as a frame of reference an other; actually in this case a reluctant other who said, "That's all (referring to the deception) — I don't think I'd like to do this kind of thing very much." The subject could tell fewer, the same, or a greater number of lies than his predecessor when giving the test.

4. The amount of ethical conflict in the two situations differed drastically. As far as we can tell, there is very little such conflict involved in guessing which one of a group of young ladies was the winner of a popularity contest. The Machiavel study, however, pointed up, for scientific reasons to be sure, the desirability of deceiving another person. Although almost all subjects complied, there was wide variability in the extent to which subjects enjoyed doing so and inferentially, in the qualms they felt while misleading someone else.

Any, or all, of these differences may have accounted for the lack of differential learning on the part of high and low Machs. However, subjects did learn and almost none could say with accuracy what cues they used in the process. We conclude that it was a fair test of their ability to learn subtle cues and that, at least in a situation in which a neutral stimulus is ambiguous, and there is no interpersonal competition and no possibility of manipulation in a face-to-face situation, neither high nor low Machs have an advantage.

The negative findings had two salutory results although it was difficult to fully appreciate them at the time. The two preceding studies had yielded positive results as did the Con Game which had been run the previous winter. We were so impressed with the superior gamesmanship of the high Machs that their failure in this study had a corrective effect. First of all, it was a relief to find that they didn't win in all situations. The second and more important reason was that the failure of high Machs to win in this particular study made us start seriously considering the limits of situations in which they did better. This is a theme to which we shall return from time to time in subsequent chapters.

SUMMARY

This study was designed to test the hypothesis that high Machs would be better learners in a situation in which the stimuli were subtle. Pictures of the contestants in Miss Rheingold contests over a 20-year period were used. The subject's task was to guess which of six contestants in a given year had won. After making their guesses they were then informed as to who the winner for a given year actually was and then went on to judge the next year's contestants.

Overall, subjects did better than chance in guessing on the first 10 years' winners and improved significantly over this score in selecting the winners for the second decade of contestants. Despite this improvement, they were unable to verbalize the cues that they had used in learning. More germane to the point of the study, however, was the fact that there was no significant difference between high and low Mach's ability to learn. A number of differences between this and earlier studies was pointed out, any one of which might indicate limiting factors on high Mach's ability to perform more successfully than lows in laboratory studies.

CHAPTER VII   **THE CON GAME** [1]

Florence Geis

In the Machiavel study (Chapter V) those who agreed with Machiavelli were more willing to manipulate their fellow man, and claimed to enjoy it. But what about the effectiveness of the manipulative attempts? To be labeled "Machiavellian," attempts at interpersonal manipulation should be performed skillfully; more important, they should end in success. This study was designed to measure the success of attempts to manipulate others.

"Successful manipulation" seems generally to mean getting someone to do something he wouldn't otherwise have done. In the simplest cases the manipulator derives direct benefit at the other's expense. (Hiring someone to perform a service is not "manipulation" by this definition, unless he would not agree to the contract on its own merits.) "Manipulation" also occurs in more socially acceptable forms. Parents induce their children to adopt conventional manners; teachers require students to read assignments; priests exhort their flocks. In such cases the "manipulation" is generally recognized as intended for the ultimate benefit of the party manipulated. Nevertheless, regardless of the manipulator's intention, these transactions involve the manipulated person's foregoing certain pleasures or subjecting himself to some discipline which he would otherwise not have chosen, and all are generally recognized as bringing "satisfaction" to the successful manipulators. In general, successful manipulation is a process by which the manipulator gets more of some kind of reward than he would have gotten without manipulating, and someone else gets less, at least within the immediate context.

Manipulation in the sense of psychological pressure tactics is not the only means of influencing the distribution of rewards among persons. Physical force is probably the most direct means, and is a form of "manipulation" as defined above. Laws and rules also govern the distribution of rewards, but manipulation has little relevance for these transactions except in defining the convention initially, or evading it later. More frequently, and especially in informal groups, the interpersonal situation is one in which physical force is not an acceptable means of distributing rewards, and existing laws, rules, or conventions are either

---

[1] This chapter is based on a Ph.D. dissertation in the Department of Social Psychology, Columbia University, 1964. Parts of the data were reported in a symposium at the annual meeting of the American Psychological Association, Los Angeles, September, 1964.

ambiguous or irrelevant. Yet frequently group members must agree or cooperate in order to realize any of the possible rewards. Such conflict of interest situations are usually resolved (and rewards allocated) by discussion, compromise, and conciliation — precisely the processes most likely susceptible to psychological pressure tactics.

The role of the "manipulator," "operator," or "con artist" has long been recognized. The purpose of this study was to find out whether individual differences in the ability to manipulate others could be predicted from Mach scale scores. More broadly, can the relative Machiavellianism of group members predict the outcome of their negotiations, specifically in terms of the distribution of rewards.

MACH SCORE AND SUCCESS AS A MANIPULATOR

How can success in interpersonal manipulation be related to self-reports on a paper-and-pencil measure? The simplest interpretation of a score on the Mach scale is that it represents the degree to which a respondent believes that people in general are manipulatable, that interpersonal manipulation is possible. This is a face valid interpretation. The items are worded in general, impersonal terms. The respondent does not claim that *he* would, or does, engage in the behaviors mentioned. He claims only that he agrees or disagrees with certain characterizations of human nature or the nature of human relations.

A further inference can be made, however. Claiming to agree with Machiavellian characterizations of human nature and interpersonal relations might imply the emotional detachment and amoral attitude toward others originally postulated by Christie. Emotional detachment, combined with lack of ethical qualms about manipulating others, might imply a willingness to attempt manipulation. This conclusion is also supported by another line of reasoning: Claiming cynical, manipulative attitudes is as contrary to conventional social norms as practicing such behavior. The emotional detachment and amorality necessary to practice Machiavellian tactics would also be necessary for admitting such attitudes when asked.

This is a testable proposition. The results of the Machiavel study (Chapter V) showed that high Machs were more willing to manipulate a supposed peer. Because of the controlled situation used in that study, the differential willingness to manipulate cannot be attributed to differential success or reward. Thus, Mach scores can be inferred to have volitional implications.

The major hypothesis of this study can now be spelled out more specifically. Theoretically, if a high Mach score indicates acceptance of Machiavellian attitudes (i.e., "in general, people are manipulatable"), if acceptance implies emotional detachment and amorality which lead to a willingness to practice interpersonal manipulation, and if practice leads to skill, then high scorers should be more skillful, hence more successful at manipulating others. And, if Mach scores do predict success in interpersonal manipulation, then, in a conflict of interest bargaining situation in which interpersonal manipulation can influence the distribution of rewards, high Machs should obtain more of the rewards.

A three-man, bargaining-coalition game described by Vinacke and Arkoff (1957) was modified to test this prediction. The three players are the potential manipulators of each other. The test situation was presented as a game to elicit serious manipulative attempts from all players, as well as serious attempts to resist being manipulated. That is, in a situation defined as a game all subjects should be willing to manipulate, so that differences in success can be attributed to differences in ability rather than willingness. Further, the value of the game was expressed numerically, and the deviation of any player's actual score from the average, or expected, value could be taken as an index of his success in the game.

The game consists, essentially, of bargaining for shares of the total payoff, set at 100 points per game. These can be won by a single player alone; they can be divided between any two players, or distributed among all three. The points can be divided, via bargaining, in any proportion agreed to by the bargainers (e.g., 50−50−0, 60−40−0, 40−40−20, 96−4−0, etc.). A subject's score over a series of games is determined by his bargaining ability (ability to enter coalitions, rather than allowing his two opponents to form one excluding him), shrewdness in bargaining (ability to get disproportionately large shares of the prize in coalition agreements entered), and dispassionate use of coalition partners (willingness to break coalition agreements, thus betraying a partner, at a strategic moment). The number of points won over a series of games provided an index of a player's ability to manipulate his opponents relative to their ability to manipulate him. Among the budding social psychologists being trained to administer this game, it came to be called "the Con Game." The name stuck.

THE CON GAME

Three players were seated around a game board on a small table. The board (Fig. VII-1) had a path divided into numbered spaces running from START at one side to FINISH in the center. The game was played with power cards, dice, and individual place markers.

To begin the game, each player was given a hand of six power cards, much like ordinary playing cards. One player always had a hand of high-value cards; another had low cards; the third had a middle-value hand. At his turn, a player tossed the dice and moved his marker toward FINISH the number of spaces equal to the higher of his two die values (a rule used simply to reduce the variance in game scores due to chances of the dice) multiplied by whichever of his power cards he chose to play at that turn. A player could use only one card at each turn, and a card could be used only once in the game. The player or

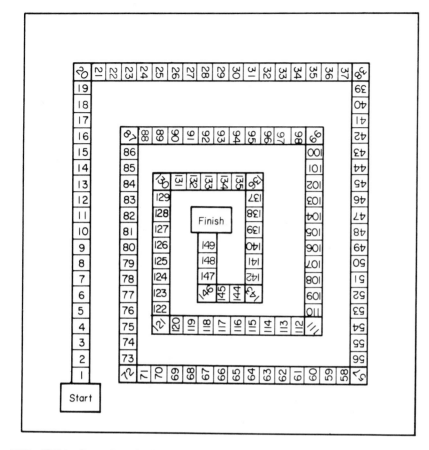

FIG. VII-1. Game board: the game boards were made of heavy cardboard, 18 in. square, and were hand printed as shown.

coalition of players to reach FINISH first received 100 points. The losing player or players received zero.

Three rules were introduced to make points accumulated over a series of games a direct reflection of success at manipulating fellow players:

1. Players could form coalitions within their triad. Coalition partners played as a single unit. At the turn of a coalition, only one toss of the dice was made, but each member played a power card. Then both moved forward, together, the number of spaces equal to their higher die value multiplied by the *sum* of the two power cards. For example, suppose A and B were in coalition. At their turn one of the two tossed the dice, and the higher face was a 4. Then A played a 5 from his hand, and B played a 2. Their move, for that turn, was 4(5 + 2), or 28 spaces. Since the power cards were prearranged so that any two players, by

forming a coalition, could beat the third one, every player had a chance to be a member of a winning coalition in every game. As a result, one way for a player to accumulate more points over the series of games was for him to be more successful than average in talking one or the other of his two opponents into forming a coalition with him rather than forming one between themselves and leaving him out.

2. A second critical rule was that each coalition agreement had to include an agreement between the partners as to how they would divide the 100 points if they should win. Players were told explicitly that they could divide the points in any way they chose. The obvious differences in the value of the power cards initially given the three players made this agreement particularly susceptible to psychological pressure tactics. The partner with the better hand was universally felt to deserve more points. But how many more? Thus, a second way for a player to accumulate more than his share of points over the series of games was for him first to succeed in getting into many coalitions, and second, succeed in talking his partner into giving him the largest possible share of the 100 points as often as possible.

3. The final critical rule was that coalitions could be made and broken at will at any time in the game. When a coalition was formed after play had begun between two players who were at different positions on the path, the two markers were moved to the point halfway between where they had been just before the coalition was formed. This meant that a player could advance on the board simply by forming a coalition with an opponent who had been ahead of him. Then, if he was skillful, he could use his advantageous position on the board to form a new coalition, giving himself a more favorable point split, with the third player, thereby breaking the agreement he had used to obtain the position.

A further, less obvious strategy should also be mentioned. As indicated, a coalition of two players got one toss of the dice at the move of their coalition. However, each partner, separately, played one of his own power cards. A player could urge his partner to play a high card. After waiting for complaince, he could then play one of his own lower cards. Thus, in coalition, he could advance largely on the contributed resources of his partner, and save his own high cards. If a player succeeded in this strategy even once or twice, he could then break the coalition at an opportune moment and, with even luck in his dice tosses, use his remaining high cards to outstrip his deserted partner, thereby winning the whole 100 points for himself.

AMBIGUITY IN THE SITUATION

An informal analysis of manipulation suggested that ambiguity in the convention governing the distribution of rewards should facilitate manipulation. If, for example, no one knows what anyone else "deserves" according to his resources or potential contribution to a coalition, and everyone knows that no one knows, knowledge of the general state of ignorance might be used for bluffing or other misleading tactics. Ambiguity, in this sense, can be thought of as a protective screen of obscurity which a skillful manipulator might use to conceal the intended effect of his strategies.

There were two previous indications that Machiavellian men might have an affinity for ambiguity, or at least less aversion to it than low Machs expressed. In a study of work-situation values among medical students (Kosa, 1961), high scorers on Mach IV valued "a well-defined work situation" less than low scorers. Using nine mixed-sex samples, Budner (1962) found that the greater the proportion of males in a sample, the larger the negative correlation in that sample between Mach score and score on a measure of intolerance of ambiguity.

If the use of ambiguity to facilitate manipulation is directly related to Machiavellianism, then, in a group of more than two persons, the highest Mach members of the group should show the greatest increase in advantage with an increase in ambiguity. And, if low Machs rely mostly on official rules and objective determinants of reward, they should be at a greater disadvantage than others intermediate in Machiavellianism.

This prediction was tested by having the triads play the Con Game under two different conditions. The hands of power cards are perceived as "objective resources" in the game. The value of the player's hand (along with his position on the board, once the game is underway) relative to the value of his prospective partner's hand roughly governs how they will expect to divide the points in a coalition agreement. To create an unambiguous situation, players were instructed to lay their power cards out in a row, face up, on the table in front of them, so that all could see exactly what power cards each of them had at all times during play. Thus, how many of the 100 points each player "deserved" as a coalition partner, as well as his desirability as a partner, were all public knowledge in the triad. For games in which the interpersonal manipulation was to take place in an ambiguous situation, the players were instructed to hold their cards as in conventional card games. They were not allowed to show their cards to each other, but were told explicitly that they could *tell* their opponents anything they wished. Thus, the ambiguous condition eliminated public knowledge of the objective power structure of the group.

POWER POSITION IN THE GROUP

A feature of the original game that seemed particularly relevant was the use of different power positions for the three players in the game. Success in interpersonal manipulation might also imply love of power, presumably accompanied by an armamentarium of strategies for the use of power. The power cards for a game were assigned so that the players perceived that the three of them started out with different power positions corresponding to different likelihoods of winning. However, the hands were prearranged so that any two players in coalition could beat the third. This meant that the perceived difference in initial advantage was a real difference only if no coalition was formed in the game. As soon as a coalition was made, according to a game theory analysis of rational strategy in terms of outcome (Luce & Raiffa, 1957), both partners were equally necessary and they should divide the prize equally, regardless of discrepancy in power position. The relevant finding in previous research in which similar games have been used (e.g., Vinacke & Arkoff, 1957; Stryker & Psathas, 1960; Shears, 1962; Chaney & Vinacke, 1960; Bond & Vinacke, 1961) is that players do not play according to the rational strategy but according to the perceived power structure of the group. In general, players' winnings correspond roughly to their relative power positions in the group, except that the player with the least advantageous position wins slightly more than his "objective" power would seem to warrant (Caplow, 1956, 1968; Gamson, 1961a).

For the purposes of the present research the problem of why subjects play according to perceived power positions rather than rational strategy was irrelevant. All that was required was that subjects perceive differences in their power positions in the group. Two questions were relevant. First, how would the different power positions affect the manipulative success of high- and low-Mach individuals? It seemed reasonable to assume that, at least when power positions were clearly defined in the group, those more skilled in using power might make more use of more power than those presumably less skilled. There were no previous data directly relevant to this assumption. A trend in pilot data, however, appeared to support it.

To summarize thus far, "Machiavellianism" should be related to "success in manipulating others." The relationship can be broken down into three components: a belief that people are in fact manipulatable; willingness to attempt manipulation; and ability or skill in manipulative techniques.

The Mach scales are assumed to measure the belief component. By inference, supported by previous data, they can be assumed to predict the volitional component as well, Theoretically, belief and willingness together should lead to attempts to manipulate others; attempts should provide practice, practice lead to skill, and skill to success.

To measure skill in manipulative techniques, a bargaining game was designed to control motivation, opportunity, and relevant objective resources for all subjects. Success in the game depended upon interpersonal manipulation, and a divisible, constant-sum payoff provided an index of relative degree of success among players.

Two additional variables were included: degree of ambiguity in the power structure of the group, and perceived power position in the group.

Three testable predictions were made:

1. High Machs would win more points in the Con Game than low Machs.

2. High Machs would win more points when the power structure of the group was more ambiguous, primarily at the expense of the low- rather than the middle-Mach group.

3. When the power positions of the players were unambiguous, an increase in the power position of high Machs would increase their winning more than the same increase in power position for low Machs would increase their winning.

PROCEDURE

These predictions were tested by having college men selected by Mach scores play a six-game tournament of the Con Game. The number of points won by each subject was taken as an index of his ability to manipulate his fellow players into partnerships and prize distributions favorable to himself. That one player's success would necessarily be at the others' expense was insured by the constant-sum feature of the game. The game also provided a direct and simple way for the experimenter to manipulate both the ambiguity of the situation for the players and the power position of each player in each game.

SELECTION OF SUBJECTS

In the first month of the fall, 1963 semester, the students in all introductory psychology and sociology courses in the General Studies division of Columbia University were given Mach IV and V, identified only as questionnaires, in their regular classrooms, and complete scales were obtained from 143 men. The two Mach scale distributions of these scores were divided separately into quartiles, as shown in Table VII-1; 122 men whose scores fell in the same or adjacent quartiles in the two distributions were called "consistent" in Machiavellianism and identified as potential subjects. The 37 whose scores fell in the fourth quartile in both distributions, or in the fourth quartile in one and the third in the other, were called high Machs. The analogous procedure for scores in the first, or first and second, quartiles identified 41 consistent low Machs. The remaining 44 consistent men whose scores fell within the limits of the two middle quartiles in both distributions were classified as middle scorers.

TABLE VII-1

Mach Scores of the Con Game Sample (n = 143 Undergraduate males)

	Mean	Standard deviation	Corrected split-half reliability		Quartile distributions	
					Mach IV	Mach V
Mach IV	98.64	15.83	.72	Q4	108–147	112–139
Mach V	103.55	11.83	.56	Q3	99–107	104–111
				Q2	89–98	97–103
	$r_{\text{Mach IV-V}}$ = .73			Q1	61–88	76–96

After eliminating 14 men who were over 29 years old, and 5 who were not fluent in English, 35 high, 34 middle, and 34 low scorers remained as potential subjects. From these pools 66 subjects were selected solely on the basis of available time. They ranged in age from 17 to 26, with mean age of 21.35; the numbers of freshmen, sophomores, juniors, and unclassified were about equal.

THE GAME TOURNAMENT: OVERVIEW

Each game was played by three subjects and supervised by a male experimenter. Each triad of players was always composed of one high, one middle, and one low Mach. Each subject played a tournament of 6 rounds of the Con Game: 3 rounds in the unambiguous condition, and 3 in the ambiguous. Each subject played in high-, middle-, and low-power position once in each ambiguity condition.

Ambiguity was varied as indicated above. For unambiguous games power cards were laid out on the table face up, in public view. For ambiguous games they were held concealed, as in conventional card games.

The power cards assigned the three players in each game were prearranged to create three power positions in each group. Each player received 6 playing cards. One player in each triad received cards with an average value of 3.00, the lowest power position in the group. (For example, in Game 1 the card values of the low power player were 1, 2, 2, 2, 5, and 6; See Table VII-2.) A second player received 6 cards that averaged 6.00, the highest power position in the group. In 4 of the 7 experimental sessions, the 6 cards of the third player averaged 5.00; in the other three sessions they averaged 4.00, making an average middle-power position of 4.57. The subjects were told that they would be given different power positions in the different games, but were not informed of the numerical relations among the positions.

CONDUCT OF THE SESSIONS

Twelve subjects, 4 each of high, middle, and low Machs were scheduled for each of seven experimental sessions. For one of these all 12 kept the appointment; the remaining 6 sessions were run with 9 subjects, 3 of each Mach classification, giving a total n of 66 subjects, 22 of each Mach classification.

Each session, of about $1\frac{1}{2}$ hr, consisted of a series of six tournament games (plus two extra games in like-Mach triads), each played simultaneously by the three or four triads of subjects present. All were conducted by a female experimenter and either three or four trained male assistants. When the subjects arrived, they were given a mimeographed explanation of the experiment described as a study of decision making. The game was introduced as an analog of real-life decision situations. Winning was described as depending on a combination of chance (dice tosses), objective resources (power cards), which would be unequally distributed in each game, and the individual player's skill in decision making (coalition formation) under the circumstances. The only experimental deception in the study was that subjects were not informed of the expected relevance of Mach scores or their use in assigning subjects to triads. The explanation concluded with a summary of the rules:

The game consists, essentially, of a race from START to FINISH. At his turn, each player tosses the dice, and moves his marker toward FINISH the number of spaces equal to the *product* of the higher of the two die faces and whichever of his power coefficients he chooses. The player or coalition unit to reach FINISH first receives the prize of 100 points for that game.

1. The experimenter in charge of your table will assign each player a set of "power coefficients" for the game. One of these coefficients must be played at each turn, and then cannot be used again in that game.

2. After the power coefficients have been assigned, players may bargain for coalitions to improve their chances in the game. Coalitions may be formed between any two or all three competitors at a table. Coalition partners play as a single unit with power at each turn equal to the sum of all individual coefficients played at that turn. For example, in a coalition of A and B, if A plays a coefficient of 2, and B plays one of 8, their coalition would have the power of 10 for that turn, and they would multiply the result of the dice toss by 10 to determine their move for that turn.

A coalition agreement is entered by consent of the players involved and must include an agreement as to how they will divide the prize of 100 points between them in the event their coalition wins the game. In the example above, if A had a set of low coefficients and B a set of high ones, A and B might have agreed that if they won, A would receive 15 points and B would receive 85. The 100 points can be divided in any way the coalition partners choose.

Coalitions can be formed at any time before the end of the game. Coalitions formed after play has begun start midway between the positions of the partners.

Coalitions can be broken at any time before the end of the game. A two-man coalition is automatically broken if either member accepts a coalition offer from the third player, or if either member makes a coalition offer to the third player and he accepts it.

3. Each player or coalition unit tosses the dice to determine order of play. The high player goes first.

4. In turn, each player tosses the dice, plays one of his power coefficients, and moves his marker toward FINISH the number of spaces equal to the product of the higher die face and his power at that turn. In coalition units, only one member tosses the dice for the coalition, each member plays a power coefficient, and all members move a number of spaces equal to the product of the higher die face and the sum of all coefficients played at that turn.

Note that since your power coefficients are used to *multiply* your die values, you will do better if you use one of your lower coefficients when you have a low die value, and save your higher coefficients for your higher die values: e.g., $(1 \times 1) + (5 \times 5)$ is greater than $(1 \times 5) + (5 \times 1)$.

5. The player or coalition unit to reach FINISH first receives the 100 point prize, and the game is over.

6. Any player may concede at any time. In this event the other two players continue the game.

7. All players record their score at the end of each game (whether they have won any points in that game or not).

8. The enforcement of these rules is the responsibility of the players, not the experimenter. However, the experimenter may intervene if he chooses, and will arbitrate if the players cannot agree among themselves.

9. The experimenter may, at any time, announce a time limit for the completion of a game. If a

time limit expires before the game is completed, the prize is forfeited and all players receive a zero for that game.

10. The experimenter in charge of each table will make notes on the conversation and bargaining that occurs during the game. To make this easier for us, please state your coalition offers in terms of the number of prize points you are offering your prospective partner.

11. Once or twice in the series of eight games the procedure will be changed in one detail. You will be told when such a change is to be made.

Remember, the objective results of your decisions will be evaluated by the number of points you succeed in winning in each individual game, and over the entire tournament. The player with the highest grand total wins the tournament.

After time to read and digest the rules, each subject was given a tag labeled A, B, or C to identify him during the tournament, and a score card. Subjects were then directed to the playing table (identified by number) indicated on their score card for game 1. Each triad always had one A, one B, and one C, one of whom was a high Mach, one a middle, and one a low. For example, in the first session run, the high Machs were A's, the middles B's, and the lows C's, as shown in Table VII-2A.

Before the beginning of the first game the assistant in charge of the table reviewed the major rules for the players. No further reviews were provided, but players could consult their own copy of the rules at will. At the end of each game the subjects' scores were recorded by the assistant at the table, as well as by the subjects themselves. When all triads had finished their first game, two players from each table were systematically rotated to two other tables, so that all subjects played their second game in a completely new triad, but again composed of one high, one middle, and one low Mach. The same procedure was followed at the end of the second game, giving a third set of new triads for the third game. Thus, over the first three games each subject played against six different opponents. For the second three-game set the same procedure was followed, so that each of the triad groupings in the first set was repeated in the second.

The order of playing in each of the conditions was counterbalanced as nearly as possible (see Table VII-2). Each subject played in each power position — highest, middle, and lowest — once in each ambiguity condition, and the sequence in which they were assigned to the three Mach groups was systematically varied (see Table VII-2). There were no differences within Mach groups between players who had different ambiguity or power position sequences, so that the various order conditions were combined for the major analyses.

The assistants who supervised the games were trained to conduct them and answer questions without suggesting ideas, strategies, or solutions to the subjects. All of the assistants knew the general idea of the study, but none knew the design in any detail, nor did any know the Mach classsification of any of the players.

At the end of the session subjects completed a short questionnaire and the experimenter offered to answer questions. After all of the sessions had been run, the entire purpose and design of the study were discussed with the students in the classes originally given the Mach scales.

TABLE VII-2A

The Experimental Conditions[a]

	Mach group	Experimental session						
		1	2	3	4	5	6	7
Identification letter	High	A	C	B	A	C	B	A
	Middle	B	A	C	B	B	A	C
	Low	C	B	A	C	A	C	B
Ambiguity condition played first		U	A	U	A	U	A	U
Middle power position used in the session (see below)		H-M	H-M	L-M	L-M	L-M	H-M	H-M

[a] The assignment of identification letters to subjects in the three Mach groups was systematically varied over the seven sessions, as indicated. The order of playing the ambiguous and unambiguous conditions was alternated from session to session. The choice of high or low middle power position was determined to balance the other conditions as nearly as possible.

TABLE VII-2B

Card Values by Power Position, Game Sequence, and Identification Letter[a]

Game sequence	Low (mean = 3.00)	Low-middle (mean = 4.00)	High-middle (mean = 5.00)	High (mean = 6.00)
1	(C) 1,2,2,2,5,6	(A) 1,3,4,5,5,6	(A) 1,4,6,6,6,7	(B) 2,6,6,6,8,8
2	(B) 1,1,3,3,3,7	(C) 2,3,3,3,5,8	(C) 3,3,3,5,8,8	(A) 3,3,7,7,8,8
3	(A) 1,1,3,3,5,5	(B) 2,2,3,5,5,7	(B) 2,3,4,7,7,7	(C) 3,5,5,6,8,9
4	(B) 1,1,3,3,4,6	(C) 2,2,3,5,6,6	(C) 2,3,5,6,6,8	(A) 3,4,6,7,8,8
5	(A) 1,2,2,2,4,7	(B) 2,2,4,4,4,8	(B) 2,3,5,6,7,7	(C) 3,4,6,7,7,9
6	(C) 1,1,2,4,5,5	(A) 2,3,3,3,6,7	(A) 2,4,4,5,7,8	(B) 3,4,5,8,8,8

[a] Power card values for the three power positions for the six-game series were chosen with two restrictions: no value higher than 9 was used, and each set averaged to the predetermined mean value for the position. The same combinations were used in all seven sessions (except that the low — middle positions were used in three sessions, and the high — middle in the other four). The sequence of power positions by player identification letter was also predetermined, as indicated, and was used in all sessions.

All tournaments were conducted in a large graduate student work area. The four playing tables were informally arranged about 12 ft apart in the center of the room; around the edges were graduate student desks, a row of calculating machines, the departmental coffee urn, assorted items of experimental equipment and banks of filing cabinets. Pilot testing had indicated that players concentrated on the game despite a variety of extraneous distractions, so no attempt was made to keep the room closed during play. Word of the game got around among faculty and graduate students, and there were often a number of informal observers standing or strolling among the playing tables during the tournaments. As anticipated, the game proved so absorbing that the subjects ignored both observers and sporadic extraneous activities around the edges of the room. In line with this informal observation, subjects' reports at the end of the session were enthusiastic, both on the questionnaires and in spontaneous comment. Requests to return and play in another tournament were frequent. For a detailed description of the bargaining interaction that took place during the games, see Chapter VIII.

RESULTS

Scores in the Con Game are not completely independent (or completely dependent) for the three subjects within a triad. At the time this research was conducted there was no known overall analysis of variance appropriate for such data. Accordingly, each of the predictions was considered separately. Each was also tested by a nonparametric method or a direct probability estimate in addition to the test reported. In no case did the results of the alternative tests differ across the .05 level from those reported.

MACHIAVELLIANISM

The major prediction was that high Machs would be more successful as manipulators of their fellow men in a live-interaction bargaining situation, as measured by scores in the Con Game. The mean scores per game, based on all six games per subject (22 subjects in each Mach classification), are shown in Table VII-3.

TABLE VII-3

Machiavellianism and Success in the Con Game (22 Ss per Mach group)

Mach group	Mean game score	Game score minus 33.33[a]	t	$p <$
High	47.32	13.99	5.56	.001
Middle	31.11	-2.22	-.97	.20
Low	21.58	-11.75	-5.58	.001

[a] The expected value per game, per subject.

Since the total value of each game was 100 points, the expected value for each subject was $33\frac{1}{3}$ points. It is immediately apparent that the high Machs, with a mean of 47 points per game, were more successful than could have been expected by chance. Since the 100 points per game was constant and the high Machs won more than an average share of them, the other subjects in the triads, necessarily, must have lost proportionately. However, the prediction that Mach scores are related directly to success in the game requires that middle Machs do better than lows. The results support the prediction. The middle Machs averaged 31 points per game, not significantly less than the expected value. It was the low Machs, with a mean of 22 points per game, who lost noticeably. These impressions are supported by the results of t tests, also shown in Table VII-3, comparing the mean score of each Mach group against the expected value of the game. These results agree with those obtained by analysis of difference scores based on subjects within triads (high versus middle Machs: $t = 3.42, p < .005$; middle versus low Machs: $t = 2.08, p < .05$).

An alternative way to evaluate the relation between self-reported Machiavellianism and success in the Con Game which includes all the subjects in one comparison is to correlate Mach scores and game scores. For this purpose the two Mach scale scores of each subject were summed. The correlation between this total Mach score and total points won in the games was .71. This approximates the correlation of .73 between the two forms of the Mach scale in this sample.

The first prediction was clearly confirmed.

AMBIGUITY IN THE SITUATION

It was assumed that ambiguity in the objective factors which ordinarily determine the distribution of rewards (in this game, power position in the group) would enhance opportunities for interpersonal manipulation. From this it was expected that high Machs would take greater advantage of their special skills when power positions were made ambiguous. On the assumption that low Machs rely least on manipulation and rely most on the objective determinants of

TABLE VII-4

Machiavellianism, Success in the Con Game, and Ambiguity (22 Ss per Mach group)

| Mach Group | Mean score per game | | t[a] | $p <$ |
	Unambiguous	Ambiguous		
High	41.83	52.80	2.12	.025
Middle	31.68	30.53	−.20	—
Low	26.48	16.67	−1.58	.10

[a] The t tests were based on difference scores (per S, between ambiguity conditions).

rewards, their power position in the group, it was expected that the increase in winning for the highs would be primarily at the expense of the low Machs rather than the middles.

That this is precisely what happened can be seen by comparing the mean scores of the three Mach groups in the two ambiguity conditions. These are reported in Table VII-4 and diagrammed in Fig. VII-2. The high Machs were more successful in winning points in the Con Game when bargaining conditions were ambiguous than when they were unambiguous ($p < .025$). The low Machs were less successful, although not significantly so.

The next step was to compare the *increase* in advantage from the un-ambiguous to the ambiguous condition of the high over the low Mach group, and the increase in advantage of the high over the middle Mach group. The relevant

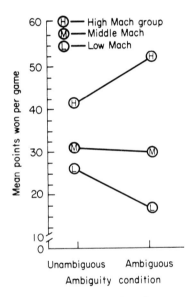

FIG. VII-2. Machiavellianism, success in the Con Game, and ambiguity (22 Ss per Mach group).

data and t tests are shown in Table VII-5. As expected, the high Machs' advantage over the lows did increase (it approximately doubled) from the unambiguous to the ambiguous games. In contrast, the advantage of the high-over the middle-Mach group did not increase significantly.

These results support the prediction that high Machs would win more points

TABLE VII-5

Machiavellianism, Success in the Con Game, and Ambiguity [a]

Mach groups compared	Mean difference in game score		t [b]	$p <$
	Unambiguous	Ambiguous		
High minus low	15.33	36.14	2.34	.025
High minus middle	10.15	22.26	1.23	.20
Middle minus low	5.20	13.86	1.09	.20

[a] Mean difference scores per game between the Mach groups in the two ambiguity conditions.

[b] The t tests were again based on difference scores (between Ss within games, between ambiguity conditions).

in the Con Game, primarily at the expense of the lows, with an increase in ambiguity in the bargaining situation.

POWER POSITION IN THE GROUP

It had been expected that the differences between the game scores of the three Mach groups would increase with increasing power position in the unambiguous condition. The relevant descriptive data, mean score per game by Mach and power position in the unambiguous condition, are shown in Table VII-6.

TABLE VII-6

Machiavellianism and Power Position in the Unambiguous games
(22 Ss per Mach group)

Mach group	Mean Score per Game (unambiguous condition)			
	Power position			
	L	M	H	All games
High	19.32	42.73	63.45	41.83
Middle	16.59	35.23	43.23	31.68
Low	14.54	23.54	41.36	26.48
All Ss	16.82	33.83	49.35	33.33

These data suggested a trend in favor of the predicted interaction: the average difference between the game scores of the three Mach groups appeared to increase from the low- to the high-power position. However, before testing the interaction, preliminary one-way analyses of variance for the effect of Machiavellianism at each power position separately were computed and are summarized in Table VII-7. Since these tests indicated that the differences between Mach groups were nonsignificant at each of the single power positions in the unambiguous condition, the interaction prediction was rejected without further test.

TABLE VII-7

Summary Results of One-Way Analyses of Variance
for the Effect of Machiavellianism at Each of
the Power and Ambiguity Conditions Separately

	F [a]	$p <$
Unambiguous condition		
Low power position	.32	—
Middle power position	2.09	—
High power position	2.38	—
Over all power positions	4.58	.05
Ambiguous condition		
Low power position	7.82	.001
Middle power position	7.46	.01
High power position	5.09	.01
Over all power positions	24.67	.001

[a] Scores of Ss in the three Mach groups at any single power position are independent, since they were obtained in different games. (In each game only one S in the triad was in a given power position.) However, the analysis of variance over all power positions combined is not strictly legitimate since it compares scores not completely independent of Ss in the same game, as well as scores of Ss from different games. The p values of the two F ratios in question, however, are probably reasonable: neither is smaller than those yielded by alternative difference score and chi square analyses.

MACHIAVELLIANISM, POWER, AND AMBIGUITY

To get a clearer picture of the relations among the variables, the mean score per game for the three Mach groups was computed by both power and ambiguity condition (one game per subject). These data are diagrammed in Fig. VII-3.

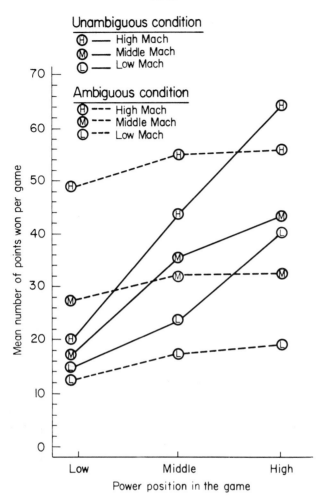

FIG. VII-3. Machiavellianism, ambiguity, and power position (one game per *S*, 22 *S*s per Mach group).

As noted above, the effect of Machiavellianism was not reliable at any of the single power positions in the unambiguous condition. But taking all games together in the unambiguous condition, the accumulated advantage of the more Machiavellian bargainers was reliable (see Table VII-7).

When bargaining conditions were ambiguous, the results were simpler. Regardless of power position in the group, success in the Con Game was directly related to Machiavellianism, as indicated by the significant F ratio for all of the possible comparisons.

DISCUSSION

High Machs succeeded notably in the Con Game, and primarily at the expense of the low rather than the middle Machs. In all six of the possible comparisons (by low-, middle-, and high-power positions in the two ambiguity conditions separately) the mean game scores of the three Mach groups were rank ordered in the direction expected (see Fig. VII-3). The probability of this pattern occurring by chance is $(1/6)^6$, or .00002. This consistency was reflected in the correlation of .71 between total Mach score and total score over all six games for all subjects.

These results are consistent with the hypotheses about Machiavellianism. Men who claimed to agree with Machiavellian attitudes on a self-report questionnaire also won more points in the Con Game, and those who claimed to disagree won less.

The game was designed to create a conflict of interest situation in a small group in which psychological pressure tactics, effectively employed, could influence the distribution of rewards. Winning in the game appeared to satisfy the rough criteria of "successful manipulation" outlined above — securing more of the rewards than chance or an equal distribution would have provided — at someone else's expense. The instructions and description of the game tournament given the subjects initially created a competitive orientation. Each subject was to try to win as many points for himself as he could. Yet the structure of the game was such that the player had to get an opponent to cooperate with him in forming a coalition and agreeing on a prize division in order to win points. To the extent that a player won more than the average, he had to get his opponents to cooperate with him rather than with the third player in the group, and further, agree to give him a little more of the prize, at their own expense, more often than not. The significant feature of this game is that the winners are those who are most successful in getting others to cooperate — at their own expense — in effecting that outcome. The extent to which such processes and outcomes are characteristic of conflict of interest situations in informal groups in general is, of course, a further question.

It should be noted that for the subjects the game was never called by name. It was presented as representing some typical characteristics of "real life" situations. Nor was the idea of "manipulation" ever suggested. The game was introduced in terms of decision making — whether to try to form a coalition, with whom, and how much to offer or accept. Subjects responded to the decision situation from the context of their own standards for reasonableness of agreements, and all had to face the psychological pressure of the group in making or breaking agreements. In these games "reasonableness" for high-Mach players appeared to be defined as, "as much as possible." This effect can be seen best in Fig. VII-3.

In the ambiguous games no one knew how much anyone else "deserved"[2] as a coalition partner. The high Machs did not have the others' expectations to support them in the high power position, or hinder them in the low power position. Instead, apparently, they used ambiguity to make high demands, and get away with them, in all power positions. The obvious effect of Machiavellianism at each power position separately in the ambiguous condition has already been noted. These results are consistent with the hypothesis that ambiguity is an asset in obtaining rewards via interpersonal manipulation to the extent that an individual agrees with Machiavellian precepts, and a liability to the extent that he does not.

The high Machs' increase in winning in the ambiguous condition is consistent with Budner's finding (1962), for males, of a negative correlation between Mach score and a measure of intolerance of ambiguity. It is of interest, however, that on the postsession questionnaire high Machs did not claim to have preferred the ambiguous games to a greater extent than middle or low Machs. A possible explanation was suggested by Draguns (1966). He compared self-reported dislike of ambiguity with a separate measure of premature attempts at closure, and concluded that these two dimensions were independent. High Machs may not like ambiguity any more (or less) than lows do, but they may cope with it more effectively.

In the unambiguous condition the player's position in the bargaining group appears to have been the major determinant of the game scores for all subjects: the higher the power position, the greater was the average winning. This observation agrees with reports of previous investigators who have studied similar situations. Kelley and Arrowood (1960), however, reported that this effect decreases with repetition of the same power structure in somewhat longer series of games. In this study one of the 66 subjects volunteered the rational strategy to the experimenter after the session: "Get into a coalition every time, and always offer or accept a 50—50 split, regardless of power position." However, on the postsession questionnaire, subjects were asked which of the power positions was most advantageous, and only 9 marked "all positions were

---

[2]As noted earlier, players form coalitions and divide the prize points according to power positions in the group. They play as if they feel that the high-power player should get the larger share of the prize points, etc. These implicit assumptions of the players can be summarized as what they perceive as "deserved" by the various power positions. These differences in power are real, though their apparent relation to the outcome of the game is specious, according to a rational analysis. However, since the players perceive them as relevant to outcome and play accordingly, they are empirically related to actual outcome. Accordingly, power positions will be referred to throughout the discussion as "objective" determinants of scores (i.e., from the players' point of view).

equally advantageous," while 36 checked "the player with the highest power."

Ambiguity virtually eliminated the effect of objective power positions. Yet the actual power positions differed as much as in the unambiguous games, and all players knew they did. Their expectations about how much they should get or offer in any particular power position should, presumably, have been similar to their expectations in the unambiguous games. Perhaps the critical element is not simply expectation, but perception or assumption of social support for expectations. When social support was eliminated in the ambiguous condition, players had only internal resources to back up their demands and counteroffers. This is speculation, of course. However, if it is correct, scores in the ambiguous condition could be interpreted as reflecting the relatively pure effects of personality in a small conflict-of-interest group when the members actually differ in resources, but have no objective criteria publicly available by which to decide on the apportionment of the rewards.

The results discussed thus far leave a number of questions unanswered. Although the objective constraints of the situation were equated for all subjects, high and low Machs differed in success. Presumably, the influence responsible was a difference in ability to manipulate fellow players. How does this ability work? This is essentially a question about the bargaining process in the games, which will be explored in Chapter VIII. Three alternative explanations for the present data are considered next.

MANIPULATIVE ABILITY OR GAME EXPERIENCE

One reason for not using a more familiar game for this study was to eliminate differences in previous experience. Still, it could be argued that greater game experience in general might have been an asset. On the postsession questionnaire subjects were asked how often they played card or dice games. Nearly half (31) of them checked the least frequent category, "Twice a year or less." (The subjects were from the College of General Studies at Columbia, and consequently were not fraternity men.) As shown in Table VII-8, 17 of the high Machs were above the total group median in card and dice playing frequency, as compared to 9 of the middle Machs and 8 of the lows. (One low failed to answer the question.) The chi square of 8.34 was significant.

This unpredicted finding is interesting in its own right. If Machiavellianism is associated with expertise in bluffing and knowing when and how to hold out for higher stakes, it should also be associated with greater rewards in poker and similar games. From this inference a simple reinforcement hypothesis would neatly predict the game playing frequencies obtained. But did the high Machs do better in the Con Game simply because more of them had more experience in card and dice games in general? An internal analysis suggested that this was

TABLE VII-8

Frequency of Card and Dice Playing
by Mach Classification

	Number of Ss in each Mach group who play	
	Twice a year or less	More than twice a year
High Machs	5	17
Middle Machs	13	9
Low Machs	13	8

$$\chi^2 = 8.34; \, p < .02$$

unlikely. The game scores of the more and less experienced subjects within each Mach classification did not differ significantly. With Machiavellianism held constant, experience was apparently not a significant asset in the Con Game.

MACHIAVELLIANISM OR INTELLIGENCE

Differences in intelligence between Mach groups could account for differences in winning. Intelligence test scores were not available, but 115 of the 143 men originally given the Mach scales had taken the General Studies (Columbia University) Screening Test with a total score based on vocabulary and reading comprehension subtests. These scores were available for 54 of the subjects. Table VII-9 shows the distribution of subjects above and below the total group median by Mach classification. The chi square of .56 was not significant.

TABLE VII-9

Achievement Test Scores by Mach Classification

	Number of Ss in each Mach group who scored:	
	Above Mdn.	Below Mdn.
High Machs	9	6
Middle Machs	11	9
Low Machs	9	10

$$\chi^2 = .56; \, p > .75$$

The same lack of relation between Mach score and academic aptitude held for the total sample. Of the 115 respondents with aptitude scores, 95 had been classified as consistent high, middle, or low Machs. Of the 28 highs 15 were above the median and 13 below; of the 38 middle scorers 17 were above and 21 below; the 29 lows split 15 and 14. The lack of relationship was obvious. This finding is consistent with previous results summarized in Chapter III.

ABILITY TO MANIPULATE OR MOTIVATION TO PLAY

If the Con Game appealed to high Machs more than lows, the resulting difference in motivation might explain the results. None of the available data support this alternative explanation. As noted earlier, the test situation was cast as a game so that low-Mach players would not be inhibited by ethics. Informal observation during the games suggested that nearly all players were enthusiastic and highly motivated. Several suggested that the experimenter should patent the game and sell it; others asked the experimenter to give them the game so they could sell it. Since these comments were not recorded systematically, they could not be used as a third behavioral index of the Machiavellian orientation of the subjects making them.

Self-report data from the subjects support these impressions. One question on the postsession questionnaire asked, "In general, how interesting or boring was the game for you?" Another asked, "In general, how hard were you trying to accumulate points while you were playing the games?" On both questions (each answered on a 7-point scale) about a third of all subjects marked the most positive response available and a second third marked the next most positive. The chi squares were not significant ($p > .10$ in both cases).

THE "GAME" EFFECT

The game context may have minimized differences in willingness to manipulate, but can success in a game be generalized to more "serious," realistic settings? Goffman (1961) has suggested that social games create exactly the social structures and tensions among participants that are significant in real, serious interactions (e.g., conflicts among obtaining rewards, interpersonal loyalties, protecting self-esteem, etc.). In this study a game was used to provide a cognitive setting that would create and legitimize a serious emotional interchange. The subjects were psychologically free to manipulate because the game rules required the role, but the game rules did not and could not prescribe the way any given individual would perform the role. The question is not how "real" was the game situation itself, but rather, how real were the interpersonal processes and outcomes it generated?

Nevertheless, the cognitive definition of a situation is undoubtedly important. One effect of increasing the seriousness of a situation would probably be a general decrease in willingness to use psychological pressure tactics. But the Machiavel study (Chapter V), in which the opportunity to manipulate was presented in a highly serious and realistic setting, indicated that high Machs were more willing to manipulate than lows. This suggests that increasing the seriousness of a situation might decrease willingness to manipulate for low Machs more than for highs. If this is true, then increasing the seriousness of the situation should increase the difference between high and low Machs in amount of rewards obtained via manipulation.

SUMMARY

Three predictions were derived from an analysis of Machiavellianism and were tested in a bargaining game designed to create a conflict-of-interest situation relevant to the personality variable. Two of the three were supported: (a) high Machs did outbargain lows and win more points in the games; (b) highs were even more successful when the bargaining situation was more ambiguous; but (c) highs failed to increase their success more than lows did with an increase in power position in their respective groups.

Perhaps the single most provocative finding was the correlation of .71 between paper-and-pencil measures of agreement with a Machiavellian outlook and success in interpersonal bargaining in a laboratory setting. This is taken as evidence that a measurable personality variable can influence the outcome of group interaction in a relevant situation. Specifically, the more Machiavellian group members in this study succeeded in getting more of the rewards.

That ambiguity in bargaining conditions would be an asset to the high Machs had been predicted, but the size of the effect deserves comment. When bargaining conditions were made ambiguous, the average difference in success between high- and low-Mach bargainers approximately doubled. Further, combining Machiavellian orientations with ambiguity in the situation virtually eliminated the effect of objective, situational determinants in distributing rewards.

CHAPTER VIII   **BARGAINING TACTICS**
IN THE CON GAME [1]

Florence Geis

The outcome of the Con Game when players were selected by Mach score was clear: the high Machs won. This chapter will explore how they did it. There are two reasons for reporting this analysis. One is that behavior believed relevant to winning was recorded to permit an examination of the tactics behind the results. The second is that these analyses led to some further experimental excursions which will be reported in subsequent chapters.

The Con Game tournament was designed to equate the objective situation for all subjects. The predictions (see Chapter VII) dealt with the outcome of the bargaining process, the number of points won. Underlying the predictions was the assumption that differences in outcome between Mach groups would be a consequence of differences in their use of opportunities and resources. Accordingly, summary records of the bargaining process were collected. At the time the study was designed there was little basis for making specific predictions about the bargaining behavior of high or low Machs. However, since Machiavelli's advice agreed with observations of high Machs' behavior in previous laboratory situations and the developing theoretical conception of "Machiavellianism," the data were examined for their relevance to these nascent hypotheses. Although tests of significance will be reported, they should be considered as descriptive and not as tests of formal hypotheses.

Machiavelli's advice might be summarized as, "Do what works — whatever works — regardless of ethical considerations; don't trust other people; by and large they can be manipulated." In the Con Game the behaviors that seemed most relevant to winning points were those associated with getting into coalitions and deciding on a division of the points between coalition partners. The following behaviors, identified by initiator and recipient, were recorded during play:

1. (P) Proposal to form a coalition. If a specific point split was suggested, the number of points the initiator was offering the recipient was recorded.

2. ($\sqrt{}$) Acceptance of a coalition proposal.

---

[1] These data were collected as part of research supported by an NSF predoctoral grant and the analyses were supported in part by NSF Grant GS-813 to the author. Some of the data were reported in an APA symposium address (Geis & Christie, 1965.)

3. (n) Rejection of a coalition proposal ("no").

4. (//) Breaking an existing coalition.

5. (Ad) "Advice," a suggestion or warning designed to influence another player.

Nine male graduate students in social psychology were trained to code and record these behaviors. At the last practice session before the study, the nine assistants were assigned to three playing tables, three to a table. Each independently recorded the interaction at his table over the course of a six-game tournament. Players were rotated to change the triad membership at each table as in the study proper. The intercoder reliabilities of the nine assistants, each one compared to two others at the same table, ranged from .65 to .87. The median reliability in the group was .82. Most of the discrepancies occurred in coding the "advice" category which will not be discussed further.

The record of a typical game is reproduced in Fig. VIII-1. This was a third game in the tournament. The "in hand" indicates that it was in the sequence of ambiguous games. That is, each player held his power cards in his hand so that none of them could see what cards any of the others held. In this session player A was low, B was middle, and C was high Mach. The low Mach was in the low-power position; the middle Mach was in the middle-power position; and the high was in the high-power position. The first recorded statement, "P–B" in column A, indicates that player A proposed a coalition to B. B did not respond to this offer, one way or the other. Next, A made a specific point-split offer to B of 50 points, provided B would promise not to break it. (In addition to the standard, coded categories, the assistants also noted other events in the game they considered significant. Promises against breaking a coalition were noted in several sessions.) B did not answer A, or before he had a chance to answer, C offered B the same deal A had offered — a 50–50 split with a promise not to break the coalition. Then (line 4) B accepted C's offer ignoring the offer from A. At this point a B–C coalition existed with a promise by B not to break it, in which the partners were splitting the prize 50–50. Then A offered C 60 of the 100 points in a prospective coalition with him. C accepted, thereby breaking his 50–50 coalition with B which he had required B to promise not to break. On line 7, B again approached C, this time offering him 70 of the 100 points. However, B apparently changed his mind and withdrew his offer (line 8). Next, the players tossed dice to determine order of play in the triad. B won the toss, and (line 10) play began with B, alone, competing against the A–C coalition. The next bargaining statement was an offer by B to give either A or C 85 of the 100 points to form a coalition with him, with a promise not to break the agreement. First C refused, and then A (line 13) followed suit. Finally (line 14) B conceded. Then, before A and C got to the goal to win together in coalition C broke the coalition (line 15). The game ended with C winning the entire 100 points for himself (line 16).

Table 3   E [Supervising Assistant]   Date 12/11

Game 3   (In Hand)

	A	B	C
(1)	P - B		
(2)	50 - B, Pr		
(3)			50 - B, Pr
(4)		v - C	
(5)	60 - C		
(6)			v - A
(7)		70 - C	
(8)		Withdraws offer to C	
(9)	3	1	2
(10)	P	L A	Y
(11)		85 - A or C, Pr	
(12)			n - B
(13)	n - B		
(14)		Concedes	
(15)			// - A
(16)	0	0	100

FIG. VIII-1.   Bargaining process protocol of a typical game of Con Game. (In this game player A was a low Mach in low-power position; B was a middle Mach in middle-power position; and C was a high Mach in high-power position.)

In this game, six coalition offers were made; two were accepted; and both were broken. The low Mach, A, made three offers and received one; the middle Mach, B, made two offers and received three; C, the high Mach, made only one offer and received three. Two coalitions were made, one between the high and middle Mach, and a second between the high and low. Neither the low nor the middle Mach broke any coalitions. The high broke two, one by accepting a better offer from the third player, and the second in order to win all of the points for himself.

In all, 132 games were played in the course of the study. Active bargaining for coalition partners and point splits occurred in most of them. The number of coalition proposals made in a game varied from zero in five games to 17 in one game. The mean number of proposals per game was 4.39. The median number per game was 3.57, or about one per player. Of the 580 proposals made, 138 were to form a coalition without offering a specific point split. Such a proposal could be meaningfully rejected, but an acceptance had to be followed by further bargaining to divide the 100 points. There were 442 (3.35 per game) of such specific offers. The number of coalitions formed (i.e., specific prize-division proposals accepted) in a single game varied from zero in 15 games to 6 in three games. The mean number of coalitions per game was 1.44. The median per game was 1.15.

Although three-man coalitions were allowed, only four proposals suggesting them were made — three in one game, and one in another, of which one was agreed to and kept. All other coalitions were two-man partnerships. Of the 190 coalitions made altogether, 96 were kept and 94 were broken before the end of the game. Of the 96 that were kept 86 were winning coalitions. The remaining 10 had been made too late in the game and were unsuccessful.

The rules of the Con Game and the structure of the social situation created by the rules placed an open-ended demand on the subject to respond to the spontaneous, ongoing behavior of others. The Con Game specified the goal for the subject, but left him to pursue it by whatever means he could. The behavior elicited by this situation appeared to differ from that of most laboratory situations in which the subject responds to a specific stimulus by choosing one of alternative predefined responses. In the Con Game, as in real life, subjects had to improvise their own responses, and they could initiate activity or not at will. The behavior elicited by these conditions was active, diverse, and frequently ingenious.

LIMITS TESTING

In the "do what works" approach to human relations the emphasis seems to be less on the "what" is to be done, and more on the "works," the result of what is done. On the postsession questionnaire completed after the games, subjects were asked whether they had used any particular strategies in playing. The response of one high Mach, verbatim and in its entirety was, "Win by any means." One way to find out what will work without relying on conventional role prescriptions is to size up the situation and then test the limits. The behavior of the high Machs in the Machiavel study (Chapter V) clearly fits this description. After the study, the experimenters were unanimous in assigning the Q-sort item, "characteristically pushes and tries to stretch limits; sees what he can get away with," to the most characteristic category for high Machs.

The tactics high Machs used to achieve their success in the Con Game appear to reflect the strategy suggested by the high Mach quoted above: any means, or all the ones recorded. As shown in Table VIII-1, the high Machs made more coalition offers, they had more of their offers accepted and more rejected; they received more offers, accepted more of them and rejected more; they broke more coalitions and kept more coalitions. However, the differences between Mach groups were not significant. High and low Machs differed significantly in only two comparisons: high Machs got into more coalitions that were kept by both partners until the end of the game, and were deserted by a partner less often than low Machs. The lack of significant difference between highs and lows held even when the two major categories, making and receiving offers, were combined.

TABLE VIII-1

Frequency of Using Bargaining Tactics[a]

Tactics	Mean frequency of use			Difference (high Mach vs. low Mach)	t	p <
	High Mach	Middle Mach	Low Mach			
No. of coalition offers made	7.50	6.59	6.00	1.50	.91	.20
No. accepted by other	3.18	3.09	2.41	.77	1.43	.10
No. rejected by other	4.32	3.50	3.59	.73	—	—
No. of offers received	7.45	6.68	6.86	.59	.50	—
No. accepted by subject	3.14	2.86	2.68	.46	.94	.20
No. rejected by subject	4.31	3.82	4.18	.13	—	—
No. of coalitions entered	6.27	5.95	5.09	1.18	1.55	.10
No. broken by subject	1.77	1.36	1.14	.63	1.24	.20
No. broken by partner	.95	1.64	1.68	-.73	-1.87	.05
No. of coalitions kept	3.55	2.95	2.27	1.28	3.66	.0005

[a]22 Ss per Mach group, six games per S.

These tabulations include only specific point-split offers. If the nonspecific proposals had been included, they would not have changed the pattern shown. For example, high Machs made 2.27 nonspecific offers to others, which would bring their total on the first line to 9.77. Middle Machs made 3.09 nonspecific offers, bringing their total to 9.68. Low Machs made 3.00, increasing their total to 9.00. The "number of offers received" would have been similarly increased for all three groups.

More offers were received than made. Occasionally a player would address an offer to both (either) of the other two. In such cases only one offer was made, by the speaker, but two were received, one by each of the other two players.

Although high Machs accepted 3.14 coalition offers, and had 3.18 of their offers accepted by others, they averaged only 6.27 coalitions entered. In the single three-man coalition, the middle Mach proposed it to the high, who accepted it; the high then proposed it to the low, who then also accepted it.

The most obvious interpretation of these data is that they represent attempts to manipulate the other players, and perhaps provide an index of willingness to manipulate in this situation. If it is assumed that they do, then clearly the high

Machs were not more motivated in the game or more willing than lows to attempt to manipulate others. This supports the argument in the previous chapter that differences in scores represented a difference in ability rather than a difference in motivation.

THE SOCIAL LIMITS OF FREQUENCY

The overall pattern of activity for the three Mach groups was provocative, and suggested a refinement of the limits-testing hypothesis. In all nine of the active categories (i.e., excluding coalitions broken by one's partner), the high Machs exceeded both middle and low Machs. This pattern of directionally consistent, but consistently nonsignificant differences suggested that these data may represent a significant nonsignificance in the behavior of the more successful manipulators. Perhaps high Machs have a built-in .05 level. Perhaps they push the limits, and their fellow man, just up to the point of becoming obvious, but not beyond. Perhaps a behavior frequency that would be significant by t test would also look significant to a fellow man. However, when manipulative intent is apparent to the victims, they may retaliate by refusing to be duped further, or by joining ranks against the would-be manipulator. Perhaps the successful manipulator is one who knows when to stop. He may test limits by pushing them, but know how not to break them.

If high Machs are attuned to some intuitive equivalent of the .05 level, how can we account for their significantly greater manipulation in the Machiavel study? The interpersonal situation in the Machiavel study differed from the one in the Con Game. In the Machiavel study the potential manipulator (the subject administering the test) was not dependent upon the test taker for cooperation, as one player was upon another in the Con Game. Nor, in the Machiavel situation, did the supposed victim have any means of retaliation, or any real alternative to remaining in the situation. In the Con Game, all potential victims did have means of retaliation. They could refuse to enter a coalition, or break it later. And they all had an alternative: if one triad member became obnoxious, a prospective victim could ignore him and try for a deal with the third player. If high Machs are limits testers, it would be reasonable to find them sensitive to the social limits of the situation.

The Con Game and Machiavel situations also differed in providing norms of others' behavior for comparison. In the Machiavel testing situation the subject had no ongoing manipulation by others, or of others, to judge whether his own activity was extreme or not. In the Con Game he had a continuous flow of interaction by which to gauge his own behavior. Perhaps a high Mach, like t-test procedure, cannot distinguish whether a particular distribution is extreme or not without another for comparison. Finally, the two situations differed in purported seriousness. Low Machs may have been more willing to manipulate in a game than while administering a test.

THE STRATEGIC LIMITS OF RAISING THE BID

The limits-testing hypothesis also described high Machs' bargaining offers, in terms of size of the point splits they offered for coalitions. A subject could offer an opponent from zero to all of the 100 points in a prospective coalition. The most extreme prize division proposed, accepted, and kept was an offer by a low Mach to give his partner 91 points, keeping nine for himself. Since any coalition had the advantage over the excluded player, a coalition was always a sure win if it was formed early enough in the game and kept till the end. And, it was the only means of winning, except for the player in high-power position who could win alone if the other two did not ally against him. Since at least one coalition was formed in the vast majority of the games, coalitions were the major means of winning.

To entice an opponent into a coalition a subject had to offer more points than the third player was willing to offer. The limit to the number of points offered was an objectively obscure but psychologically compelling sense of how much each player "ought" to get on the basis of the strength of his hand of power cards relative to the hands of his opponents. For example, no subject consistently offered 90 points, game after game. Such offers might have insured a coalition in every game, and one which the subject's partner would be unlikely to break. However, such a tactic would have given the player an average score of 10 points per game, far less than the expected value of $33\frac{1}{3}$ points. The dilemma faced by the player was how to offer a prospective partner more than the third player was willing to offer, but still keep as many points for himself as possible.

Again, high Machs kept within the .05 level, as shown in Table VIII-2. They did not differ from lows in making either very large or very small offers to prospective partners. They tended to make slightly more offers of 50 points, and slightly more of 51 through 60 points. Low Machs slightly exceeded highs in offering opponents 40 through 49 points. Again, however, the differences were not significant. Perhaps subjects obviously willing to raise their bids more than others in the group would acquire the reputation of easy marks. This would be a disadvantage in future bargaining.

Combining offers in the size categories listed in Table VIII-2 did reveal some significant differences. Highs made more of the larger-middle size offers (50 – 60 points) than lows did ($p < .05$). The interaction between Mach group and size of offer was also significant. Highs made more larger than smaller offers compared to lows' making more smaller than larger offers ($p < .01$). These patterns can be seen best in Fig. VIII-2. Nevertheless, the predominant pattern was for the differences between high and low Machs to be consistent in direction and, equally consistently, just short of the .05 level.

TABLE VIII-2

Size of Offers Made to Opponents

Size of offer[a] (points)	Mean number of offers of each size, per subject			Difference (High Mach minus low Mach)	t	p <
	High Mach	Middle Mach	Low Mach			
61–99	1.23	1.32	1.14	.09	—	—
51–60	1.86	.86	.86	1.00	1.61	.10
50	2.32	1.86	1.55	.77	1.41	.10
40–49	.86	.91	1.32	−.46	−1.20	.20
1–39	1.23	1.64	1.14	.09	—	—

[a] Offers were categorized by the number of points offered by a subject to his prospective partner.

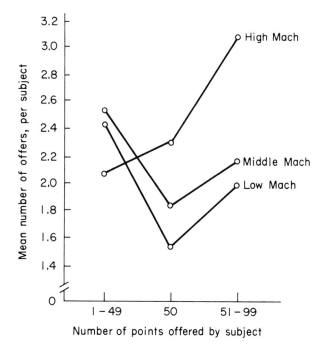

FIG. VIII-2.   Number of small, middle, and large offers made to opponents.

High Machs appear to be limits testers. They used all the bargaining tactics recorded slightly but not significantly more than other subjects; they made slightly but not significantly better offers to opponents. Perhaps in a situation that requires cooperation from others they know how to test and stretch the limits without breaking them.

TIMING OF TACTICS AND OPPORTUNISM

One requirement of doing what works in interpersonal relations is a sense of timing. This might also be interpreted as opportunism. What will work at a given moment may have been premature a minute before, but a few seconds later the opportunity may have passed. As noted above, the three Mach groups did not differ significantly in how frequently they used the various bargaining tactics. Yet empirically the high Mach tactics worked, while lows, using the same tactics almost as often, were unsuccessful.

For example, there was no significant difference between high and low Machs in the number of coalitions they broke. Highs broke 1.77 each over their six games; lows broke 1.14 each. However, the subject's final score in a game can be compared to the number of points he was to receive in the most valuable coalition he broke in that game. These data are presented in Table VIII-3. When a high Mach broke a coalition, he ended up with a higher score than he would have made by keeping it. High Machs who broke coalitions averaged 18 points per game better than the best coalition they broke would have brought them. (They either made another coalition in which they got more points than they were getting in the one they broke, or they had withheld some high power cards while in the coalition, and then broke it, using the hoarded cards to finish first and get all of the points for themselves.) For low Machs breaking coalitions turned out to be disastrous. Those who broke coalitions lost 28 points a game, compared to what they might have won if they had not broken them. A more conservative test would be to average the total gain or loss of each subject over all six of his games (rather than just those in which he actually broke a coalition), and include all 22 subjects in each Mach group (rather than just those who actually broke coalitions). This procedure gives the mean gain or loss due to coalition breaking per subject, per game, for all subjects. When this was done, again comparing only the *best* coalition a subject broke against his actual score at the end of the game, the 22 high Machs gained 3.50 points per game by this tactic ($p < .005$); the middle Machs lost 1.59 points per game ($p < .05$); and lows lost 3.91 points per game ($p < .01$).

How can this be possible? It might have been due to timing. For example, if a player broke a coalition too early in the game and failed to replace it with

TABLE VIII-3

Breaking Coalitions and Score in the Game: The Difference between a Subject's Score at the End of the Game and the Point Value to Him of the Most Valuable Coalition He Broke in that Game

Mach group	No. of Ss who broke coalitions	Mean points per game (over games in which S broke a coalition) per S				
		Value of best coalition S broke	Score after breaking	Difference	t	p <
High	(15)	50.87	69.00	18.13	2.67	.01
Middle	(12)	55.25	39.08	-16.17	-1.75	.10
Low	(13)	61.23	33.62	-27.61	-2.72	.01

another, his deserted partner could form a coalition with the third player. The new coalition, though initially behind, could move faster than the single player, and had a good chance of beating him.

A player could also break a coalition too late in the game. If two players in coalition were only two or three moves from winning, the excluded player, trying to avert a total shutout, might offer one of them a much better point split to form a new coalition with him. If the recipient accepted, he had to move halfway back to meet his new partner, perhaps leaving his deserted partner close enough to the finish line to get there first, alone, in spite of moving now more slowly than the new coalition.

Timing was also important in accepting or rejecting offers. As noted above, high Machs did not receive significantly more offers than low Machs. Further, an analysis of the size of offers received (how many of the 100 points were offered to a subject) indicated that high Machs did not receive better offers than low Machs. The mean size of all offers received by highs was 50.92 points, by lows 51.92 (n.s.). Yet, when the value of the best offer a subject received but did not accept was compared to his actual score at the end of the game, it turned out that highs averaged 2 points below the best offer they refused, while lows' scores at the end of games in which they rejected offers averaged 32 points lower. These comparisons are in Table VIII-4. Again, if game score compared to best offer refused in the game is averaged over all games and all subjects, the results are the same ($-.45$ of a point for high Machs, n.s.; -5.36 points for middles, $p < .005$; -12.86 for lows, $p < .0005$).

TABLE VIII-4

Rejecting Offers and Score in the Game: The Difference between a Subject's
Score at the End of the Game and the Point Value to Him of the Most Valuable
Coalition Offer He Rejected in That Game

Mach group	No. of Ss who rejected offers	Mean points per game (over games in which S rejected an offer), per S		Difference	t	p <
		Value of best offer S rejected	Score after rejecting			
High	(19)	51.37	49.05	-2.32	-.44	—
Middle	(19)	57.63	38.79	-18.84	-3.03	.005
Low	(20)	53.35	21.05	-32.30	-6.62	.0005

In summary, the low Machs received as many offers as the highs, the offers
they received were as advantageous as were those of the highs, they accepted and
rejected as many offers as the highs, and broke as many coalitions, but
apparently they did all these things at the wrong time, while the high Machs
timed their tactics to pay off. Although these data provide only indirect evidence
for the timing hypothesis, it seems the most likely explanation for them.

INITIATION AND CONTROL OF STRUCTURE

In watching subjects play the Con Game the first noticeable regularity was
that the high Mach usually ended up with at least half of the points. This effect
had been predicted, and why it should occur was accounted for by theory. *How*
they managed to do it, though, was at first obscure. In the search for possible
explanations, a too-frequent coincidence became apparent. Both the low and
middle Machs in the triad seemed to direct most of their bargaining to the high.
He argued with each of them, and they responded to him, but seldom turned to
each other.

CONTROL OF COALITION MAKING

These impressions were confirmed by the data. Figure VIII-3 shows the
number of coalition offers subjects made to the higher Mach of their two
potential partners compared to the number they made to the lower Mach of the

two. It is clear that the high Machs did not discriminate between middle- and low-Mach players in making offers. The middle- and low-Mach players, however, did discriminate between the high Mach in the triad and each other. They averaged 3.73 coalition offers each to the high Mach, compared to 2.98 each, to each other ($t = 2.46$, $p < .01$). When the number of offers a subject made to the higher Mach of his two available opponents was compared to the number he made to the lower Mach of the two, the choice of the higher over the lower Mach of the two possible recipients was reliable for all subjects combined.

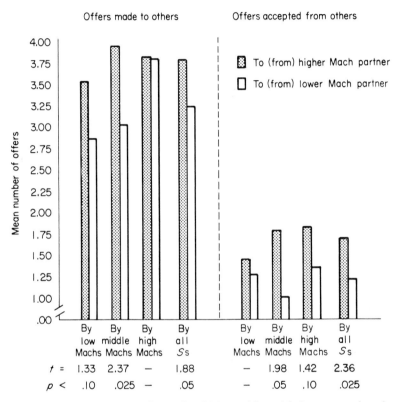

FIG. VIII-3. Number of coalition offers made to higher- and lower-Mach partner, and number of offers from higher- and lower-Mach partner accepted. ("Higher" and "lower" Mach of partners was determined by the relative Mach scores of the two available partners, not by comparison with S's own Mach score: e.g., for the high-Mach S, the middle Mach was his higher-Mach partner and the low was his lower-Mach partner.)

There was some brief speculation about reviving an animal magnetism notion, which was not pursued. Also relevant, and more fruitful, was the "great-man" theory of leadership (Borgatta, Couch, & Bales, 1954) and studies of emergent leadership in group discussions. A consistent finding is that the leader talks to the followers and they to him, more than they talk to each other. According to the bargaining records, the high Machs had been more active, although not significantly so. However, the acts recorded were only a portion of the interaction. Also, leadership in the usual sense was not an issue in the Con Game. The point is that the high Machs seemed to be acting in a way, or exerting some force, analoguous to leadership in discussion groups. The common element in the leadership and Con Game situations seemed to be the function of initiating and controlling structure for the interaction in the group. Somehow, in the bargaining triads the high Mach always seemed to be in control. Both of the other players appeared to act as if he were the preferred coalition partner. They followed his suggestions and accepted his offers over those from each other. For example, in the game protocol shown at the beginning of the chapter both the low and high Mach offered the middle Mach a 50−50 coalition, and it was the low who had spoken first. The middle ignored the low and accepted the high.

The middle Mach in the example (Fig. VIII-1) was typical. Before the data are presented, though, consider the steps by which the final outcome in the triad was determined. Each of these steps, in sequence, was a turning point for creating, maintaining, or altering the structure of relationships relevant to the final distribution of points. First, a coalition offer had to be made. Then it had to be accepted by the recipient. At this point the group was structured into a coalition of two against one, and the structure between the two partners was determined by the point-split agreement they had made. However, coalitions could be broken. In order for a coalition to determine the final structure, it had to be kept by both partners. However, some coalitions were unsuccessful, especially those made frantically at the last minute, and the lone player won by himself. In order to be successful, a coalition had to have been made early enough in the game and maintained by both partners against all blandishments from the excluded player.

In summary, the turning points that determined the final reward structure were: (a) making an offer; (b) accepting an offer; (c) keeping the coalition rather than breaking it; (d) having the coalition win. These steps in determining group structure necessarily followed each other sequentially in time. However, they do not represent exclusive time periods in the game. At any point in the development of structure, a player could return to the first step by making a new offer. If it was accepted, the structuring sequence began anew. This often happened a number of times in the course of a single game.

At the first step in creating structure, making offers, high Machs did not differ from the other players except for virtually imperceptible tendencies to make more and better offers. Even without statistically discernible salience, however, they somehow elicited significantly more offers from each of the other two members of the triad than either of them drew from the other, as shown in Fig.

VIII-3. At each succeeding step in determining the final group structure, the controlling influence of the higher Mach in the group was apparent. This influence increased from the earlier, less certain, to the later, more definitive stages in determining the final structure.

After making and receiving offers, the next step in creating structure was accepting an offer, or getting one accepted. The number of offers accepted by the Mach group of the player accepting and the one offering is also shown in Fig. VIII-3. Again, more offers were accepted from the higher Mach of the other two players in the triad. Again, the middle Machs most sharply discriminated between their high- and low-Mach opponents. It might be assumed that middle Machs' acceptance of more offers from high than low Machs was simply a function of the number of offers they received from highs and lows. But middle Machs accepted 46% of all offers they received from a high Mach, versus 38% of those from a low.

The tendency of high Machs to accept more offers from middle Machs than from lows should also be noted. Although it was small, and not statistically significant ($p < .10$), it was the first indication of discrimination by high Machs in favor of the more Machiavellian of their two opponents. Accepting an offer involved a more complex social interaction than making one. First, there had to be a coordination of timing. An offer had to be received at a time when the player was ready to accept one. Second, the size of the offer had to be acceptable from the point of view of the two players' relative advantages and disadvantages at the time. Third, the player receiving the offer had to notice or attend to the one offering. On each of these counts middle Machs tended to surpass lows as prospective partners. In all of the data on timing the middle Machs fell between the highs and lows in effectiveness. In making more larger offers and fewer smaller ones the middles were again between the highs and lows. Finally, they were clearly higher than the lows in Machiavellianism, and therefore, if the present hypothesis is correct, more apt to initiate and control structure, or be the kind of person attended to and desired as a partner.

Obviously, the high and middle Machs preferred each other as coalition partners. The pattern of mutual choices can be seen in Fig. VIII-4. In this figure the number of offers accepted by the subjects in each Mach group is combined with the number of their offers which were accepted by others, to show the total number of coalitions they entered with members of each of the other two Mach groups. Again, it was the middle Machs who discriminated most. They made 3.55 coalitions with high Machs, as compared to 2.36 with lows ($p < .01$). Consistently, the highs again showed an almost-significant preference for coalitions with the higher Mach of their two opponents — 3.55 with middles, as against 2.68 with lows ($p < .10$). When the preferences (i.e., difference scores) for all subjects were combined, the preference for coalitions with the higher- rather than the lower-Mach opponent was obvious.

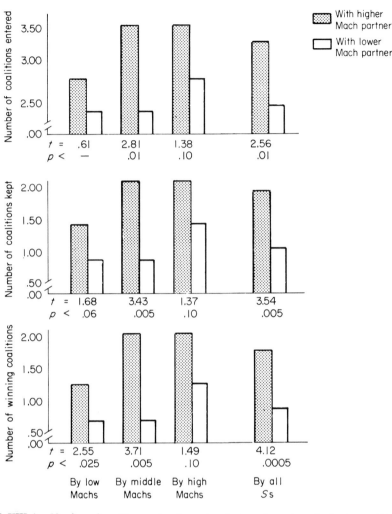

FIG. VIII-4. Number of coalitions entered, number kept, and number of winning coalitions between subjects in each Mach group and their higher- versus lower-Mach partner in the triad.

The mean number of coalitions made by high Machs with middles is, of course, the same as the number made by middles with highs, but the two distributions of difference scores are different. This is because triad membership was changed from game to game. For example, a particular high and middle Mach pair might have made a coalition in their first game in the tournament. The high Mach of the pair could, in the remainder of the tournament, make an unlimited number of coalitions with other middle Machs, while the middle Mach of the original pair might not make any further coalitions with high Machs.

Nevertheless, each coalition that was made is counted twice, once for each of the partners.

involved. Psychologically this makes sense; each coalition required two independent acts of commitment.

Statistically, the comparisons for any two of the Mach groups are independent of each other. Since subjects were free to make as many coalitions as they wished in a game, the number high Machs made with middles, compared to the number they made with lows, for example, in no way constrained the difference between the number of coalitions middle Machs made with highs compared to the number they made with lows. However, given the mean difference scores for any two of the groups, the mean difference for the third group is determined (but the size of the variance is not determined). To compensate for the partial lack of independence, the degrees of freedom for each distribution were reduced by one-third, both in computing the value of t, and in entering the t table for the associated p value.

The comparison for all subjects combined is obviously not independent of the three separate Mach group comparisons. It is the average of the three. The variance for the distribution, however, is the sum of the variances for the three separate distributions. Again, the degrees of freedom were reduced by one-third — from 65 to 43.

The comparisons for "Coalitions Kept" and "Winning Coalitions" are further constrained by the fact that only one coalition could win or be in effect at the end of the game in each triad. This limitation in no way constrains the *relative* representation of higher- and lower-Mach partners within each comparison. Again the "total group" degrees of freedom were reduced by one-third.

Not all of the coalitions that were made were kept. Some subjects in all three Mach groups broke coalitions. In order for a coalition to determine the final structure of the triad, it had to be kept by both partners against all offers from the excluded player. The number of coalitions kept until the end of the game, by Mach group of the partners, is also shown in Fig. VIII-4. Still, the high Machs' tendency to prefer middle- over low-Mach partnerships hovered short of the .05 level. However, both the middle and low Machs, separately, kept more coalitions with a high Mach partner than with the available lower Mach partner (i.e., with each other). The tendency among all subjects combined to keep more coalitions with the higher Mach of their two opponents (1.86 vs. 1.02) was also significant.

Not all coalitions that were kept were winning coalitions. A few had been made too late in the game, and although the partners remained loyal, the excluded player won alone. At this final, definitive step in the control of structure, high Machs had more successful coalitions with both middle and low Machs separately than either of them had with the other. See Fig. VIII-4.

The data on players' behavior at each of the steps leading to the final group structure have been described in terms of a preference for the higher Mach of the two possible partners. Obviously, such preferences must have been determined jointly by the contrast in attractiveness between the two alternative partners and by the personality of the chooser. It is the contrast in attractiveness as a partner that is relevant to the structure-controlling hypothesis. In fact, "attractiveness as a partner" may be simply an alternative description of the fact of controlling the structure in the group.

The time trend in this analysis of the gradual formation of group structure in terms of winning points fits with the data discussed earlier in connection with the limits-testing and timing hypotheses. At the initial stage — making offers — the high Machs did not discriminate in favor of the higher Mach of their two opponents. At this stage their control was inferred from their being preferred as the recipient of an offer by the other two players. Thereafter, in accepting offers, entering coalitions, and keeping coalitions, they showed consistent tendencies to prefer middle over low Machs. Consistent with the limits-testing data, the significance of these tendencies hovered just short of the .05 level.

The timing pattern for low Machs is less clear-cut. They tended to discriminate in favor of high Machs over middles in making offers, but did not discriminate in accepting offers. At the two final stages — keeping coalitions and keeping coalitions that won — they discriminated significantly in favor of the high Mach. The present hunch is that low Machs always preferred the high — when he was available. The high was always available as a recipient of offers. And once a low had made a coalition with a high, the low did not break it. Lows broke only 10% of all their coalitions with a high Mach, but they broke 37% of all their coalitions with a middle Mach.

The pattern of preference for the higher- over the lower-Mach opponent was most dramatic among the middle-Mach subjects. At each step in the determination of structure they definitively chose the high over the low as the partner with whom to share the opportunity. If Mach scores are correlated with a controlling or attracting (or compelling) influence, as hypothesized, then the middle Mach subjects would be in the position of having a choice between two partners with the greatest contrast on this dimension.

CONTROL BY COALITION BREAKING

Coalitions were the major means of controlling structure in the triad. One way to control structure was making and keeping them; another was breaking them. There were three ways a player could break a coalition. One was by being bribed away from an existing coalition by a more attractive offer from the third player. A second way was to make an offer to one player while in a coalition with the other, and have it accepted. In both of these kinds of breaks, the partner to be deserted had warning of the impending threat. In either case, he had a chance to make counteroffers and come out of the situation as well off as he started, sometimes better off. High and low Machs did not differ in breaking coalitions in either of these ways.

There was a third way to break coalitions. A player could simply break his existing coalition by fiat, without warning. This was felt to be a dirty trick, possibly because it changed the structure with a jolt. It could be dangerous. After such a move neither of the other players would be likely to accept a new coalition with the traitor. But it could also pay off. The subject had to keep his coalition until just a few moves before the end of the game, and meanwhile hold back a couple of his highest power cards, simultaneously urging his partner to play his highest remaining card at each turn. Then if he broke the coalition and tossed dice values at least as high as his former partner, he could use his hoarded high cards to get to the finish line first, thereby winning the entire 100 points for the game. Such maneuvers were infrequent, as can be seen in Table VIII-5. However, to the extent that they were attempted, they were more characteristic of high Machs than lows.

TABLE VIII-5

Three Types of Coalition Breaking: Number of Coalitions Broken by Being Bribed Away (Accepting Another Offer), by Proposing and Making Another Coalition, and by Individual Fiat

| Type of break | Mean no. of coalitions broken | | | Difference (highs vs. lows) | t | $p <$ |
	High Mach	Middle Mach	Low Mach			
Accepting another offer	.73	.64	.77	-.04	—	—
Proposing another coalition	.23	.36	.14	.09	—	—
Individual fiat	.77	.45	.23	.54	2.32	.025

CONTROLLING STRUCTURE WITHIN THE COALITION

High Machs not only controlled the triad structure by controlling coalition partnerships, they also controlled the structure of the prize division within their coalitions. They maneuvered into the most advantageous position by the end of the game more often than either of the other two groups of subjects. These data are shown in Table VIII-6.

A High Mach won 1.09 of his 6 games alone, compared to .41 won alone by a low Mach. A one-way analysis of variance showed a significant effect of Machiavellianism ($F = 5.27, p < .01$). However, analysis of variance for these data is questionable. A median split was approximated by classifying subjects as winning one or more games alone versus winning none alone. Eighteen of the 22 high Machs, 10 middles, and 9 lows each won one or more of his six games alone ($x^2 = 9.01, p < .02$). One way to win alone was to be in high-power position in a game in which the other two players did not form a coalition. At least one high Mach attempted to insure this structure for himself. At the beginning of the game, he simply proposed to the others that they all agree not to make any coalitions during the game.

TABLE VIII-6

Five Degrees of Success in the Con Game: (1) Winning Alone (100 points); (2) Winning in Coalition (51– 99 points); (3) Tying in Coalition (50 points); (4) Scoring in Coalition (1 – 49 points); and (5) Being Shut Out (no points)

Game outcome	Mean number of games (out of six games, total, per subject)			
	High Mach	Middle Mach	Low Mach	All Ss
Won alone (100 points)	1.09	.59	.41	.70
Won in coalition (51–99 points)	1.32	.82	.68	.94
Tied in coalition (50 points)	1.00	.50	.59	.70
Scored in coalition (1–49 points)	.95	1.32	.68	.98
Total games scored	4.36	3.23	2.36	3.32
Shut out (no points)	1.64	2.77	3.64	2.68

High Machs tended to be in winning coalitions in which they received more than half of the 100 points more often than middle and low Machs. ($F = 2.15, p < .05; X^2 = 4.02, p < .25$). This sheds further light on the ability of high Machs to influence structure. The Mach groups differed only slightly in the size of offers they made opponents, but highs tended to make more of the better offers. This tendency, together with the strong preference for highs as coalition partners, might have suggested that highs were giving points in return for partnerships. And so they might have, at least near the beginning of the game. However, many of those who did obviously managed to rearrange the structure in their own favor over the course of play.

Although it was not possible to collect systematic evidence of any such Machiavellian intention, all subjects were asked on the postsession questionnaire, "Did you use any particular plan or strategies in the game? If you did, please explain briefly." The most articulate high-Mach response was, verbatim, "I learned to make any coalition, however extravagant, at the start of the game — that gave me insurance of not getting stuck on bad dice rolls. However, I held onto my high coefficients [power cards] in anticipation of going on my own at the finish." The response of another high was more of a Machiavellian aphorism: "Use your opponent's greed." Low Machs tended to claim that they had not used strategies. The tone of those who said they had was quite different. The most articulate low answered, "When I had a good hand, said so, to get a better share, acted quickly to form coalitions whenever possible so as to get at least some of the points." Another confessed, "After the first few games I realized the value of coalitions and tried to make them when it seemed helpful. Often, however, I wasn't successful in making a coalition."

The high Machs showed a tremendous margin over both middle and low Machs in keeping winning coalitions in which the partners divided the points equally. It will be recalled that according to a game theory analysis, this is the rational solution to the prize-dividing problem. There were only 23 winning coalitions in the entire study in which the points were divided equally. High Machs were a member of 22 or 96% of these. Although the chance probability that a subject in a particular Mach group would be a member is two-thirds, the high Machs' 96% is statistically larger than two-thirds — even with a sample of only 23 cases.

A final way to initiate structure in the bargaining situation is to do it literally: step in and take over before someone else does. The first step in creating structure was making a specific point-split offer to another player. There were 54 games (41% of all games) in which play was initiated by a direct point offer, rather than other, less decisive beginnings. Of these 54, 32 were initiated by the high Mach ($\chi^2 = 20.34$, $p < .001$). One high Mach mentioned initiating negotiations in reply to the strategy question on the questionnaire.

The structure initiating and controlling hypothesis also seems to fit the data from other studies. In the study by Exline et $al.$ in Chapter IV, high Machs looked an interrogator in the eye longer than lows while denying cheating. A direct gaze while maintaining one's innocence could be interpreted as the best attempt the subject could make, under the circumstances, to structure the situation so it would support his claim of innocence. The high Machs' behavior in the Machiavel study (Chapter V) could also be interpreted in terms of initiating and controlling structure.

THE IMPORTANCE OF AMBIGUITY

One of the best examples of high-Mach limits testing, use of timing, opportunism, and structuring is their use of ambiguity. When the power structure in the triad was made ambiguous, the effect on the outcome of the bargaining process was clear. Although high Machs won in both conditions, they approximately doubled their margin over the lows under cover of ambiguity.

OPPORTUNISM

The high Machs adapted their bargaining tactics to the social limits of the situation in the ambiguous games more than low Machs did. In the unambiguous games all subjects played by their power position in the group. When they were in the low-power position, they made large offers to the other players and accepted small ones. In the high-power position they made small offers and accepted large ones. The mean value to the subject (the number of points he was to receive) of all coalitions he entered in each power position is shown in Table VIII-7. Since not all subjects made a coalition in each power position, the number of subjects upon which each cell mean is based is given in parentheses. In the unambiguous games the value of coalitions to the subject varied from 37 points in low-power position to 62 points in high-power positions. This pattern was uniform across all three Mach groups.

TABLE VIII-7

Point Value to the Subject of his Coalitions [a]

Mach group	Mean value of coalitions						Mean difference [b] (high−middle −low power)		t	$p <$
	Power position in the game									
	Low		Middle		High					
Unambiguous condition										
High	(17)	38	(17)	53	(14)	63				
Middle	(15)	33	(19)	53	(11)	61				
Low	(14)	39	(16)	53	(11)	61				
Ambiguous condition										
High	(18)	51	(19)	51	(13)	51	(19)	.16	—	—
Middle	(19)	43	(15)	56	(10)	52	(16)	8.50	2.24	.025
Low	(14)	45	(14)	48	(11)	55	(13)	6.69	2.69	.01

[a] The number of Ss upon which each cell mean is based is given in parentheses.
[b] Mean of difference scores of Ss who had coalitions in at least two power positions.

As an alternative test, subjects were classified as either playing by power position in the ambiguous games, or not playing by power position. Subjects who had coalitions in all three power positions were classified as playing by power position if the mean value of their coalitions in high power was greater than the mean value in low power. If a subject had coalitions in only two power positions, the comparison was between the mean coalition values in those two positions. Subjects who had coalitions only in the low- or high-power position were classified as playing by power position if the mean value of their coalitions was below or above, respectively, the grand mean of all coalitions in the ambiguous condition. (Subjects who had coalitions only in middle power were excluded from the analysis.) This classification was possible for 21 high Machs, 20 middles, and 19 lows. Of the 21 highs 10 were classified as playing by power position, and 11 not. Fifteen of the 20 middle Machs played by power position and 5 did not. Sixteen of the 19 low Machs did and three did not ($\chi^2 = 6.71, p < .05$).

In the ambiguous games, however, when power cards were hidden, all subjects were less dominated by their own power positions, or relied less on them. High Machs disregarded power position altogether. Low Machs compromised. The shift in tactics by highs could be interpreted as opportunism, or limits testing, or both. High Machs demanded and accepted exactly as much in low power position — 51 points — as they did in middle or high power. They were apparently quite ready to disregard the official or external grounds for demands, and rely instead upon their ability to influence and control the social process. In contrast, although power cards were hidden in the ambiguous games, coalition agreements by low Machs clearly reflected their power positions. They entered coalitions for 45 points when they were in low power position, 48 points in middle power, and 55 points in high power. Low Machs were apparently either less able or less willing to disregard the objective determinants of rewards. Or, not being limits testers or exploiters of the possible, they were guided by what seemed salient to them.

High Machs were characteristically opportunistic in both the unambiguous and ambiguous conditions. In both, they exploited a salient feature of the situation. When the low Machs in the unambiguous condition had publicly verifiable, objective evidence to back up their demands, they did not differ from high Machs in agreeing to prize divisions according to the value of their power cards. However, in the ambiguous games social support for demands based on power position was not available. Nevertheless, the low Machs appeared to be striving for justice.

CONTROL OF STRUCTURE BY BREAKING
AND MAKING COALITIONS

Otherwise, the bargaining tactics of high Machs in the ambiguous games seemed to be the same as those noted previously, only more so. For example, the three Mach groups did not differ in the number of coalitions they broke, overall. In the ambiguous games, however, the high Machs tended to break more coalitions than either of the other two groups (1.05 vs. .45 for middles, .55 for lows; $p < .10$). In the ambiguous condition when power cards were concealed, it was easier to withhold high cards while in a coalition. This was the recognized preparation, at least among several high Machs who mentioned it on the postsession questionnaire, for breaking the coalition just before the end and using the high cards to win alone. No low Mach mentioned such a strategy.

A major line of evidence for the controlling influence of high Machs was the preference of all subjects for the higher Mach of their two possible coalition partners. This attractiveness of the higher-Mach players was stronger, at each of the steps described before, in the ambiguous games than in the unambiguous ones. For example, Table VIII-8 shows the number of winning coalitions by Mach group of the partners broken down by ambiguity condition of the game. These figures show that while the higher-Mach partner was preferred in both conditions, the preference was stronger in the ambiguous games. In the unambiguous games the power relations in the triad provided cues for structuring the situation. In the absence of these external sources of control in the ambiguous games, the effect of the dominant member's personality increased. In answering why he had preferred games in which the power cards were hidden or public, a high Mach explained, "I feel that I had the opportunity to use resources beyond my power to better advantage when they were not public."

TABLE VIII-8

Number of Winning Coalitions with Higher versus Lower Mach Partner

	Mean number of winning coalitions				
	With higher- Mach partner	With lower- Mach partner	Difference: with higher minus lower Mach		
Ambiguous condition	.92	.32	.61		
Unambiguous condition	.80	.53	.27		
Difference: ambiguous				t	$p <$
minus unambiguous	.12	– .21	.33	1.91	.05

"Higher" and "lower" Mach of partners was determined by the relative Mach scores of the two available partners, not by comparison with S's own Mach score. E.g., for a high Mach S, the middle Mach player was his higher Mach partner, and the low Mach player was his lower Mach partner.

The t test was computed on the distribution of difference-of-difference scores for all subjects, combined ($n = 66$). The number of winning coalitions a subject made in the unambiguous games with the lower Mach of his two partners was subtracted from the number he made with the higher Mach of the two. This difference score was then subtracted from the analogous difference score for the same subject with the same opponents, in the ambiguous games. Again, the degrees of freedom were reduced by one-third.

DEPERSONALIZATION OF OTHERS

In Chapter I it was proposed that the manipulator would be unlikely to invest affect in others or empathize with them, and that he would have little concern for conventional morality. The bargaining data relevant to these two descriptions seemed to fit together into a single characterization, a tendency to depersonalize others, their concerns, and the interaction process. The first face-to-face experience with this tendency occurred in the Machiavel study, in which the experimenter knew the Mach classification of the subject.

High Machs can be charming immediately. Low Machs, telephoned to participate in an experiment or upon arriving at the laboratory, often appeared more reticent and less spontaneous than the highs. Later in the session, however, the experimenter delivered a memorized script intended to convey to the subject that manipulating the test taker was permissible but not required.

Low-Mach subjects responded as if they understood thoroughly and would cooperate to the best of their ability. In delivering the same instructions to a high Mach, with equal care and emphasis, the experimenter usually failed to discern a response of any kind. Looking back at this situation, in terms of the interpersonal relationship between the subject and experimenter, it appears that the highs either did not sense the experimenter's concern or chose to ignore it. The lows did sense the concern and responded to it.

There is some evidence that the two assistants in that study had similar impressions. They did not know the Mach classification of any subject, but after working with each one they recorded a guess as to whether he had been a high or low Mach. As the basis for guessing, they were told that high Machs would show little concern or involvement with the other student but would perform their manipulations with enthusiasm and verve, while lows would be more concerned and involved with the test taker, but perform their manipulations in a flat and colorless way. Either by these descriptions or some other unrecognized cues the assistants guessed better than chance which subjects had scored high and which low on the Mach scale.

AFFECTIVE DETACHMENT

The same kind of difference between high and low Machs showed up in the Con Game. All subjects appeared to be involved in the game, but the high Machs looked impersonally task involved, while the lows looked ego involved.

For example, some subjects asked for promises that a prospective coalition, if agreed to, would not be broken. This was not surprising. The game had been introduced as an analog of real, conflict-of-interest situations. Low Machs played the game as if it *were* those situations; highs played the situation as a game. There were four cases recorded in which a low Mach required his partner to promise not to break a coalition. ("Promising" was not a formal scoring category, but the observers had been asked to note any "significant events" not covered by the standard categories.) In each of these cases, the low Mach kept the coalition as faithfully as the partner he had bound with a promise. In all seven recorded cases of a high Mach requiring a promise of his partner not to break a coalition, the high himself subsequently broke it. It appeared that low Machs were assuming an unspoken rule of reciprocity: a promise was as binding upon him who demanded and accepted it as it was upon the one who made it. No high Mach ever broke a (recorded) promise he had made. For high Machs a promise evidently bound only the one who gave his word explicitly.

A further indication that low Machs may have played the game as if it were a real conflict-of-interest situation is shown in Table VIII-9. They alone refused more offers from a prospective low-power partner than they refused from a prospective high-power partner. (All subjects received more offers from low-than high-power opponents.) High Machs rejected 68% of all the offers they received from low-power opponents, and 79% from high power opponents. For middle Machs these figures were 67 and 76%. Low Machs, however, refused 78% of all offers from low power opponents, and only 58% from high-power opponents. In most situations the efficacy of a coalition is related to the resources of the partners. An alliance with a strong partner is more effective than one with a weak partner. The low Machs' refusal of more offers from low- than high-power partners may reflect their transferral of this principle to the game situation. However, in the Con Game all coalitions were equally effective. In general, a coalition with the low-power player netted the bargainer more points than one with the high-power player.

TABLE VIII-9

Mean Number of Coalition Offers from Low-, Middle-, and High-Power Partners Refused

Refused by	Power position of offerer			Difference: low offerer minus high offerer	t	$p <$
	Low	Middle	High			
High Mach	2.00	1.55	2.05	−.05	—	—
Middle Mach	2.27	1.82	1.86	.41	—	—
Low Mach	2.82	1.59	1.36	1.46	2.59	.01

A distinction suggested by these examples is that high Machs approached the game situation cognitively, while low Machs had an emotion or value-oriented approach. High Machs played by what they knew — the specific game rules, and the definition of the situation as a game. Low Machs knew the game rules equally well, but played by what they felt. They responded to the personal, emotional, and value implications that the interpersonal relations in the game would have had outside the game.

Some of the data presented earlier also fit these descriptions. Figures VIII-3 and VIII-4 presented evidence showing a strong preference for the higher Mach in the triad as a coalition partner. This discrimination must have been based on a discriminable personality difference between the two available partners. Both middle and low Machs, separately, discriminated significantly between the high Mach and each other. Among high Machs, however, preference for the middle over the low Mach never exceeded the .10 level of significance. The depersonalization hypothesis proposes that high Machs' lack of discrimination was due to not perceiving the difference, or disregarding it in favor of impersonal strategy considerations, rather than a real lack of perceptible difference between the middle and low Machs.

The significant discrimination by low Machs indicates that they did respond to the personality differences between their two partners. An illustration of focusing on personal characteristics rather than on strategy was provided explicitly by a low Mach. In response to the postsession questionnaire item on using strategy, he answered, "No — it wasn't possible because our opponents in every game were different people." No high Mach gave a reply even vaguely similar.

The difference in the way high and low Machs broke coalitions also supports the impersonal, detached characterization of highs compared to the more involved, person-oriented characterization of lows. Lows usually broke a coalition only to enter another one. This involved switching loyalty from one partner to another, but not breaking off alliances altogether. Highs switched partners too, but they could also break off a partnership cold, without any replacement. As shown in Table VIII-5, they did this significantly more often than lows.

The cool, detached characterization of high Machs, compared to the more emotionally ego-involved characterization of lows is also consistent with the results of Exline *et al.* in Chapter IV. After cheating on a test, subjects were confronted and accused in a face-to-face interrogation by the experimenter. Low Machs responded to the pressure and confessed more than highs.

THE UNIMPORTANCE OF ETHICS

Low Machs appeared to personalize the value implications of power positions. In bargaining, they often appealed to fairness as the criterion for deciding on prize divisions. As noted earlier (Fig. VIII-2), low Machs made more small than large offers to prospective partners, compared to high Machs making more large than small offers. In accord with justice, low Machs offered prospective partners in lower power positions less than half of the prize points. This insistence on fairness may have made their bargaining position seem rigid. This may be part of the reason that high and middle Mach players disregarded them. Or, high and middle Machs may have shied away from the player who seemed to take the terms of agreements too personally.

The contrast between high and low Machs in the meaning of power positions was particularly evident in the ambiguous games. In these games, as shown in Table VIII-7, high Machs disregarded power positions altogether in the size of offers they made and accepted. The low Machs did not disregard them. For them these values remained real considerations. The importance of the power values and honesty in dealing with them were expressed by a low Mach on the postsession questionnaire. Subjects were asked to explain their answer to the preceeding question on preferences for the ambiguous or unambiguous games. His reply was, "Whether or not the coefficients [power cards] were hidden did not seem extremely important because one could discuss them freely. However, the game seemed more open when the coefficients were public." The second sentence may also imply a feeling that some of his partners were not entirely open when power cards were hidden. In fact, in response to the strategy question a high Mach replied, "I endeavored to reveal as little as possible of my resources and personal feelings in my dealings with the other players."

High Machs expressed little concern for fairness or justice. They tended to make and accept more 50−50 offers than lows, regardless of their own power position, or their partner's. They were significantly more willing than others to keep the 50−50 coalitions (Table VIII-6). This could be interpreted as an expedient solution to the problem of getting into a coalition that one's partner would be unlikely to break. It certainly disregarded the individual worth of partners in terms of power positions.

Earlier in this chapter, high-Mach tactics were compared to statistical evaluation procedures. Statistical tests are decision devices designed to compare two or more distributions, relegating all irrelevant deviations within distributions, however individually interesting, to an error term. The behavior of high Machs in the bargaining situation appeared to follow similar rules. The metaphor was used initially to describe their sizing up of the situation and testing of the limits without using any one tactic so excessively that other players might notice and retaliate. In addition to this somewhat fancifully ascribed sensitivity to distribution differences, however, they also appeared to disregard individual personality differences between potential partners, and play instead by game rules and strategies geared to the situation, not to the person. They did not personalize the value implications of power positions and ignored them in the ambiguous games when they could not exploit them. Their inclination for the 50−50 coalitions would fit the same impersonal, probability-based orientation to interpersonal relations in the bargaining situation.

None of these data provide direct evidence of depersonalization. However, the inferential evidence suggests that one of the ways high Machs succeeded in the Con Game was through an impersonal, cognition-dominated approach to the social situation, in contrast to a personalized, feeling-dominated approach among lows.

RELATION TO OTHER THEORIES AND RESEARCH

A number of psychologists and sociologists have been interested in tactics of interpersonal control. Thibaut and Kelley (1959) distinguished between fate control, a potential of all Con Game players, and behavior control, which could be attempted by persuasion or threat. They also listed a number of compliance-gaining techniques, among them devaluing the worth of the other's compliance, and expertise — obtaining compliance by convincing the other that his outcomes will be improved if he follows the expert's advice. The high Mach's impersonal detachment may have appeared to devalue compliance, and may have been interpreted by the other players as evidence of expertise.

Goffman's (1959, 1961) descriptions of the ways of presenting and defining oneself in relation to others are clearly social control techniques. Subsequently, Weinstein (1965; Weinstein & Deutschberger, 1963) pointed out that people not only define their own position; they may also attempt to define roles and identities for others which in turn pressure the others to respond congruently. (This is a special case of the technique described by Thibaut and Kelley (1959) of reducing the other's alternatives.) This technique of casting the other into a role is called "altercasting." Obviously, individuals might reasonably differ in adeptness at casting the other into a role supporting their own purposes rather than his.

Other investigators have also been concerned with control or compliance-gaining techniques (e.g., Parsons, 1963; French & Raven, 1960; Jones, 1964; Kelman, 1961; Etzioni, 1961; Marwell & Schmitt; 1966; Skinner, 1953). Many of the proposed differences in interpersonal control techniques have been based on differences in the situations in which control occurred, or differences in the relationship of the controller and complier. The analyses in this chapter were focused on differences in technique between individuals in the same situation, and specifically between individuals who differed in Machiavellianism.

COALITION THEORY

There is one area of theory and research to which the Con Game data are directly relevant. Simmel (1950) originally observed that a triad was likely to break up into an alliance of two against one. Caplow (1956, 1959, 1968) proposed a theory based on power relationships to explain the observation and derived predictions as to the most likely coalitions. He described several different power structures, including the one used in the Con Game — all members unequal in power, and any two in combination more powerful than the third. For this power structure, Caplow predicted that coalitions between the low- and middle-, and low- and high-power members would be overrepresented. Gamson (1961a, 1961b) extended the theory and predictions to n-person groups. Using the concept of "cheapest winning coalition," he predicted that coalitions between the middle- and low-power players should be overrepresented.

The data supported the predictions of these theorists, as shown in Table VIII-10. In this sample, coalitions between players in the low and middle power positions were significantly overrepresented. This was true for coalitions accepted, and for those kept till the end of the game (47% of all coalitions in both cases), but not for coalitions proposed. There appears to have been a trend for the predicted coalitions to be selected for acceptance from among those proposed. Further, the overrepresentation of the low–middle-power coalition appears to have been stronger in the ambiguous condition. This observation is interesting in view of the fact that most studies designed to test Caplow's and Gamson's theories have used situations similar to the unambiguous condition in these games.

TABLE VIII-10

Number of Coalitions Proposed, Made, and Kept,
by Power Positions of the Partners in 132 Games

	Power positions of partners						
	High & middle power		High & low power		Middle & low power		
	No. of coali-tions	% of total	No. of coali-tions	% of total	No. of coali-tions	% of total	Total coali-tions
Coalitions proposed							
Unambiguous condition	(76)	33%	(82)	35%	(74)	32%	232
Ambiguous condition	(68)	29	(72)	31	(90)	39	230
Total	(144)	31	(154)	33	(164)	35	462 [a]
Coalitions accepted							
Unambiguous condition	(30)	31	(24)	25	(43)	44 [b]	97
Ambiguous condition	(22)	24	(25)	27	(45)	49 [b]	92
Total	(52)	28	(49)	26	(88)	47 [b]	189 [c]
Coalitions kept							
Unambiguous condition	(18)	36	(11)	22	(21)	42	50
Ambiguous condition	(9)	20	(12)	27	(24)	53 [b]	45
Total	(27)	28	(23)	24	(45)	47 [b]	95 [c]

[a] Twenty offers made to both opponents are counted twice, once for each offerer-recipient pair.

[b] Significantly larger than 33% by Z test $(z = p - P \div \sqrt{PQ \div N})$.

[c] One three-man coalition excluded.

For the Z test used in Table VIII-10 each offer (or coalition) is counted only once, regardless of the subjects making them. However, this means that not all offers (or coalitions) are independent. Most subjects made more than one offer and entered more than one coalition over their six games. Accordingly, an alternative test was made. A proportion score was computed for each subject. For example, for the category of coalitions made (i.e., accepted), the number of coalitions a subject made when he was in the low-power position with a middle-power partner was combined with the number he made in middle power with a low power partner, and this sum was divided by the total of all the coalitions he made. (Each coalition was attributed to only one partner, the one who had proposed it initially.) The mean of the distribution of proportion scores was then compared by t test against the null hypothesis mean of .33.

By these tests, the proportions of offers, coalitions made, and coalitions kept between low- and middle-power players were all significantly larger than one-third, and the average proportions were all larger than those shown in the table. This was because subjects who made few offers, overall, during their six games tended to make the few they did make in low- or middle-power position, and direct their offers to the player in middle or low power (thus, many of their proportion scores were 1.00). On the other hand, those subjects who made many offers during the tournament tended to make offers in all power positions, and to divide them more equally between their two possible partners. For example, as shown in the table, 35% of all coalitions proposed were between middle- and low-power players. The mean proportion per subject of proposals involving middle- and low-power players was .43. However, when subjects were divided at the median by the total number of offers they made, the mean proportion per subject for the more active players was .35; the mean proportion for the less active players was .51.

Finally, it should be noted that coalition theory and predictions based on individual differences in Machiavellianism are in no way contradictory. It was in the ambiguous games that the coalition theory predictions were more strongly supported. It was also in the ambiguous condition that all players showed the greater preference for the high-Mach over the low-Mach opponent as a coalition partner and that the high Machs showed the greater margin over the lows in winning points.

SUMMARY

The bargaining tactics recorded as subjects played the Con Game were analyzed for their relevance to five hypotheses intended as first steps in explaining how Machiavellians differ from non-Machiavellians in interpersonal tactics. High Machs appeared to size up the situation and then test the limits of how much they could get away with, but not to the point of becoming obvious to others in a position to retaliate. The evidence for this hypothesis is equivocal, since it consists of strings of directional but not-quite-significant differences showing that high Machs did slightly but not significantly more of nearly everything recorded.

It was proposed that high Machs must have an acute and opportunistic sense of timing in social situations. This sense of timing is probably not based on sensitivity to the other person, or his needs or wishes. It is more likely to be based on a sense of what is the logical next step — that will work — at that point in the social process.

High Machs appeared to initiate and control the structure of bargaining interaction in the group. They were overwhelmingly the dominant, decisive, and sought-after member of the triad. This is the best supported of the five hypotheses. The relevant data represent diverse behaviors, and many were relatively direct measures of structure initiation and control.

High Machs thrive especially when ambiguity obscures the claim of low Machs to fair play and justice. The tactics they used to achieve the increased success, however, seemed to be flexible, opportunistic adaptations of the same kind of tactics they used in nonambiguous games. It is as if the high Machs took advantage of the general confusion produced by ambiguity to be slightly more Machiavellian than might have been astute when others had fewer distracting concerns.

High Machs appeared unresponsive to personal or ethical concerns of others. Rather, they appeared to depersonalize the social interaction and approach it instead from a cognitive–probabilistic orientation. In contrast, lows appeared to personalize the situation and respond primarily from an emotional–ethical orientation.

CHAPTER IX

THE TEN DOLLAR GAME

Richard Christie and Florence Geis

The results of the Con Game were interpreted in terms of success in manipulating other people. Still, it could be argued that for sophisticated college men, bargaining for points might be like playing poker without money. In fact, at the end of some of the Con Game sessions, some subjects suggested playing for money. We must add, however, that it was usually those who had collected the lion's shares of the points who made such suggestions. Asides aside, the argument is interesting. Would the results have been the same if the subjects had been playing for more tangible rewards?

Playing for money stakes would make the game a more serious situation. "Seriousness" often seems to mean the extent to which the outcome of a situation has future implications. A situation whose outcome affects the future welfare of a person is more serious than one whose outcome has no such effect, or a smaller one. Playing a game for money is more serious than playing without money because winning and losing have future implications: the winners will be richer, the losers poorer. (If the stake is provided by an external source, only the winners have an objective change in future welfare; the effect on the losers is relative.) Finally, increasing the amount of money at stake in a game should increase the seriousness to the players.

Would high Machs be as successful at outbargaining lows with $10 at stake as they were in deciding on a division of 100 points? Clearly, if the theoretical descriptions presented so far are correct, they should be. Further, if low Machs respond to the value implications in a situation, and highs to the cognitive definition of it, an increase in seriousness should affect the behavior of low Machs, but not highs. To investigate these questions a new game was adapted from one described by Rapoport (1960).[1] It was essentially similar to the Con Game, except that it was simpler and crucially, it was played for money and for keeps. Three subjects were again seated around a table, this time with a female experimenter, and given the following mimeographed instructions:

THE TEN DOLLAR GAME

This is a bargaining game in which you will have a chance to make some money if you are good at bargaining. Ten $1 bills will be placed on the table in front of the three of you. The money will

---

[1] We are indebted to Professor David Marlowe for bringing this game to our attention.

belong to any *two* of you who can agree with each other as to how you will divide the $10 between you. (You will not be allowed to divide the money among all three of you.) The two prospective partners can divide the $10 any way they choose. For example, they might split it 5 and 5, 8 and 2, or any other split. Of course, the third man, who at the time is being left out of the agreement, can also make offers to either of the two bargainers, and try to win one of them over to making the agreement with him. The game is over when any two players have made an agreement which the third player cannot get them to break. The money belongs to the two who have made the agreement and is divided accordingly between them.

Since the experimenter was present during the entire bargaining sequence, it was not possible for the subjects to make a private agreement to split the $10 on a different basis after they left the laboratory.

The psychological decision situation created by this game was similar to that in the Con Game. Again, the subject found himself in a triad in which a coalition between any two members would win. Again, winning depended upon getting into the final coalition, and getting in on terms as favorable as possible. The situation differed from the Con Game in three important ways: (a) real money, in a sizable but not overwhelming amount was at stake; (b) there were no arbitrarily assigned power positions to lead two members to prefer each other as partners over the third man; (c) each triad played only one game, and the subjects were told that it would be the only one. After they had read the instructions, the experimenter emphasized, again, that the game was "for real," that the two who had the final bargain would indeed keep the money they had won.

Theoretically, this is an endless game since the excluded player can always make a better offer to one of the two who have reached an agreement, until exhaustion or other appointments force an end to the game. In actual practice, the game was resolved in from 2 to 17 proffered coalitions. This closely approximated the Con Game in which the number of offers made in a game ranged from zero to 17.

Only subjects who had participated in the previous study were used for this one. This ensured that all subjects would be equally familiar with bargaining and coalition formation in a triad with "no-holds-barred" rules, and that all had a similar previous experience in which to learn relevant interpersonal strategies. An attempt was made to schedule subjects for each triad who were unacquainted, and had not participated in the same session before to avoid effects of previous alliances or antipathies. The second condition was imposed after we had to discard the results of a triad in which conduct in the previous game, six months earlier, became an issue of debate in choosing coalition partners. Three subjects of differing Mach scores were scheduled for each session. The mean and median total Mach scale scores for the subjects who were highest, middle, and lowest in their triad are given in Table IX-1. Seven uncontaminated triads were observed in this game.

TABLE IX-1

Mean and Median Total Mach Scale Score for the
Highest-, Middle-, and Lowest-Mach Subject in
the Triad, for the Seven Triads

	Mean score	Median score
Highest	112.71	113.50
Middle	98.99	96.63
Lowest	85.36	83.00

RESULTS

On the basis of results from the Con Game, we would expect the highest Mach-scale scorer in the triad to be successful in talking his way into the final coalition more often than chance, and the lowest scorer to be included less often than chance. The number of subjects in each Mach group who were included in the final coalition, and the number excluded, are listed in Table IX-2. In all seven of the triads, the highest Mach-scale scorer in the group was a member of the final coalition. Since the probability of any player being a member of the final coalition is $\frac{2}{3}$, the chance probability of the high Mach being a member seven times in seven sessions is

$$\binom{7}{7,0} (\tfrac{2}{3})^7 (\tfrac{1}{3})^0 = .059.$$

The middle-Mach players, again as in the previous game, just about held their own, being included in five of the seven final coalitions and excluded twice

$$\binom{7}{5,2} (\tfrac{2}{3})^5 (\tfrac{1}{3})^2 = .307.$$

Again, it was the lowest Mach-scale scorer in the triad who lost more often than would have been expected by chance. Lows were included in the final coalition only twice and excluded five times

$$\binom{7}{2,5} (\tfrac{2}{3})^2 (\tfrac{1}{3})^5 = .038.$$

(The probability that a low would be included two or less times in seven trials is

$$[\binom{7}{2,5} (\tfrac{2}{3})^2 (\tfrac{1}{3})^5 = .0384] + [\binom{7}{1,6} (\tfrac{2}{3})^1 (\tfrac{1}{3})^6 = .0064]$$
$$+ [\binom{7}{0,7} (\tfrac{2}{3})^0 (\tfrac{1}{3})^7 = .0004] = .045.)$$

The pattern of coalition partnerships by Mach classification of the members was also far from random. Five of the seven final coalitions were between the two highest-Mach players in the triad; the other two were between the highest and

TABLE IX-2

Number of Subjects in each Mach Category Included in
the Final Coalition and Excluded from it
($n = 7$ Triads)

Mach category	Included	Excluded	$p =$
High	7	0	.059
Middle	5	2	.307
Low	2	5	.038

For this overall pattern, or any more extreme in the predicted direction,
$p = .016$.

lowest men in the group. Since the chance probability of each of the three possible partnerships, by Mach category of the partners, is $\frac{1}{3}$, this pattern of results is highly significant

$$\binom{7}{5,2,0} \; (\tfrac{1}{3})^5 (\tfrac{1}{3})^2 (\tfrac{1}{3})^0 \; = \; .010,$$

and the chance probability of obtaining this pattern, or any more extreme in the predicted direction is .016 (the sum of the probabilities for high−middle, high−low, and middle−low coalition frequencies of 5, 2, 0; 6, 1, 0; 6, 0, 1; and 7, 0, 0). Even if the two coalitions between the high- and low-Mach members are disregarded, the chance probability that as many as five of the seven partnerships would be between the two highest-Mach members of the triad is only .045.

Since the number of subjects in this study was small, we did an alternative analysis, dividing the subjects into only two Mach-scale groups, high and low. Subjects were assigned to their classification from the previous study, except that those who had been classified as middle scorers were now grouped either with the highs or lows, on the basis of the median total Mach score in the original middle group. On this basis, 9 of the 21 subjects were called highs and 12 lows. Five of the seven triads were composed of one high and two lows, the remaining two of two highs and one low. Since in each game two players had to win and one lose, a random distribution of winning and losing would place about two-thirds of each group in the winners' column. The actual distribution, presented in Table IX-3, is clearly not random. All nine of the high-Mach players were winners, and non losers, while of the 12 low-Mach players, only five were winners and seven were losers. Further, all five of these low-Mach winners were in triads composed of one high- and two low-Mach subjects. That is, they were in a triad in which one of the two low-Mach subjects *had* to win.

TABLE IX-3

Number of Winners and Losers, by Mach
Classification, in the Ten Dollar Game[a]

	Winners		Losers
High Mach	9		0
Low Mach	5	$\chi^2 = 5.36, p < .05$	7

Comparisons of the amount of money won by the players are presented in
Table IX-4. Five of the seven splits were even, each coalition member receiving
five dollars. In both of the uneven splits, the higher-Mach partner obtained the
larger share of the money. One of these was a $6-4$ split, the other an $8-2$ split.
The seven high scorers averaged \$5.57 each; the middle-Mach group averaged
\$3.14; and the seven lows averaged \$1.28. The mean of each group was
compared by t test with the theoretical mean winning of \$3.33. Results for the
highs and lows were significant. Again, as in the Con Game, highs won, and at
the expense of the lows rather than the middles.

TABLE IX-4

Mean Amount of Money Won in the Ten Dollar Game
by Mach classification ($n = 7$ subjects per classification)

Mach classification	Mean (\$)	Mean minus \$3.33 [a]	t	$p <$
High	5.57	2.24	5.21	.005
Middle	3.14	-.19	-.28	—
Low	1.29	-2.04	-2.45	.05

[a] The expected value of the game.

DISCUSSION

The pattern of winning when subjects were bargaining for a division of \$10
was the same as in the Con Game when they were bargaining for a division of
100 points. Highs won; middles drew; lows lost. Again, of course, the scores or

winnings of the three subjects within a triad are not completely independent. However, the extent to which scores are dependent in no way forces this particular distribution. Even given that high Machs win excessively, the loser in the triad, if losers were randomly distributed, should be a middle Mach-scale scorer as often as a low. Clearly, neither winning nor losing is randomly distributed. Winning, via bargaining, appears to be directly related to Machiavellianism, and losing, inversely related.

The money won by the three Mach groups in the Ten Dollar Game can be compared with the numbers of points won in the Con Game. These data are shown in Table IX-5. If the decimal points in the Ten Dollar Game scores are moved one place to the right, to equate total payoff in the two situations, the three sets of scores are strikingly similar. In both sets of scores from the Con Game, as well as those from the Ten Dollar Game, the difference in winning between the high- and middle-Mach groups is larger than the difference between the middle- and low-Mach groups.

TABLE IX-5

Dollars and Points Won in Bargaining Triads
by High-, Middle-, and Low-Mach Subjects

Mach classification	The Con Game (points) (22 Ss per group)		Ten Dollar Game ($) (7 groups)
	Unambiguous condition	Ambiguous condition	
High	41.83	52.80	5.57
Middle	31.68	30.53	3.14
Low	26.48	16.67	1.29

This can be seen in Table IX-6 in which the difference between the mean scores of adjacent Mach groups (high minus middle, and middle minus low) are shown for the two games. In the Con Game, analysis of the difference between scores of subjects in the same triad showed high Machs differing from middles by a greater margin than the one separating middles and lows. In the Ten Dollar Game, analysis of difference scores (in terms of dollars won) between the high and middle Mach in the same triad yielded a t of 2.43, significant at the .05 level; the t value for the distribution of differences between the middle and low Machs was 1.85, which just missed the .05 level.

TABLE IX-6

Differences between Mach Groups in Average Winning in the
Con Game and the Ten Dollar Game

Mach groups compared	The Con Game (22 Ss per group)		The Ten Dollar Game[a] (7 groups)
	Unambiguous condition	Ambiguous condition	
High–middle	10.15	22.27	24.30
Middle–low	5.20	13.86	18.30
Average difference	7.67	18.07	21.40

[a] For winning in the Ten Dollar Game, decimal points have been moved one place to the right to equate total payoff to the 100 points available in the Con Game.

The pattern of difference scores between Mach groups in Table IX-6 poses another interesting question. Why were the difference scores in the Ten Dollar Game as large as those in the ambiguous condition in the Con Game? In the unambiguous condition in the Con Game, the average difference between the Mach groups was 8 points. In the ambiguous condition, this average difference rose to 18 points. The increase in difference scores between Mach groups in the Con Game was attributed to the high Machs' taking advantage of ambiguity for bluffing or other psychological pressure tactics. When the payoff in the Ten Dollar Game was multiplied by 10 (to equate it with the Con Game for total payoff available), the average difference between the Mach groups was 21. This was at least as large as the average difference in the ambiguous condition of the Con Game, and much larger than the average difference in the unambiguous condition. Since all of the Ten Dollar Game subjects had participated in the Con Game, it was possible to compare the score of each one in the Ten Dollar Game (multiplied by 10) with his average score in the Con Game. The tendency of the high Machs to win more in the Ten Dollar Game than they did in the Con Game, compared to the opposite tendency of lows to win less, closely approached significance ($t = 1.53; p < .10$).

One possibility, of course, is that the subjects available to play the Ten Dollar Game differed more in Mach score than the original three Mach groups from which they were selected. The evidence is to the contrary. The mean combined Mach IV and V scores for the original high, middle, and low groups of subjects who played the Con Game were, respectively, 116, 102, and 87. The mean scores for the Ten Dollar Game groups were 112, 99, and 85. The Ten Dollar Game subjects were also representative of their Con Game groups in winning points. The mean Con Game score of the seven highs was 47.43, compared to 47.32 for all highs in the Con Game. The mean score of the seven lows was 21.29, compared to 21.58 for all lows in the Con Game.

A second possible explanation is an interaction between Machiavellianism and the effect of the previous experience in the Con Game. High Machs may have increased in manipulative skills more than lows as a consequence of the earlier practice. Since all Ten Dollar Game subjects had the previous experience, there were no data to test this possibility directly. However, there was no difference between scores in the first and second halves of the Con Game tournament for any of the three Mach groups.

The most obvious explanation for the large differences between Mach groups in winning in the Ten Dollar Game is that the psychological situation was again ambiguous. Again, subjects had no external criterion by which to decide which two of them should be included in the final coalition, and which one excluded. This was similar to the ambiguous condition of the Con Game, in which no external criterion for making these decisions was *publicly* available. However, a criterion did exist in the Con Game, and the subjects knew it did. In that situation the three players had hands of power cards which differed quite obviously in value (see Table VII-2). Coalitions were made most often between the middle- and low-power players, and the partner with the better hand often got more than half of the 100 points in the coalition bargain. What made the ambiguous games ambiguous was knowing that the three of them had hands differing in value, but *not* knowing which of the other two was the more desirable partner, or, once a partnership was formed, which of the two should get the larger share of the points.

The Ten Dollar Game situation was ambiguous in that there was no external criterion by which to decide on partnerships or dollar divisions, but it was unambiguous in that subjects knew there was none, and knew that all of them were on equal footing. In order to create a comparable situation with the Con Game paradigm, subjects would have to know beforehand that each of them had exactly the same hand.

There is another possible explanation for the large difference between Mach groups in winning in the Ten Dollar Game, as compared to the Con Game. Since money was involved in the Ten Dollar Game, it may have been perceived as a more serious situation. Theoretically, increasing the seriousness of a game should affect the behavior of low Machs more than highs. It was proposed in the previous chapter, as one of the reasons for high Machs winning in the Con Game, that they played by impersonal strategies adapted to the cognitive definition of the situation, while lows became personally involved with value implications. Increasing the seriousness of the situation by ten dollars would have little effect on the definition of the situation as a game, or a rational, impersonal approach to bargaining. It would have an effect on emotionalized value implications. Perhaps low Machs did poorly in the Ten Dollar Game because they were distracted by moral conflict. Worrying over the ethical dilemma posed by the more serious situation might make it difficult to make bargaining offers sound convincing, especially in competition with opponents unhampered by such qualms.

It is also possible that as the seriousness of the situation increases, low Machs become increasingly reluctant to try to manipulate others. One of the reversed Mach scale items reads, "One should take action only when sure it is morally right." As a situation becomes more serious, morality becomes more salient. High Machs disagree with the item; for them morality is not a relevant criterion for action. As morality becomes more salient for lows, they should become increasingly less willing to take advantage of others. There is some empirical support for this argument. In the Con Game, in which there were no consequences of the game outside of the game itself, high and low Machs did not differ in willingness to attempt to manipulate others as measured by number of manipulative attempts made. However, in the Machiavel study (Chapter V), in which subjects were given a legitimized, but optional, chance to manipulate a supposed fellow student in a purportedly genuine testing situation, low Machs did in fact make far fewer manipulative attempts than highs.

There are no data to distinguish between these two possibilities. By either explanation, high Machs would be little affected by an increase in seriousness. Lows would do less well in more serious situations either because they are less willing to try to manipulate, or because their attention to ethical concerns interfers with bargaining effectiveness, or both. In either case, the results of the three studies together support the formulation that the difference between high and low Machs in obtaining rewards via manipulation will increase as the seriousness of the situation increases.

The behavior of two of the seven low Machs in the Ten Dollar Game illustrates this interpretation. In one triad, as soon as the subjects finished reading the instructions, had been reminded that this was the only Ten Dollar Game they would play, and that the winners would indeed keep the money, the high Mach turned to the middle scorer and offered him $4. The middle immediately accepted. The low Mach then suggested that they wait a minute, consider the situation, talk it over, and see if they couldn't arrive at some fair way of dealing with it. The other two gave minimal responses. The low kept talking. He appeared to take the situation personally and seriously — "I don't like to fight over money." Over and over, he emphasized the need to find a fair way to handle the money situation. The high and middle remained unresponsive. Finally, the low suggested that the other two divide the money between them, and agree to take care of him in the next game. (The subjects knew that they would next play another, different game, but did not know whether it would involve money or not, what sort of game it was, or whether they would have any control over who won.) In effect, the low Mach talked himself into giving the other two the money. This is similar to the finding of Exline *et al.* in Chapter IV. Low Machs did more explaining than highs in response to the interrogation after cheating, and confessed more. The authors suggested that the lows literally talked themselves into confessing.

In another triad, the game ended with the high and low Mach dividing the money equally between them. After the session, as the subjects were leaving, the low Mach handed his winnings to the experimenter. The experimenter handed the money back, explaining that it was his to keep. The low protested that it was only an experiment, and that the money did not rightfully belong to him. The experimenter protested that it was not her money, that it came from a grant fund specifically allocated to provide the stake in the game. The low protested that he had agreed to participate in the experiment as a personal favor to the experimenter, and in the interests of advancing science, and he would not consider accepting pay for it. This bargaining contest with the experimenter was one of the few such encounters we've seen in which a low Mach clearly and forcefully won. He placed the money on the table, and simply walked out.

In this game the high Machs won by getting into the final coalition. All seven of the high Machs were members of the final coalition in their triad, but only two of them arranged a division of the $10 giving themselves more than half of the money. In the Con Game (Chapters VII and VIII) the coalition partners tended to divide the 100 points unequally between them. The partner in the higher-power position, as determined by the value of his hand of playing cards, usually took the larger portion of the prize. In the Ten Dollar Game there were no external cues, e.g., power cards, indicating that one player might deserve more than another. All were on equal footing. This power structure in the triad (all equal in power) was described by Caplow (1956) and tested by Vinacke and Arkoff (1957). Vinacke and Arkoff reported that when coalition partners had equal power weights they were more likely to divide the prize equally between them.

The behavior of the high Machs can be seen as another example of their tendency to test the limits of a situation without breaking them (see Chapter VIII). The data of Vinacke and Arkoff suggest that the social limit is a 50–50 split when players know they are all on equal footing. The limits-testing hypothesis proposed that high Machs test and find the limits, and then concentrate on doing what works. They may have concentrated on getting into the coalition rather than on trying to break the limits and get more money at the risk of being excluded. This interpretation is consistent with the Con Game data on differences in high Mach strategy between the unambiguous and ambiguous conditions. In the ambiguous condition, when power positions in the triad were public knowledge, high Machs, like the other subjects, made and accepted prize-division offers in accord with their power position. However, in the ambiguous condition, when power positions were hidden, high Machs, unlike the others, disregarded power positions completely. In general, high Machs seem to be opportunistic. Whatever the situation, they appear to concentrate on success in achieving the possible.

The high Machs' ability to get into the final coalition supports the hypothesis, proposed in the previous chapter, that high Machs initiate and control the structure of relationships in their group.

The bargaining data also support the structuring hypothesis. In this study an attempt was made to record some of the bargaining conversation content. For example, the first task-relevant statement made by any subject in each triad was systematically recorded. Six of the seven opening statements were made by the high Mach in the group. Five of these six were direct, dollar-split offers, unprefaced by preliminary agreement seeking or polite generalizations. The one high-Mach opening which was not a point-blank money offer was a good natured, but not joking "Ok, who wants to make the first offer." (It was a statement, not a question.) The low Mach in the group immediately responded by making the high an offer. In one of the seven triads the middle Mach beat the high to the verbal draw. His opening statement was, "How does it start?" This could be interpreted as a request for structure. The high Machs in the game, on the other hand, clearly did not look to others for structure. They provided it, without hesitation, and apparently unselfconsciously, typically by the direct and obvious technique of making an offer.

In another triad, immediately after the game (in which the high and middle Machs had divided the money equally between them), the high Mach was explaining the rational strategy (the $50-50$ prize division) to the low. He spoke in terms of "we," including his partner, the middle Mach, as an active participant in planning and executing the strategy (in effect, controlling the structure of rewards in the group). The middle Mach, perhaps truthfully, denied it. "I didn't have anything to do with it," he said. "You made the offer and I agreed."

In conclusion, the data from the Ten Dollar Game support the findings in the Con Game. However, since the same subjects were used in both studies, these new observations cannot be considered independent tests of the hypotheses. They can be considered a rough approximation of the test—retest reliability of bargaining tactics and outcomes in similar situations six months apart.

SUMMARY

Seven triads of subjects, selected by Mach score, played a three-man, bargaining-coalition game. The stake was $10, to be divided between any two of the three players in any way they chose. The high Machs won overwhelmingly.

No high failed to be a member of the winning coaliton. Lows lost. The highs were even more successful at outbargaining lows in this game, when the stake was a tangible and sizable reward, than they were in deciding on the division of the points in the previous study. It was proposed that the real stake made the situation more serious. This would not affect the behavior of high Machs, but it would put lows at a greater disadvantage in bargaining.

The bargaining observations collected in this study were also consistent with the tactics descriptions of the bargaining data from the previous study. Although these observations are not independent tests of the hypotheses, they do indicate that these subjects were consistent over the intervening six months in using the same kinds of tactics. Again, high Machs appeared to control the structure of interaction in the triad, and thereby the structure of the final distribution of money. Again, in contrast to low Machs, highs played impersonally and opportunistically.

CHAPTER X   **THE PENNY—DOLLAR CAPER**[1]

Richard Christie, Kenneth J. Gergen,
and David Marlowe

The past ten years have seen a rapid increase of interest in the application of game theory to experiments in social interaction. Since Machiavellians are hypothesized to be interpersonal game players, the two lines of inquiry almost inevitably had to merge. In two of the previously reported studies, the Con Game and the Ten Dollar Game, high Machs did in fact outbargain low and middle Machs for both points and dollars when placed in face to face situations in which they were members of triads.

One of the most popular games stemming from mathematical game theory has been the Prisoner's Dilemma or variations of it (Rapaport & Orwant, 1962). This two-person nonzero sum game, as it is called in the language of the game theorists, differs from the ones we had used earlier in that it deals with a dyadic relationship and, more important, is not necessarily face to face and does not allow negotiation.

The Prisoner's Dilemma is played by two persons who independently make one of two choices. Player A can choose either α_1 or α_2; Player B can choose either β_1 or β_2. There are four possible outcomes: $\alpha_1\beta_1$, $\alpha_1\beta_2$, $\alpha_2\beta_1$, and $\alpha_2\beta_2$. Values $(x_i x_j)$ can be attached to these outcomes to change the utility of various simultaneous choices.

The classic Prisoner's Dilemma game is defined by the following matrix and restrictions.

Player B

		β_1	β_2
	α_1	(x_1, x_1)	(x_2, x_3)
Player A	α_2	(x_3, x_2)	(x_4, x_4)

Restrictions:

1. $2x_1 > x_2 + x_3 > 2x_4$,
2. $x_3 > x_1$,
3. $x_3 > x_2$,
4. $x_4 > x_2$.

[1] The authors joined in an informal consortium, to use a popular current term, not to be fashionable but to divide costs. This study was supported by their respective grants from the National Science Foundation: NSF GS814, NSF 562, and NSF 1223,

In translating these symbols to the situation faced by subjects who are playing the game it is illustrative to use an actual payoff matrix. In this example (Marlowe, Gergen, & Doob, 1966), α_1 and α_2 (and β_1 and β_2) are referred to as black and red choices, respectively. The $x_{1...4}$ choices refer to the payoff values associated with them. The first number in the parentheses refers to the number of points which can be acquired by Player A, the second to those which can be acquired by Player B.

The matrix is:

		Player B	
		Black	Red
Player A	Black	(3,3)	(0,5)
	Red	(5,0)	(1,1)

In a typical experiment each player has a console in which a switch or buttons are mounted. He can choose either red or black. The other player has a similar option. After each makes an independent choice, they are informed as to the joint outcome. If both choose black, each receives 3 points (or the equivalent). If Player A chooses black and Player B chooses red, the first get no points and B receives 5 points. If Player A makes a red choice and B chooses black, the respective payoffs are 5 and zero. If both opt for red, both receive only 1 point. In this matrix, which meets the formal restrictions specified above, the red strategy is dominant. If Player A played red for 10 trials and B played randomly, A would win 30 points ($5 \times 5 + 5 \times 1$) and B only 5 ($5 \times 0 + 5 \times 1$). Since the matrix is symmetric, the opposite pattern of choices would result in opposite payoffs. However, if both players chose black on all 10 trials, each would win 30 points; if both chose red, each would receive 10 points. Red choices are commonly viewed as competitive since the person making the choice can win more points than the other player but can never win fewer. Black choices are commonly viewed as cooperative since mutual choices of black can maximize joint payoffs but never give one relative advantage over the other player in terms of points won.

There are a number of reasons why variations of this game are popular among experimental social psychologists, aside from the fact that it pits competitive and cooperative strategies against one another in a simplified form. It permits legions of variations. It can be run on a one-shot basis or iteratively and the *x*s (payoffs) can be varied to make the red or competitive strategy more or less tempting than the black or cooperative strategy. A further experimental attraction has to do with the independence of choices. Two subjects can be in visual interaction with one another but neither knows the other player's choice until after it has been made. Usually they are separated and have no clues as to the other player's behavior until after the simultaneous choices have been made. This opens the door to a variety of experimental deceptions which usually take the form of having subjects meet other subjects in the initial stages of experimentation and, after being separated, being given either true or false information about the other player's choice of red or black for each trial. In some instances experimenters have reported truthfully the responses of the other player. The more usual practice is to give the subject incorrect information about the other player's choices upon some experimentally devised rationale.

For example, in the experiment by Marlowe *et al.*, six subjects met one another and each was assigned to a separate booth. They were informed that they were playing the game with one of the other persons and that their mutual choices would be indicated to each of them after each trial. In fact, this was not done. Each subject was given a programmed series of alleged choices by the other player in which the other chose black on 80% of the trials and made a competitive or red choice on 20%. Despite the fact that the other player was, as could be inferred from the feedback, 80% cooperative, the subjects themselves made over 80% competitive or red choices. (This was in an experimental condition typical of most such situations in which the subjects met one another before the game-playing situation, were separated from them during the game, and had no expectation of meeting the other afterwards.)

It is a truism that it is difficult to uncover the effects of individual differences in situations in which everyone behaves similarly. Although it is difficult to disentangle main effects from particular treatments when there are small numbers of subjects in each cell, a series of experiments reported by Lowe (1966) illustrates the point. He found no significant differences in Mach scores as to proportion of red choices in a matrix in which the payoff values strongly favored cooperation (only about 20% of the choices were for red). With a different matrix in which almost half the choices (46%) were red, high Machs were significantly more competitive than low Machs.

In view of these findings the three authors decided to join forces in what promised to be an expensive but intriguing experimental study. In the first place, Lowe's tentative findings suggested that the possible relationship between Machiavellianism and exploitation in a Prisoner's Dilemma type of game would be worth following up. Second, it was of considerable interest to find what effects a substantial monetary incentive would have on the choice of red versus black by high versus low Machs. This latter point, aside from Machiavellianism, had implications relevant to the area of bargaining and decision making generally.

In a situation in which the choice of red and black strategies might be affected by individual differences in Machiavellianism and differences in the amount of payoff (money rather than points), it was deemed advisable to use a matrix in which neither Red nor Black were dominant. We therefore employed the following matrix which violated restriction 4 as given above since x_4 is not greater than x_2. It is, consequently, a variant rather than a true Prisoner's Dilemma game. The matrix employed was:

		Player B	
		Black	Red
Player A	Black	3, 3	1, 4
	Red	4, 1	0, 0

If the opponent plays randomly, a player wins 20 points over 10 trials whether he plays red or black. Neither strategy is dominant in terms of the player's own winnings.

In their review of the literature, Gallo and McClintock (1965) could find no studies in which substantial or significant monetary rewards had been employed. Evans (1964) had compared results in a Prisoner's Dilemma game in which using imaginary money versus points added to an examination grade as incentives led to no significant differences. A more recent study (Wrightsman, 1966) conducted about the same time the present study was carried out did use a substantial monetary incentive. It differed from the present one in several respects. First, the subjects were predominantly females. Second, in one condition each subject was told that after her first choice, her partner would be informed as to the choice she had made before making her own choice. After the subject was told of the partner's first choice, and the first trial had been completed, a second and final trial was run. In the second trial both the subject and partner chose without information concerning the other's choice. This procedure differs from the customary pattern of successive independent trials in which each subject finds out the other's choice at the end of the trial. Wrightsman's matrix also differed in that it violated the first restriction of the Prisoner's Dilemma game, that $2x_1$ ($2 \times \$3 = \$6$) be greater than x_2 plus x_3 ($0 + \$6 = \$6$). Under these conditions it was found that it made no difference whether subjects played for real or imaginary money although when using real money, it was possible to win as much as $12.00.

In essence, then, virtually all the generalizations made about bargaining and the extrapolations made from such studies to behavior in the domain of daily interaction have been based on results obtained under conditions in which the stakes were trivial. It was our intention, in the present study, to play a game of the standard experimental sort in which the payoffs were of real significance to the subjects.

Our decision as to what payoff would be significant to subjects was determined in part by our knowledge of undergraduate finances and by the limitations imposed by our combined budgets. We decided to run 10 trials in which the values in the matrix could represent either pennies or dollars. This meant that as far as the subject in the dollar condition knew, he could make as much as $4 a trial, and although he did not know how many trials there would be, he could presumably win as much as $40 in the space of a few minutes.

·Before embarking on this costly and somewhat venturesome excursion into financial largesse, it seemed prudent to engage in a certain amount of pilot work. First, we wanted to test the matrix on subjects who would be roughly similar to those who would be playing for cash to see if the proportion of red choices was in fact close to the desired 50% level. We also wanted to find out whether or not high-Mach subjects behaved more or less exploitatively under trivial payoffs on this matrix. Finally, we wanted to determine whether the various strategies used by the programmed partner made any difference.

In the pilot study, 120 subjects were run for 30 trials each on the above matrix in a 2 × 2 × 3 factorial design. Half the subjects were run at Harvard with the assistance of George Goethals, Jr. and half at the University of California at Berkeley with the assistance of Jonathan Cook. These schools were selected because of their convenience and because their student populations approximated in general sophistication the one at Columbia University where the study itself was to be conducted. There were three major variations: one was whether the subject was told he would meet his "partner" after the game or not; the second, of course, was high or low Machiavellianism; the third was the strategy played by the "other player" which was preprogrammed so that the "other" played 20, 50, or 80% black choices.

The overall findings were clear. In neither sample, combined or alone, did any of the major variables make a significant difference. The percentage of Red choices was 57 as contrasted with the 50% expected in terms of the matrix. High-Mach scorers did become more exploitative (red) over the 30 trials at the .05 level but the overall difference between high and low Machs was not significant.

THE PENNY – DOLLAR CAPER

At this point the stage was set for our major undertaking. Since it made no difference in the pilot study whether or not subjects were told they would meet their presumed partner, we decided to use the no-meet condition to eliminate the extra time taken in giving instructions and in the debriefing. The finding that the presumed other player's strategy made no difference meant that any one of the programs was equally effective or ineffective in influencing the behavior of the subjects and we decided for simplicity's sake to program all other players as 80% cooperative. If playing for money increased exploitive tendencies, it could be expected to become more apparent against a cooperative other.

We were now in the strange position of having designed an experimental situation for which we had no clear-cut hypotheses. We were committed to using a matrix in which there was no game playing advantage in being either exploitive or cooperative — assuming that the subject was playing a game against nature or a random other. But the "the other" was not a random other; he was another person who, unknown to the subject, was going to play a predetermined 80% cooperative strategy. We had decided to run 10 trials for points and then switch to playing 10 trials for pennies or dollars.

In this situation it was possible to advance two alternative hypotheses. In both the pilot study and Lowe's research high Machs became more competitive than lows as the game progressed. A simple extrapolation would suggest that the same would be true in the present experiment. But there was one crucial difference. In one condition both the subject and the other player would be playing for dollars not points or pennies. We assumed that playing for dollars *might* have a different meaning for subjects and that it *might* have a different interpretation for high and low Machs.

What is the rational strategy in such a situation? During the first ten trials the presumed other played a basically cooperative strategy. For some reason, he opted for the red choice twice in the 10 trials. Was this by chance, from boredom, or because he was playing a secret strategy? After a break in which he was asked to evaluate the play in the game thus far, the subject was told that he would continue playing with the same person. The only change was that the ante was now raised to a dollar a point. Would the subject reevaluate the situation and shift his own strategy so that he could win a substantial sum of money very quickly? And assuming that the subject would like to win as many dollars as possible, would he also assume that his unknown partner was similarly motivated and might change his strategy also?

Consider the situation faced by the subject. He could win the most money if the other played black and he played red consistently. He would then win $4 a trial and the other only $1. Assuming that dollars are not trivial, it is unlikely that any other player would be so magnanimous as to take so little while the subject piled up dollar bills. If, on the other hand, the other played a consistent red strategy, there would be little point in the subject's gratuitously allowing him to accumulate dollars by playing black and ending up with little himself. We are suggesting that the most rational strategy in this situation for one who is interested in making as much money as possible is to play black and by his sequence of choices to encourage the other to play black as well. In this way, they can both win $3 a trial rather than engage in a divisive and mutually profitless competition.

This line of reasoning would suggest that in this case high Machs would be more self-serving by being more cooperative, i.e., they would make more black choices under the dollar condition than would low Machs. This is, of course, in direct conflict with the evidence about the greater competitiveness of high Machs as reflected in increasing red choices over trials when the play is for points. It is also contrary to other research on their general exploitive characteristics, unless the object of exploitation is seen as including the situation as a whole (including the experimenter) rather than just the experimenter-defined "opponent."

Although we could argue for either of two possible outcomes, there simply was not enough previous research to permit a choice of two opposing predictions. Our curiosity exceeded our need for theoretical elegance so we proceeded.

METHOD

SUBJECTS

Students in all sections in introductory psychology and sociology courses at Columbia College and the School of General Studies at Columbia University in the fall of 1965 were asked to fill out a volunteer schedule sheet in class. In some classes students filled out an "opinion inventory" which included Mach IV and Mach V; in other classes, they took the scales home and returned them to their instructors. Over 300 scorable protocols from males were obtained. Since we, for reasons discussed shortly, wanted to run the experiment quickly, we did not select subjects randomly from this potential pool, but used two criteria: their Mach scores and their availability. Scores on both Mach IV and V were split at the median and those students who scored above on both scales were classified as highs (101 on Mach IV and 120 on Mach V); those who fell below the median on both scales were considered lows. (Students with mixed-Mach scores were not used.) The class schedules of those meeting these criteria were examined to see if any free hours were listed for the days on which the experiment was to be run. If not, they were automatically excluded. Everyone meeting these criteria was listed as to whether or not they had indicated a willingness to serve as subjects. Since we planned to run about 40 subjects, telephone calls were made the evening before the experiment until enough subjects had volunteered. They were asked to help us by participating in a study which they would find interesting and told that there would be a chance to make some money — at least $2 for an hour of their time. Actually of 43 reachable potential subjects, 41 agreed to come but one arrived too late and could not be included.[2] The final sample consisted of 21 high and 19 low Machs.

---

[2] We are indebted to Drs. Florence Geis, Dolores Kreisman, and Alice Singer for so capably persuading potential subjects to volunteer. Each had previously proved highly successful in recruiting students and graciously agreed to help us.

APPARATUS

Each subject was seated in one of ten booths. These were ranged along a wall so that no player could see the display box of the other subjects. On the table in each booth was a small box which had a switch which could be turned from its neutral position to either a red or black choice. A display panel was mounted above the switch which reproduced the matrix. After all subjects made their choices, the quadrant of the matrix which represented the joint payoff was lighted so that each could see how much he and the other player had won on that particular trial.

Each subject's choice was also recorded on a master panel in an adjoining room so that an experimenter could send the appropriate panel lighting back to each subject on his display panel.

PROCEDURE

It was deemed desirable to run the experiment as quickly as possible. Even on a campus as large as Columbia, there was the possibility that word that one could make as much as $40.00 in less than an hour would spread through informal conversation. Every effort was made to minimize the possible effects of such a happening by conducting the study as quickly as possible and admonishing the subjects to maintain secrecy. The sessions were run as follows: 9 A.M., first day, three highs and four lows for pennies; 11 A.M. five highs and four lows for dollars; 1 P.M., six highs and four lows for dollars; second day, 11 A.M., five highs and four lows for pennies; 1 P.M., two highs and three lows for dollars. Exigencies of scheduling during subject's available time were responsible for differing ns in each session. The spacing between sessions was planned to minimize informal contact between subjects leaving and arriving. As far as possible, subjects in the session were selected from different classes in order to minimize possible extralaboratory contact with each other. As far as could be determined, no subject knew the nature of the study or payoffs in advance.

When participants arrived, they remained in a waiting room until escorted into the experimental room. They were seated and told that they would be engaged in a study of decision making. They were also told that they would be playing with one of the other students whose panel was electrically connected with his through a central control board. If an odd number of subjects were being run, a young male of the appropriate age was included to prevent any suspicion connected with having an odd man. The instructions specifically did not contain words referring to competition, opponent, or any other possible exploitive inducing set.

The nature of the choices was explained and subjects were given a few practice trials to familiarize themselves with the details of the payoff matrix. After questions were answered, the game was started. Each player was required to have his switch on neutral at the start of each trial. He then made a choice of red or black. When all had made their choices, the experimenter in the control room lit their panels so they could see the results for each trials. Subjects were instructed to write down their own and the other player's payoff at these points and return their switches to the neutral position in preparation for the next trial.

At the end of the first ten trials this procedure was interrupted. Each subject was asked to fill out a sheet requesting information about the strategy he was using and about the other's style of playing. After these forms were filled out and collected, the experimenter announced that, "to make things more interesting" further games would be played for a penny (or dollar) a point and that there would be an immediate payoff after every trial. It was made clear that the money was theirs to keep. No mention was made of how many trials would be played but each participant's score sheet had spaces for recording the scores of 20 additional trials.

At the end of each trial, the experimenters went down the row of players giving each the appropriate number of pennies or dollars. As soon as this process was completed and all subjects had recorded their scores and returned switches to neutral, the next trial began. At the end of the second series of 10 trials, the game was terminated and all subjects filled out a postquestionnaire of the game. Players in the penny condition were given $2 in addition to their winnings.

The preprogrammed other player responded with black on every trial except the fourth and seventh trials in the initial 10 trial games for points. He also gave red choices on the third and eighth trials when playing for money. This procedure was, of course, uniform for all subjects.

RESULTS

The first independent variable — level of Machiavellianism — was taken care of by the preclassification of subjects, who were fairly evenly distributed among the various experimental sections. The other variable in which we were interested, the effects of a significant amount of money, was handled by immediate payoff in cash. Players in the dollar condition actually won from 26 to $33 for a few minutes of game-playing time. We have two reasons for supposing that this was a significant sum to them. They were asked the following question, "Over and above your basic living expenses (tuition, room, board, books) how much money do you have to spend each month?" The answers varied from zero to $175, with a median of $37. The second was the alacrity with which most participants accepted the money. Some put their dollars into their billfolds on every trial after counting them; others stacked them neatly in bundles but a few more casual ones did let them pile in disorder on the table beside the recording sheet. It should also be noted that one subject, despite all our previous assurances, still asked if he could keep his winnings at the end of the session. In general, however, as far as we could tell, the amount of money in the dollar condition did represent a welcome and meaningful incentive. One young man was so carried away — it was impossible to determine whether this was from interest in the experiment or the amount of loose cash changing hands — that he wanted to know what undergraduate courses he should take to prepare himself for graduate work so he, too, could become a social psychologist.

Despite all the enthusiasm for money, the shift from points to money did not make any difference overall. On the first block of 10 trials for points the percentage of red choices was 54.7, on the second 10 trials for money it was 54.8%. These obviously do not differ from one another and they are very close to the 57% obtained in the pilot study. The major results are presented graphically in Fig. X-1: It can be seen that the strategies used by high and low Machs did not differ in the first 10 trials for points and that the introduction of money on trials 11–20 did not significantly affect the behavior of low Machs. However, when monetary stakes were introduced, high Machs switched to a less-exploitive strategy. The overall analysis of variance is presented in Table X-1. In this analysis, a difference score was used for each subject so that the comparison is between the number of red choices made on the first block of trials minus the number of red choices in the second block of trials. There was no main effect difference for pennies or dollars. There was, however, a main effect for Machiavellianism, the shift depicted in Fig. X-1 being significant at the 0.25 level.

Although the overall pattern of differential shifting in strategies is clear, it is somewhat obscured by the fact that on the trials following the other's red moves a number of subjects signaled or retaliated by switching from black to red. Note the peaks on trials 14 and 19. The shift from the preceding trials is most marked for the high Machs but they were playing fewer reds previously so that there was a greater opportunity to shift. Actually, on the first trial for money the high Machs

TABLE X-1

Analysis of Variance of Change Scores from
Game I to Game II

Source	SS	df	MS	F
Mach (A)	39.83	1	39.83	6.27 [a]
Money (B)	.5981	1	.5981	—
A × B	1.61	1	1.61	—
Error	228.52	36	6.35	—

[a] Significant at the .025 level.

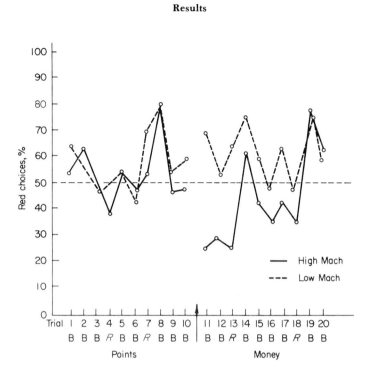

FIG. X-1. Trial-by-trial comparisons of high and low Machs' exploitative choices (red).

points for Fig. X-1.

Trial	High	Low	Trial	High	Low
1	.524	.632	11	.238	.684
2	.619	.526	12	.286	.526
3	.524	.474	13	.238	.632
4	.381	.474	14	.619	.737
5	.524	.526	15	.429	.579
6	.476	.421	16	.333	.474
7	.524	.684	17	.429	.632
8	.810	.789	18	.333	.474
9	.476	.526	19	.762	.789
10	.476	.579	20	.619	.579

played significantly less red (at the .05 level by chi square) than the lows and the difference on trials 11−13 is also significant. If we had known this in advance, we could have saved a considerable amount of money by eliminating the last seven trials.

There is one finding which is not revealed in Fig. X-1. For the sake of graphical clarity, we did not plot highs and lows separately under penny and dollar conditions. During the first 10 trials for points there was no difference between highs and lows, nor was there any significant difference for the lows between the point, penny, or dollar conditions. High Machs, however, performed more like low Machs for pennies, but changed their strategy in the dollar condition. It was primarily the high Machs playing for dollars who were responsible for the overall Mach difference. High Machs playing for pennies tended ($p < .10$ by t test) to be less exploitive than their low-Mach counterparts but high-Mach dollar players were much less exploitive than low-Mach dollar players ($p < .01$).

DISCUSSION

In this study we were neither damned by having a wrong hypothesis which was disconfirmed nor blessed by knowing what would happen. The data indicate that — in this particular experimental situation with a unique sample from which no generalizations can be legitimately made — the introduction of high stakes in the game did not have an overall effect. This supports the findings of Evans (1964) and also of Wrightsman (1966). However, more germane to the understanding of Machiavellianism is the finding that high Machs behaved less competitively when the stakes were changed from points to pennies and even less so when the ante was raised to dollars. It evidently does make a difference who is playing the game and what the stakes are.

Again, these effects may be specific to the particular matrix used and the value of the payoff. The results certainly do not lend credence to the notion that high Machs are more exploitive, whatever the objective situation. They tend to support the second of the two alternatives suggested, i.e., high Machs are more rational game players. We incline to this interpretation.

If out interpretation is correct, it is testable by using a matrix in which the exploitive strategy is dominant and by providing a substantial payoff. High Machs should be more exploitive than lows when it is rational to be so. As noted, there is a trend for high Machs to be more prone to exploitation in a true Prisoner's Dilemma game where the red strategy is dominant and the payoff is in points or pennies. We would predict that this tendency for highs to be more exploitive than lows would be increased if dollars or substantial payoffs were introduced.

Even when the matrix fosters dominance of one strategy over another as in the original Prisoner's Dilemma game, game theorists have problems over the rational strategy in repeated games. For example, Luce and Raiffa (1957, p. 101) whose classis treatise is primarily responsible for behavioral scientists' interest in game theory observed,

If the Prisoner's Dilemma game is played but once, we feel that it is "reasonable" to single out $(\alpha_2\beta_2)$ as the "solution" to the game provided there is no preplay communication . . . In contrast, we do not think it "reasonable" to single out (α_2,β_2) as the "solution" when the game is iterated n times. . . It is not "reasonable" in the sense that we would predict that most intelligent people would not play accordingly.

We would go a step beyond Luce and Raiffa and reiterate the previous argument that when the matrix does not make one strategy dominant it is even less "reasonable" to assume that one is playing against nature or a fool, rather than against a reasonable opponent. None of our previous evidence indicates that high and low Machs differ in terms of IQ but high Machs do report playing and enjoying games more than low Machs. What is important for our argument is that they not only enjoy playing games with others, but that they apparently make assumptions about the unknown fellow students who have become others in this particular situation. Their switch to a cooperative strategy once the payoff is changed implies that they assume that the other player is equally aware of the mutually unsatisfactory nature of the red strategy.

Some support for this point of view comes from written replies by high Machs to questions after the game was over. "At the start, we both realized, I think, that pushing the black button would be the most profitable for both of us. . .it is better to insure the $3 each trial rather than to stab each other in the back for an extra dollar. Unfortunately, he twice tried to make that dollar but realized the chaos that would be caused and returned to all black." Another said, "At one point he tried to gain by playing red (I did, too) but both of us realized less fortune. Then we worked together."

The trial by trial results in Fig. X-1 also tend to support this explanation. The high Machs' basic black strategy switched to red on the trials after the preprogrammed Other defected and played red instead of black (see trials 14 and 19). Red on these choices apparently was a retaliative attempt to steer the partner back to a black strategy. It must be remembered that if the high Mach could get his partner to play black, he would be in a better position to exploit him on the final trials by suddenly playing red. One high Mach said as much, "I used this (black strategy) to start out to provide money for both of us without 'quarrel' and at the end to make a minor 'killing.' " (Such a strategy would, of course, depend on guessing which trials would be last.)

Another factor involved is that high Machs are generally more suspicious of others (see Chapter III) and that they tend to ascribe higher Mach scores to others (Chapter XII). This would lead us to expect that the high Machs would have views of the other which emphasize the potential manipulativeness of his partner to a greater extent than low Machs. Realizing the capacity of the other to exploit, and feeling that the other would be likely to exploit, the high Mach may have been more attuned to the necessity of keeping his partner cooperative for their mutual benefit. Ratings of the other obtained both before and after the money trials supported this line of reasoning. After the game was over, the highs rated the partner as significantly less "trustworthy" than did the lows ($p <$ .025). In the dollar condition the highs were also more likely to see the partner as "greedy" ($p <$ .05) and as more "ambitious" ($p <$ .05). This view of the other differed among highs and lows, even though they were playing an identically programmed other who was generally cooperative but who defected twice in each series.

In effect, given the high Mach's picture of the other player as untrustworthy, greedy, and ambitious, it would not have been rational to engage him in a contest to see who could outexploit the other since then the subject would walk away with very little or no money when cooperation would have meant a fast and certain mutual killing.

The results are reminiscent of the earlier bargaining study carried out by Marlowe *et. al.* (1966). In that study, the perceived personality of the partner was systematically varied. Half the subjects played a partner described as domineering and egoistical, while the remainder were led to believe that he was self-effacing and humble. Under conditions similar to those in the present experiment, in which no further interaction was anticipated with the partner, the humble partner was exploited more than the egoist. In the present study we did not experimentally manipulate the perceived personality of the other but selected groups on the basis of Mach scores, knowing that they had different views of others. The high Machs played as though the other was an egoist, the low Machs as if he were meek and full of humility.

One interesting sideline of the present study has to do with the actual amount of money won under the dollar condition. Because of the values in the matrix and the nature of the program, a subject who played red consistently would win $32 (8 RB at $4 plus 2 RR at $0). A subject who played black consistently would win $26 (8 BB at $3 plus 2 BR at $1). The high Machs' preference for the black strategy (except on the trials after the other defected) led them to mean winnings of $29.01 as against the lows' winnings of $30.63. What is even more striking is that the (hypothetical) other was clobbered by low Machs, winning an average of only $15.55 while the high Machs' others won $23.23. Comparing the difference in earnings between low Machs and their others and high Machs and their others indicates that the high Mach's others won significantly more (hypothetically, to be sure) than the low Machs' others ($p <$ .05, Mann–Whitney, two tailed).

The "spiking" or retaliatory behavior displayed after the other player's defections on trials 13 and 18 is consistent with results found in two other games. Lake (1967) used the Hornstein and Deutsch products game (1967) and found that high Machs responded to aggressive behavior with counteraggression to a greater extent than lows.

Wahlin (1967) had high- and low-Mach subjects assigned to either rows or columns in an asymmetric matrix:

| | | Player B | |
		Black	Red
Player A	Black	15, 25	0, 15
	Red	25, 5	−25, 10

Player B could not lose if he played competitively and stayed with the red choice and would always make more points than Player A. If he played cooperatively, he could not lose in absolute number of points, but he could lose relative to Player A if the latter played competively. In this situation the programmed Player A made two initial black moves and then switched to a red move, back to black, etc., so that in 24 trials there was a total of nine red and 15 black choices. High and low Machs did not differ significantly in the number of points won (there were no money stakes) under this condition in which it was possible to ream Player A by always choosing red. In fact, high Machs were slightly less likely to play Red than low Machs.

The more interesting condition was that of subjects randomly assigned to be Player A. They were at the mercy of Player B. If the latter played competitively, then they could not possibly win, absolutely or relatively. Wahlin devised a diabolic contingency program for the other. On the first trial B was programmed to make a red choice. If the row-playing subject, A, made a black choice, the programmed other made a black choice on the second trial and remained on black until the subject made a red choice. At this point the program went into a red sequence for from one to three trials. If Player A made a black choice on the last of the program's red sequence, the other player would return to black and remain theire until A made another red choice which would trigger off a new sequence of red choices on the part of the programmed Player B.

This program was designed to lead row Player A to believe his unseen partner was vindictive and was punishing A for daring to play Red. The partner was willing to lower his own gain for the sake of thwarting the subject. The other player could also be viewed as trying to manipulate A by trying to guide him back to black choices so that B could maximize his own absolute gain.

Eighteen low-Mach row-playing subjects did not fight the programmed other (Player B) and *won* a mean of 188.9 points in the 24 trials. The 20 high Machs in this situation fought back and *lost* a mean of 38.8 points. This difference is significant at better than the .01 level. As will be noted in a review of 50 experimental situations in Chapter XV, this is the *only* experiment in which high Machs did not do as well as, if not significantly better than, low Machs. In this situation they were responding to an aggressive game-playing strategy by counteraggression but unknown to them, the other player was programmed to take advantage of the asymmetric payoff matrix so that counteraggression was a losing strategy.

These two games differed from the present one in that Lake's subjects played for pennies and Wahlin's for points. Whether the same behavior would have occurred for high Machs under dollar conditions is a moot point.

The present results of the high-Mach decrease in red choices from the first to the second block of trials differs from all known studies in which such an analysis has been made. Scodel, Minas, Ratoosh, and Lipetz (1959) and Minas, Scodel, Marlowe, and Rawson (1960) explored the parameters of red and black choices in a variety of matrices and noted that in all cases (except one in which a discussion of strategies was allowed) there was an increase in the choice of red during the second block of trials (in nine cases this was significant at the .05 level or better; in three, only a trend was noticed). This was also found in our original pilot study. These studies and the present one had in common the fact that the matrix remained the same throughout but differed in that there was no interruption at the midpoint to introduce a change in the value of the payoff.

It is of interest, therefore, to note that the low Machs in the present study showed a shift similar to that of subjects in other studies. They increased he proportion of red choices over time (although not significantly) and were seemingly not affected by the change in reward to pennies or dollars. Lake (1967, p. 127) found a similar lack of responsiveness by lows in his study, noting in conclusion, "There was also a tendency for high Machs to respond more quickly, and to respond more in kind, to changes in the Other's bargaining."

We conclude wiser but poorer. Unlike the earlier studies where there was face to face interaction and negotiation, high Machs do not have the same advantage in outmaneuvering the other player in the present game. They did play differently than low Machs, however. They showed more counteraggression in this and other non-face-to-face bargaining studies and are more responsive to changes in procedure. What is most striking, however, is that in this particular matrix, they shift behavior significantly as compared to lows when money is introduced as a reward. We have argued that, given the particular circumstances, they have adopted a rational strategy, even though it was cooperative rather than exploitive.

SUMMARY

A two-person, nonzero sum game, similar to the Prisoner's Dilemma but differing in that there was no dominant strategy, was devised. It was pretested with another player programmed for 80, 50, and 20% cooperative strategies. The exploitive (red) strategy was slightly favored (57% of the choices) across all programs whether or not the player expected to meet the other player after the game. There was no main effect for Machiavellianism although Ss classified as high Mach did become significantly more exploitive over trials.

The experiment proper used the 80% cooperative program under no-meet conditions. Ten games were played for points. The payoff was then changed to either pennies or dollars a point. Although the introduction of money had no overall effect upon cooperative or exploitive choices, it did significantly affect the choice behavior of high and low Machs. High Machs became significantly more cooperative. It is argued that in this particular experiment, cooperative behavior was more rational.

CHAPTER XI

PLAYING LEGISLATURE: COOL HEADS AND HOT ISSUES [1]

Florence Geis, Sidney Weinheimer,
and David Berger

A puzzling conclusion from the analyses of tactics used by high and low Machs in the Con Game and Ten Dollar Game (Chapters VIII and IX) was that high Machs' tactics worked, but low Machs failed when trying the same techniques. This led to a search for more general principles which could account for the difference in outcome. This study was designed to pursue one interpretation of the depersonalization hypothesis, proposed in Chapter VIII. In the previous bargaining games all players had been instructed to maximize their winnings. The high Machs appeared to concentrate on this goal. The low Machs, given the same objective situation, appeared to become involved with personal values, such as "being fair." It was proposed that these emotional concerns distracted them from a single-minded pursuit of winning.

If high and low Machs do differ in a tendency to become affectively involved, their differences in winning in competitive bargaining situations could be related to studies of emotional arousal. In general, arousal has been found to facilitate performance of previously well-learned routines (Zajonc, 1965). On the other hand, arousal usually inhibits learning on cognitive tasks involving analysis of complex stimuli. The kind of activity required for winning in a bargaining contest clearly fits the learning– analyzing pattern better than the performance pattern.

The previous studies provided some evidence relevant to this hypothesis. One of the strongest impressions that emerged from watching high- and low-Mach subjects in the Con Game and Ten Dollar Game was that high Machs were task involved in the problem of winning, not personally ego involved in the situation, or with the other players. They appeared to be guided by cognitions — the definition of the situation as a game, the game rules, and general strategy considerations. Lows, on the other hand, appeared to take the situation more personally. They appeared to invest themselves emotionally in the demands they made, the offers they accepted, and the coalition relationships they formed. The evidence for these impressions was discussed in Chapter VIII.

---

[1] Parts of this research were reported (Geis, Weinheimer, & Berger, 1966) at the annual meeting of the American Psychological Association, New York, September 3, 1966.

Although the previous bargaining data were consistent with a distraction hypothesis, they provided no direct measure of differential effects of distraction on the behavior of high and low Machs. The present study was designed to vary conditions leading to personal involvement, and measure their effect on success in bargaining. James Coleman's (1965, personal communication) Legislature game was adapted to test bargaining effectiveness. In this game subjects play the role of congressmen whose goal is to get reelected by their respective constituencies. The only way a congressman can get reelected is to have congress pass bills that his constituency favors and defeat those that his constituency opposes. The wishes of each player's constituency were predetermined and assigned by the experimenter. "Congress" consisted of all players present, so the bargaining process consisted of each player's trying to get the others in the group to vote his way on the bills crucial for his success, usually in return for a promise to support them on their bills.

In the Con Game and Ten Dollar Game two sources of affective involvement seemed to distract the low Machs. One was a concern for fairness and justice in deciding on the terms of the bargain. The other seemed to be a concern with others as persons as compared to the high Machs' impersonal strategy-oriented approach to others.

To test the generality of the affective distraction hypothesis, a different kind of personal value was used in this study — commitment to social ideals and principles outside of the immediate interpersonal bargaining context. At the same time, an attempt was made to eliminate the previously noted sources of distraction for low Machs. All subjects had equal power and resources at all times, and the game structure was designed to make fair, equitable agreements easy to find and make. Further, the bargaining in this study did not involve a direct, competitive dividing of the prize, but rather a trading of mutual support. Finally, a seven-man group was used. This reduced the likelihood of personal commitment to a single partner. Since multiple partnership opportunities were provided, players could restrict themselves to fair, mutually advantageous exchanges and still pursue their own self-interest effectively.

The possibility of being distracted by value implications was varied by changing the content of the bills in the game. Each group of subjects played three games of Legislature. In one, all of the bills for all subjects involved real or potentially real and important issues. For example, one was to abolish the Peace Corps; another was to institute immediate universal military conscription; another was to abolish all civil rights legislation. If, as we suspected, non-Machiavellians cannot, or do not, detach themselves from value implications, emotional involvement with the content of such issues might well distract them from single-minded pursuit of voting support. On the other hand, if high Machs can detach themselves from personal commitments, or can disregard them for strategic purposes, the issue content should not affect them.

To check whether or not it was the emotionally involving issue content that would be responsible for the anticipated difference in bargaining success, a control condition was used. In another of the three games, all the issues were utterly prosaic. Some examples are issuing a new postage stamp, moving the Bureau of Documents to a new location, changing fiscal deadlines, etc. Such issues were unlikely to evoke strong emotional responses in any of the subjects. Since the structure of the game minimized emotional conflict and provided multiple opportunities for fair and mutually advantageous bargains, no difference in success between high and low Machs was expected in the control games.

For half of the groups the issues with high emotional content were used in the first game, and the trivial issues in the second. For the other half this order was reversed. For the third game in all groups subjects were allowed to choose their own issues. The third game was included to investigate the effect of interaction over time on success in bargaining.

PROCEDURE

SELECTION OF THE EMOTIONAL ISSUES

Seven emotionally involving issues were needed. To minimize any differential advantage between high and low Machs due to the subject's own position on the issues he was assigned in the game, we decided to use issues on which there would be nearly unanimous agreement in the entire subject population. The second criterion was that the issue content should be important to the subjects so they would be strongly committed in their own positions. Ten issues were selected for pretesting: (1) the Peace Corps; (2) civil rights; (3) military draft requirements; (4) financial support of the United Nations; (5) unilateral disarmament; (6) social welfare services; (7) socialized medicine; (8) the minimum voting age; (9) the minimum driving age; (10) the minimum drinking age.

Two statements representing opposite positions on each issue were prepared: e.g., "We should abolish the Peace Corps" and "We should expand the Peace Corps"; "We should lower the minimum voting age to 18" and "We should raise the minimum voting age to 25." Two forms of the pretest were prepared, each containing one of the two position statements for each issue. Respondents indicated whether they agreed or disagreed with each statement, and how involved or strongly committed they felt about their answer. Questionnaires were distributed to 121 undergraduate males, roughly comparable in age and diversity of college major to the later, different sample of experimental subjects.

Fifty-six responses were obtained on one form, and 65 on the other. For each of the 20 items an index of unanimity was computed by dividing the number of respondents who gave the more popular response (agree or disagree) by the total number answering the form. Items were selected by unanimity of opinion. Ties were resolved in favor of the item eliciting stronger involvement.

The seven most unanimous positions were all "disagree," with unanimity varying from 96% (opposition to raising the minimum drinking age) to 83% (opposition to raising the minimum voting age). It is clear that this sample agreed more in opposing restrictive changes than in approving their opposites. Most important, it seemed safe to conclude that most of the subjects assigned the "anti" position on these issues would have to argue in favor of their own beliefs in the game, and those assigned the "pro" position would have to argue against their own beliefs.

SELECTION OF EXPERIMENTAL SUBJECTS

Male subjects were recruited from the introductory psychology course (required of all undergraduates in the Colleges of Arts and Sciences, Commerce, and Education) at New York University. Experimental participation fulfilled a course requirement. At the beginning of the 1965 spring semester 60 subjects were given Mach IV and V. The mean score on Mach IV was 101.25, the standard deviation was 17.65, and the split-half reliability was .88. For Mach V these figures were, respectively, 105.93, 13.31, and .64. Since the correlation between scores on the two forms was relatively high (.87), the two scores for each subject were averaged and the distribution of these total scores was divided into sextiles, as shown in Table XI-1.

TABLE XI-1

Mean Combined Mach Score Sextiles for 60 New York University
Male Students in Introductory Psychology

Sextile	Mean total Mach scores
6	120–140
5	110–119
4	104–109
	Median
3	96–103
2	86– 95
1	77– 85

Seven subjects, representing as nearly as possible the range of scores in the population tested, were scheduled for each experimental session. Eight sessions were run. Twice, a subject failed to show up and was replaced by a stooge who played passively. In all, 25 high Machs (sextiles 4, 5, and 6) participated, and 29 lows (sextiles 1, 2, and 3).[2] All sessions were conducted by a male experimenter who did not know the Mach classification of any subject in the group.

THE EXPERIMENTAL SESSION

When subjects arrived, they were seated in an informal circle with the experimenter, in one corner of a large room. Each was assigned an identification tag (a number from 1 to 7 to be worn throughout the session) and given a questionnaire containing the opinion issues to be used in the emotional issues game. Since we anticipated that most subjects would disagree with most of the position statements, three filler items were interspersed to inhibit response set. After the questionnaire, the following tape recorded instructions were played to the group.

> This is a study of the psychological aspects of the legislative process. We are interested in studying some of the psychological factors that determine how and why some bills pass and others do not. Specifically we are interested in studying (1) how a congressman responds to his constituency and (2) in particular, the bargaining and log-rolling process that occurs among the congressmen themselves. Your behavior will be evaluated by how successful you are as a congressman. You will be asked to play a game called Legislature which is designed to simulate the actual legislative process. Each of you will play the part of a congressman. We have had to simplify the legislative process in order to study it in a laboratory setting. Nevertheless, we think that you will learn something about the problems involved. *We* are trying to learn something about legislative voting. It is important to follow carefully all instructions given you. As you know, procedural rules are important in debate in actual legislatures. Here are the rules of the game.
>
> Image that you are a newly elected congressman. Your goal in the game is to keep getting yourself reelected by the largest plurality you can obtain. Each of you wants to be your party's candidate for president. According to the rules of this game, the congressman who manages to win the most votes from his constituency will be his party's presidential candidate. The people back home, your constituents, will decide whether or not to vote for you depending on whether or not you succeed in getting certain issues passed or defeated in congress.
>
> To begin the game, each of you will be given five cards which will state your constituency's position on five issues. Each card will also tell you the net number of votes you will get from your constituency if you succeed in getting congress to act on the issue in accord with their wishes. That is, you can interpret the number of votes listed on the card as the difference between the number of voters who hold the position stated and the number opposed. You will note that sometimes your constituents want bills passed and sometimes they want bills defeated. If you succeed in getting congress to adopt the position stated on your card — that is, if you get the bills passed that they want passed and defeat the bills they want defeated — you will automatically receive the number of votes listed on the card from your constituency.

---

[2] This is the only laboratory study we know of in which more low than high Machs showed up for experimental appointments. This is also the only study for which high- and low-Mach subjects were telephoned separately for experimental appointments by two different callers. Since we believed on the basis of previous experience that low Machs would be more difficult to schedule, and more likely to fail to keep appointments, they were contacted by the more experienced caller.

After you have received the cards reporting your constituency's wishes, each of you, if you wish, will have a chance to make a 30-sec statement addressed to your fellow congressmen. You may use this opportunity to make whatever remarks seem to you to be most likely to help win votes from your fellow congressmen, or you may decide to make no statement at all. When these opening remarks have been completed, congress will adjourn for 10 min. This is your opportunity to make contacts with your fellow legislators and to bargain with them for votes. During this open cloakroom bargaining period, you will be free to circulate around the room engaging in whatever activities seem most advantageous to you.

After the bargaining period, congress will reconvene. Then you will all vote on the issues as they are brought up. The experimenter will call on one congressman at a time. That congressman will name an issue that has not yet been voted on. Then if he wants, he will have 15 sec to urge congress to vote as he wishes. In addition, one speaker for the opposite point of view will be recognized and will also have 15 sec to argue for his point of view. Then, all of you will vote on the issue. Voting will be by show of hands. Unlike real legislators, however, everyone must vote on every issue.

In all, we will hold three complete legislative sessions. Your performance in the game will be evaluated by the number of votes you get from your constituency. *Remember, your goal in the game is to get as many votes from your constituency as possible* — in each session and over all three sessions. At the end of the third session, your total votes will be added up. The congressman with the greatest number of votes wins the presidential nomination. If you have any questions, be sure to ask them now. Once the game has begun, no questions will be permitted.

After the subjects' questions were answered, each was given his constituency's wishes for the first game. Each player's constituency had a position on five issues. Two of these had high value to the subject — 50,000 constituency votes for each if congress voted according to the constituency's wishes. For one of these high-value issues, the constituency favored a bill before congress; on the other, it opposed a bill. Two other issues had low value to the congressmen — 30,000 constituency votes each. Again, one would pay off if congress passed the bill, the other if congress defeated the bill. The fifth issue given each subject was a pork barrel item of still lower value — 20,000 votes, which his constituents wanted passed. Thus, for each game, each subject had an interest in five bills: two of high value to him if congress passed one and defeated the other; two of low value to him, again one if passed and the other if defeated; and a final pork barrel issue he wanted passed. Each issue was typed on a 3 × 5 card which also stated whether the constituency wanted the bill passed or defeated, and the net number of constituency votes the subject would win if congress acted accordingly.

Subjects were given no information about the distribution of issue interests in the group. In fact, except for the pork barrel issues, there were four players in the group assigned a payoff position on each of the issues. For one player, the issue had high value if congress passed the bill; for another it had high value if congress defeated the bill. Two other players held the low-value positions, one in favor, and the other opposed. The remaining three players had no payoff position on the issue. For the purpose of the game, they were uncommitted. Thus, effective bargaining consisted of a subject's finding those who were uncommitted, and getting their support for his position before his opponents got to them.

The specific issues assigned a subject were determined by his identification number. Seven different constituencies were preestablished, and numbered from 1 to 7. A constituency was defined, for the purpose of the game, by a set of issue positions. The seven "constituencies" in the emotional issues game are shown in Table XI-2. Each subject was assigned the issues and payoff positions corresponding to his identification number. For example, subject number one won 50,000 points ("constituency votes") if congress voted to revoke civil rights, another 50,000 if congress defeated the unilateral disarmament bill, another 30,000 if congress passed the bill abolishing minimum age requirements for driver's licenses, and another 30,000 if congress defeated the bill to abolish the Peace Corps. In addition, he won another 20,000 pork barrel votes for getting aid to commuter railroads.

TABLE XI-2

Assignment of Issues and Payoff Positions in the Emotional Issues Game[a]

Bills before Congress	Issues and payoff positions[b] of each constituency						
	1	2	3	4	5	6	7
Revoke previous civil rights legislation, and pass no more of it.	Hi+	—	—	—	Lo-	Lo+	Hi-
The U.S. will disarm unilaterally, even if other nations do not disarm.	Hi-	Hi+	—	—	—	Lo-	Lo+
Abolish the minimum age requirement for driver's license.	Lo+	Hi-	Hi+	—	—	—	Lo-
Abolish the Peace Corps	Lo-	Lo+	Hi-	Hi+	—	—	—
Raise the minimum drinking age to 25 years of age.	—	Lo-	Lo+	Hi-	Hi+	—	—
Establish universal, compulsory military conscription.	—	—	Lo-	Lo+	Hi-	Hi+	—
Raise the minimum voting age to 25 years of age.	—	—	—	Lo-	Lo+	Hi-	Hi+
Seven different pork barrel issues	P_1	P_2	P_3	P_4	P_5	P_6	P_7

a Each subject was assigned one of the seven constituencies described.

b "Hi+" indicates that the player would win 50,000 constituency votes if congress passed the bill, zero if the bill failed to pass. "Hi-" indicates that the player would win 50,000 constituency votes if congress defeated the bill, zero if the bill were passed. "Lo+" and "Lo-" indicate the 30,000 vote payoffs for passing or defeating the bill, respectively. Each constituency had a position on four of the bills, and had no position (no payoff, one way or the other) on the remaining three bills. The pork barrel item of each constituency payed 20,000 points if passed.

It can also be seen in Table XI-2 that for each of the contested bills held by a subject, a different set of three other players in the group was uncommitted. Thus, for player number 1, players 2, 3, and 4 were uncommitted (i.e., held no payoff position) on one of his issues; players 3, 4, and 5 were uncommitted on another; players 4, 5, and 6 on a third; and players 5, 6, and 7 on the last. For each player two of the others were uncommitted on three of his four contested issues; two others were uncommitted on two of them; and the remaining two were uncommitted on one each. Thus, no matter which of the others in the group a player approached, the pair could find at least one issue for each of them, in addition to their pork barrel items, on which they could agree to trade support.

The issues and positions in the neutral issues games were assigned in the same way. The seven contested bills were (in their entirety):

1. Approve the appointment of James Hester [then President of New York University] as chairman of the Rules Committee.
2. Issue a new postage stamp.
3. Change the procedure for reporting committee actions.
4. Change fiscal deadlines from the 10th to the 15th of the month.
5. Change the specifications for sewer pipes.
6. Relocate the Bureau of Documents.
7. Approve a pay increase for civil service employees.

Again, each constituency had its own, different pork barrel item. The neutral issues had been pretested informally. The seven selected were chosen for unanimous lack of interest in having them resolved one way or the other.

Each subject was first classified by the sextile of his scoring position on the Mach scales. The identification-constituency numbers were distributed randomly among the seven subjects in each group with the restriction that (over succeeding groups of subjects) no number was assigned to subjects of the same Mach sextile twice, until it had been assigned once to a subject in each of the other sextiles. Thus, in each session the two allies on each issue position (i.e., the two subjects assigned the same position on a given issue) could be two high Machs, two lows, or a high and a low Mach.

All the data for the study were tabulated separately by the particular issues involved. In no case within the emotional or neutral condition did the two Mach groups differ on one issue more than another, nor did any issue elicit a pattern of responses from the group as a whole different from any other issue. It seems safe to conclude that the particular content of the issues within conditions had little effect on the results.

After the subjects received their issue assignments for the first game, each was allowed to make a 30-sec statement to the group, if he wished. Most players did use this opportunity to mention one or more of their payoff issues; some elaborated more extensively and managed to include some persuasive appeals for their positions, as well. (The 30-sec time limit was imposed during pilot testing to curtail the more enthusiastic participants and keep the session within the allotted time limits.) These statements by fellow players provided the first indication to the subject that he had both allies and opponents in the group on at least some of his payoff positions. Although formal rebuttals were not allowed in this period, nonverbal signs of approval and disapproval were frequent, and occasionally accompanied by a vocal exclamation.

After all players had a chance to speak, congress recessed for a 10-min "cloakroom bargaining session." This was the subject's opportunity to find those who were uncommitted on his issues and trade his support for one of their issues for their agreement to support him on one (or more) of his issues. In this period players were free to move about the room as they wished, and talk to whomever they could corner. Monitoring and enforcement of the agreements made in this period were left entirely to the discretion of the players. There were no external constraints to prevent a subject from agreeing to vote against the driver's license bill, for example, in making a deal with one of the others, and then promising to vote for it in an exchange with another.

After 10 min the experimenter reconvened congress. The players reassembled in the circle of chairs, and each was called upon in turn around the circle to propose a bill for vote if he wished. When a subject proposed a bill, he was allowed 15 sec to argue for his position. Then one 15-sec statement for the opposite position was allowed. Then all congressmen voted on the bill. No abstentions were allowed. Voting was by show of hands, so all could see how each of the others voted. Decision was by majority vote. This procedure was repeated, proceeding around the circle of players, until all of the issues in the game had been voted on by the group. The bills introduced by each subject, all statements he made, his vote on each bill, and his score on each of his own issues were all recorded by trained observers.

After all bills in the first game had been voted on, the issues for game two were distributed, and the whole procedure was repeated. In half of the sessions the emotional issues were used in the first game, and the neutral issues in the second. In the other half of the sessions this order was reversed. After the first game and again after the second players were given a brief information test on the meaning of their own issue assignments in terms of winning, and the structure of the game. The entire session, from the beginning of the first game to the end of the third, lasted 2 hr.

CHECK ON THE MANIPULATIONS

The first concern for the emotional issues game was that both high and low Mach subjects should have equally strong private opinions on the issues. The questionnaires administered at the beginning of each session showed that this condition was fulfilled. Each item was answered on a five point scale, from "strongly disagree" (scored as 1) to "strongly agree" (scored as 5). As shown in Table XI-3, both high and low Machs disagreed with all seven items. The mean scores of highs and lows did not differ significantly on any item, or overall. Clearly, low Machs did not indicate stronger initial private feelings than highs. In fact, on six of the seven items the directional difference was for high Machs to express stronger disagreement than lows.

TABLE XI-3

Private Presession Opinion on the Seven Emotional Issues by Mach of Subjects [a]

| | Mean score per issue | | |
Issues	High Machs	Low Machs	Difference
Revoke civil rights.	1.48	1.55	-.07
Disarm unilaterally.	1.52	1.59	-.07
Abolish minimum age for driving.	1.36	1.52	-.16
Abolish Peace Corps.	2.08	1.62	.46
Raise minimum age for drinking to 25.	1.24	1.52	-.28
Compulsory universal military conscription.	1.60	2.17	-.47
Raise minimum age to vote to 25.	1.68	1.83	-.15
All seven issues	1.57	1.68	-.11

[a] ns = 25 high Machs, 29 lows; scoring for each issue was from 1 for strong disagreement to 5 for strong agreement.

The second concern in the emotional issues games was that high and low Machs should be equally balanced in being assigned payoff positions with which they privately agreed and disagreed. Each subject was assigned a payoff position on four of the seven issues, the pro position on two, and the anti position on the other two. Comparisons between subjects' own beliefs on the presession questionnaire and the positions they were assigned in the game are shown in Table XI-4. These shows that high Machs had no initial advantage over lows from not having to argue against their own beliefs in order to win points, from having more issues they privately endorsed, or more on which they were neutral.

TABLE XI-4

Private Belief on Assigned Payoff Positions [a]

Private opinion on assigned payoff position	Mean Number of assigned positions		Difference	*t*	*p* <
	High Mach	Low Mach			
Endorsed	1.76	1.71	.05	.33	—
Opposed	2.12	1.93	.19	1.36	.10
Neutral	.12	.36	−.24	1.50	.10

[a] Mean number of assigned positions in the emotional issues game which subjects endorsed, opposed, or on which they were neutral. *N*s = 25 high Machs, 29 lows; four assigned issues per subject.

TRANSFORMATION OF SCORES

Payoffs on the issues were presented to the players in multiples of 10,000 (i.e., 50,000, 30,000 and 20,000) to approximate numbers of net "constituency votes" a congressman might find significant. However, to simplify discussion of the results (as well as tabulation and calculations) each payoff was divided by 10,000. Thus, in the remainder of the paper, high-value issues will be called 5-point issues; low-value issues will be worth 3 points; and pork barrel items will be 2 points.

RESULTS AND DISCUSSION

High Machs were expected to win when the issues under discussion were emotionally loaded, but not when they were neutral. The structure of the game was designed to give high Machs no particular advantage: Assigning each subject at least two issues (his pork barrel and one contested issue) that were different from those held by any other given player suggested fair and mutually advantageous trading of support on a one-to-one basis. The multiple opportunities for such bargains in the group of seven further enhanced players' tendencies to restrict themselves to even trades. The only difference between the neutral and emotional issues games was in the content of the issues the players had to discuss in bargaining. In the emotional issues games it was expected that low Machs would become ego involved in the issue content, and that this involvement would distract them from single-minded pursuit of support.

The average pattern for all subjects was to win their pork barrel issue and two of their four contested issues. Each held four contested issues with a total value of

16 points, two 5-point issues, and two 3-point issues. Since each contested issue was won by two players in the group — one who held the 5-point position, and another holding the 3-point position — the expected score in the game on contested issues was 8 points. In addition, 93% of all pork barrel issues (2 points per subject) were passed. The mean game score for all subjects, then, was 8.00 plus 1.86, or 9.86 points. Actual scores ranged from no points won at all (by four players, all in neutral-issues games) to the highest possible score in a game, 18 points (all five issues won, by four players in emotional-issues games, and by six others in neutral-issues games).

As expected, deviations from the average pattern depended upon the Mach classification of the subject and the type of issues used in the game. Figure XI-1 shows the mean score per game of the two Mach groups for the game in which all the issues were emotionally neutral, compared to the game in which all the issues had value-laden implications. When trivial issues were used, the low-Mach bargainers did just as well as the highs. In fact, the directional difference was in favor of the lows (10.21 points per game, compared to 9.32 for the highs), although it was not significant ($p < .20$). However, these same subjects, given emotional issues to discuss, behaved quite differently. In the emotional issues games the high Machs averaged 11.24 points a game; the lows averaged 8.86 points ($t = 2.00$, $p < .03$). The interaction was obviously also significant. Clearly, the major hypothesis was supported.

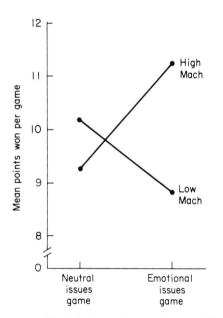

FIG. XI-1. Mean game score by Mach of subject and type of issues used in the game (ns = 25 high Machs, 29 lows).

The low Machs' losing in the emotional issues games had been predicted. The rationale for the prediction was that emotional involvement with the content of these value-laden issues would distract them from effective pursuit of voting support. Additional data support this interpretation and provide some further hints about how distraction affected the low Machs.

VOTING AGAINST A PAYOFF POSITION

Voting against one's own payoff position in the game could be considered an index of distraction. The group voting immediately followed the bargaining session in which players discussed their own and others' issues in the process of trading support. If a subject became involved with an issue in the bargaining session, his interest might interfere with recalling his payoff position on it when it came up for vote. Subjects kept their issue assignment cards during the voting so that they could check their payoff positions if they wished. Thus, voting against one's payoff position must have represented a specific misrecall of the position, or failure to recall having an assigned position. Such slips of memory could be caused by a generalized state of arousal, or a predominating concern with the content of particular issues.

Exactly half of the subjects (27 of the 54) consistently voted in accord with their payoff positions on every issue, regardless of type of issues used in the game or whether they privately agreed or disagreed with their assigned position. The other half of the subjects voted against their payoff position on one or more of their ten issues over the two games. Again, voting against one's own position depended upon both Machiavellianism and type of issues used in the game. Table XI-5 shows the number of votes against the player's own payoff position. In the emotional issues games the low Machs voted against themselves more than high Machs did. (Since one-tailed tests will be used for the sake of consistency, the .025 level will be required to call unpredicted differences significant.) The difference between Mach groups in the neutral issues game was not significant. Further, the low Machs tended to vote against themselves in the emotional issues game more often than they did in the neutral issues game ($t = 1.98, p < .05$), while the difference for high Machs between the two conditions was insignificant.

It cannot be argued that the low Machs' voting against themselves in the emotional issues game was due to their being less bright than the highs or having a less adequate understanding of the game. If either of these were true, the effect should have been equally strong in the neutral issues game. Further, high and low Machs did not differ in intellectual understanding of the structure of the game and the meaning of payoff positions in terms of winning points, as measured by the information tests administered after the first game and again after the second.

TABLE XI-5

Voting Against Own Payoff Position by Mach and Type of Issues Used in the Game [a]

| Type of issues | Mean number of votes against own position | | | | |
	High Mach	Low Mach	Difference	t	$p <$
Emotional issues	.32	.83	−.51	2.13	.025
Neutral issues	.36	.48	−.12	.60	—

[a] ns = 25 high Machs, 29 lows.

It might be supposed that in the emotional issues games subjects voted against assigned payoff positions out of principle. The evidence is to the contrary. Of the eight votes by a high Mach against an assigned payoff position, four were in accord with the voter's private belief, and the other four were against the voter's private belief as well as his payoff position. Of the 24 cases of a low Mach voting against his payoff position, 13 were in accord with private belief. In the other 11 cases the subjects' private belief was in accord with his assigned position, and he voted against both, or (in four cases) the subject was privately neutral on the issue.

When the structural complexity of the game was the only problem the subject had to keep track of, as was true for high Machs in both games, and for lows in the neutral issues game, relatively few votes were cast against payoff positions. The only cell mean out of line in Table XI-5 is the one for low Machs in the emotional issues game. It was for these subjects, in this condition, that a distracting factor of affective involvement with issue content had been predicted.

EMOTIONAL VALUE VERSUS POINT VALUE

In this game an efficient bargaining period strategy designed to assure a player the maximum number of points would be first to line up support on his high-value issues, and then work on his low-value issues if time allowed. If all players pursued this strategy, each would win one of his two high-value issues, on the average. And, in fact, the data from the neutral issues game appear to follow this pattern. The high Machs' average score on high value issues was 2.20 points per issue, not significantly different from the low Mach's average of 2.59 points.

In the emotional issues game a low Mach who became involved with the content of an issue might have become engrossed in discussing it, even if it had only low value for him in the game. Or, he might have become involved in discussing another player's issue which had no point value for him at all. If this is in fact how the low Machs were distracted while highs were cooly pursuing the strategy of "high-value issues first," then we would expect to find the highs winning and lows losing primarily on the high-value issues in the emotional issues game. As shown in Table XI-6, high Machs won 3.30 points each on their two high-value (5-point) issues, while lows won only 1.89 points ($p < .005$). No such discrepancy appeared on the low-value (3-point) issues.

TABLE XI-6

Game Score in the Emotional Issues Game by Mach of Subject and
Point-Value of Issue [a]

Point value of issue	Mean score per subject, per issue		Difference	t	$p <$
	High Mach	Low Mach			
High value (5 pts. ea.)	3.30	1.89	1.41	3.02	.005
Low value (3 pts. ea.)	1.32	1.60	-.28	.97	—

[a] ns = 25 high Machs, 29 lows.

This finding was also tested by chi square. Each subject was classified as winning both, one or neither of his high value issues. Of the 25 high Machs 10 won both of their high-value issues; 13 won one; and 2 won neither. For the 29 low Machs these frequencies were, respectively, 5, 12, and 12 ($\chi^2 = 8.60, p < .02$).

The most plausible reason for low Machs' not also losing their low-value emotional issues was the method of assigning issues to subjects in the group. For every high-value position assigned a high Mach, the chances were 3/6 or 4/6 that the corresponding low-value position on that issue would be held by a low Mach. Since high Machs won their high-value issues predominantly, roughly half of these outcomes would necessarily bring a low-value win to a low Mach.

DISTRACTION OR CONSCIENCE

It cannot be argued that low Machs simply refused to seek support for positions they privately opposed in the emotional issues game. If conscience were the cause of their undoing rather than a more general state of arousal, they should have done as well as the high Machs on issue positions they endorsed, and should have lost primarily on those they opposed. As noted above, all of the emotional issues were worded to evoke nearly universal private opposition. And, in fact, all players won more of the issues on which they were assigned the popular (anti) position than those on which they were assigned the unpopular (pro) position. However, as shown in Table XI-7, low Machs did less well than highs on high-value emotional issues, regardless of position. However, it was precisely on popular positions, for which the player had to argue in favor of a position he privately endorsed, that the low Machs lost most decisively to the highs ($p < .005$).

TABLE XI-7

Score on High Value (5-Point) Issues in the Emotional Issues Game by Mach and Popularity of Payoff Position [a]

Payoff position on the issue	Mean score per subject, per issue		Difference	t	$p <$
	High Mach	Low Mach			
Popular (anti) position	4.20	2.41	1.79	2.98	.005
Unpopular (pro) position	2.40	1.38	1.02	1.55	.10

[a] ns = 25 high Machs, 29 lows; one popular and one unpopular position per subject.

The result was the same when the data were tested by chi square. Each subject had one high-value issue on which he held the popular position. Accordingly, each was classified as winning or losing this issue. Twenty-one of the 25 high Machs won their high-value popular issues, and 4 lost it. Of the 29 lows, 14 won their high-value popular issue, and 15 lost it (χ^2 with Yates' correction = 6.03, $p < .02$). The results were the same when issues were classified by subjects' private endorsement rather than by popularity of the position. Clearly, endorsement of assigned payoff position was no asset to the low Machs nor was private opposition a special liability.

This finding strongly supports the involvement—distraction rationale. It was proposed that low Machs are influenced by emotional involvements while highs are not, or control them more effectively. It seems reasonable to assume that defending one's own position on an important issue would be more involving than arguing against it for clear utilitarian purposes. If the lows' losing in the emotional issues games was due to the distraction of emotional involvement with the issue content as proposed, it would make sense to find them losing more decisively on positions they agreed with — precisely because for them these positions were more involving.

Again, it cannot be argued that the low Machs failed to understand the importance of high-value issues. At the beginning of the game, after receiving their issue assignments, all subjects were permitted an unrestricted 30-sec statement. Low Machs consistently mentioned high-value positions more than low-value positions (.86 high-value positions mentioned per subject to .38 low-value mentions per subject in the neutral issues game; and .66 to .34 ($t = 1.97, p < .05$) in the emotional issues game). High Machs, on the other hand, mentioned popular positions in the emotional issues game more than unpopular positions (.76 to .20; $t = 3.65, p < .005$) and ignored the distinction between high value and low value issues (.56 to .40, n.s.). Low Machs ignored the popularity distinction (.55 popular to .45 unpopular, n.s.).

Lest this comparison cast doubt on the high Machs' intellectual grasp of the importance of high value issues, it should be noted that after the bargaining session the experimenter called on subjects in turn to propose an issue for vote. All players more often proposed one of their own high-value issues at this more crucial point. In the emotional issues game the mean frequencies of proposing high- and low-value issues were .72 and .36 for high Machs, and .83 and .10 for lows. (The frequencies don't add up to 1.00 because all four of the player's contested issues were sometimes proposed by others before his turn.)

High Machs mentioned popular issues in the introductory period, but worked on high value issues in the bargaining and voting periods when it counted. Low Machs attended to their high value issues in the introductory and voting periods — when they were not distracted by getting involved in conversations with others. These data, combined with the results of the information tests mentioned earlier, show that low Machs understood the game as well as highs did. However, they were unable to use their intellectual grasp of the situation to their own advantage when emotionally involving conversations distracted them.

Can the low Machs' losing when discussion focused on emotionally involving content be attributed to their greater susceptibility to "arousal"? Zajonc (1965) used the term to account for the facilitating effect of the presence of others on performance of previously well-learned routines (usually motor tasks). In this study others were present and interaction among subjects occurred in both conditions, but the low Machs did not lose in the neutral issues condition. Evidently, whatever "arousal" accompanies the presence of others cannot alone account for the lows' losing. On the other hand, neither can the intrusion of issue content *per se* explain it. It seems more likely that the lows' (presumed) greater susceptibility to arousal functioned as a state of readiness to invest energy, but the actual investment was only elicited by the situation which provided appropriately ego-involving issue content.

The question the data cannot answer is whether the source of the low Machs' distraction was simply the emotional issue content itself, or whether the emotional issue content served as a focus or "releaser" or object in which to invest a generalized "arousal" accompanying the presence of others.

GAME PLAYING, EMOTIONALITY, AND SERIOUSNESS

The fact that the high Machs did not win in the neutral issues game indicates that, in this sample at least, high Machs were not simply better game players than lows. The neutral issues game was, if anything, even more clearly "just a game." It required the same understanding of the game rules and the same bargaining. It was, if anything, more complicated for the players than the emotional issues game because the issues were not salient. In this situation the low Machs were at least as effective as highs. It may still be true, however, that high Machs are more likely to win in most games occurring in the world outside of the laboratory. This is because most games contain some potentially ego-involving elements irrelevant to winning.

Scores in the neutral issues game also demonstrate that low Machs are not simply more emotional or more confused in general than highs. The results indicate that lows are more susceptible to emotional involvements, but this is specific to situations in which the potential for distracting involvement exists. Given a situation in which such potential is minimal, low Machs function as efficiently as highs.

It has been proposed in previous chapters that high Machs have an increasing advantage over lows in competitive bargaining as the situation becomes more serious. Since the emotional issues in the present study could be considered more relevant than the trivial ones, the results support that formulation also. As noted previously, the seriousness of a situation is usually defined by the number or importance of the values at stake in it. Clearly, as situations become more serious, their potential for evoking distracting arousal also increases.

NONINDEPENDENCE OF SCORES

Player's scores in this game are not independent. Two players had to lose and get a score of zero on each contested issue; two others had to win, one receiving 5 points and the other 3. However, the method of assigning issues and positions to subjects should have *minimized* differences between Mach groups, and could never have produced a difference spuriously. The two players assigned the same position on an issue were as often one high and one low Mach as they were two highs or two lows. Further, when a high Mach was assigned one position on a bill, one or both of his two assigned opponents could also be high Machs.

How, then, did the high Machs manage to win in the emotional issues games?

As in the previous studies, it appears again that they took advantage of whatever they could. For example, there were only five instances in the emotional issues games in which two high Machs were assigned allies on an issue, and the two opposing positions were both assigned to low Machs. In four of these five cases, the high Mach pair won.

There were 11 cases in which a high- and low-Mach pair opposed another high—low pair, but the high on one side held the high-value position, while the opposing high held the low-value position. In this situation, the pair in which the high Mach had the high-value position won 7 of the 11 decisions. Similarly, when one pair consisted of a high and low Mach, and the opposing pair were both lows, the high—low pair won 9 of 11 decisions, but they won consistently (5 out of 5) when the high Mach had the high-value position and the low Mach the low-value position.

It appears that the high Machs, in these emotional issues games, were opportunistic. They may have tried to win all four of their contested issues, but if they could not win them all they more often won their high-value issues. Low Machs, in contrast, won most often when they had a high-Mach ally, and when it was the high who got the most points for winning.

ORDER EFFECTS AND GAME THREE

There were no significant order effects. When the type of issues was disregarded and games were classified by the order in which they were played, the directional difference was in favor of the high Machs in each of the three games, but in no case was it significant, nor was there a sequence effect. High Machs who played the emotional game first and the neutral game second did not differ in either type of game, or over both, from highs who had the opposite order, nor did low Machs who had the two sequences differ. Scores in game three were not strictly comparable to those in the first two games since subjects were allowed to choose their own issues. The mean scores of high and low Machs in game three were 9.40 and 9.34 points, respectively.

SUMMARY

This study was designed to test the hypothesis that one of the reasons high Machs win in bargaining is that low Machs invest emotional energy in personal value implications which arise in the bargaining context, and that these involvements distract them from undivided concentration on winning. In contrast, high Machs were expected to be detached from potential involvements or to control them for the purpose of devoting full attention to a cognitive analysis of the situation and strategies for winning.

A bargaining game designed around legislative log rolling was adapted to minimize intrinsic distractions. The hypothesis was tested by using trivial issues of consequence to none of the subjects in one game, and important issues on which all subjects privately held strong opinions in another. Fifty-four subjects participated in mixed-Mach groups of seven. Since the game structure minimized emotional conflict, no difference in winning between Mach groups was expected in the trivial-issues game. In the emotional-issues game it was expected that low Machs would become involved with the content of the issues, with a consequent loss of bargaining efficiency.

The results supported the hypothesis. High and low Machs did not differ significantly in the neutral issues game, but high Machs won in the emotional issues game.

The low Machs' losing in the emotional issues game was not due to failure to understand the game intellectually, to refusing to seek support for a position they privately opposed, or to voting in accord with conscience rather than payoff position. They lost to the highs by the greatest margin on issues they most strongly endorsed, not those they privately opposed.

The results of the study, together with those of previous studies, clearly support the notion that one of the significant advantages of high Machs in competitive bargaining with lows is that the lows become distracted by potentially ego-involving elements in the bargaining context, while high Machs remain detached from such concerns and concentrate on winning.

CHAPTER XII

THE EYE OF THE BEHOLDER [1]

Florence Geis and Marguerite Levy

If beauty is in the eye of the beholder, perhaps other characteristics also are attributed differentially to others, depending upon who is looking at them. Specifically, the perceiver's interpersonal orientation may influence how he looks at others, which in turn could influence what he perceives of them. Such problems are familiar ones to researchers in the area of interpersonal perception.

Machiavellianism implies distinctive interpersonal attitudes. High Machs are assumed to have a detached, impersonal orientation toward others. This leaves them freer to analyze the situation dispassionately and proceed according to strategy; in contrast, low Machs can be distracted by emotional or personal involvements. The Legislature study (Chapter XI) tested the rational versus emotional distractibility part of the characterization. The present study, using the same subjects, was designed to investigate personal versus impersonal orientations more directly. The initial question was, what are the implications of personal versus impersonal orientations for accuracy in perceiving others?

The major results of previous studies gave no unambiguous clues. High Machs' demonstrated manipulative skills could have been based on accurate perceptions of others, but it is equally possible that they were the result of insensitivity and disregard of others. Similarly, while the cognitive-strategic orientation of high Machs could be assumed to yield more accurate appraisals of others, the personal orientation of lows could equally reasonably be assumed to lead them to greater accuracy. However, as Cronbach (1955) and others have pointed out, there are different ways to be accurate.

One way is in perceiving what people in general are like. That is, regardless of whether the perceiver is right or wrong on particular details, or for particular target persons, the sum of his judgements gives an accurate picture of what most of the targets are like on most of the judging dimensions. In his review of the social perception literature, Taft (1955) concluded that people who are cold, unsympathetic, and not socially oriented are more accurate, in general, in their evaluations of others. This description fits high Machs better than lows; it

---

[1] Parts of this research were reported (Geis, Levy, & Weinheimer, 1966) at the annual meeting of the Eastern Psychological Associatin, New York, April 14, 1966.

squares with our characterization of highs as impersonal, cognitive, rational, "cool," and strategy oriented rather than person oriented. This led us to expect that high Machs would be more accurate, overall, in describing others.

A second way to be accurate is perceiving how one person differs from another. If low Machs have the more personal, empathizing orientation toward others that we have assumed, they should be more sensitive to individual differences. Data from the Con Game bargaining protocols (Chapter VIII) support this assumption indirectly. In that study, the middle- and low-Mach members of the triad both chose the high Mach over each other as a coalition partner, but the high Machs did not discriminate between their potential middle- and low-Mach partners. This suggests that low Machs are more responsive to individual differences. The question was whether their behavioral discrimination was based on a perceptual discrimination. If it was, what cues were being used? A perception that two potential partners differed could have been based on either an accurate or inaccurate appraisal of how they differed. For example, the low Machs might have seen the high Mach as more intelligent. This could account for their preferring him as a partner, but the perception would have been false. Nevertheless, the finding that low Machs did discriminate between others who actually differed was consistent with our growing impression that they have an empathic orientation which focuses on others as persons rather than objects.

The emerging theoretical descriptions of high and low scorers on the Mach scales, together with previous data, suggested that high Machs should be more accurate in appraising others in general, but low Machs should be more sensitive to individual differences between others.

PROCEDURE

Data to test these assumptions were gathered at the end of the Legislature sessions, described in Chapter XI. Male subjects pretested on the Mach scales interacted together for 2 hr in groups of seven. The subjects for each group were selected to represent the range of Mach scores in the sample initially tested, and all were strangers to each other at the beginning of the session. The Legislature game was designed to create mixed-motive bargaining interaction. Subjects were in competition, but winning at each subsequent step required the temporary cooperation of some erstwhile opponents. The game provided opportunities for interaction among all subjects in the session.

Since most people form their impressions of others without the benefit of expecting to be tested for accuracy afterwards, we did not inform the subjects in advance that a perception test was to follow, or in any way cue them to attend to the personality characteristics of fellow players. The instructions for the Legislature game were task oriented — designed to teach the subjects the game rules and motivate them to try to win. Accordingly, when the person perception task was introduced after the games, the subjects had to rely on whatever impressions they had formed about others incidentally during the preceding interaction.

A perennial problem in assessing accuracy in interpersonal perception is the criterion problem. By what criterion does the experimenter decide whether a subject's judgements about another are accurate or not? The most relevant information we had about the subjects was their Mach scale responses given one to two months previously, so these were used as criteria. The task given the subjects was to guess the responses previously made by another person in the group on the Mach IV scale. The task of guessing another's responses to attitude items is similar to tasks employed by previous investigators. It has been suggested in the literature that there is little evidence of perceptual accuracy because such tasks are too difficult or not relevant. In this case the task was relevant, as is explained below. However, it did seem difficult in view of the relatively short acquaintance period during which subjects' attention was presumably focused on winning in the game, not on getting to know their fellow players. In an attempt to counteract the difficulty of the task we followed a procedure suggested by Stanley Lehmann (1964). Subjects were allowed to choose whomever they wished in the group as the person whose responses they would try to guess.

Immediately following their final round of Legislature, the seven subjects in each group were seated in a circle apart from but in sight of each other. Each still wore the numbered identification tag used in the preceding games, and subjects were asked to identify their chosen target person by this number. Each subject was given a copy of the Mach IV Scale with the following instructions:

> Finally, we want to find out how *accurate* you are in forming impressions of others. Each of you has taken, previously, a questionnaire dealing with attitudes and opinions on various social issues. What we would like you to do now is pick the one person in the group whom you think you can most accurately size up, and answer the questionnaire as you think he did when he took it.
>
> The questionnaire directions and items are reproduced below. You can look over the questions first, before you choose the person, if you want. Remember, your job will be to answer the questions exactly as you think he did when he answered them.

It should be noted that none of the 20 Mach scale items directly mentions "manipulation of others," nor was this ever mentioned in the instructions for the preceding games. Some items describe behavior that can easily be interpreted as manipulative; others simply refer to general characteristics of human nature. Thus, the "perception" task given the subjects actually required inference based upon live, face-to-face interaction of a sort designed to be relevant to the dimension on which judgements would be assessed.

It should also be noted that we are using the term *perception* loosely. Presumably, different subjects were using varying combinations of sensations, cognitive organizing principles, memories, and assumptions in making the Mach scale guesses for their chosen target. We do not intend to imply any specific definition of the processes involved by labeling them *perception*. Inferences about these processes derived from the data are discussed in context.

There were eight laboratory sessions which yielded 51 Mach scale postdictions of one subject by another. Two of the Legislature sessions were run with only six subjects and a stooge replacing the seventh who had failed to show up; and three subjects (one high Mach and two lows) chose a stooge as their target person. The data from these three subjects were excluded from the analyses, leaving 24 high Mach judges, and 27 lows.

RESULTS

OVERALL ACCURACY

Since high Machs were assumed to have a cognitive, impersonal orientation toward others, they were expected to be more accurate in estimating the Machiavellianism of others in general. The best index of a judge's estimate of his target's Machiavellianism is probably the average degree of Machiavellianism he attributed to his target over all 20 items. (Judges made guesses only on the Mach IV scale.) Accordingly, we scored the judge's guesses and compared this "predicted" (actually postdicted) Mach score with the actual Mach IV and V scores of the target person he had chosen. Both Mach IV and Mach V have a range of 120 points; the standard deviations in this sample were 17.65 points on Mach IV and 13.31 on Mach V. As shown in Tables XII-1A and XII-1B; the high Machs were not only more accurate as compared to lows; they hit their targets' actual Mach scores almost exactly. The scores computed from their guesses averaged 1.17 points below the actual Mach IV scores of their target persons, and .92 of a point below their targets' Mach V scores. In contrast, the low Mach judges' average attributed score was 13.81 points below their targets' actual Mach IV average, and 14.81 points short of their targets' Mach V. Clearly, the first prediction was confirmed. The high Machs as a group were more accurate in approximating the average Machiavellianism of their target persons, overall.

TABLE XII-1A

Overall Accuracy:
Mach Scores of Judges, Targets, and Judges' Estimates for Targets
(ns = 24 high judges, 27 lows)

		Mean Mach Scores		
		Judges' own score	Judges' estimate for target	Targets' own score
High-Mach judges	Mach IV	114.63	107.79	108.96
	Mach V	116.25	–	108.71
Low-Mach judges	Mach IV	87.85	92.89	106.70
	Mach V	95.15	–	107.70

TABLE XII-1B

Overall Accuracy:
Judge's Estimate for Target Minus Target's Own Score

Target's score on	Judge's mean error		Difference	t	$p <$
	High-Mach judges	Low-Mach judges			
Mach IV	-1.17	-13.81	12.64	2.12	.025
Mach V	-.92	-14.81	13.89	4.34	.005

PERCEIVING INDIVIDUAL DIFFERENCES

Since low Machs were assumed to have a more personal orientation toward others, and had discriminated between high- and middle-Mach partners in face-to-face bargaining previously, they were expected to be sensitive to individual differences in Machiavellianism. Thus, we can ask, did the judges discriminate between high- and low-Mach target persons? We cannot evaluate any single judge's ability to discriminate, since each one made guesses for only one target. However, we can separate judges who chose high Mach targets from those who chose lows, and compare the Mach scores attributed to the two groups of targets. These data are shown in Table XII-2.

TABLE XII-2

Perception of Individual Differences:
Mean Mach Score Computed from Judge's Guesses for High- and Low-Mach Targets [a]

Score Predicted by	Mean Mach score predicted for		Difference	t	$p <$
	High-Mach targets	Low-Mach targets			
High-Mach Judges	(14) 107.14	(10) 108.70	-1.56	—	—
Low-Mach Judges	(16) 97.56	(11) 86.09	11.47	2.18	.025

[a] The n for each cell mean is given in parentheses.

Low-Mach judges who chose high-Mach targets predicted a mean Mach score of 98 for them; those who chose low-Mach targets guessed responses yielding a mean score of 86. The low-Mach judges did discriminate significantly whether the person whose responses they were guessing was relatively higher or lower in Machiavellianism. High-Mach judges, on the other hand, predicted a mean score of 107 when they had chosen a high-Mach target person, and a mean score of 109 for low-Mach targets. Clearly, the high-Mach judges did not discriminate between high and low Mach target persons.

Figure XII-1 shows how high Mach judges achieved their overall accuracy without making any discrimination whatever between high and low Mach targets, and how low-Mach judges did discriminate between high- and low-Mach targets even though they made larger errors on the average over all targets.

DISCUSSION

The person perception data suggest that high and low Machs are "accurate" judges of others in strikingly different ways. What do these differences suggest about differences in the quality of the interaction process experienced by highs and lows during their contact with others in the preceding Legislature game? The judging task outcomes indicate that high Machs were accurate in estimating the Mach scores of others in general, without discriminating at all whether the particular person whose responses they were guessing was higher or lower in Machiavellianism. The low Machs significantly underestimated the Mach scores of their targets overall, but they did accurately guess high Machs as more Machiavellian than lows. What were the processes high and low Machs used that led to these different outcomes?

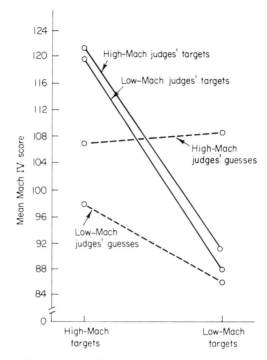

FIG. XII-1. Targets' Mach scores and judges' predictions (*ns* are the same as in Table XII-2).

OVERALL ACCURACY

SIZE OF ERROR REGARDLESS OF DIRECTION. The average of the Mach scores computed from high-Mach judges' guesses matched the average of their targets' actual scores. Further analyses suggest that this accuracy did not reflect sensitivity to others as individuals but rather, at least partly, an absence of directionally consistent misconceptions among the high-Mach judges as a group. An example will illustrate: Suppose three high Machs guess Mach responses for three target persons. Judge A overestimates his target's score by 20 points; B and C underestimate their targets' scores by 12 and 8 points, respectively. When these three error scores are summed algebraically, the mean error of "the group" will be zero. In contrast, if three low-Mach judges made errors of exactly the same sizes — 20, 12, and 8 points, respectively — but all in the same direction, for example, underestimating their targets' scores, the mean error of their group would be 13.33 points.

However, if the absolute values of the error scores were used rather than the algebraic values, the mean error of both hypothetical groups in the example above would be 13.33 points. This procedure allows errors in both directions to add up rather than cancelling out. It answers the question of how far, regardless of direction, the judges' estimates missed their targets' scores. By this measure, high Machs missed their targets' Mach IV score by 17 points on the average and lows by 22 points, but the difference was not significant ($p < .20$).[2] However, the high Machs' estimates (on Mach IV) did come closer to their targets' Mach V scores than those of lows' did. By this criterion highs erred by 13 points, lows by 21 points ($t = 2.36, p < .025$).

Why did the high Machs' guesses on Mach IV come closer than lows' to their targets' scores on Mach V, but not Mach IV? (In Table XII-1A the judges' and targets' Mach IV and Mach V scores are shown separately, along with the judges' estimates for their targets on Mach IV.) Mach IV, in agree–disagree Likert format, is transparent. The subject can shape the image his answers are giving. In contrast, the forced-choice Mach V is more devious (see Chapter II). If the target's Mach V score was less subject to willful distortion, or if it related more closely to behavior in the preceding interaction than Mach IV did, then the high-Mach judges may have been estimating how Machiavellian their targets actually were (or had acted) rather than guessing how their targets had presented themselves on the more obvious Mach IV format.

However, the high Machs' greater accuracy by the Mach V criterion could also be an artifact. In general, high scorers on the Mach scale make similar scores on the two forms, but low scorers characteristically score higher on Mach V than Mach IV (see Table XII-1A). As can be seen in Fig. XII-1, high-Mach judges overestimated the scores of low-Mach targets. Their greater accuracy by the Mach V criterion could reflect only the fact that most of these low-Mach targets made higher scores on Mach V.

ACCURACY ON THE TEN MOST DISCRIMINATING MACH IV ITEMS. The Mach IV–Mach V comparison is difficult to interpret. The high Machs may have done better by the Mach V criterion because it in fact discriminated better, or they may have done better simply because low-Mach targets generally scored higher on Mach V. An alternative test of accuracy on discriminating items which keeps (in fact increases) the size of the scoring difference between high- and low-Mach targets can be made by using only the most discriminating items from Mach IV. The ten Mach IV items that had discriminated most among high, middle, and low scorers at the initial testing of the sample were identified (Mach IV items numbered 3, 6, 7, 9, 10, 11, 16, 18, 19, and 20 in Table II-3). The target's score on these ten items was then compared against the score of his judge's guesses on them. The high-Mach judges' average absolute error was 8.92 Mach scale points; the lows' was 13.93 points ($t = 2.14, p < .025$).

_____

[2] One-tailed p values are reported throughout the chapter for the sake of consistency. Unpredicted differences are called significant if the one-tailed value is .025 or smaller.

The high Machs were just as accurate on the more discriminating half of the items as on the less discriminating half. They were in error by 9 points on the former, 8 on the latter. In contrast, the low Machs' average absolute error was 14 points on the more discriminating items, approximately twice the size of their error (7½ points) on the less discriminating items. Clearly, the high Machs were not significantly more accurate in terms of absolute size of error on the total Mach IV because the lows were just as accurate on the *less* discriminating items. The implications of this finding for low Machs are explored further below. The high Machs' consistency suggests a relatively accurate conception of how their targets had answered the more discriminating items, as well as the others. This relative accuracy in estimating the average popularity of items corresponds roughly to what Cronbach (1955) called stereotype accuracy.

Thus far, it appears that one part of the explanation of high Machs' superiority to lows in overall accuracy — as judges of others in general — was that the low Machs as a group consistently underestimated targets' Mach scores while highs were more variable. Some overestimated targets' scores and other underestimated, so when the error scores of individual high Machs were averaged algebraically across the group, their errors cancelled out. However, this is apparently not the whole story. Even when the effect of the low Mach's directional bias was eliminated by using absolute values of the error scores, the high Machs came significantly closer than lows to their target's scores on Mach V and the more discriminating half of Mach IV. Before further interpretation, however, one final analysis should be considered, the extent to which the judge's guesses on specific items matched his target's responses, respectively.

ITEM-BY-ITEM ACCURACY. From the point of view of the judge, his job was guessing his target's previous responses to particular items. No subject was aware, either in answering the items initially or in making guesses for his target, that a total score would be computed from his responses.

For an item-by-item analysis, we compared the judge's guesses with his target's previous Mach IV responses. An average squared error score for each judge was computed by squaring the difference between his guess on each item and his target's actual response to it, and then averaging across the 20 items. This procedure penalizes the judge heavily for large errors and very little for small errors. High and low Mach judges did not differ. The highs' average squared error was 7.06 points per item; the lows' was 7.11 (n.s.).

The average squared error reflects the *size* of errors, regardless of direction. We can also correlate the judge's guesses with his target's responses across the 20 items. This relates the two *patterns* of responses, regardless of any constant distance between them. To evaluate group tendencies, the correlation for each judge–target pair was tranformed into its equivalent Fisher's z value, and the mean was computed for each Mach group. These means, converted back into r

values, were .16 for the high Machs and .06 for the lows. Neither group showed any consistent accuracy. These results indicate that neither the high Machs' greater overall accuracy nor the lows' accurate discrimination was due to greater accuracy in guessing their target's specific item responses.

The total Mach score computed from a judge's guesses is equivalent to the average Machiavellianism of his estimates for his target over the 20 items. Although the judge might be dead wrong in guessing which particular items his target had answered "high" or "low," if he duplicated his target's *proportions* of high and low responses, his total score estimate would be accurate. Hastorf, Richardson, & Dornbusch (1958) have pointed out that few people except psychologists characteristically view others in terms of their probable responses to specific items. However, people do characteristically have global impressions of others. A judge could be accurate in his general impression without being correct on the specific components of it taken singly.

HIGH MACHS' AVERAGE ACCURACY. High Machs' interpersonal strategies have been compared previously to statistical computation procedures partly because their tactics appeared to be detached, objective, and more attuned to population parameters than to the particulars of individual variation. (The "populations," of course, were those present, or in the same experimental situation in other groups.) Again, in the present situation, the simplest description of the high Machs' overall accuracy is a statistical analogy — the averaging process. The more high Machs' responses were averaged, the more accurate they became. High and low Machs did not differ in guessing the specific item responses of their targets. However, when the judge's guesses were summed across items, the the highs' estimates came closer than lows' to their targets' scores on both Mach V and the more discriminating half of Mach IV. The total score measure allows a judge's underestimates on some items to compensate for overestimates on others. One further averaging process — algebraically averaging the total score errors of individual judges — made the highs significantly more accurate than lows on all possible comparisons. That is, the total score errors of some high-Mach judges were opposite in direction to those of others so that the average of their estimates coincided with the actual average of their targets' scores on both Mach IV and Mach V. The low Machs were more consistent in their directional errors, and consequently less accurate on the average.

The prediction that high Machs would be more accurate judges of others in general was supported by the data examined from a number of different perspectives. Their accuracy appeared to reflect their knowing where targets in general were on the dimension — how the target had answered the type of item, not how he had answered particular items. Similarly, high Machs' estimates came closer to the actual scores of all their targets as a group without discriminating (accurately or otherwise) between high- and low-scoring targets. These findings provide inferential support for the hypothesis that high Machs view others impersonally. Presumably, impersonal detachment provides perspective which in turn permits an unbiased, if global, assessment. The results are also consistent with Taft's (1955) conclusion that cold, unsympathetic people are more accurate judges of others in general.

It should be noted that none of the evidence so far considered indicates definitively that the highs' "accuracy" as judges of others reflected accurate perceptions of their designated target persons. Their performance could equally well have reflected accurate *conceptions* of the Machiavellianism of "others in general" (i.e., fellow students). This question is considered next.

REAL SIMILARITY AND ASSUMED SIMILARITY

A problem in interpreting accuracy scores is that subjects tend to guess the same responses for another that they gave for themselves initially. In the person perception literature this has been called the tendency to assume similarity. For example, suppose a judge with no perceptual accuracy of any kind blindly attributed his own previous responses to a target person; if the target happened to have given responses that were actually similar to those of his judge, the

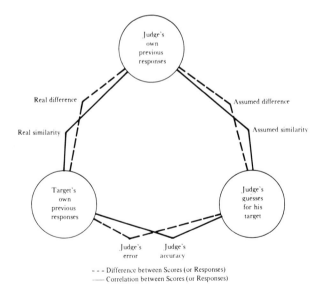

FIG. XII-2. Similarity, difference, and accuracy measures.

judge's guesses would falsely appear accurate. Real similarity between judge and target, combined with a judge's tendency to attribute similarity indiscriminately, necessarily produces apparent accuracy indistinguishable from genuine accuracy. To untangle these effects we must compare the amount of difference that actually existed between a judge and his target (e.g., in Mach score) and the extent to which the judge then correctly estimated the difference. Figure XII-2 shows the three sets of responses — the judge's and target's own previous responses, and the judge's guesses for his target — and the measures derived from each of the three possible comparisons.

The data for the overall comparisons are shown in Fig. XII-3. The distance AB represents the real difference in Mach score between high-Mach judges and their targets; the distance AC represents the amount of difference from themselves high Mach judges attributed to their targets. (The distance BC is the high-Mach judges' mean error, the difference between their estimates and the actual scores of their targets.) All comparisons in this section are based on Mach IV scores only.

The data in Table XII-1 and Fig. XII-3 suggest that the high Machs may in fact have chosen targets closer to themselves in Mach IV score than lows did ($AB - DF$ in Fig. XII-3: $t = -1.92, p < .05$). While the high-Mach judges only tended to differ from their targets ($AB > 0$: $t = 1.86, p < .05$), the low Machs clearly differed from theirs ($DF > 0$: $t = 4.90, p < .0005$). However, the high Machs' estimates reflected the full difference that actually existed. They accurately tended to attribute less Machiavellianism to their targets than they

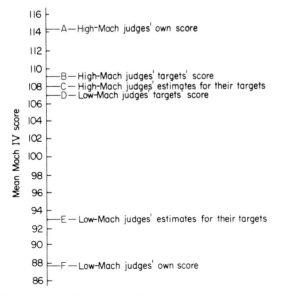

FIG. XII-3. Real and assumed similarity: difference in Mach score between judge and target, and amount of difference estimated by judge ($ns = 24$ high-Mach judges, 27 lows).

had claimed for themselves originally ($AC > 0$: $t = 1.81, p < .05$). On the other hand, low Machs underestimated the difference between themselves and their targets ($DF - EF$: $t = 2.83, p < .005$). In fact, low Machs' guesses for targets were indistinguishable from their own previous self-reports ($EF > 0$: $t = 1.59, p < .10$). These comparisons indicate that although high Machs tended to choose targets closer to themselves in Mach score than lows did, the highs were accurate in estimating the actual differences. In contrast, the low Machs failed to estimate any significant difference between themselves and their targets.

The data provide a number of other ways of comparing a judge's tendency to "assume similarity" with the extent to which his target person was actually similar. These further comparisons, which are described next, corroborate the conclusion above, that high-Mach judges did not assume similarity indiscriminately, that low-Mach judges did, and in most cases to a significantly greater extent than the highs.

AMOUNT OF SIMILARITY REGARDLESS OF DIRECTION. Real and assumed similarity can also be evaluated in terms of the absolute size of the difference in Mach scores, disregarding algebraic signs of direction. By this measure high- and low-Mach judges differed equally much from their targets (15 vs. 18 points; $t = .98, p > .10$). The two groups also estimated scores for their targets equally distant from their own (14 points and 13 points). Again, however, the high Machs estimated as much difference as actually existed (14 of 15 points), but lows placed their targets 5 points closer to themselves in Mach score than they actually were ($t = 2.82, p < .005$). Alternatively, we can disregard amount of difference and consider only direction. Seventeen of the 24 high Machs correctly called their target a higher or lower Mach than themselves ($p = .047$). Low Machs guessed no better than chance; 14 were right, 13 were wrong.

From the point of view of absolute differences in Mach scores, the high Machs chose targets as far removed from themselves as the low Machs did. However, while the highs were accurate in estimating both the amount and direction of difference between themselves and their targets, the lows were not. It seems safe to conclude that the high Machs' overall accuracy was not due to indiscriminate assumptions of similarity fortuitously coupled with real similarity. Clearly, it was the low-Mach judges who assumed unwarranted similarity. Equally clearly, it was their tendency to assume similarity which doubled their error on the more discriminating items (those they themselves had answered differently from middle and high Machs at the initial testing) compared to their error on the less discriminating items.

ITEM-BY-ITEM SIMILARITY COMPARISONS. The predicted differences in guessing accuracy between high- and low-Mach judges appeared in the total score comparisons, but not at the item-by-item level. It was therefore surprising to find the pattern of high Machs estimating differences accurately and lows assuming similarity also appearing at the item by item level. Table XII-3 shows the average squared discrepancy measures for real and assumed differences at the item-by-item level.

TABLE XII-3

Real Differences and Assumed Differences

Real Difference Between Judge and His Target (Based on Their Previous Self-Descriptions) and Assumed Difference (Judge's Guess for His Target Versus the Judge's Own Self-Description) Over All 20 Mach IV Items

		Mean squared discrepancy per item				
		High-Mach judges			Low-Mach judges	
Guesses for	(n)	Real Difference (between J and T)	Assumed difference (J's guess for T and J's prior self-description)	(n)	Real difference (between J and T)	Assumed difference (J's guess for T and J's prior self-description)
High-Mach targets	(14)	7.86	5.70	(16)	9.36	4.48
Low-Mach targets	(10)	6.68	5.01	(11)	6.14	4.43
All targets combined	(24)	7.37	5.41	(27)	8.04	4.46
Correlation between real difference and assumed difference		.51 ($p <$ .01)			−.08 (n.s.)	

These data indicated that targets as a group differed from their judges more than the judges assumed they did (Real Difference for each judge—target pair minus Assumed Difference for the same pair: $t = 5.58$, $p <$ .0005); but, as in the total score analyses, this bias tended to be more characteristic of low than high Mach judges ($t = 1.76$, $p <$ .05).

Most important, as in the total score analyses, the Real Difference measure can be used to interpret the Assumed Difference measure. The question is: did the judges' assumptions of how their targets differed in answering the Mach items represent a perception of real difference, or were they unrelated to real differences? To answer this question, we can say that the assumed differences reflect accurate perception if judges who chose an actually similar target then guessed him as being similar, while those who chose an actually different target guessed him as differing more from themselves. To measure the extent to which guessed similarity varied with real similarity we correlated the Real Difference measure for each judge–target pair with the Assumed Difference measure for the same pair. For the high-Mach judges this correlation was .51 and respectably significant. (For the extreme high Machs — n = 16 — it was .62.) Apparently, high Machs' assumptions of similarity and difference, even at the item-by-item level, reflected accurate perceptions or inferences of real similarities and differences. Among the low-Mach judges the correlation between real and assumed differences was −.08. (In the lowest-Mach third of the judges — n = 18 — it was −.01.) Clearly, the Assumed Difference scores for low Machs represented a bias of the judge unrelated to actual characteristics of the target.

The item-by-item correlation measures, shown in Table XII-4, tell the same story. These measures show the extent of similarity between two patterns of responding across the 20 items. (All operations were performed on Fisher's z transformations; final results were converted back into r values.) First, as shown in Table XII-4A the responses middle and low Machs attributed to their targets correlated with their own responses, while high Machs showed no significant tendency to assume similarity. Second, since there was a z score representing each of the correlation measures for each judge–target pair, it was possible to correlate them with each other. As shown in Table XII-4B, high Mach judges' assumptions of similarity in response pattern tended to correlate with real similarity between them and their targets (r = .43, p < .05). For low-Mach judges, however, this correlation was approaching significance in the negative direction (r = −.40, p < .05). Apparently, the low-Mach judges tended to "perceive" more similarity the *less* it actually existed.

TABLE XII-4A

Guessing Accuracy, Real Similarity, and Assumed Similarity

Mean Correlation Between Judge's and Target's Responses,
Item by Item, Over All 20 Mach IV Items

	Mean item-by-item correlations		
	Guessing Accuracy J's guesses for T & T's own prior responses	Real Similarity J's own prior responses & T's own prior responses	Assumed Similarity J's guesses for T & J's own prior responses
High-Mach judges (n = 16)	.25	.22	.23
Middle-Mach judges (n = 17)	.07	.15	.50 (p < .025)
Low-Mach judges (n = 18)	.01	.16	.35 (p < .10)

TABLE XII-4B

Guessing Accuracy, Real Similarity, and Assumed Similarity

Correlations Between Pairs of Correlations [a]

	Real similarity and assumed similarity	Guessing accuracy and real similarity	Guessing accuracy and assumed similarity
High-Mach judges (n = 16)	.43 ($p < .05$)	.20	.21
Middle-Mach judges (n = 17)	-.18	.58 ($p < .01$)	-.29
Low-Mach judges (n = 18)	-.40 ($p < .05$)	.51 ($p < .025$)	-.28

[a] Computed on Z transformations.

The only other correlations that were significant in both the squared discrepancy measures and the correlation measures were between Real Difference and Prediction Error (Real Similarity and Prediction Accuracy) for the middle- and low-Mach judges. These suggest that for these judges accuracy in guessing targets' specific responses depended upon real similarity. Thus, apparent accuracy reflected assumed similarity, but was not related to it because there judges tended to assume similarity for all targets, while only some were actually similar.

HIGH MACHS SIZE UP OTHERS IN RELATION TO THEMSELVES. The high Machs were consistently accurate in estimating how others differed from themselves, while the lows were equally consistent in underestimating differences. The highs were accurate in guessing both the direction and amount of difference in Mach score between themselves and their targets as a group. However, they were also accurate in guessing the direction in which their specific target person differed, and how much he differed. The same pattern turned up in the item-by-item analyses. The extent to which high Machs attributed similar item responses to their targets correlated with the extent to which the target had actually given similar responses previously. These correlations could not have been a statistical artifact of the highs' more accurate conception of the average popularity of each item. Consistently guessing the popular response to each item would make them more accurate in guessing which *items* targets generally had answered more like they had previously, and which less. But it could not account for their discriminating which *targets* were more similar, over all 20 items, and which less.

The highs' accurate discrimination between their target persons and themselves appears to provide clear evidence of accuracy in perceiving specific, designated target persons. That is, the highs' guesses were apparently influenced by some actual characteristics of their target persons as well as by their own internal judging processes. This finding indicates that their performance could not have been based solely on an accurate conception of others in general, or even on the judge's accurate conception of how others in general differed from himself.

This finding appears to pose a paradox. Our initial prediction was that highs would be more accurate judges of others in general, but would be less apt to detect individual differences. In fact, their guesses did not distinguish high- from low-Mach targets. How, then, did they manage to peg the individual differences between the particular target and themselves? To resolve the paradox we have to distinguish between what high Machs do and the incidental consequences of what they do that were detected by the task. The results of the task would seem to indicate that highs are accurate in locating others with respect to themselves, but we propose that what high Machs actually do is size up where *they* stand in relation to others and in fact attend to what others are like only incidentally in the process of locating themselves. If the high Machs characteristically sized up where they stood vis-a-vis the competition in the preceding Legislature games (while lows were more absorbed in the issue content and specific conversations), subsequently when the person perception task was introduced, the highs would already have a basis for then, on the spot, making the reverse inferences — from "where I stand, vis-a-vis him" to "where he, therefore, must be vis-a-vis me."

This formulation is consistent with the assumption that high Machs are more detached in their view of others, and also more detached in viewing their own attitudes and values (as indicated in the Legislature study in Chapter XI). Detachment implies keeping the self (in the sense of personal feelings) out of evaluative judgements. If high Machs see themselves and others objectively, this would give them the perspective to see exactly where they stand with respect to others, and then infer, if necessary, how others differ from themselves. The accumulation of such experiences with fellow students over time would account for their accuracy in placing "others in general" on the Mach dimension. Low Machs' assumed inclination to become emotionally involved, on the other hand, would reduce their detachment, objectivity, and perspective. This distinction will be examined further.

PERCEIVING INDIVIDUAL DIFFERENCES

Although low Machs underestimated the Machiavellianism of others in general, they accurately described high-Mach targets as more Machiavellian than low-Mach targets. This is consistent with our impression that low Mach's orientation toward others is more open, emphatic, somehow in touch with who or what the other is as a person, distinct from other persons.

The low Machs' accurate differentiation of high- and low-Mach targets was not due to their targets' being actually more discriminable. The mean scores of their high- and low-Mach targets, shown in Fig. XII-1 and Table XII-5, differed by 32 points; those of the highs' targets differed by 30 points (n.s.). The low Machs' discrimination could not have been due to their assumptions of similarity, either, since there was no tendency for the higher of the low-Mach judges to choose higher Mach targets. The correlations between the initial Mach scores of judge and target were .09 (n.s.) for the low-Mach judges, and .03 for highs. And, although the high-Mach judges as a group did estimate higher scores for their targets than lows did, in neither group of judges considered separately did the judges' estimates correlate with their own scores. These correlations were .20 (n.s.) for the low Machs, and .004 for the highs.

An alternative way to measure differential responses to high- and low-Mach target persons is to correlate the actual score of the target with the score computed from his judge's guesses. As might have been expected, this correlation for the group of high-Mach judges was effectively zero ($r = .10$, n.s.). For the low-Mach judges it was .29 ($p < .10$). For the extreme low-Mach group (sextiles 1 and 2, $n = 18$), it was .39, still only approaching significance at the .10 level. Thus, low-Mach judges discriminated individually whether their specific target person was relatively higher or lower in Machiavellianism, as shown in Table XII-2 and Fig. XII-1, but they were less consistent *as a group* in guessing how much higher or lower he was than other targets. This again suggests that they shared no consensual conception of how Machiavellian others are in general against which they then compared their specific target. Apparently, the low Machs' accuracy was specific to the particular judge—target pair.

It was noted above that the high Machs' overall accuracy could have been based on realistic inferences about fellow students in general, rather than accurate descriptions of their chosen target persons. On the other hand, the low Machs' relative accuracy in differentiating high- and low-Mach target persons could not possibly have been solely the result of private conceptions about students in general. Clearly, their guesses for their targets must have been influenced, somehow, by reference to the particular person whose responses they were trying to guess.

The high Machs' accuracy in detecting differences between themselves and particular targets also implies perception. The difference between the high and low Machs' judging accuracy appears to be that the highs' accuracy was specific to themselves as a reference point. The low-Mach judges were inaccurate in pegging the other's scoring position and his particular item responses in relation to their own position and responses, but were more accurate in guessing targets' scoring positions in terms of where the target himself actually was.

SYSTEMATIC VERSUS UNSYSTEMATIC ACCURACY

The high Machs as a group showed no consistent error tendencies. They neither over- nor underestimated targets' Machiavellianism, nor did they attribute similarity to their targets indiscriminately. They were as accurate on the more discriminating items as on the less discriminating ones, and were as accurate for low-Mach targets as for highs. In short, their errors appeared to be random, and appeared to be randomly distributed around an accurate central conception. Most of the low Machs' consistencies were error tendencies. They tended to attribute similarity to their targets indiscriminately. Consequently, they underestimated others' Machiavellianism. Since their assumptions of similarity were indiscriminate, what accuracy they showed (in approximating actual scores of targets) was related to real similarity. Consequently, they were less accurate for high- than low-Mach targets, and less accurate on the more discriminating items in the scale. Most of these error tendencies appeared in the item-by-item comparisons as well as in the total score analyses. Yet, in spite of the low Machs' systematic error tendencies and the highs' lack of them, there was no difference between the two groups in guessing their target's specific item responses. Somehow the lows compensated for their systematic errors but not by any systematic accuracies we were able to detect.

These differences again suggest that the low Machs' accuracy was specific to particular items for particular targets. In contrast, the high Machs' lack of consistent error tendencies, together with their lack of greater accuracy in guessing targets' specific item responses is consistent with the interpretation that they disregard individual differences. They deal with others, and the task of guessing their responses, cognitively from an accurate general conception rather than empathically, and are more accurate on the average than in particular.

How can we explain low Machs' pervasive error tendencies in the response-guessing task? From the *post hoc* perspective of subsequent research, the best explanation seems to be that guessing another's response to an attitude item is a cognitive task, and low Machs' empathy is noncognitive in nature (see Chapter XIV). Forced by the task to translate empathic feelings of closeness into cognitive attitude descriptions, the low Machs tended to attribute their own responses to their targets. This interpretation says that the low Machs' feeling or intuition for what kind of person the target was pulled their guesses in the right direction for their particular target person, sometimes on the right items. Whether these empathic feelings should be labeled perceptual or not depends first upon how perception is defined, and second, upon a more precise specification of the proposed empathy.

This is not to imply that low Machs are less cognitive than highs. Recall that it was they, not the highs, who accurately translated the difference between high- and low-Mach targets into its cognitive representation on the Mach scale. Low Machs do appear to be more emotionally involved with their cognitions, and, as shown by the Legislature study (Chapter XI), they can be distracted by such involvements. From this point of view, their assumption of similarity can be seen as a distraction created by involvement with their targets. This would imply that low Machs' personal orientation had two different effects. First, it led to a kind of empathy or openness which put the low Mach in touch with what the other was actually like. Second, it made the low Mach more susceptible to becoming involved with the other, which distracted him in translating what he sensed the other to be like into the terms required by the task. Thus, in translating their perceptions of the target resulting from empathic openness the low Machs interwove a constant error — they also translated the feeling of empathy itself into the cognitive terms of the task — attitudinal similarity. These speculations are consistent with the contrast between high and low Machs' performances in this study. The highs, assumed to have an impersonal orientation toward others, showed none of the positive results of empathy (awareness of how high and low targets differed on the Mach scale). They clearly showed no evidence of distraction (involvement) in the form of assumptions of similarity.

In summary, it is proposed that the low Mach sees where another is in his own right, but is too personally involved to see how the other differs from himself. In contrast, the high disregards individual differences between others, but is uncannily accurate in locating others in relation to himself, both in general and in particular. Or alternatively, the high Mach assesses his *own* standing vis-a-vis the competition, and attends to what the other is like only incidentally in the process.

This speculation also makes sense of some apparently contradictory data. Danielian (1964) studied perceptual accuracy using five of the Cline and Richards (1960) movies of target persons being interviewed, and found low Machs superior to highs in detecting individual differences, as we did, but also (though not significantly) in estimating the average responses of all targets. In Danielian's study, the judges had no live, face-to-face interaction with their targets. If the high Machs' accuracy depends upon assessing the other in relation to himself, and if this requires direct interaction, this difference alone could account for the difference in results. Similarly, because of the lack of live interaction, Danielian's low Machs may have become less involved with their targets.

Up to this point we have considered how high and low Machs differed as judges of a fellow subject. However, high and low Machs also differed as target persons. Although no predictions were made for these data, the more interesting comparisons will be presented for their heuristic value.

HIGH VERSUS LOW MACHS AS TARGET PERSONS

DECEPTIVELY UNTRANSPARENT HIGH MACHS. High Machs were overchosen as target persons. The average Mach score of all the target persons (each counted as often as he was chosen) was 107.96, higher than the average score (102.77) in the group of judges from which they were selected ($t = 2.31, p < .025$). The ns in Table XII-2 show that this was due to a general tendency of both high- and low-Mach judges to choose more high Machs as targets. Out of 25 high Machs and 29 lows available altogether, 30 judges chose a high Mach as a target, and only 21 chose a low (three chose a stooge). In fact, the highest Mach scale scorer available was significantly overchosen over the eight groups of subjects run ($p < .025$); the eight lowest scorers were somewhat but not significantly underchosen ($p < .10$). Recall that subjects had been instructed to select the one other member of the group whom they thought they could size up best. The high Machs evidently *appeared* most predictable.

Ironically, these apparently transparent high Machs turned out to be harder to predict. The judges' over- and underestimates for their targets are shown in Fig. XII-4. The Machiavellianism of high Mach targets was underestimated (by 18 points) more than that of lows was overestimated (by 7 points, $p < .025$). The high-Mach targets were underestimated by both high-Mach judges ($t = 3.61, p < .005$) and by low-Mach judges ($t = 4.38, p < .0005$). Low-Mach targets were overestimated by high-Mach judges ($t = 3.78, p < .005$), but were guessed almost exactly by fellow lows.

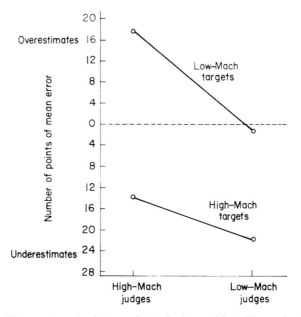

FIG. XII-4. High machs are harder to predict: judges' mean Mach IV error for high- and low-Mach target persons.

Tables XII-5A and 5B show the data represented in Fig. XII-4. All judges as a group made smaller errors for target persons similar to themselves in Machiavellianism, and larger errors for opposites. However, this was due almost entirely to the low-Mach judges; it was not true of highs. The results were the same when absolute values of the judges' errors were used. Again, for low-Mach judges, the high-Mach targets were clearly more difficult ($p < .005$). Again, for high-Mach judges high- and low-Mach targets were equally difficult ($p < .20$). By either measure, high-Mach targets were more deceptive for low-Mach judges than low-Mach targets were for high-Mach judges ($t = 2.11\ p < .025$). The results were the same when the target's Mach V score was used as the criterion, and also appeared in item-by-item analyses.

TABLE XII-5A

High Machs are Harder to Predict:
Mean Mach IV Scores of High- and Low-Mach
Target Persons, and their Judge's Estimates

	High-Mach targets			Low-Mach targets		
	(n)	Target's score	Judge's estimate	(n)	Target's score	Judge's estimate
High-Mach judges	(14)	121.43	107.14	(10)	91.50	108.70
Low-Mach judges	(16)	119.62	97.56	(11)	87.91	86.09
All judges combined	(30)	120.46	102.03	(21)	89.62	96.86

TABLE XII-5B

High Machs are Harder to Predict:
Judge's Estimate Minus Target's Score (based on figures in Table XII-5A)

	Mean judging error for		Difference in size of error	t	p<
	High-Mach targets	Low-Mach targets			
High-Mach judges	-14.29[a]	17.20	2.91	—	—
Low Mach judges	-22.06	-1.82	20.14	2.78	.01
All judges combined	-18.43	7.24	11.19	2.16	.025

[a] -14.29 = 107.14 minus 121.43 (from Table XII-5A).

The high Machs' deceptiveness was not due to their differing from their judges more than low-Mach targets differed from theirs. The high targets averaged 16 points higher than their judges; lows averaged 10 points below theirs ($t = 1.27$, $p < .10$). In terms of absolute discrepancies, the highs differed from their judges by 19 points, lows by 14 ($t = 1.39$, $p < .10$). Rather, the high-Mach targets appear to have been simply less transparent. The correlation between the amount of difference in Mach score separating the judge and his target and the amount of difference estimated by the judge tended to be positive for judge–target pairs in which the target was a low Mach ($r = .37$, $p < .05$); but for pairs in which the target was a high Mach this correlation was literally zero ($r = .002$).

Why where the high Machs overchosen as targets? They had won in one of the preceding games, lost (nonsignificantly) in another, and tied in the third. Further, observers' records of the bargaining during the games showed no differences between high and low Machs. The finding that high Machs were overchosen as prediction targets with no reason for which we have evidence is similar to the finding in the Con Game (Chapter VIII) that high Machs were overchosen as coalition partners without having made more or better coalition offers than others had. We have long suspected that high Machs are visible to the naked eye. In the Machiavel study (Chapter V) observers alerted to the dimension were able to identify high- and low-Mach subjects. In two studies since then naive subjects have chosen high Machs over lows for different purposes and in quite different situations. And a major finding of the present study was that low Machs, although not highs, clearly separated high- and low-Mach target persons on the appropriate descriptive dimension.

Why were the high Machs harder to predict? They did not differ from their judges in Mach score more than lows differed from theirs. Yet, judges who chose a low-Mach target tended to be accurate in estimating how much he differed from themselves, while those who chose a high were not.

Obviously, the high Machs had "given off" information that led to their being overchosen as targets. Evidently, the information they gave bore little relation to their actual attitudes as tapped by the Mach scale. Perhaps part of the high-Mach strategy is to act open, honest, and transparent. Or, perhaps high Machs are open, honest and transparent, but others just cannot believe how Machiavellian they really are. Conversely, the information given off by low Machs evidently gave a more accurate picture of where they stood on such issues. Combining the findings for judges and targets, we would bet now that high Machs size others up in relation to themselves, but do not give others the kind of information to do likewise. Low Machs, on the other hand, give off exactly the kind of information another can use to locate them, both absolutely and in relation to himself, and lows can locate others' relative positions in the population, but not in relation to themselves.

OTHER IMPLICATIONS

The group of target persons chosen by high-Mach judges did not differ in average Mach score from those chosen by low Machs (108.96 vs. 106.70, n.s.). Since the two groups of targets did not differ, the difference in the judges' estimates sheds some light on high and low Machs' images of their interpersonal environment. The average Mach score computed from high Machs' guesses was 108, 8 points (roughly half a standard deviation) above the theoretical neutral point on the scale, and an almost veridical approximation of the average score in the low Machs' group of targets as well as in their own. However, the mean score computed from low Machs' guesses was 93, 7 points below theoretical neutral, and 15 points (approximately one standard deviation) less Machiavellian than the highs' more accurate image ($t = 3.69, p < .005$).

These contrasts shed some light on high Machs' interpersonal effectiveness. By conventional standards they gave an unflattering picture of others. Apparently, they assume that people in general are not to be trusted. However, they had given an even less flattering picture of themselves initially; they were also accurate in describing others as not quite as Machiavellian as themselves. Although we have no data on whether this was done knowingly, our hunch is that most high Machs are aware that they are more Machiavellian than others. An even more subjective impression is that they accept the difference at least with equanimity and more frequently as an evidence of astute common sense. On the other hand, low Machs apparently assumed, incorrectly, that people in general are non-Machiavellian and can be trusted. This more idealistic image of their interpersonal environment would appear to be unrealistic.

The differences between high and low Machs as target persons fits in with the same picture. Although high Machs were overchosen by all judges, and were more difficult to predict for all judges combined, they were especially and consistently more deceptive for low-Mach judges. This undoubtedly reflects the low Machs' tendencies to assume similarity. The question is whether it reflects a tendency to assume similarity in general or only on tests of person perception. If low Machs generally attribute non-Machiavellian motives to the high Machs' Machiavellian behaviors, this would account for the highs being more difficult for them to size up accurately. It would also have an obvious bearing on the highs' success as manipulators.

In this study there were two indications of significant accuracy that can clearly be attributed to perceptions of the relevant target persons. One was that low-Mach judges did discriminate between high- and low-Mach target persons. The most puzzling evidence of accuracy was that high Machs' assumptions of similarity and difference correlated with real similarities and differences between themselves and their targets.

Multiple significance tests on the same data were reported. These should be regarded as different views of a single finding. An equally dire statistical sin is that the observations were not all independent. The same person, usually the highest Mach in the group, was often selected as target by two or three of the other group members. Since this particular person was usually also more difficult to predict, the judges who chose him would have a selective disadvantage. This probably did not seriously distort the comparisons between high- and low-Mach judges since both chose more high- than low-Mach targets, but it could distort the average picture of accuracy which might be inferred. On the other hand, our judges may have had a significant advantage compared to those in previous research, since ours were allowed to choose a single target person from six potential candidates.

Finally, no evaluation of the unanticipated findings can be offered. Obviously, conclusions must depend upon replications.

SUMMARY

The results of this research suggest that Machiavellianism is related to accuracy in perceiving others. After playing a semicompetitive bargaining game in a seven-man group for 2 hr, subjects were instructed to select one member of the group whom they thought they could size up most accurately, and fill in the Mach IV scale as they thought their target person had previously.

High-Mach subjects saw others as more Machiavellian than lows saw them, and it was the highs who were accurate. Their estimates of their target's Machiavellianism came closer to their specific target person's Mach V score than lows' did, and the average of their estimates for their targets matched the actual average of their targets' scores on both Mach IV and Mach V.

Although low Machs consistently underestimated their target's Machiavellianism, they did accurately describe high-Mach targets as more Machiavellian than low-Mach targets. High-Mach subjects made no such discrimination. In spite of this possible perceptual accuracy of the low Machs, they were less accurate than highs on most of the derivative measures.

High Machs were most consistently superior to lows in detecting similarities and differences between their targets and themselves. While low Machs did no better than chance in guessing whether their target was higher or lower than themselves in Machiavellianism, misjudged how much or little he differed from themselves in Mach score, and assumed similarity indiscriminately, the high Machs were more accurate in each of these details. This suggested that low Machs see how a particular other differs from others in general, but are too personally involved to see how he differs from themselves. In contrast, highs see how others differ from themselves both in general and in particular, but pay little attention to how a particular other differs from others in general.

A second unanticipated finding was that high and low Machs differed as target persons. These differences in how they were seen by others, combined with their differences as judges of others, shed some light on the high Machs' success as manipulators. First, highs were estimated as less Machiavellian than they actually were. Second, they were apparently perceived as more transparent, understandable, or predictable. In fact, they were less predictable, especially for low Machs. These same deceptively untransparent high Machs were, in turn, not deceived about others. Although they did not discriminate how one target differed from another, they were accurate on the average, and they were also accurate in estimating others as less Machiavellian than themselves.

CHAPTER XIII   NO DISSONANCE
FOR MACHIAVELLIANS [1]

Karen Bogart, Florence Geis,
Marguerite Levy, and Philip Zimbardo

"Dissonance," in situations like the one in this study, is the uncomfortable state of having just done something without quite enough justification. Social psychologists have been interested in this situation primarily because one of its consequences is attitude change. Volumes of research (e.g., Brehm & Cohen, 1962; Festinger, 1957; Zimbardo, 1969) show that once caught in this bind, most people try to save face. Saving face typically involves bolstering the justification for what they did by altering what they know or believe. Thus, having "voluntarily" argued against a belief, they change the belief to fit the argument. In other words, belief-behavior inconsistency leads to dissonance reduction in the form of attitude change.

The present study sheds some light on getting into the state of dissonance as well as getting out of it, in terms of the Machiavellianism of the subject involved.

Such dissonance situations are by definition irrational. The person allows himself to be persuaded into "freely choosing" to do something he would not have done otherwise — with inadequate justification. Reducing the dissonance created by the irrational behavior then compounds the irrationality by a further distortion of reality — changing the initial belief to make it consistent with the irrational behavior. What this boils down to, as Festinger originally pointed out, is that cognitions representing private opinions are often easier to change than those representing publicly verifiable actions.

Previous research (the Legislature study, Chapter XI, and The Eye of the Beholder, Chapter XII) indicated that high Machs are less likely to be distracted from a cognitive analysis of the situation by emotional involvements, but there were no data on how they might respond to conflicts among cognitions. In fact, two opposite predictions could have been made.

(1) Since high Machs are less distracted by emotional involvements, they should be able to avoid dissonance better than low Machs; since they are less personally involved with their cognitions, they should show less need to save face by changing cognitions when they do violate them.

---

[1] This research was originally reported (Geis, Bogart, & Levy, 1967) at the annual meeting of the Eastern Psychological Association, Boston, April 7, 1967.

(2) On the other hand, if high Machs attend to cognitions, and rely on them more consistently than low Machs do, a conflict among cognitions might have a greater effect on them so that they would show more dissonance reduction than lows.

The present study began as pure dissonance research based on Zimbardo's (1960) proposal that an unattractive communicator might be more effective than an attractive one in producing private attitude change in a forced-compliance situation. After complying with a request by an attractive persuader, subjects could use his attractive characteristics to justify having violated their own beliefs. With their overt behavior justified, there would be no dissonance, and consequently no need to change their private attitudes to support their behavior. However, the opposite should be true of complying with a request from an unattractive source. With no justification provided by characteristics of the persuader, the complying subject should be more likely to justify his action by changing his private attitude to support it. Both Smith (1961) and Zimbardo, Weisenberg, Firestone, and Levy (1969) demonstrated this effect. Asked to eat fried Japanese grasshoppers, complying subjects reported liking them more when the request had come from a negative communicator than when it had come from a positive communicator.

The question was, would the same effect hold when the source of persuasion was a peer group rather than an authority figure? Much group dynamics research indicated that in groups that are more attractive to their members more members conform to group norms. (In this research, the group's attractiveness was called "cohesiveness"; see Cartwright & Zander, 1960.) For example, Back (1951) manipulated attractiveness in three different ways and found that more influence was attempted and accepted in the more attractive groups regardless of the reason for the group's attractiveness. The general import of this and other studies was that more attractive groups have more influence on members' attitudes. But according to dissonance theory, complying with an attractive group can be justified in the same way as complying with an attractive persuader. The subject can violate his own beliefs and do as the others want because, for example, he likes them and wants them to like him. On the other hand, complying with an unattractive group would leave the subject with no such justification. One of the ways he could justify his behavior would be to change his private attitude to support it.

A problem in testing this prediction was how to prevent subjects who complied with an unattractive group from increasing their feeling of attraction to the group, rather than changing their attitude toward the behavior induced. The first part of our solution was to use a socially questionable act, cheating, as the dissonant behavior. In spite of rumors and suspicions about students' classroom behavior, most observations (e.g., Orne, 1962; Rosenthal, 1964; as well as our own informal observations) indicate that the norm for students in the role of subjects in an experiment is to comply with what the experimenter is perceived as wanting. To prevent the subject from increasing his liking for his group rather than increasing his endorsement of cheating, a "personality" test was given first. Then, just preceding the experimental session, the subject was given feedback on these test results for his group. These showed that the subject himself had extremely desirable personality characteristics and, for the high dissonance (unattractive group) condition, that the other group members were clearly inferior — definitely not the kind of people one would seriously like or want to emulate.

In pretesting, both three-person groups (a naïve subject and two experimental confederates) and two-person groups (a subject and one confederate) were used. Since the two-person groups were sufficiently effective in obtaining compliance, and were more efficient, only dyads were used in obtaining the data to be reported.

Thus far this is a pure dissonance experiment. The basic paradigm was simple. Subjects were put in a dissonant situation by having their team partner urge them to cheat on a test in an experiment. For half the subjects the partner was a liked, high-prestige person; for the others he was an unliked, low-prestige person. To create the unattractive partner condition, the subject was led to believe that his partner was not particularly bright and had serious personality defects as well. Cheating in this condition could not be justified by liking or admiring the partner. Consequently, and theoretically, it should be justified by attitude change. The subject should become more favorable toward cheating, or see himself as less honest than before. In the low-dissonance condition the subject was led to believe that his partner was a superior person in all respects. Subjects who cheated in this condition should not have to change their attitude about cheating or honesty; they could comply simply because an attractive partner urged them to.

Machiavellianism became a variable for two reasons. First, the cheating situation presented an ideal opportunity to test unexpected findings of Exline *et al.* (Chapter IV) that high Machs did not cheat more than lows in a similar situation. This was surprising, since high scores on the Mach scale clearly represent rejection of conventional morality. Exline proposed that the high Machs were more successful in resisting their partner's attempt to manipulate them. However, Exline's induction was powerful. The subject found himself implicated in his partner's cheating whether he liked it or not. From the inference that high Machs resist being manipulated, we predicted that in a cheating situation modeled after Exline's, if the subject had a genuine choice about going along with his partner or not, the high Machs would actually cheat less than lows.

The second reason for injecting Machiavellianism into dissonance was as a measure of attitude change. The dissonance prediction required pre- and postmeasures of attitudes toward cheating and honesty. Since cheating is socially condemned, it was felt that attitudes on the less-specific dimension of conventional morality in general might be more sensitive to attitudinal changes. [McGuire (1960) has shown that attitude change on a specific issue generalizes to logically implicated statements.] Although no Mach scale item specifically refers to cheating on tests, scores on the Mach scale can be interpreted as representing a continuum from endorsement to rejection of conventional morality.

The experimental design had a high- and a low-dissonance condition, created by describing the subject's partner as either unattractive or attractive. Within each dissonance condition high- and low-Mach subjects, classified by initial Mach score, were observed. The dissonant behavior, urged by the subject's partner, was cheating on the experimental task. Two behaviors were of interest: first, the frequency of cheating by high- and low-Mach subjects; second, cognitive change, measured by change in Mach scores, from before to after cheating.

PROCEDURE

At the beginning of the spring semester, 1966, 74 male undergraduates, recruited from the subject pool of the introductory psychology course at New York University were pretested on the Mach scales. They were told it was a "personality test." To convince even the skeptics that it really was a personality test, it was prefaced by four original inkblots to interpret. In this sample the mean score on Mach IV was 102.70, with a standard deviation of 13.73. The mean and standard deviation on Mach V were 106.00 and 11.21. Since scores on the two forms correlated .70, the two scores of each subject were averaged, and the distribution was divided at the median, 104.22, giving 37 high Machs (mean score = 113.11) and 37 lows (mean score = 95.02).

Sixty-one subjects — 33 high Machs (mean score = 114.09) and 28 lows (96.07) — subsequently participated. The remaining 13 either could not be located or scheduled, or failed to keep appointments. Each session was conducted by a female experimenter. The naive subject was paired with a pretrained male confederate playing the role of the other subject. Subjects were told that the purpose of the experiment was to determine whether teams of people who are similar in personality are more or less efficient than teams who are dissimilar, and that accordingly some of the teams for the experiment were selected so that the two members were very much alike, and other teams would have two members very different from each other.

The subject was then, privately, given the "results" of his own personality test — a mimeographed page titled "Individual Diagnostic Evaluation," containing scales labeled Creativity, Self-Actualization, Neurotic Tendencies, Intelligence

Estimate, etc. The subject's name appeared at the top, and the scales were marked to show a highly attractive personality picture. This manipulation was an attempt to prevent subjects from identifying or sympathizing, later, with the unattractive partner, but was administered identically to all subjects.

The dissonance manipulation was a description of the subject's partner, given to the subject by the experimenter.

HIGH-DISSONANCE — UNATTRACTIVE-PARTNER CONDITION

For the high-dissonance condition, in which the subject was to have little external justification for cheating because of having an unliked, low-prestige partner, the experimenter continued, after giving the subject his own personality results:

> Now I suppose you are also wondering what your partner is like. You have been assigned to work with a partner who is pretty much *similar* to you, except that, unlike yourself, he did very poorly on this particular personality test, and has some weaknesses in some areas of psychological functioning. In view of the fact that the two of you are going to be working as partners, we feel that it is only fair to the both of you for you each to know something about the other. So what I have here is a description of some characteristics of each of you which I'll show you now and then your partner will see it when I talk to him.

The subject was given a page with the following information about his partner:

> NAME: [stooge's name appeared here]
> SCHOOL: School of Education
> FIELD OF SPECIALIZATION: Industrial Arts
> INTERESTS AND HOBBIES: [This and the following lines were left blank]
> PRIZES AND HONORS:
> ORGANIZATIONAL MEMBERSHIPS:

The same items of information about the subject, taken from his own previous report, appeared on the same page.

LOW-DISSONANCE — ATTRACTIVE-PARTNER CONDITION

For the low-dissonance condition, in which the subject was to have relatively good justification for cheating, because of having a liked, high-prestige partner, the experimenter gave the same introductory sentence, but continued: "You have been assigned to work with a partner who is pretty much *different* from you in personality, except that, like yourself, he did very well on this particular personality test. In view of the fact that the two of you are going to be working as partners..." (etc., as in the high-dissonance condition). The further information about this partner showed that he was a graduate law student whose hobbies were amateur photography and football. "Phi beta kappa, cum laude" was given as his prizes and honors, and he belonged to the American Photographer's Association.

The reader may have wondered why the unattractive partner was described as similar to the subject and the attractive partner as different, when traditionally groups have been made attractive to the subject by telling him that the others are like himself, and have been made unattractive by telling him they are different. Apparently either times have changed or the sophisticated undergraduates at this metropolitan university were a deviant group. Subjects in a pilot group used to standardize the partner-attractiveness manipulation were unanimously attracted to the partner who was "different," and were indifferent to outright disappointed at having a similar partner. So for the high and low attraction conditions, we simply switched the "similar" and "different" around.

After one or the other of the two partner descriptions had been given, all subjects were treated alike. Immediately after the partner attractiveness manipulation, a check on it was obtained on the pretext that attitudes and feelings toward partners might be needed to analyze the results of the team efforts. The stooge knew the two partner descriptions used in the study, but never knew which of them had been used; he was totally unaware of the Mach variable. He believed that the purposes of the "personality test" (Mach scales) were (a) to provide a rationale for giving alleged results to manipulate self-esteem during the session, and (b) to provide pre- and postmeasures of attitudes toward conventional morality.

THE CHEATING SESSION

After the second subject had also (presumably) been given his personality results and the summary description of the naive subject, the experimenter brought the two together for the experimental task, a specially constructed multiple-choice human relations problems test. Each item described a problem situation and was followed by three multiple-choice questions. In the first group of three problems (nine questions) the answers were obvious and reasonable. An example of an item and one of the three associated questions is:

> A man has a very ambitious wife. She wants him to try for a promotion to a higher position in his firm. The man is at present a junior executive. He is not altogether happy where he is but fears the extra responsibility that a higher position would entail. The wife suggests that he obtain psychotherapy to overcome his feelings of inferiority. The man feels ashamed to do this.

> 1. Who is most likely to have the best solution to the problem?
>   A. The man.
>   B. His wife.
>   C. Both of them together.

The second group of three problems was more difficult. In the last third of the test, the problems had no solution. For example:

Two children, a white boy and a Negro girl, ages 8 and 9, run up to a newspaper and candy stand operated by a blind vendor in an interracial neighborhood. They grab as many candy bars as they can carry and run off without paying. It is midafternoon. Observing are a housewife pushing a cart of groceries, a postman making his rounds, an appliance salesman on his way to work, a Negro college student on his way to school, and a middle-aged man walking a dog. The blind man does not know what has happened.

1. Who is most likely to have the best solution to the problem?
    A. The housewife.
    B. The appliance salesman.
    C. The postman.

In the test instructions subjects were warned that this was not a test of opinion; they were to answer strictly on the basis of the facts given in the problem.

As the two subjects finished the first set of problems, the experimenter received an apparently unexpected telephone call obviously demanding her presence elsewhere, at once. This device and parts of the following procedures were adapted from Exline *et al.* (Chapter IV). After first protesting that she was in the middle of a testing session, she finally acquiesced. In obvious consternation and confusion, she asked the subjects to continue the test alone. As a desperate afterthought she explained that she might be gone for some time, and finally asked the naïve subject to bring the test papers to her, on another floor of the building, when they finished.

She left, with footsteps echoing down the stairway, and the two subjects worked in silence on the second set of problems. Shortly after beginning the impossible problems (three situations, nine questions in all) the stooge sighed, groaned, wriggled in his seat, and looked generally distressed. Breaking his pencil, he went to get another from the experimenter's desk, and discovered the answer key to the test. He announced his find, hesitated, and said, "I'm going to use it. I don't want to look stupid."[2] He used the key and offered it casually to the naïve subject: "You wanna look?" If the subject refused, the stooge used it

---

[2]One additional manipulation was included in the design. Half of the high- and low-Mach subjects in each dissonance condition were told that they would work as a team first and individually second; the other half expected the reverse sequence. Since there was no second session, half of the subjects had the individual condition, and the other half had the team condition. For the individual condition, each answered all the questions alone on his own answer sheet, and the stooge's opening remark was the one given in the text. For the team condition the two subjects worked on the same answer sheet, but alternated in answering the questions. In this condition the stooge substituted, "I don't want our group to look stupid." It had been expected that cheating in the individual condition would make the subject feel more responsible and therefore more dissonant than cheating in the team condition. However, there were no differences in either compliance or attitude change between these two conditions overall, nor did they appear in any significant interactions. Accordingly, the data were combined to analyze the group attractiveness and Mach effects.

alone, but offered it again on the next problem: "You better look." If the subject still refused, the stooge continued cheating alone. At the final opportunity for the subject to cheat, the stooge said, "You'll *never* get this one. You've *gotta* look." At no time did the stooge announce answers out loud, or otherwise force or trick the subject into cheating. The stooge's pressure consisted of offering the answer key, advising and then urging the subject to use it, and setting the example, but the subject did have a choice about whether to comply or not. Subjects who accepted and looked at the proffered key were classified as complying. (No subject accepted it and then failed to look at it.) Since we were interested in how many high Machs would comply as compared to lows, the pressure situation was empirically constructed during pretesting so that about half of all subjects, overall, would comply.

When the naïve subject appeared at the appointed place with the test papers, he was given a second administration of the Mach IV scale. The difference between the subject's score just after the cheating session, and his Mach IV score at the beginning of the semester provided a measure of change in attitude toward conventional morality. After the Mach scale came a second check on the partner-attractiveness manipulation, then an open-ended opportunity to express suspicions and confess cheating, and finally a full explanation of all the procedures.

CHECK ON THE MANIPULATION

The partner-attractiveness manipulation was successful. Immediately after receiving the description of their partner from the experimenter, and before meeting him, subjects were asked, "How much do you like your partner, personally?" The same question was asked again after the session in the past tense. As shown in Table XIII-1, subjects given the attractive partner description liked their partner, both before and after the cheating session, significantly more than those given the unattractive description. Most important, subjects with the unattractive partner did not like him any more after the cheating session than they had before it. Thus, subjects who complied did not reduce dissonance by perceiving their partner as more attractive.

RESULTS

The only prediction involving Machiavellianism was that high Machs would comply less than lows when their partner urged them to cheat. After the

TABLE XIII-1

Check on the Attractiveness Manipulation:
"How well do you [did you] like your partner, personally?"[a]

	(n)	Attractive partner	(n)	Unattractive partner	t	p <
		Mean attraction to partner				
Presession ratings						
All Subjects	(29)	6.42	(32)	4.77	8.92	.01
Subjects who later complied	(17)	6.36	(11)	4.52	6.76	.01
Postsession ratings						
Subjects who had complied	(17)	6.29	(11)	4.81	3.93	.01
Difference						
Post minus pre for compliers	(17)	-.07 (n.s.)[b]	(11)	.29 (n.s.)[c]	—	—

[a] Answered on a 10-point scale: 1 = not at all; 10 = very much.
[b] t = .16, n.s.
[c] t = .83, n.s.

compliance data are presented, the dissonance theory prediction of attitude change will be examined.

COMPLIANCE IN CHEATING BY HIGH AND LOW MACHS

In spite of the difference between high and low Machs in endorsing conventional morality, the high Machs did not cheat more than the lows. Sixteen of the 33 high Machs cheated and 16 refused. (One became suspicious of the bogus telephone call, forcing an end to the session before the cheating induction.) Thirteen of the 28 low Machs cheated, and 15 refused. The lack of differential cheating between high and low Machs clearly supports Exline's (Chapter IV) finding, and equally clearly fails to support our own prediction that highs would cheat less than lows.

SELECTIVE COMPLIANCE. However, high and low Machs cheated and refused differently in the two dissonance conditions, as shown in Table XIII-2. Low Machs cheated as urged about half the time, regardless of condition. High Machs discriminated.

It proved almost impossible to induce the high Machs to cheat in the high-dissonance condition in which there was little justification for compliance. Only 5 of 18 complied, and even this proportion is questionable. Since we wanted to analyze attitude change data, we kept running high Machs in the high-dissonance condition until 5 could be classified as complying, and then stopped.

TABLE XIII-2

Number of Subjects Who Complied (Cheated) and Refused to Comply, by Mach and Dissonance Condition

	High Machs			Low Machs		
	Cheated	Refused to cheat	Total	Cheated	Refused to cheat	Total
High dissonance (low justification)	5	13	18	6	8	14
Low dissonance (high justification)	11	3	14	7	7	14
Total	16	16	32	13	15	28
	$\chi^2 = 6.22, p < .02.$			$\chi^2 < 1.00$, n.s.		

In contrast, high Machs rarely failed to cheat in the low-dissonance condition in which the attractiveness of the partner provided some reasonable justification for going along with him. Of the 14 run in this condition 11 cheated. And of the 3 who refused, 2 indicated on the postsession questionnaire that they had become suspicious during the session.

Further, the 5 high Machs who did comply in the high-dissonance condition tended to be lower in initial Mach scores than the 13 noncompliers ($t = 2.01, p < .10$). There was no significant difference between high-Mach compliers and noncompliers in the low-dissonance condition, or between low-Mach compliers and noncompliers in either dissonance condition. Combining this trend with the data on frequency of compliance, it appears that cheating was negatively related to Machiavellianism in the high dissonance condition.

MACH IV CHANGE AFTER CHEATING

According to dissonance theory, cheating at the suggestion of the attractive partner could be justified by liking him and seeking his esteem in return. Further, the attractive law student could have been viewed as a competent accomplice in a risky venture. On the other hand, subjects had little justification for cheating with the unattractive partner. Consequently, according to dissonance theory, those who did should change their private attitudes to make them consistent with being a cheater. They should describe themselves as less moral afterwards, compared to subjects who had complied with the attractive partner. The pre- and postadministrations of the Mach IV scale provided data on changes in endorsement of conventional morality.

Eight suspicious subjects, 7 noncompliers and 1 complier, were excluded from the attitude change analyses. Changes in Mach IV scores from before to after the experimental session for all nonsuspicious subjects ($n = 53$) are shown in Table XIII-3. The mean change in score for all subjects who cheated (combining those in the high and low dissonance conditions) was effectively zero ($+.04$ of a point on the Mach scale). Apparently cheating, in and of itself, had no simple overall effect on Mach scores.

When all nonsuspicious compliers (16 high Machs and 12 lows) were considered together, the dissonance theory prediction was supported, although the effect was extremely weak. The 11 subjects who cheated in the high-dissonance condition went up in Mach score (1.91 points) compared to the 17 in the low-dissonance condition who went down (by 1.29 points: $t = .87, p < .20$, one tailed).

This overall trend, however, was due entirely to the low Machs, as shown in Fig. XIII-1. The bar graphs show the net change in Mach IV score for all nonsuspicious subjects.[3]

High and low Machs who cheated showed opposite patterns of attitude change. The dissonance prediction was confirmed for low Machs. Lows who cheated in the high-dissonance condition with the unattractive partner providing low extrinsic justification lowered their endorsement of conventional morality; those who complied in the low-dissonance condition with the attractive partner providing more justification increased their endorsement. Although we had only 12 low Machs for this analysis, 6 in each condition, the difference in Mach IV score change between these two groups was significant ($p < .01$). Further, low Machs who complied in the high-dissonance condition described themselves as less moral compared to the combined group of noncompliers ($t = 5.95, p < .001$), while lows who cheated in the low-dissonance condition did not differ significantly from the noncompliers ($t = .66$, n.s.).

High Machs, on the other hand, showed exactly the opposite pattern. Those who cheated in the high-dissonance condition, without external justification, claimed to be more rather than less moral afterwards (although not significantly more moral), and those who cheated in the low-dissonance condition with some justification based on the partner's attractiveness did not change at all. The

---

[3] Only the Likert-format Mach IV was used after the session. Change scores for each subject were computed from his presession Mach IV to his postsession Mach IV. An *increase* in Mach score was assumed to represent a decrease in endorsement of conventional moral standards, and vice versa. In view of the unanticipated results, two-tailed p values are reported throughout the chapter, except as noted.

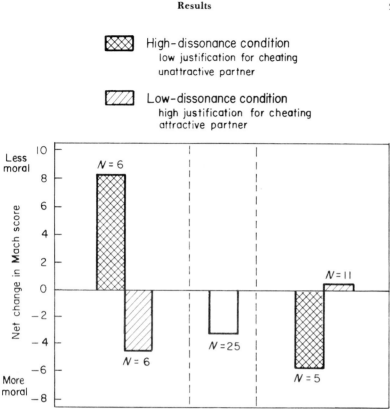

FIG. XIII-1. Mach IV change after compliance: net change in Mach score after cheating or refusing to cheat. High versus low dissonance for low-Mach compliers, $p=4.35$, $p < .01$; for high-Mach compliers, $p=2.10$, $p < .10$. High versus low-Mach compliers: in the high-dissonance condition, $p=4.05$, $p < .01$; in the low-dissonance condition, $p=1.95$, $p < .10$.

effects of the two conditions on the high Machs did not differ significantly $(p < .10)$. Further, those who cheated in the high-dissonance condition did not differ from the combined group of noncompliers $(t = 1.05$, n.s.$)$, while the non-changing cheaters in the low-dissonance condition did $(t = 2.11, p < .05)$.

MACH IV CHANGE AFTER REFUSING TO CHEAT. Twenty-five nonsuspicious subjects, 10 high Machs and 15 lows, refused to cheat. These subjects tended to increase their endorsement of conventional morality from before to after the cheating session, as would be predicted by dissonance theory. They dropped 3.08 points in Mach score $(p < .10)$. Again, this trend was due primarily to the low Machs (see Table XIII-3). The 8 who refused to cheat in the high-dissonance condition went down in Mach score (by 4.63 points; $t = 2.51, p < .05$). The high Machs who refused in the high-dissonance condition

TABLE XIII-3

Mean Change in Mach IV Score[a] from Before to After Experiment
for All Nonsuspicious Subjects

		All nonsuspicious subjects: n = 53, mean change = -1.43 (n.s.)						
		Cheaters				Noncheaters		
	(n)	Mean change	t	$p <$	(n)	Mean change	t	$p <$
All *Ss*	(28)	.04	.02	—	(25)	-3.08	1.92	.10
High Mach	(16)	-1.38	.65	—	(10)	-3.20	1.49	—
Low Mach	(12)	1.75	.63	—	(15)	-3.00	1.30	—
High-dissonance condition								
All *Ss*	(11)	1.91	.61	—	(17)	-3.47	2.37	.05
High Mach	(5)	-5.60	1.21	—	(9)	-2.22	1.04	—
Low Mach	(6)	8.17	3.74	.02	(8)	-4.63	2.51	.05
Low-dissonance condition								
All *Ss*	(17)	-1.29	.67	—	(8)	-2.50	.59	—
High Mach	(11)	.55	.25	—	(1)	-12.00	—	—
Low Mach	(6)	-4.67	1.31	—	(7)	-1.14	.25	—

[a] Positive numbers indicate a net increase in Mach score; negative number indicate a decrease.

showed no significant decrease (2.22 points; t = 1.04, p > .10), nor did low Machs in the low-dissonance condition. Only one nonsuspicious high Mach refused in the low-dissonance condition. These results are the same as those for complying subjects. Low Machs who refused to cheat in the high-dissonance condition, like those who did cheat, changed their beliefs to support their behavior. High Machs did not change their beliefs to support their behavior, and this was true for cheaters and noncheaters alike, and in the high- as well as the low-dissonance condition.

High Machs resisted getting into our dissonant situation, and the few who were enticed showed no dissonance reduction in the form of changing their beliefs to support their behavior. These results had not been predicted. Consequently, they inspired first a spate of *post hoc* theorizing to account for them, and second a replication study to test it. These will be considered next, but in the reverse order.

A REPLICATION

The replication (Bogart, 1968) used a similar cheating situation and experimental paradigm with a tighter control on the partner and his influence attempt. The experiment was presented to subjects as being concerned with whether more persuasive arguments could be produced by an individual or by a two-man team. Once again the teams were allegedly preselected to pair either similar or different partners, and high- and low-dissonance conditions were created as before. This time, though, subjects believed they were one of a group of six, so that there were, they thought, three two-man teams competing against each other in each session. However, each subject was in an individual booth and although given information about his partner, as before, never actually saw him. First, each subject planned and delivered a persuasive argument individually, and heard and evaluated five other presentations presented over the intercom system. In the second round, each planned an argument for his partner to deliver. The naive subject received a plan, supposedly from his partner, and delivered an argument. Then the proceedings were interrupted "temporarily" (actually to collect the postmeasures). Subjects believed that after the "midway break" their partner would deliver the argument they had prepared for him, and were also promised a third round in which they would work face to face with each other in both planning and delivering the argument.

Evaluations of the presentations after each round were promised, and were actually given after the first round. The subject received five evaluations of his own presentation, and five of his partner's from the supposed other subjects present. These showed that while his partner had done well in presenting a position the group already agreed with, he had not done well on one they opposed. (Subjects had a rigged tally of their group's opinions on all issues.) For the second round, the subject again drew a position contrary to the audience's belief. The written plans for his second-round presentation, supposedly from his partner, pointed out the obvious relation between agreeing with the audience and getting a favorable evaluation, and directly urged the subject to break the rules of the experiment (explicitly spelled out to subjects in taped instructions at the beginning of the session) and defend the opposite position. This was followed by three reasonable arguments in favor of the urged, opposite position. Subjects were then given time "to elaborate or revise" the plans sent by their partners, and then gave their presentations.

Subjects for this study were classified as high or low Mach on the basis of their scoring position above or below the median (104) on Mach V. Changes in endorsement of conventional morality were measured by changes in Mach IV score from two weeks before the experimental session to immediately following the subject's second speech in which he had either cheated, as urged, or refused to cheat. Eighty-seven male subjects, again recruited from the introductory psychology subject pool at New York University (spring, 1967), participated.

The results differed from the previous ones in one respect. This time the high Machs cheated more often (27 out of 41) than the lows (19 of 46; overall $\chi^2 = 4.30$, $p < .05$). The major results, however, held up. Again high Machs discriminated between the high- and low-dissonance conditions (the unattractive and attractive partner descriptions) in complying with the cheating suggestion. They complied significantly more often than they refused with the attractive partner. ($\chi^2 = 6.25$, $p < .05$), and refused as often as complying with the unattractive partner ($\chi^2 = .37$, n.s.). Again, low Machs did not discriminate. Nine of 21 cheated in the low-dissonance condition; 10 of 25 cheated in the high-dissonance condition.

The Mach IV change results also replicated. Low Machs showed the expected dissonance effect; highs did not. Lows who complied with the unattractive partner went up significantly in Mach IV score (i.e., endorsed conventional morality less) compared both to those who complied with the attractive partner ($F = 7.50$, $p < .05$), and compared to the noncompliers ($t = 2.45$, $p < .05$). High Machs who complied in the high-dissonance condition did not differ in Mach IV change from highs who complied under low dissonance ($F < 1.00$, n.s.) or from noncompliers ($t = 1.33$, n.s.).

These results are also supported by those of an independent investigation by Epstein (1969) using a different dissonance situation. Subjects in favor of fluoridating city water supplies were subtly pressured to "volunteer" to tape record an argument against fluoridation for an educational radio program for a college audience. A low-dissonance condition was created by having subjects silently read a prepared rational argument against fluoridation. In this study dissonance reduction was measured by attitude change on the fluoridation issue. Again low Machs showed a strong dissonance effect. They changed their attitudes, in the antifluoridation direction, more after role playing than after silent reading. High Machs did the opposite. They showed no change after role playing, and a significantly larger change in the direction of the arguments they had read silently.

DISCUSSION

The one distinction that seems to account for both the compliance data and the attitude change data is that high Machs decide for themselves what they will or will not do, and then act on their decision, while low Machs can be distracted by personal or emotional involvements which can lead them into agreeing to something they did not decide to do. This distinction can be derived from the detached, cognitive orientation of high Machs, compared to the personal, emotional orientation of lows, discussed in preceding chapters.

ON AVOIDING DISSONANCE

RATIONAL STRATEGY VERSUS EMOTIONAL DISTRACTION. The high-dissonance condition was designed to provide inadequate justification for cheating as the partner urged. It is this defining characteristic that makes dissonance situations irrational at the outset. One rational way to avoid dissonant behavior is to refuse to engage in it. This is not to imply that low Machs are less rational than highs. Rather, as in the Legislature study (Chapter XI), it appears that they can be distracted by emotional involvements. The distraction in the present situation was their partner's presence and his obvious desires. In Epstein's study, as in dissonance experiments generally, it is the experimenter's presence and desires.

COGNITIVE ANALYSIS VERSUS PERSONAL INVOLVEMENT. While high Machs refused to cheat in the high-dissonance condition, they showed no such reluctance in the low-dissonance condition or in Bogart's replication. Thus, their behavior was not a consequence of moral principles. They were quite willing to cheat when given greater justification. The image conveyed by the experimenter's description of the law student was both attractive and competent. The image of the metal shop student was made unattractive and not particularly competent as a partner in a risky cheating venture. Clearly, high Machs cheated or refused according to the cognitive, descriptive labels given them by the experimenter. They acted according to a decision based on *ideas about the person.* Low Machs' cheating and refusing to cheat was unrelated to the partner's label. We propose that they acted according to their *feeling for the person himself.* The stooge, of course, was the same *person* in both description conditions.

Then why did the low Machs cheat at all in the replication study in which they never saw their partner face to face? In fact, they did cheat slightly but not significantly less. To apply the distraction explanation, we must argue that involvement does not require face-to-face interaction. That is, involvement can occur by imagination. In the replication study informal observation suggested that all subjects believed they had a real partner. They had been told they had a partner, were given a description of him, reported on a form how much they liked him, heard him make a presentation in the first round, received evaluations of his presentation from the group, planned an argument for him to deliver in the second round, received plans from him for their own second-round presentation, and were told they would meet him face to face in the third round. It was evidently this image of a partner that some low Machs became involved with enough to comply.

This interpretation says that high Machs decided whether to cheat or not on the basis of the cognitive justification available, and acted on their decision. On the other hand, low Machs tended to be influenced by personal involvement with their partner. Thus, high Machs' behavior was independent of their partner's behavior; it depended upon their own decision based on prior information — the cognitive labels describing the partner. The low Machs' behavior was not independent of their partner; they were influenced by him, as a person, in the cheating situation, in addition to being influenced by their cognitions about him afterwards. We will return to the implications of these differences for understanding high and low Machs' interpersonal behavior after considering the differences in attitude change.

ON CHANGING COGNITIONS

The difference in Mach IV score changes between high and low Machs suggests that dissonance leads to attitude change by using a noncognitive, personal influence process to produce cognitive change. High-dissonance conditions are explicitly set up so that all the cognitive cues lead to a clear conclusion. However, there is also an experimenter, or assistant, or partner, who wants the subject to do exactly what all reason says he should not do. This person carefully gives the subject no *reason* (that is, no cognitive justification) for the irrational behavior, and in addition gives the subject the clear cognition that if he does do it, it is by his own choice. We propose that low Machs comply by their own choice only in the technical sense of the word. In fact, they comply because the other wants them to.

Actually, there are two behaviors involved. One is complying, doing as the other wishes, satisfying the other's needs. This is the choice low Machs make. However, complying also involves an overt activity which is irrational or counterattitudinal (e.g., cheating, eating grasshoppers, enduring electric shock, etc.). It is this *activity* that low Machs do not choose but perform only because it is a necessary concomitant of going along with the other's wishes. Typically, however, the induction to comply is phrased in terms of the activity. Once the low Mach accepts the experimenter's definition of his choosing to comply as a choice of the activity involved in complying, he has redefined the behavior to which he is committed — and reports the redefinition on the posttest.

The high Mach in the high-dissonance condition has a number of alternatives, all provided by detachment from others and from his own cognitions. One, discussed above, is simply to refuse to do what is urged. This should be a preferred alternative when the stakes are high — such as getting caught cheating — *and* when the pressure is minimal. The interpretation that low Machs choose to comply even when the activity involved is counterattitudinal, while highs are more likely to refuse, can also be applied to the results of a study by Jones *et al.* (1962). After feedback indicating that an interviewer disapproved of them as they had described themselves, low-Mach girls changed their self-descriptions, but high-Mach girls did not.

Suppose, however, that the potential cost to the subject is not high and the pressure is strong. The high Mach can acknowledge complying with a personal request and separate his compliance from endorsement of the activity involved. This argument is consistent with Epstein's reasoning. She pointed out that high scores on the Mach scale imply pragmatism: telling people what they want to hear, not giving real reasons, etc. Since such principles imply assertions contrary to belief, she argued that high Machs should be able to make counterattitudinal statements without changing their private belief more easily than lows. Our interpretation says the same thing in a different way: high Machs are more detached from the implications of their behavior; they can separate the content of a behavior from the reasons for engaging in it.

But there must certainly be some high Machs who would succumb to a noncognizable personal pressure and also accept the implicit definition that it was the activity and not just the compliance they had chosen. This is the predicament that leads to dissonance-reducing attitude change for low Machs. The highs' emotional detachment makes face saving less necessary. High Machs characteristically admit more socially undesirable attributes, and cognitive inconsistency may be motivating partly because it is socially undesirable. High Machs also *claim* to be masters of their own fate less than lows (see Chapter III), so they can admit to having done something inconsistent more easily than lows who think they have internal control. This argument is also in line with informal observations of subjects' reactions to learning that they have been deceived in an experiment. It is the low Machs who are more likely to be upset or angry until the reasons for the deception — and the reasonableness of their behavior in light of all they knew at the time — have been clarified. The high Machs' initial response is more likely to be appreciative curiosity and an increase in enthusiasm for the whole experiment. High Machs appear to be less upset at finding that they have been conned, have acted foolishly, or made a mistake. Thus, they do not have to try to justify their foolish behavior by changing their cognitions to support it.

In summary, high Machs have three ways of coping with what, for low Machs, is dissonance. All depend upon their detachment from others and from their own behavior. First, they can more easily refuse a request. Second, they can comply with a request and separate the choice to comply from endorsement of the activity involved. Third, if they do get caught, they can acknowledge it and maintain their initial position anyway.

HOW TO INFLUENCE A HIGH MACH. High Machs have appeared immune to persuasion by the subtleties involved in dissonance manipulations in three experiments, but it cannot be concluded that they are less persuasible than lows. In fact, they were consistently influenced by the *low*-dissonance conditions. In the two cheating experiments, they were more likely than low Machs to follow the suggestions of the attractive, high-prestige partner. And in Epstein's study they showed more change after silently reading the prepared rational argument against fluoridation than after role playing. This suggested that attitude change for high Machs may be predicted better by the Janis and Gilmore (1965) model of attitude change, which is essentially an incentive or learning theory model. The more reason, incentive, or reward high Machs are given for changing, the more they change. With smaller incentives or greater costs they change less or in the opposite direction. In our original study the high Machs who cheated with the attractive partner maintained their initial attitudes; those who cheated with the unattractive partner subsequently rejected such behaviors slightly (but not significantly) more than they had initially. This model also handles Epstein's results. In her situation the incentive was the prepared rational argument. Not only did the high Machs comply more with the greater incentive provided by the low-dissonance condition in all three studies, but they also complied more than lows overall when the cost of cheating — the objective risk of getting caught — was reduced from one study to the next. Again, we are not suggesting that low Machs do not also learn and change their beliefs for rational reasons. The difference seems to be that it is peculiarly they who can be induced to change for irrational reasons as well.

COGNITIONS AND CATHEXES

The finding that high Machs went along with the attractive partner more than the unattractive one, while lows complied with the stooge equally often under both labels suggested that high and low Machs were responding to different sets of cues. In the original study all subjects had two sources of information about their partner. One was the label — the verbal description and printed "demographic" information provided by the experimenter. The other source was seeing the actual person who played the role of their partner, being in his physical presence, with no verbal interchange at all prior to the cheating induction. This second source of information was carefully constructed to provide no relevant cognitive cues. The high Machs apparently ignored the "non-cognitive" cues, or were insensitive to them, and acted on the basis of the cognitive cues provided explicitly by the experimenter. The low Machs heard the same descriptions, and these did influence their cognitions, as was seen in the attitude change data. However, the low Mach's cognitions about the kind of person their partner was were not related to their overt behavior with him. Thus, we proposed that they cheated or refused at least partly on the basis of some personal feeling for their partner which developed in the face-to-face interaction between them.

These data can be compared with previous findings. In the present studies high Machs discriminated significantly between two allegedly different partners, but low Machs did not. In the Con Game (Chapter VIII) and in the Eye of the Beholder (Chapter XII), it was the lows who had discriminated between others who were different, while the highs did not. The difference between the two previous situations and the present ones was in the kind of cues available about the other person. In the previous studies subjects were given no explicit cues to discriminate, but the others were in fact different people. The reverse was true in the present studies. Although explicitly different cues were given, the others were in fact the same. In each case, then, low Machs' interpersonal behavior has been specific to the particular others in the situation, without authoritative cues that they differed, and in spite of false cues. In contrast, high Machs failed to discriminate between actually different others when given no explicit clues beforehand, and they did discriminate when given cues, even though no real difference existed. This pattern had held over three studies using different samples of subjects and different test situations: high Machs act by what they know, low Machs by what they feel.

The compliance data from the present studies can also be contrasted with the attitude change data. In complying, the high Machs responded according to the stooge's label but lows did not. However, in the attitude change data the lows responded differently to having cheated with the differently labeled stooges, while highs did not. The compliance data were based on the subject's overt actions in the physical (or imagined) presence of another, in the course of interaction, and in direct response to his stated desires. It is in this direct and overt responding that low Machs ignore labels and highs use them to guide their responses. The Mach IV change data, on the other hand, were measures after the fact of the subject's private cognitions.

If this contrast can be generalized, it would say that low Machs' overt action in the course of interaction does not follow systematically from their cognitions, but their subsequent cognitions are influenced by prior cognitions about their own behavior and the situation. On the other hand, high Machs use their cognitions to guide their actions but do not allow cognitions about their actions to influence their subsequent cognitions. This suggests that high Machs may have a very cognitive approach to the relations among their cognitions. Strictly on the basis of logic there is no reason why one should do only what he believes in, or should believe in everything he does. The feeling that actions and beliefs should be consistent is itself a belief. Low Machs apparently accept the "ought" in the consistency formula; high Machs apparently do not.

This interpretation also clarifies high Machs' relative rejection of conventional morality on the Mach scales in relation to their lack of indiscriminate cheating in the present studies. A high Mach who disagrees with the item, "Honesty is the best policy in all cases," is not thereby endorsing the principle of dishonesty in all cases.

MACHIAVELLIANISM AND CHEATING

We had predicted initially that high Machs would cheat less than lows when pressured by a partner. Obviously we had underestimated the inducing power of an attractive, prestigious partner. However, we can now formulate a more refined hypothesis in light of the data: high Machs will cheat more with an increase in incentive, and less with an increase in risk; low Machs will cheat more when the inducement is made more personal and offered repeatedly, and less if there are conflicting personal inducements.

In both of our studies, high Machs cheated more in the low-dissonance conditions. The intelligent and skillful partner presumably made getting caught appear less risky. Comparing the initial study in which half of the high Machs cheated and the replication in which two-thirds of them did provides some further hints. First, in the replication cheating was made to appear less risky, regardless of partner. Second, in the initial study the suggestion to cheat was given little rational support. In the replication the partner's note first stressed the reason for cheating (our audience only gives favorable evaluations to arguments supporting what they already believe), and went on to note the improbability of getting caught. Third, after receiving the suggestion subjects were allowed time "to elaborate or revise" the plans. This gave the subject time to evaluate the pros and cons of cheating, and arrive at a decision based on strategy rather than impulse.

For low Machs we proposed that cheating depended less on reasons or risks and more upon personal involvement. Lows cheated as often as highs in the initial study but less often in the replication. In the initial study the pressure to cheat came in a face-to-face situation in which personal involvement would presumably be greater for lows, while in the replication it came via written message. Second, the private decision situation which gave the high Machs time to decide to cheat gave the lows time to decide *not* to cheat. In the initial study the partner's series of increasingly strong urgings presented a series of opportunities to give in to the impulse to go along with him. If the low Mach once made the decision not to cheat in the replication, he was safe. There was no repetition of inducements.

Cheating as a general principle is more counterattitudinal for low Machs than for highs. However, the lows can be induced to cheat if someone they are involved with really wants them to and keeps urging. High Machs, although unencumbered by a policy stand on the matter, are also less susceptible to distractions of personal involvement. They can be induced to cheat not as an impulsive gesture of togetherness but as a strategy if they decide the situation warrants it.

ALTERNATIVE INTERPRETATIONS

SUSPICIOUS HIGH MACHS. We have noted in previous chapters that high Machs tend to be suspicious of instructions and procedures. Since we wanted to eliminate suspicious subjects from the attitude change analysis, the open-ended postsession questionnaire provided opportunities to express suspicion, and the debriefing session always opened with questions designed to elicit suspicion. Eight of the 61 subjects expressed suspicion. Seven of the 8 were high Machs. Although the proportion was large, the chi square (7 out of 33 high Machs versus 1 out of 28 lows) was not significant with Yates correction.

The breakdown of suspicion by dissonance conditions was clearly not significant. Five suspicious subjects came from the high-dissonance condition. These were all high Machs who had refused to cheat (but 9 other nonsuspicious highs had also refused). The other 3 suspicious subjects came from the low-dissonance condition. Two were high Machs who had refused to comply. The single suspicious low Mach was also the only subject to become suspicious after complying.

WAS CHEATING DISSONANT? It could be argued that cheating was dissonant for low Machs but not highs. This argument does little to alter the interpretation above. First, it should be noted that cheating *per se* was not dissonant for low Machs either. If it were, they should have shown dissonance reduction — i.e., change in attitude toward being less moral — after cheating with the attractive as well as the unattractive partner. What was dissonant was cheating with *inadequate* justification.

On the other hand, cheating as a general principle should be less counter-attitudinal for high Machs. This can be inferred from their initial Mach scores and from their willingness to cheat in the low-dissonance conditions. However, their overwhelming resistance to cheating in the high-dissonance condition indicates that there must have been something about cheating in this condition that they rejected. Presumably this was the lack of justification for it.

It might also be noted that had we used a standard dissonance-type measure of attitude change, we would have asked a question such as, "How much do you believe in cheating in experiments?" Although we did not ask, we venture that high Machs as well as lows would have disclaimed cheating in experiments. Some indirect evidence for this was obtained in Bogart's replication. A control group of 7 high and 10 low Machs was run with no cheating suggestion. These subjects had all the incentives to cheat that the others had, but their partner's second-round message contained no cheating suggestion, only a set of arguments in favor of the unpopular position assignment they had drawn. None of these subjects cheated on his own initiative.

Finally, it is not clear that behavior must be counterattitudinal for dissonance to occur. A number of dissonance studies have shown attitude change in the form of greater endorsement of an initially nonpreferred or less-preferred alternative. Clearly, cheating in an experiment was not a spontaneously preferred alternative for high Machs, and cheating in the high-dissonance condition was clearly nonpreferred for them. Finally, in Epstein's study the "dissonant" behavior was as counterattitudinal for high Machs as for lows. Still there was no evidence of dissonance reduction from the highs.

BIASED AND UNBIASED SAMPLES. It could be argued that our attitude change data for high Machs were unrepresentative. Since most of our high Machs in the high-dissonance condition refused to comply, it is possible that the few who did differed from the majority in some way other than having slightly lower Mach scores. Since we were as interested in compliance frequency as in attitude change, our data provide no way to answer this question. However, Epstein was interested only in attitude change. Her inducement to perform the "dissonant" behavior was subtle but powerful, and virtually all subjects complied. However, this unbiased sample of high-Mach compliers still showed no change.

CHANGE SCORES WERE NOT ARTIFACTS. Our attitude change data cannot be explained by assuming that Mach scores at the second testing tended to regress toward the mean. According to the regression explanation high Machs should score lower at the second testing and low Machs higher. This is what happened only for complying low Machs in the high-dissonance condition. However, complying highs showed no significant change in either condition, and low Machs who complied in the low-dissonance condition scored even lower on the second testing than initially. Nor was the high Machs' lack of change at the second testing an artifact due to the ceiling on Mach scores. The highest Mach IV score in our group of subjects was 140, 20 points below the ceiling at the initial testing.

IMPLICATIONS FOR DISSONANCE RESEARCH

One way for a subject to avoid dissonance is to refuse to comply with the induction. Usually at least a few subjects are lost in dissonance experiments for this reason. The data in Table XIII-2 suggest that high-Mach subjects are more likely to be lost in the high- than the low-dissonance condition. Further, it was the highest of the high Machs who refused to comply in the high-dissonance condition, and the lower-scoring minority (those who would be middle Machs in a trichotomous classification) who complied. Although it would be rash to generalize from our results, based on a weak manipulation, to results obtained with the stronger manipulations usually employed in dissonance studies, it is possible that low Machs have been at least to some extent overrepresented in attitude change data for high dissonance conditions. It is low Machs who give the attitude change data which support the dissonance prediction.

SUMMARY

The results of this study suggest that there are predictable individual differences in response to dissonance situations. The dissonant situation used was engaging in risky behavior — cheating in an experiment — at a team partner's suggestion. Justification for compliance was manipulated by varying the attractiveness of the partner. High-Mach subjects were more likely to refuse than cheat when justification was minimal, but they rarely failed to comply when given justification. Further, among those who did comply, cognitive change from before to after compliance was counter to dissonance theory predictions. Low-Mach subjects complied with their partner's suggestion as often as highs, but regardless of the justification available. After complying, they changed their cognitions to support their behavior, as predicted by dissonance theory.

These results were interpreted as reflecting high Machs' emotional detachment from others and their wishes, and from the implications of their own behavior as well. It was proposed that attitude change for high Machs may be predicted more accurately by incentive theory. In contrast, low Machs' greater susceptibility to emotional involvement with others makes it more difficult for them to refuse the dissonance induction, and their greater emotional investment in maintaining a consistent self-image leads them to restore consistency after complying, as predicted by dissonance theory.

CHAPTER XIV   ENCOUNTERING:
                WHAT LOW MACHS DO [1]

James E. Durkin

The relation to the Thou is direct. No system of ideas,
no foreknowledge, and no fancy intervene between I and Thou.
The memory itself is transformed, as it plunges out of its
isolation and into the unity of the whole.
                    Buber, *I and Thou*

What do low Machs do while high Machs are busy implementing cognitive strategies designed to insure the task outcomes documented in the preceding chapters? It has been proposed that lows get distracted from task goals by empathic involvements with cosubjects. It has been proposed that lows have a personal orientation to others as compared to an impersonal instrumental approach among highs. It appeared that lows were more likely to become absorbed in group processes which were task irrelevant. This research is designed to show that low Machs are more than just incapable of "Machiavellianism," but are individuals who become engrossed in their own characteristic mode of interpersonal functioning. It was designed to focus on low-Mach process rather than high-Mach outcome. The description of this process, called encountering (Durkin, 1966), sheds some light on such concepts on "empathy," "spontaneity," and "treating others personally."

Encountering is a process by which we change through direct contact with one another. Encountering happens when we open up to one another, that is, when we lay aside the layers of cognitive insulation that usually isolate us within separate (although roughly equivalent) frames of reference. As encountering happens, we move together with reference to each other rather than with reference to ourselves and get carried away spontaneously in the process of interaction, often in directions irrelevant to any previous intentions. The theory of encountering attempts to distinguish two modes of relating: (a) encountering, a nonsymbolic mutual communion; and (b) cognitive exchange, a reciprocal

---

[1] Presented in modified form under the title "Empathic orientation in physical encounters" at the annual meeting of the Eastern Psychological Association, Boston, April 1967.

symbolic communication. It also attempts to identify the sources, mechanisms, and outcomes of each process. Because encountering is a noncognitive process operating outside of cognitive awareness, we must avoid confusing our cognitions concerning the outcome of the process with the process itself.

In most naturally occurring transactions between individuals the two processes operate together. The balance between them depends jointly upon the dispositions brought into the group by its members and upon the situation with which the group must cope. This study will focus upon personality dispositions, specifically the degree of Machiavellianism. For example, in bargaining both high and low Machs typically hold private cognitions about how much each should give and get in an agreement. However, the low gets moved away from his private conception. He does not "decide" to give in; he simply responds, follows the action, and is moved. Lows lose unexpectedly, and in terms of meaning, inexplicably.

Situations such as social dancing in which both individuals must coordinate their physical responses on a moment-to-moment basis to form a single activity system are encounter controlled to a great extent, even though both partners are usually also guided by common cognitions concerning the dance step and the tempo of the music. The brief mutual glance which we unexpectedly exchange with a stranger, and in which we become engrossed for a fleeting second before we turn away or begin to stare intentionally, is a relatively common encounter experience (Durkin, 1967b). We sometimes find ourselves in unpremeditated angry encounters with our children or spouses which we would have avoided if we were acting under cognitive control. Perhaps the purest encounter is lovemaking, at least that form of lovemaking that arises spontaneously and continues for its own sake rather than being managed as a means to some predetermined end. The common element in these examples is the uncognized mutual action response of the participants. Such a tendency to *act,* directly triggered by another's act, without cognitive mediation, could explain how low Machs gets "distracted" from task goals.

Encounters have always been recognized in everyday language. Slang usage describes the encounter experience as "turning on to," "tuning in on," or "swinging with" other individuals. Concepts such as empathy and rapport suggest the operation of a noncognitive process in which individuals participate with each other. Statements such as "I was moved by his presence" articulate the concept of action without meaning. Although attempts have been made to study empathic processes, the literature in the area is inconsistent. From the point of view of encounter theory, most of these previous attempts have measured cognitions resulting from empathic experiences rather than measuring the nonsymbolic, dynamic action process itself.

In situations where either encountering or cognitive exchanging can be utilized to guide the interaction process, high Machs characteristically choose cognitive control by which they converge on achieving individual task goals, while lows gravitate toward encounter control in which they get carried away in the process of interaction. All of the relevant evidence suggests that low Machs are more sensitive to individual characteristics of others than highs are. For example, in the Con Game (Chapter VIII) low Machs discriminated between high and middle Machs in the bargaining interaction, but highs showed no consistent preference between lows and middles. In the Eye of the Beholder study (Chapter XII) low Machs discriminated accurately between actually different high- and low-Mach target persons, but highs made no such discrimination. From the point of view of encounter theory, the lows' performance represented the cognitive residue of their encounters during the preceding interaction.

In the dissonance study (Chapter XIII) the same individual, sometimes labeled as a high-status person and sometimes as a low-status person elicited label-contingent compliance from high-Mach subjects, but not lows. On a subsequent, private attitude change measure, however, the lows reacted differently to the two labels, rather than the highs. This contrast suggested that high Machs use their cognitions to guide their overt behavioral action rather than allowing their behavior to shape their cognitions. For low Machs, on the other hand, cognitions about a person might affect their subsequent cognitions about him, and affect their interpretation of their relation to him, but have less effect on their overt behavioral interactions with him.

All the data suggest that the behavior of low Machs in interaction depends upon the behavior of the particular person with whom they are interacting, and that this differentiation of behavior emerges in the process of interaction rather than depending upon prior cognitive sets brought with them into the situation. High Machs, although highly effective in implementing subtle strategies for dealing with others in general, do not respond differentially to different others unless guided by explicit distinguishing cognitive cues.

The low Machs' characteristic "distraction" in interpersonal interaction fits the description of encountering: (a) the personal response is a particular response; (b) it is a response based on behavioral contact rather than cognitive information; (c) it is based on a tendency to receive rather than to give influence; (d) it is based on participation with others rather than objective perspective on them; and (e) the behavioral experience influences subsequent attitudes but is not determined by previous attitudes. In short, since low Machs appear to be more open and thus more vulnerable and emotionally responsive to others, they should be open to empathic, encounter experience to a greater extent than high Machs.

More precisely, it is hypothesized that low Machs are encounter prone; high Machs are encounter blind.

A basic question, of course, is how can this spontaneous mutual responsiveness of the encounter process be measured? One way is to use a subjects-by-subjects factorial design. This design is a variation of the standard treatments-by-treatments factorial design except that combinations of group members are systematically varied over common or comparable experimental treatments rather than combinations of treatments being systematically varied over a common or comparable sets of experimental groups. The dependent measures are, of course, group performance scores. Note that the interaction term in such a design refers to interaction between specific combinations of people rather than between specific combinations of treatments. For example, consider two men and two women, all equally skillful dancers. Call the women A and B and the two men C and D. Further, suppose that woman A and man D "turn on" to each other and dance together superbly, whereas woman A and man C can perform the steps equally efficiently but together they lack flair. On the other hand, woman B and man D give a competent but wooden performance on the dance floor, while woman B and man C almost outshine the AD combination.

If judges were evaluating these dance team performances, say on a zero-to-100 scale, we could show each pair's score in one of the boxes of a fourfold table, as shown in Fig. XIV-1. The two men, C and D, are at the head of the two columns, and the two women, A and B, are on the rows. The score of 75 in the upper right-hand box is the score of team AD. These scores can also be plotted graphically. In the situation described above, in which A does well with D and poorly with C, but B shows the opposite pattern, the resulting crossed profiles show the familiar factorial interaction effect. The line connecting A's two scores with the two different men is not parallel to the line for B's scores. The amount of interaction in the tetrad can be calculated by taking the difference of differences in the four team scores. When there is a significant interaction, it means that A's performance depends on who her partner is, and so do B's, C's, and D's. This is an operational representation of what is meant by an encounter interaction, since differences in the teams' performances could not be wholly accounted for by differences in the individuals' knowledge about the dance steps, but depend upon a process that emerges in the particular pair combinations. Note that this noncognitive encounter interaction can be represented by the ordinary model of statistical interaction.

In contrast, suppose that in the same dancing contest there was another foursome. We'll call the women J and K and the men L and M. Each of them

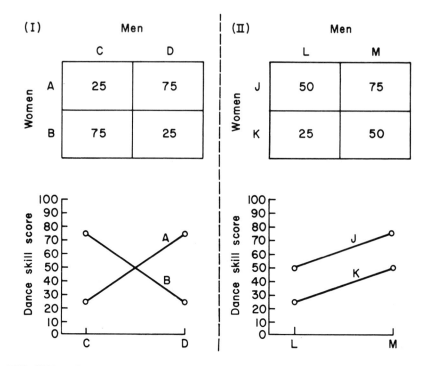

FIG. XIV-1. The subjects-by-subjects factorial design, (I) All subject-by-subjects interaction, teams AC, AD, BC, and BD dance skill scores. (II) No subjects-by-subjects interaction, teams JL, JM, KL, and KM dance skill scores.

(I) Calculation of interaction scores	(II) Calculation of interaction scores
(AD - AC) - (BD -BC)	(JM - JL) - (KM - KL)
= (75 - 25) - (25 - 75) = 100	= (75 - 50) - (50 - 25) = 0
= (50) - (-50) = 100	= 25 - 25 = 0
= 50 + 50 = 100	

also dances with both possible partners, and these four teams receive the scores on the right hand side of Fig. XIV-1. The differences in team scores in this group can be accounted for by the fact that J is a better dancer than K no matter who she is with and that M is consistently better than L. The graph of these results show the parallel profiles of the no-interaction situation.

In terms of the hypothesis that low Machs are open to the others and encounter prone while high Machs treat others alike and are encounter blind, it would be expected that tetrads of low Machs would show the encounter interaction effect as in the ABCD tetrad, while the high Machs would show the no-interaction pattern as in the JKLM tetrad.

PROCEDURE

APPARATUS

Instead of dancing contests, tetrads of subjects were observed in pair combinations on the ball-and-spiral task. The ball and spiral used was a large Plexiglas spiral ramp with a track about 3 in. wide (see Fig. XIV-2). At the base the ramp was 3 ft in diameter and wound 3½ turns up and around to a goal cup at the top. The ramp rested on a wooden platform with handles so that the two team players could coordinate their responses to tilt the apparatus to any angle. A tennis ball was placed at the bottom of the ramp at the start of a trial. The two-person task was to change the tilt of the apparatus continuously to roll the ball around the ramp up into the goal cup. If the ball fell off the ramp, the trial was over. The score for each trial was the number of quarter turns travelled by the ball from the starting point.

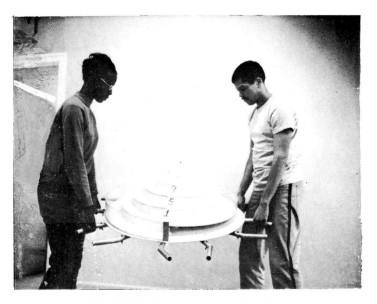

FIG. XIV-2. The ball and spiral in play.

The task requires mutual coordination between team members. If the apparatus is tilted too suddenly or with poor timing, the ball falls off. This is essentially a mutual tracking task in which partners can pick up the joint system feedback signal through the apparatus. Verbal interactions other than groans, sighs, and screams of agony or triumph drop out quickly, for by the time a task instruction can be formulated, transmitted, decoded and enacted by the partner, the situation has changed so much that the information is obsolete. This task, like social dancing, involves direct physical coordination between team members. Unlike social dancing, however, there is no established pattern of steps and no given tempo which the team members can utilize individually but in common to guide their behavior. This leaves only a relational frame of reference within which the team can coordinate their efforts to keep the ball on the ramp and moving. The task is characterized by dynamic interactions.

SELECTION OF SUBJECTS

At the beginning of the spring semester, 1966, 173 students, 61 males and 112 females, in an introductory psychology course for nonpsychology majors at Queens College filled out the Mach IV and Mach V scales. The means and standard deviations are shown in Table XIV-1. The correlation between scores on the two forms was .66. The two scores of each subject were averaged as an estimate of his individual Machiavellianism.

TABLE XIV-1

Means and Standard Deviations on Mach IV and Mach V for 173 Queens College Students (61 Males and 112 Females, Combined)

	Mean score	Standard deviation	Split-half reliability
Mach IV	96.25	15.19	.75
Mach V	102.10	10.30	.54
Mach IV and V, combined	99.17	11.65	—

Two males and two females were scheduled for each experimental session. Twenty-three tetrads (92 subjects) were observed. To classify groups as either high or low Mach, the individual Mach scores of the four members were averaged, and the distribution of these 23 means was divided at the median, 95.50, giving 11 high- and 12 low-Mach groups. Thus, the measure of the independent variable was a single index for each tetrad representing the degree of Machiavellian orientation in the foursome as a whole.

THE EXPERIMENTAL SESSION

Eleven different experimenters, 8 males and 3 females, were used in the study. All were trained to conduct the sessions according to a standardized routine;

none knew the Mach classification of his or her group; but each ran approximately the same number of high- and low-Mach groups.

Each session was conducted by two experimenters in adjoining experimental rooms, each containing a ball-and-spiral device. First, the two male subjects were taken to one room and the two girls to the other for training trials. Each pair practiced with the help and encouragement of their experimenter until they reached a criterion of 15 min of practice or three goals (getting the ball to the top and into the goal cup), not necessarily consecutive, whichever came first. Upon completion of training, they were each randomly assigned to a partner of the opposite sex for a block of ten trials. The order of partnerships was counterbalanced in *abba* fashion. That is, each individual played four blocks of ten trials, the first and fourth blocks with one partner, and the second and third with the other. One block with a given partner was played in one experimental room, with one of the ball-and-spiral devices, and supervised by one of the experimenters. The other block with the same partner was played in the other room, with the other experimenter and other device. This counterbalancing procedure was designed to compensate for any experimenter, room, or device effects as well as any linear practice effects not eliminated by the training trials.

A trial began when the experimenter placed the ball in position at the base of the spiral. A trial was terminated if the ball fell off the edge of the ramp to a lower level, but not if it rolled backwards without falling off. Reaching the goal cup, of course, also terminated a trial. When a trial ended, the experimenter recorded the score for the trial, and placed the ball back at the base of the ramp for the next trial. Subjects were permitted to talk at will and to rest as long as they chose between trials. As it turned out, the task was so engrossing that there was relatively little talking or resting.

The score for a trial was the number of quarter turns from the base the ball attained before falling off. Since the spirals had $3\frac{1}{2}$ turns, a score of 14 indicated that the team rolled the ball all the way up to the goal cup, but then it fell off the outer edge of the ramp rather than into the cup. Scores of 15, 16, or 17 indicated that the team got the ball to the top and into the goal cup. The actual number of points alloted for a goal depended upon how many goals the team made in that block of ten trials. Teams that made more goals were given more points for each goal they made. The reason for this scoring procedure was the assumption that pairs who made relatively many goals would otherwise have had their true score depressed by the ceiling on the task. Had the ramp gone further, they could have kept the ball on it. The score adjustment was an attempt to compensate for these ceiling effects. Teams with 1 to 3 goals in 10 trials got 15 points for each goal. Teams making 4, 5, or 6 goals in their 10 trials received 16 points for each goal, and those making 7 or more goals received 17 points for each. This adjustment had the effect of making a more nearly flat distribution of trial scores in the sample. That is, with the adjustment, the frequency of trial scores from zero to

17 was approximately flat; there were about equal numbers of each of the scores.

The final score for each pair was the mean of their 20 trial scores over their two blocks of trials together as a team. Two measures of ball-and-spiral performance were computed for each tetrad, one representing the average skill level of the group, the other representing the amount of group system interaction between team members. The skill score for each tetrad was simply the average trial score over the four teams. The subjects by subjects interaction measure was the difference of differences between the four team scores in each tetrad. Since the study predicted differences in the magnitude of the group system effect rather than in its direction, each tetrad interaction estimate was made positive through the assignment of consistent letter designations to each member of the group. The girl observed to show more of a difference in performance between her two boy partners was designated A, and the girl who showed less, B. The boy who performed worse with A was called C and the boy who did better was called D. Then the magnitude of interaction was calculated by the formula (AD − AC) − (BD − BC). Thus, interaction scores varied only from zero upward.

RESULTS

This study tested the hypothesis that low Machs would respond to others individually to a greater extent than high Machs, who were expected to treat all others the same. The tendency to respond to different others the same or differently was measured by the amount of interaction within tetrads, as outlined above. That is, differences between low Machs' ball-and-spiral skill scores from one partner to another were expected to reflect effects of the two particular people in combination that could not be accounted for by differences in individual skill level. In contrast, differences between high Machs' ball-and-spiral skill scores from one partner to another were expected to reflect primarily individual differences in skill among the four members of the tetrad. The interaction score for the tetrad, the differences of differences between team scores eliminates the effect of differences in individual skill. It is a measure of deviation from both participants' average skill as a result of being paired together, and in this sense is a measure of how personally the members of the tetrad respond to each other. Accordingly, this interaction score was expected to be larger for low Machs than for highs.

This prediction was confirmed. As shown in Fig. XIV-3, the team scores of low-Mach groups showed a greater interaction between members (A, B, C, and D) than those of high-Mach groups (J, K, L, and M). The interaction score of each group, computed as indicated above, is shown in Table XIV-2. The mean magnitude of interaction for the 12 low-Mach tetrads was 2.38, compared to a mean of 1.01 for the 11 high-Mach tetrads ($p < .01$).

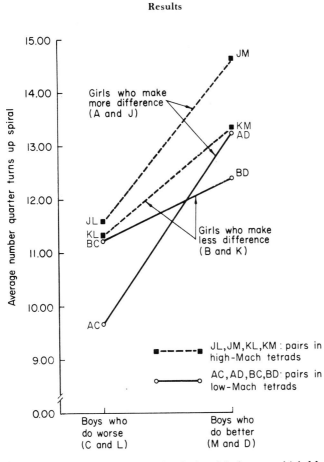

FIG. XIV-3. Subjects-by-subjects interaction in low-Mach versus high-Mach groups.

BALL-AND-SPIRAL SKILL COMPARISONS

A ball-and-spiral skill index was computed for each tetrad. This was simply the average of the trial scores of the four teams in each tetrad. Scores for each trial could vary from zero to 17, as explained above. This ball-and-spiral skill index provides an estimate of how skillful the four teams or, equivalently, the four individuals in the tetrad were, on the average, in trying to roll the ball up the ramp into the goal cup at the top.

No predictions were made relating Machiavellianism to skill *per se* in the ball-and-spiral task. If it is a task in which noncognitive, encounter-controlled processes dominate, then low Machs should do better than highs. That is, the openness of the low-Mach partners to each other should enable them to

TABLE XIV-2

Ball-and-Spiral Interaction Scores: Absolute Difference of Differences Between Team Skill Scores in the Tetrad [a]

Individual tetrad interaction scores				
Low-Mach groups (n = 12 tetrads)	High-Mach groups (n = 11 tetrads)			
5.70	2.55			
4.05	2.05			
3.30	1.20			
3.15	1.15			
2.85	1.00			
2.70	.85			
2.40	.75			
1.25	.65			
1.15	.65			
.85	.25			
.85	.10			
.25		Difference	t	p <
Mean interaction 2.38	1.01	1.37	2.61	.01

[a] The absolute difference between one girl's scores with the two boys minus the difference between the other girl's scores with the same two boys taken in the same order.

accommodate to each other's style on the task, and they should gravitate toward a *modus vivendi* which would make efficient use of whatever skills they have. The high Machs, with their individualistic orientation, should have difficulty sharing control. On the other hand, if the ball and spiral does create an encounter situation, it does so precisely by engrossing the partners in the encounter with each other. To the extent that they become absorbed in responding to each other, they might fail to concentrate on keeping the ball under control. The fact that high Machs were expected to be less susceptible to these mutual response engrossments, together with their previously demonstrated task orientation, would suggest that they might actually be more efficient at the task than lows. The probability of these mixed tendencies made prediction impossible.

In fact, as shown in Table XIV-3, high- and low-Mach groups did not differ in average skill. Clearly, amount of Machiavellianism had no simple, dominant effect on skill at the task. This was true when individuals were classified according to their tetrad classification, as well as when they were classified according to their individual Mach scores.

TABLE XIV-3

Ball-and-Spiral Skill Scores: Mean Score Per Trial[a]

Mean skill score per trial				
High-Mach tetrads	Low-Mach tetrads	Difference	t	p
12.69	11.64	1.05	< 1.00	n.s.

[a] Each score point represents one quarter-turn around the spiral; a single trial score could range from zero to a maximum of 17.

THE RELATION BETWEEN SKILL AND INTERACTION

The analysis of variance model upon which the subjects-by-subjects design is based assumes that main effects are independent of interaction effects. In the subjects-by-subjects design, this would mean that skill level should be independent of interaction score in the tetrad. To check this assumption, the skill level of each tetrad was correlated with its interaction score. This correlation, over the 23 groups, was +.027. Thus, there was no relation between the average skill level of the four teams in a group and the amount of interaction between the members within tetrads. This suggests that equating the model of factorial interaction whose properties are thoroughly understood with the phenomenon of encounter interaction whose properties at this point have only been speculated about is not entirely without empirical justification.

DISCUSSION

Low Machs showed more subjects-by-subjects interaction on the ball-and-spiral task than high Machs. This finding supports the hypothesis that low Machs respond to others more personally. The basic characteristics of encounter process suggest what the specific *mechanisms* of treating another personally might be, and how they can be measured.

(1) Encountering is a mutual group system effect, while cognitive exchange consists of two (or more) independent reciprocal individual effects.

(2) Encounter process is spontaneous and divergent in direction and thus predictable only in its magnitude, while cognitive exchange is convergent and thus predictable in its direction and outcome.

(3) The psychological mechanism controlling encounter process is a non-cognitive mutual-feedback performance process, while the cognitive exchange is a symbolically mediated learning process.

High Machs maintained their individual orientation in a group, regardless of who their partners were; lows were influenced by the particular persons serving as partners. These conclusions are implicit in the results by the logic of the subjects-by-subjects design. In the two-way factorial design the total variance is decomposed into four additive components: (a) the grand mean which represents the overall task difficulty level; (b) the row effect; (c) the column effect — the deviations, respectively, of the designated row and column from the grand mean; and (d) the row − column interaction which is the residual value after the other three independent components have been subtracted from each cell mean and thus completely partialed out.

Just as the total variance may be partitioned into independent components, each separate team observation may be similarly decomposed. The component variances are logically equivalent to the variance components of each observation. The equivalence provides a means of studying the encounter process even though it is embedded in unitary team scores and thus not observable in pure form in behavior.

In the subjects by subjects design, the main effects for rows and columns logically reflect consistencies within individuals. The row and column means provide an unbiased estimate of characteristic performance, irrespective of partner, and irrespective of interactions. These individual skill consistencies accounted for the team scores of high Machs, but not lows. That is, high Machs' behavior on the task was influenced primarily by their own individual attitudes and skill levels. Accordingly, high-Mach team performances represented a simple additive combination of the two members' individual skills.

What psychological processes contribute to these within-individual row and column averages? They represent stable skills such as strength, balance, and tracking ability. They also represent stable learned traits and attitudinal factors transferred from other contests of skill. The averaging process is sensitive to consistent central tendencies. The host of long-term influences which operate to maintain a consistent definition of the person in relation to his task environment is generally termed personality. Thus, the personality or style of performance which remains relatively consistent from partnership to partnership is represented by this within-individual estimate. The finding that the summed within-individual estimates of the partners could account for the scores of the high-Mach group supports the notion that highs are able to maintain self-defined goals in the face of disturbances presented by others.

Factorial main effects are deviations from the overall grand mean. Factorial interactions are deviations from these deviations. In terms of actual ball-and-spiral performance, the interaction effect characteristic of low-Mach pairs could be said to represent the extent to which the group is more (or less) than the sum of its parts, the extent to which who works with whom is more important than simply who works, the degree to which compatibility or incompatibility effects are operating, the extent to which psychological processes such as "turning on," empathizing, or being *en rapport* caused the participants to do better or worse than their "potential." These are familiar terms, but they do not explain the processes which produced the effects.

Some clues as to *how* encounter process works can be derived from *when* and *where* it operates, based on properties of the interaction term in the subjects by subjects design. First, the interaction is not carried into the group performance by either participant; rather it emerges out of the specific interaction process that occurs only when the particular participants come together. Furthermore, the process is not generated *within* each of the participants separately; rather, it develops *between* them — it is an effect of the group as a unitary system. The outcome of this emergent between-individual process is spontaneous in the sense that it cannot be predicted from observations on the participants working with other partners. (These were the predictions estimated by the row and column main effects described above.)

The logical structure of the factorial design is such that the average responses of the row and column members are functionally related to the difficulty of the task as estimated by the grand mean, but that the between-member combination responses operating within the cells are not. Internal group maintenance behavior is independent of task behavior. Recall that the correlation between interaction and skill in the tetrad was $+.027$. Encountering is concerned with internal group system maintenance; cognitive exchanges are concerned with external task adaptation. Thus, the data indicate that low Machs have a disposition to get carried away in these maintenance processes while highs are more strictly task oriented.

CONVERGENT VERSUS DIVERGENT BEHAVIOR DYNAMICS

The dynamics of a behavioral process describe the trend of its change or development over time. The distinction between convergent and divergent behavior dynamics clarifies the attributes of spontaneity and unpredictability which characterize encounters. The actual mechanisms by which convergent cognitive exchange processes which guide individual high Machs and the divergent encounter process which carries low-Mach pairs away in interaction with each other will be suggested below. The purpose here is to present a general model by which behavior process such as encountering can be described or measured even though it seems to lack direction, stability, or intention in terms of its content. The outcome or direction of convergent behavior can be predicted by sampling because deviations tend to center around the given path. In divergent behavior the variations accumulate and feed back to change the original course. Viewed from a stable reference point, convergent behavior appears consistent and regular; divergent behavior appears improvised, creative, spontaneous and unpredictable.

The convergent–divergent distinction was employed by Langmuir (1943) to call attention to singular, nonrepeatable events in the physical world. It was used by Magorah (1963) to separate biological regulatory processes that maintain stability as opposed to those which generate growth. It was used by Guilford (1966) to distinguish analytic rule-following intellective processes from synthetic, creative, rule-modifying intellective processes. The principles of convergent and divergent regulatory processes have been developed in the field of systems engineering to analyze dynamic physical systems.

Convergent and divergent dynamics can be observed in human social systems such as ball-and-spiral teams. Convergent dynamics operate within the individual to maintain a consistent definition of himself and of the situation and a consistent response to it in the face of environmental vicissitudes including those generated by a partner. High Machs' performances were convergent. Divergent dynamics occur when dynamic interactions with the environment operate on an individual to change his basic style of performance. In encounter process small, possibly chance responses from one individual, rather than being filtered out by the other through compensatory actions, "move" that other to amplify and reflect the response. In turn, the original partner amplifies the return response and adds more divergence. The pattern builds up through the circular casual process and consistent individual response patterns are left far behind.

Encounters are divergent by theoretical definition. Empirically, encountering was measured by subjects-by-subjects interaction. This necessarily represents a divergence of the team scores from the characteristic skill levels of the partners involved.

COGNITIVE VERSUS NONCOGNITIVE BEHAVIOR CONTROL

In encountering, the dynamics of the behavior are divergent rather than convergent, and behavior is controlled by noncognitive rather than cognitive processes. As shown in Fig. XIV-4, these two dimensions are theoretically independent. That is, both convergent and divergent processes can be either cognitive or noncognitive. However, encounter theory postulates that all divergent group system interactions between people are also noncognitive.

A number of thinkers have described noncognitive interindividual processes related to the encountering idea. Martin Buber's (1958) distinction between I–Thou and I–It relations is extremely close to the distinction between encountering and cognitive exchange. G. H. Mead (1934) conceived of a primitive conversation of nonsignificant gestures as a precursor of reciprocal symbolic communication. Church (1966), following Werner (1948), distinguished a more primitive physiognomic mobilization process from the

The Dynamic Path of the Process

		Convergent	Divergent
The Mechanism of Behavior Control	Feedback (noncognitive)	Individual skilled performance	Encountering
		Proprioception, homeostasis, symbiosis	Natural selection
		Servomechanisms, e.g., a thermostat	Spontaneous behavior
			Conversions, ecstasies
	Cognitive	Instrumental learning	Scientific creativity
		Finding right answers	Asking new questions

FIG. XIV-4. Two theoretical dimensions of behavior process.

learned, cognitive, classifying-knowing process. In *Fights, Games, and Debates,* Rapoport (1960) described fights as wholly noncognitive interactions in contrast to games which are more cognitive in nature. Richardson (1960) developed a differential equation approach to the theoretical description of divergent noncognitive response spirals such as arms races. Finally, the currently proliferating, so-called "encounter groups" (Schutz, 1967) deal for the most part in noncognitive physical contact exercises. Unfortunately, none of these workers has proposed a means of measuring the encounterlike processes they dealt with, with the possible exception of Richardson.

On the other hand, statistically sophisticated psychologists have developed quantitative methods for analytically disentangling unitary group system effects from individual member effects in raw group performance scores. "Group system" effects were noted by Comrey (1953) using partial correlations; Cattell (1953) using factor analysis; and Runkel, Keith-Smith, and Newcomb (1957) employing a subjects-by-subjects factorial design similar to the one used in this study. None of these measuring people reported speculations on the source or nature of the psychological process generating their empirical effects, even though the effect in each case occurred in at least a partially noncognitive action situation. The basic encounter theory hypothesis (i.e., that the process which welds a group whose members who are open to each other into a unitary action system is controlled by noncognitive behavior mechanisms) is testable with these measurement methods. Encounter theory weaves these two traditions of investigation together.

Evidence that the group system effect is mediated by noncognitive contact processes can be inferred by comparing a pair of studies, one a specific replication attempt of the other, and each employing a subjects-by-subjects factorial design. Rosenberg, Erlick, and Berkowitz (1955) used the ball and spiral with three-man combinations of air crewmen and found a significant group system effect. The study was replicated by Roby and Lanzetta (1961). They made the minor "improvement" of substituting an almost purely cognitive task involving a proper sequence of binary switch responses distributed among group members under the following rationale:

Whereas the ball and spiral is essentially a motor skills task, the present task presents primarily a cognitive problem. One might expect individual motor skill to be relatively more impervious to influence by co-workers' behavior than intellectual functioning and, thus, would predict a larger [group system] effect on the cognitive task.

The results were unequivocal. There was no group system effect whatever. It seems that noncognitive direct action tasks generate subjects-by-subjects inter-action but that cognitive tasks do not.

More direct verification from a single experiment has recently been presented (Durkin, 1968). An interpersonal reaction time paradigm was used to compare the group system effects in cognitive and noncognitive situations. Three subjects sat face to face at close quarters each holding a handle fitted with shock plates and either one or three response buttons, depending on the experimental condition. In each trial one of the three subjects, selected at random, received a shock after a random interval. The victim had to signal his unshocked partners to press their buttons to turn his shock off. Thus the group was "wired" in series. The raw scores (time from onset of shock to the victim to offset of shock by a savior) were then transformed to group-system effect scores by the method of Runkel *et al.* (1957).

Cognitive and noncognitive situations were created by using choice and simple reaction time tasks. In the choice condition, there were three buttons on the handle, and a savior response was valid only if the button pressed was the one designated for the particular victim getting shocked. This was a cognitive situation since the savior had to first discriminate which of the others was the victim and then apply the symbolically encoded "if–then" rule to press the appropriate button. In the noncognitive one-button situation each handle had a single response button to be pressed for any victim. In this condition there were no discriminations between victims or buttons to process cognitively, only an action response to be triggered by any outcry. The greater group system effect in the one-button condition ($t = 4.00$, $p < .0005$) supported the prediction that noncognitive tasks generate more subjects by subjects interaction and the general encounter theory hypothesis that interaction in the group system effect sense is nonsymbolically mediated.

Turning from task situations to personality dispositions once again, we have argued that low Machs get carried away in encountering, a process of mutual responding which emerges between rather than within individuals, which is specific to them as a unitary group system, which diverges from the convergent tendencies initially characteristic of each of them, and which is a direct action response rather than a symbolically mediated cognitive response. If these responses are not cognitively controlled, how are they guided? This is the problem dealt with next.

MUTUAL FEEDBACK CONTROL, AN ALTERNATIVE TO RECIPROCAL COGNITIVE CONTROL OF BEHAVIOR

High Machs have been described as maintaining an instrumental cognitive attitude toward others and a convergent orientation to the task at hand. They are cognitively sensitive to the definitional characteristics of others and of the situation, and are relatively impervious to "irrelevant" distractions. These characteristics are typical of the cognitive control process. Cognitive control operates through informed decisions made by a cognizing subject about the meaning of a given object with respect to a set of alternatives already represented within his memory system. Effective cognitive exchange with another depends upon the development within each individual of reasonably accurate cognitions about the other's cognitions. Common language and cultural norms facilitate such inferences. It is essential, however, that the actual work of processing these cognitions remain isolated within each cognizer and not be confounded with either the objects to be represented or the independent cognizing process of the other individual. The cognitive frame must remain as a fixed reference against which cognitions *about* the other can be compared. On the ball-and-spiral task cognitive high Machs convergently maintained their own style of play, and the characteristic skill level associated with it, and filtered out the influence of the partner as a mere disturbance to that style.

The efficiency of cognitive control is amply demonstrated by our ability to process information and to generate useful decisions based on it in coordination with others. However, there are certain situations which even the most powerful cognitive systems cannot in principle handle. These are situations generating dynamic interactions in which the objects of cognition are changing so rapidly that informed decisions become obsolete before they can be enacted and because the cognitive process itself changes the object of cognition. Encounters are essentially dynamic interactions; here mutual feedback control is more appropriate.

We are now ready to deal specifically with the mechanisms in which low Machs engage while highs are cognizing and implementing decisions. The evidence suggests that they are operating under mutual feedback control. A semantic ambiguity must be disposed of at the outset. Traditionally in psychology the term "feedback" has been equated with knowledge of results or, more generally, with reinforcement. On the other hand, the term *feedback control* refers to a kind of structural configuration in a behavior system where a portion of the output response of the system is fed back as an input or excitation of that same system. In the first use feedback refers to the meaning of information while in the second a physical configuration is described. Encounter theory employs the second sense of the term, and an encounter configuration is a mutual feedback configuration between individuals.

The basic encounter configuration, the one low Machs fall into and highs avoid through cognitive control, is one in which people are "open" to each other. Our operational definition of openness is the emergence of subjects by subjects interaction, but a more graphic image would be of two individuals who have opened up psychological "holes" in each other's presence and begun direct contact. Let us be clear about holes. A hole that is empty *does* nothing and a hole that is full *is* nothing. Furthermore, a hole passes everything through while a device that passes some things and not others is a filter. A hole is best seen as a process. As a dynamic process it is best characterized by the rate at which things pass through it rather than its state at any moment. Thus, holes provide noncognitive channels for contact between people.

How does feedback control handle these situations of mutual openness? How does it explain how encounter participants get carried away into a divergent group system interaction? In a feedback-controlled system a portion of the output of the system is looped around back into the input of the system in a circular causal process, and used to modify its own output. For example, in ball-and-spiral operation the output, what the ball is doing, is fed back into the team and influences their inputs, what they do with their hands to tilt the platform. The feedback signal is used to modify the tilting responses in such a way as to maintain optimal ball rate. Three general principles of feedback control can be used to clarify the mechanism of encountering.

THREE PROPERTIES OF FEEDBACK CONTROL. First, feedback systems are critically dependent on the very same dynamic interactions with their environment that constitute the major stumbling block for cognitive systems. In feedback systems the action response of the environment and the output of the system which produced the response become completely confounded in the feedback signal.

Second, a feedback system can maintain dynamic equilibrium in the face of a wide range and infinite pattern of environmental disturbances on a purely noncognitive physical basis. Although many complex hardware systems basically controlled by feedback loops can also contain cognitive information processing systems as components, a purely physical configuration without memory storage is sufficient to do the job. In the ball and spiral the eyes are used, but not to gather information for cognitive decision making. We might develop cognitive perceptions or conceptions about the encounter process apart from or after the process, but the process itself is noncognitive.

Third, feedback systems operate spontaneously. Operating noncognitively, they have no need for memory or learning and hence, no intention, discrimination, reinforcement or other time binding functions. A feedback system behaves as it does because of what it is and how it is put together, not because of what it knows. A feedback system is spontaneous in the sense that it operates on a moment-to-moment basis in the present without regard to past or future. It has an equilibrium point built into it (like the 72-degree set point on a thermostat) where output ceases, but this set point is never represented as a fixed goal state as the actual state of the system varies around it in process. Feedback system responses are determined equfinally. At any moment the system output gravitates toward the response which maximizes the *rate* of convergence on the goal state by whatever behavior may be necessary, no matter what the system was doing a moment before. This kind of spontaneous improvised dynamic process might be termed a natural-behavior selection process analogous to Darwin's natural selection process applied to species. The behavior of a ball rolling down a hill exhibits natural behavior selection as it "spontaneously" improvises the most downhill path to the bottom. So too, ball-and-spiral play can be improvised in order to do whatever you have to do to keep the ball going up.

MUTUAL FEEDBACK SYSTEMS. While the major problem of cognitive systems is how to handle ambiguity, the major problem of feedback systems is how to handle instability. Instability develops when the feedback response acts to increase rather than decrease the distance between the present state of the system and the equilibrium state. In such a case a convergent system is carried away into a divergent system which "takes off" on the wings of its own attempts to stabilize itself. This process is especially apt to occur when two responsive feedback systems come into contact with each other, as in encountering.

In the basic encounter configuration two open and responsive individuals come into contact with one another. As individuals, each has learned to maintain the integrity of his own control system while moving to satisfy his goals in the face of environmental obstacles. Cognitive functions such as learning are particularly useful in dealing with nonresponsive objects, which "hold still" long enough for cognitions to do their work. High Machs have learned to succeed by transforming responsive other persons into cognitive objects. Low Machs let holes open up in their cognitive insulation and fall into dynamic interactions with others. Their goal state in the presence of others seems to be "go along with the other equifinally wherever he happens to be." Divergent encounters arise precisely because two individuals each try to go along with the other wherever he happens to be and the pair gets carried away in a spiral of mutual attempts to respond to each other's responding. In the ball-and-spiral task, if both participants attempt to converge on one goal, doing it in their partner's way, they will diverge to a way of doing it which is characteristic only of the group interaction system, and the performance score will be unrelated to estimates based on their performances with other partners. If one of the partners does not open up, but rather retains his individual style, the open one will converge upon him and no interaction process will take place.

Encountering must be mutual. A group cannot diverge together if one of the members converges separately. What happens when a low Mach is open in the presence of an unopen high? Encounter theory would predict that the low would diverge from his individual style and converge on the high's. This idea can be examined by comparing the encounter effect in groups in which all members were homogeneously low in Machiavellianism against groups in which members varied more in Mach score among themselves. A Mach heterogeneity index was computed for each tetrad by summing and averaging the four absolute differences between the Mach scores of the four boy–girl teams, and the resulting tetrad heterogeneity distribution was split at the median (ten scale points). Unfortunately most of the homogeneous groups were also low in Machiavellianism on the average, and most of the heterogeneous tetrads were high. Since the two-way classification (by Mach and homogeneity of Mach) yielded grossly discrepant cell frequencies, a factorial analysis seemed unwarranted. However, the mean group interaction score (2.98) of the eight tetrads that were both low and homogeneous in Machiavellianism was significantly larger than the average of the interaction scores (1.06) of all other groups (high-Mach groups high and low in homogeneity, and low-Mach heterogeneous groups; $t = 4.11$ $p < .0005$). That is, most of the encountering (i.e., large interaction scores) occurred in groups that were both homogeneous and low in Machiavellianism, as would be predicted by encounter theory.

LOW MACHS ARE ENCOUNTER PRONE; HIGHS ARE ENCOUNTER BLIND

Previous research has suggested that high Machs do better than lows in bargaining and other tasks because lows get distracted from the task by interpersonal group maintenance processes surrounding it. The focus of interest in this report, however, has been upon the interaction process rather than the task outcome because encountering is independent of task outcome both in theory and in the present data. From the process point of view high Machs can be seen as being distracted from encountering by the demands of the task.

The hypothesis of this study can now be restated more precisely. Certain types of group members, low Machs, in certain types of situations, relational tasks, find psychological "holes" in their cognitive insulation and get carried away divergently in a certain type of noncognitive interaction process, encountering, which is mediated by a certain type of behavior control, feedback control. On the basis of these concepts and the encounter theory hypothesis that links them together, we consider some questions which are central to an understanding of what the Mach scale measures.

LOW MACHS TREAT OTHERS AS PERSONS; HIGHS TREAT THEM AS OBJECTS. What is a personal process? Encounter theory, the subjects-by-subjects interaction response, and the distinction between divergent feedback control and convergent cognitive control can clarify the assertion that low Machs are disposed to be personal, and highs impersonal, in their relations with others. One way to treat others personally is to treat them particularly. The subjects-by-subjects interaction reflects particular responses of particular pairs to each other. Since low-Mach groups showed significant interactions and highs did not, these data support the hypothesis that lows treat others as persons in particular while highs treat others generally as cognitive objects. Treating others personally means treating them openly. It is not how the subject influences the other that defines how personal he is being, but rather how he is influenced by the other. High Machs influence others without taking them personally. Lows are influenced because they are personally influenced.

Low Machs treat others personally through the mediation of feedback control. High Machs treat others impersonally through the mediation of cognitive control. Encounter theory provides an interesting view of the rather striking findings of the person perception study (Chapter XII) which suggested that highs attain greater overall accuracy through a process of perceiving others in relation to themselves as a fixed point of reference. The lows, on the other hand, differentiated between high- and low-Mach targets despite their seemingly deleterious tendency to assume similarity. Perceiving is a knowing process and person perception is a kind of knowledge. In terms of encounter theory highs and lows acquire knowledge of others of two basically different kinds, kinds that correspond with the distinction between cognitive exchange and encountering as modes of relating to others.

Let us term these two kinds of knowledge *analytic* and *analog* knowledge. Knowledge is a relationship between the knower and the known. The convention of defining knowledge as objective, i.e., independent of the knower, applies to analytic knowledge which would be impossible to attain if knower and known fell into dynamic interactions. In analog knowledge, however, the knower and the known are fused into a unitary action system. Analog knowledge, like knowing another in the biblical sense, consists of moving in behavioral coherence through time and space. Analytic knowledge is symbolic information about an object in terms of a set of alternatives encoded within the memory system of the knower. Analog knowledge is the nonsymbolic physical fact of moving together with the object. Analog knowledge has no memory; it stops when the process of knowing stops, when the knowers cease to be a unit.

The high Mach gains analytic knowledge over his target only because he can keep dynamic interactions out of the exchange. Thus, he remains fixed, avoids assuming similarity, and fails to differentiate between high and low targets because his measuring rod is in subjective units with himself as point of origin rather than objective (i.e., experiential) units of how far he had to go out to get to where the other person was.

Lows relate to others through analog knowledge and their later analytic responses to the person perception task reflect this. According to the encounter theory view, the process of "assuming similarity" was not an assumption but a fact, and was not detrimental but necessary for their differential accuracy later. Encounter prone, lows know others by moving into contact with them. They do not stand off, maintaining the integrity of their own cognitive frame, but open up to and get carried away by the influence of the other. They differentiate between highs and lows because they actually experience going in different directions, depending on where they must move to meet their targets. The similarity is real, not assumed, because they actually go themselves to where their targets are rather than sending out their cognitions to do the job of knowing analytically.

WHAT GOES ON WHEN ONE GETS "MACH'D"? Lows characteristically get "mach'd" by highs in bargaining. The lack of correlation between Mach scores and IQ rules out the possibility that highs win through intellectual superiority. It is more in mobilizing what he knows than in learning what is going on that the low fails. He appears to have a performance rather than a learning deficit. Zajonc's (1965) resolution of the perennial social facilitation problem dovetails with the encounter theory explanation of low-Mach bargaining. Zajonc demonstrated that the presence of others facilitates the performance of dominant responses. Encounter theory asserts that the moment-to-moment feedback-controlled regulation of interaction process that we have called encounter is a performance rather than a learning variable and that it operates more potently in lows than highs.

The low brings the dominant response of being willing to go along with others into the bargaining situation, while the high, undistracted by this process, pursues the task goals of maximizing his gain. In general, it looks as if the lows are more heedless than helpless. They are taken unaware, and before they know what has happened they find themselves in a new position, often a worse one. Gradually the low discovers not only that he has been disadvantaged on the task, but also that the high is not reciprocating in the interaction as he has assumed. Once the situation has crystallized, there is little the low can do except grin and bear it or complain about the "unfairness" of the situation. The low gets "mach'd" by leaving himself open to an encounter which is unreciprocated.

This feedback model of getting "mach'd" is a special case of attitude change, a problem that has traditionally been examined from the outcome point of view. But by what process do we move from one set of cognitions or beliefs to another set? In the dissonance study (Chapter XIII) low's attitudes were changed after counterattitudinal behavior. Their attitude change was interpreted as a consequence of their wish to go along with the other in spite of the particular behavior involved, even though they themselves accepted the external cognitive definition that it was the overt behavior they had chosen. The present data support this interpretation, and encounter theory describes the behavioral processes involved. We would say that they went along with their partner in openness for an encounter and then later had to interpret their noncognitive behavior to themselves in cognitive terms.

The encounter process was described as an unintentional improvisation whose dynamic course is determined by following along with one another. How does the low experience an unreciprocated encounter attempt? An apt analogy might seem to be falling off a cliff, i.e., having no internal behavior control. However, feedback control is simply a different form of behavior control from cognitive control. A better analogy is that being "mach'd" is like being hypnotized. Under hypnotic control subjects feel aware of what is happening and free to do what they want. It is just that the suggestions of the hypnotist are so salient that it would be unthinkable to countermand them. The hypnotist defines "the way things are" and the subject goes along. Just so, high Machs orient cognitively to external task demands and proceed to initiate control over the interaction structure by defining the way things are. Lows, open to the personal presence of the highs and ready to follow along, fall into the highs' structure and then emerge from the process forced to face up to the reality of the way things have become.

SUMMARY

It was hypothesized in this study that low-Mach groups performing on the ball and spiral would be open and get carried away in divergent dynamics through a noncognitive interaction process called encountering asserted to operate under mutual feedback control. In contrast, high-Mach groups would retain reciprocal cognitive control on the task, thus remaining convergent on their expected individual levels of performance.

Twenty-three two-boy two-girl tetrads were assembled and run in the four boy—girl pairs in counterbalanced fashion on the ball and spiral. The average Mach scale score for the tetrad was calculated and the tetrads split at the median. The skill level on the task was calculated by taking the average number of quarter turns reached by the ball before it fell off the spiral over the 80 trials each tetrad played. The subjects-by-subjects index of encountering was calculated by taking the difference of differences between the pair scores within each tetrad. Low-Mach tetrads showed more encounter interaction than the highs, but no more skill than the highs. The encountering effect was strongest in those tetrads which were both low and homogeneous in Mach scale score. Encountering estimates were found to be statistically independent of skill estimates in the data.

The subjects by subjects factorial design was demonstrated to provide a way of analytically disentangling group system effects from individual group member effects, even though the two cannot be observed separately in behavior. The group system effect was deduced to represent divergent group-maintenance behavior while the individual effects were deduced to represent convergent task-oriented behavior. Empirical evidence was reviewed, indicating that cognitive group tasks are mediated by cognitive behavior control while relational action tasks operate under noncognitive mutual feedback control.

Insights have emerged within the framework of encounter theory about what low Machs do, not only on the cooperative ball-and-spiral task, but also in the mere presence of others, in attitude change situations, in person perception, and in bargaining with high Machs. The encountering concept has also helped to clarify such terms as empathy, spontaneity, treating others personally, and getting "mach'd."

The basic messages of this research are: (a) low Machs are encounter prone and high Machs are encounter blind; (b) interaction between individuals in the group system sense is noncognitive; and (c) encountering can be empirically measured and theoretically understood as a divergent, noncognitive, mutual-feedback process.

CHAPTER XV

OVERVIEW
OF EXPERIMENTAL RESEARCH

Florence Geis and Richard Christie

The preceding chapters have given an account of how Machiavellianism was explored in the laboratory. Eleven studies have been reported in detail; others have been mentioned; and yet others have been done or discovered more recently. To the best of our knowledge the Mach scales have been used in 38 different experimental studies. Although many are related in that new research sprang from puzzles and hunches generated by previous ones, the accumulation of results has modified and expanded some of the conclusions. In this chapter we will pause and consider the major themes of the experimental work to date: what do high and low Machs do and how do they go about doing it?

In some situations high and low Machs have behaved differently; in others they have not. These differences appear to be related to characteristics of the situation which may either facilitate or mask the dispositional differences. The situational characteristics we believe relevant are:

1. face-to-face interaction,
2. latitude for improvisation,
3. arousing irrelevant affect.

The personal characteristics of high and low Machs which are hypothesized as accounting for the difference in outcome when these situational characteristics are present are currently seen as related consequences of a general difference in orientation. We have labeled the interpersonal stance of high Machs "the cool syndrome" and that of lows "the soft touch."

Dispositional Differences

High Machs: the Cool Syndrome	Low Machs: the Soft Touch
Resistance to social influence	Susceptibility to social influence
Orientation to cognitions	Orientation to persons
Initiating and controlling structure	Accepting and following structure

The personal characteristics of high and low Machs which interact with the situational variables are considered in more detail after the evidence for the situational characteristics is presented.

EXPERIMENTAL CONDITIONS UNDER WHICH
HIGH MACHS "WIN"

The 38 known studies involving 50 experimental conditions among them are summarized in Table XV-1. These studies involved more than the 50 conditions listed, but variations not relevant to our present classification system are not reported separately. Those not discussed in other chapters are marked with a dagger and described briefly in Appendix B. Each study or experimental condition has been categorized as to the presence or absence of the three situational conditions, and was also characterized as to outcome.

Before describing these concepts as we presently understand them, it should be noted that although our present labels are *post hoc,* their referents are not completely so. We will sketch in briefly how each of them was clarified and redefined over the course of experimentation. These accounts are not intended to exhaust the list of studies which support the importance of the variables, since this is the purpose of the tabulation to follow.

FACE-TO-FACE INTERACTION

If the subjects were not in each other's physical presence, or had no opportunity to observe and communicate with the person with whom they were interacting the studies were coded "no." If physical confrontation occurred they were coded "yes."

When high Machs won more money in face-to-face bargaining in the Ten Dollar Game (Chapter IX) but did not win more in the Penny–Dollar Caper (Chapter X) in which subjects were not playing a live opponent, the face-to-face variable became salient. Earlier, the high Machs' greater willingness to manipulate in the face-to-face Machiavel study (Chapter V) had suggested an ability to size up subtle social cues. This was tested in the Rheingold study (Chapter VI) in which the cues were pictures of the Miss Rheingold contestants, not face-to-face contact with them, and high Machs did not guess more winners. Although the lack of an opportunity to improvise could also account for these contrasts, the face-to-face variable had turned up in other contexts. In the Eye of the Beholder (Chapter XII) after 2 hr of face-to-face interaction, high Machs were more accurate than lows in guessing the Mach scores of others in their group, while in a previous study by Danielian (1964†) highs had been no more accurate than lows at describing others they had seen in a filmed interview. Subsequently, Durkin's encounter analysis (Chapter XIV) suggested that low Machs, but not highs, get caught up and carried away in a social response process which emerges in the action components of face-to-face interaction.

LATITUDE FOR IMPROVISATION

Situations were coded low on this variable if the subject had to choose one of two or more predefined alternative responses, usually at a given signal or decision point. For example, in the Miss Rheingold study the subjects had to guess the winner among a set of six contestants; in the Penny–Dollar Caper they had to choose between a red and black button. If the subject had to improvise both the content and timing of his responses, the situation was characterized as providing latitude for improvisation.

The earliest recognition of this variable was that of Exline *et al.* in Chapter IV. They suggested that high Machs were superior in situations in which subjects have to think on their feet. This was made an explicit characteristic of the Machiavel testing situation, and the manipulation category that captured the biggest difference betwen high and low Machs was one labeled "Innovative Manipulations." These were tactics clearly fabricated by the subject himself.

A related variable under yet a third label was manipulated in the Con Game study (Chapter VII). A hunch about low Machs' reliance on "objective" resources and an externally given structure for getting what they "deserved" compared to highs' reliance on manipulation was conceptualized as a difference in ability to take advantage of ambiguity. High Machs doubled their winning margin over the lows when the guidelines for how many points a player got in the game were more ambiguous. "Latitude for improvisation" indicates that the structure of the social interaction is open ended, not specifically predefined in terms of content or timing. "Ambiguity" in the Con Game referred to the absence of public criteria for allocating rewards among competitors. Obviously, ambiguity would be of little advantage to high Machs unless "improvisations" on their part could influence the distribution of rewards and conversely, improvising would be fruitless if rewards were determined by objective criteria beyond the subject's control. Latitude for improvisation implies both that subjects must improvise and that improvisation can influence outcomes.

It has been suggested (Chapter VIII) that the high Machs must be superior in timing their responses. We know of no study to date that has evaluated the effectiveness of high Machs' timing of responses independent of content. Our present category includes improvisation of both content and timing.

Perspective suggests that we should limit "latitude for improvisation" specifically to *cognitive* improvisation. We have no reason to believe that high Machs would be better lovers than lows. The highs were no more skillful on the ball-and-spiral task (Chapter XIV) although it required moment-to-moment physical improvisation between partners. Similarly, we would not expect high Machs to be better at "improvising" on a musical instrument. Further, since no differences in IQ between high and low Machs have been found, it may be true that highs do better only in situations in which cognitive improvisation can make a difference *and* irrelevant affect distracts otherwise comparable low Machs. For example, we would not expect Machiavellianism to be an asset in such intellectual improvisations as theoretical physics (although it might be an asset in promoting recognition of contributions).

IRRELEVANT AFFECT

This was the hardest of the three categories to code. Most interpersonal situations involve affect to some degree. The critical question is whether or not the affect distracts the subject from concentrating on the operations which lead to success as measured by the experimenter.

When high Machs won in the Con Game, the obvious question was how did they win, since they had not used any of the coded tactics significantly more often than lows. Retrospect provided some clues. One was that low Machs seemed to take the situation more seriously, becoming personally and emotionally involved with their partners and also with moral concerns elicited by the situation, while highs showed little evidence of such concern. This was consistent with the initial formulation of the characteristics of high Machs (Chapter I) — that they would not be likely to invest affect in others. This suggested that becoming affectively involved could "distract" a subject and interfere with effective pursuit of task goals, and the Legislature study (Chapter XI) supported this interpretation.

An early notion related to the irrelevant affect variable might be noted. In the Ten Dollar Game (Chapter IX) we needed only seven triads of subjects to demonstrate statistically that high Machs won. The difference between bargaining for money in this situation and for points in the previous Con Game triads was conceptualized as a difference in the "seriousness" of the situation. Seriousness was defined as the importance of values at stake in the situation with consequences extending beyond it. "Values with consequences" are, obviously, prime candidates as affect arousers.

CLASSIFICATION OF OUTCOME

The studies are grouped in the table roughly in terms of the kind of behavior that was being measured. Those in the first group, "Manipulation," involved ·situations in which the major activity was conning or manipulating a peer (Machiavel, Children's Dice, Chapter XVI), several peers [Con Game; Oksenberg Wheel (Oksenberg, 1968†)], a supposed partner (all of the Prisoner's Dilemma-type studies), and in one case the experimenter (Exline *et al*). In all of the studies marked with an asterisk the subjects were competing against each other and knew what they were competing for (points in a game, pennies, dollars, M&M candies, winning debates, course grades, etc.). When high Machs won significantly more than lows, the outcome is classified as "yes." In the unasterisked studies, in which subjects were not knowingly competing with each other, or did not know what was being measured, the outcome is classified as "yes" if high Machs manipulated more.

In the second group of studies, "Persuasibility," the behavior that was being measured involved compliance or attitude change. In each, the subject's belief or attitude about something was measured before and after an experimental treatment. Outcome is classified as "yes" if high Machs changed significantly less than lows, i.e., if they were *less* persuasible. The two studies listed under "Persuasiveness" measured the ability of one subject to persuade another or others. Outcome is classified as "yes" if high Machs were more successful as persuaders than lows.

In the miscellaneous studies, the outcome is classified as "yes" if high Machs did better at the task than lows, and otherwise if the results were consistent with the investigator's predictions. In one case (Jones & Daugherty, 1959†) the investigators interpreted the results as confirming their conceptualization, but our reinterpretation is that the findings were negative and we have so classified them. In another (Blumstein & Weinstein, 1969†), the authors' prediction was not confirmed, but our own, stated previously and unknown to the authors, was confirmed, so we classified the outcome in that case as "yes."

It should be emphasized that outcome was coded "yes" only if the high Machs won or behaved as predicted significantly. In only one of the 25 instances coded "no" [Wahlin's "bottom dog" condition (Wahlin, 1967†)] did they lose significantly contrary to prediction. In two cases (Durkin's ball-and-spiral study and Geis and Leventhal's detection condition, 1966†) the lows' significant superiority had been predicted, and in several control conditions the prediction was for no difference.

Each of the authors coded all of the studies. We then compared notes and discussed the few cases of disagreement. In some it was difficult to tell and we left a question mark which we counted as a "no" in summarizing. In general we tried to err on the side of caution. Although it might be possible to quibble about certain decisions, most of them were relatively straightforward.

EXPERIMENTAL CONDITIONS
AND RESEARCH OUTCOME

The classifications presented in Table XV-1 are summarized in Table XV-2. In 13 of 14 instances in which face-to-face contact, latitude for improvisation, and irrelevant affect were all judged present, the high Machs won more, were persuaded less, persuaded others more, or behaved as predicted significantly compared to low Machs. In all 11 cases in which none of these variables was present, there was no significant difference in favor of the highs. In 7 of the 12

TABLE XV-1

Overview of Situational Parameters in Experimental Studies [a]

	Situational parameters			
Studies	Face to face	Latitude for improvisation	Irrelevant affect	Outcome
Manipulation				
1. Visual Interaction (Exline *et al.*, Ch. IV)	X	X	X	Yes
2. Machiavel (Geis *et al.*, Ch. V)	X	X	X	Yes
ᵃCon Game				
3. Ambiguous	X	X	X	Yes
4. Unambiguous (Geis, Ch. VII)	X	X	X	Yes
5. ᵃTen Dollar Game (Christie & Geis, Ch. IX)	X	X	X	Yes
ᵃLegislature				
6. Hot Issues	X	X	X	Yes
7. Cold Issues (Geis *et al.*, Ch. XI)	X	X	0	No
ᵃClassroom Mach				
8. Leader within group	X	X	X	Yes
9. Grades between groups (Geis, 1968 [†])	X	X	X	Yes
10. Altercasting (Weinstein, Berkhouser, Blumstein, & Stein, 1968 [†])	X	X	X	Yes
ᵃDeception				
11. Deceiving	X	X	X	No
12. Detecting (Geis & Leventhal, 1966 [†])	X	0	0	No
13. ᵃChildren's Dice (Nachamie, Ch. XVI)	X	0	?	Yes
14. Dominoes Tactics (Edelstein, 1966 [†])	X	0	?	Yes
15. ᵃCollege Dice (Metze, 1967 [†])	X	0	?	No

TABLE XV-1 (continued)

| Studies | Situational parameters | | | Outcome |
	Face to face	Latitude for improvisation	Irrelevant affect	
Manipulation (cont'd)				
*Penny Dollar Caper				
16. Dollars	0	0	X	No
17. Pennies	0	0	0	No
(Christie *et al.*, Ch. X)				
*Asymetric Prisoners Dilemma				
18. "Bottom Dog"	0	0	X	No
19. "Top Dog"	0	0	0	No
(Wahlin, 1967 [†])				
20. *Prisoners Dilemma	0	0	X	No
(Wrightsman, 1966 [†])				
21. *Ethnic Prisoners Dilemma	0	0	0	No
(Vejio & Wrightsman, 1967 [†])				
22. *Products Game	0	0	?	No
(Lake, 1967 [†])				
23. Problem-Solving Wheel	0	X	0	No
(Oksenberg, 1968 [†])				
24. *Exchanging Chips	0	0	?	No
(Daniels, 1967 [†])				
Persuasibility				
25. Change Self-Description	X	X	X	Yes
(Jones *et al.*, 1962 [†])				
26. Leaderless Group Discussion	X	X	0	Yes
(Geis *et al.*, 1965 [†])				
27. Group Risk Taking	X	X	?	Yes
(Rim, 1966 [†])				
28. Waiting for Godot	X	X	X	Yes
(Harris, 1966 [†])				
Persuasive Communications				
29. Social Influence	0	0	X	Yes
30. Factual Influence	0	0	0	No
(Harris, 1966 [†])				

TABLE XV-1 (continued)

Studies	Situational parameters			Outcome
	Face to face	Latitude for improvisation	Irrelevant affect	
Persuasibility (cont'd)				
Devil's Advocate Dissonance				
31. Role Playing	0	0	X	Yes
32. Silent Reading (Epstein, 1969 [†])	0	0	0	No
Cheating Dissonance I				
33. Unattractive Partner	X	0	X	Yes
34. Attractive Partner (Bogart, Ch. XIII)	X	0	X	No
Cheating Dissonance II				
35. Unattractive partner	0	0	X	Yes
36. Attractive Partner (Bogart Ch. XIII)	0	0	X	No
Debating Dissonance				
37. Dissonant Position	X	0	X	Yes
38. Consonant Position (Feiler, 1967 [†])	X	0	X	Yes
Persuasiveness				
39. Cracker Pushing (Braginsky, 1966 [†])	X	X	X	Yes
ª Debating Persuasiveness				
40. Sincere Argument	X	X	X	Yes
41. Insincere Argument (Novielli, 1968 [†])	X	X	?	No
Miscellaneous				
42. Ball-and-Spiral Encounters (Durkin, Ch. XIV)	X	X	0	No
43. Eye of the Beholder (Geis & Levy, Ch. XII)	X	0	X	Yes
44. Movie Judgements (Danielian, 1964 [†])	0	0	?	No
45. ª Redress of Injustice (Blumstein & Weinstein, 1969 [†])	X	0	X	Yes

TABLE XV-1 (continued)

Studies	Situational parameters			Outcome
	Face to face	Latitude for improvisation	Irrelevant affect	
Miscellaneous (cont'd)				
46. Expected Interaction (Jones & Daugherty, 1959 [†])	0	0	?	No
47. In and Out of Role (Jones *et al.*, 1961 [†])	0	0	0	No
48. Skin Deep (Oksenberg, 1964 [†])	0	?	X	No
49. Miss Rheingold (Christie & Boehm, Ch. VI)	0	0	0	No
50. Opinion Disagreement (Thornton, 1967 [†])	X	X	0	No

[a] X, variable present; 0, variable absent; *, competition present or implied;
[†] , study described in Appendix B.

cases in which two of the variables were present high Machs did better. But they won in only 5 of the 13 instances in which only one of the variables was present. Such a finding is striking. A chi square test indicated that our classification scheme separated situations in which high Machs won and failed to win at the .001 level.

It might be asked whether any one of the variables alone was primarily responsible for the combined results. Each of them was independently related to outcome at better than the .025 level as tested by chi square. However, it is difficult to separate their effects. For example, in 39 of the 50 cases, face-to-face interaction and latitude for improvisation were jointly present or absent, in 32 conditions face-to-face interaction and irrelevant affect covaried, and in 29 latitude for improvisation and irrelevant affect covaried. Thus, there are relatively few cases in which outcome can be compared with the presence of one and the absence of another. Although conceptually the three variables are independent, they obviously tend to vary together empirically. Face-to-face interaction tends to arouse affective involvement which may be irrelevant to the task outcome defined by the experimenter. Improvising a conversation or deciding what to do in an unstructured situation can have the same effect.

These variables do not tell the whole story. As in the Geis and Leventhal deception condition (1966†), it is possible that even when all three variables are

TABLE XV-2

Outcomes of High and Low Machs by Number of Situational Parameters Present

No. of cases in which:	Number of parameters present				
	0	1	2	3	
High Machs win	0	5	7	13	25
High Machs do not win	11	8	5	1	25
Total	11	13	12	14	50

$$\chi^2 = 22.28, p < .001$$

judged present high Machs will not be more successful. Our position is that these three situational factors are significantly related to the relative outcome of high and low Machs in the experimental situations analyzed to date and that any future research should take them into account.

PERSONAL CHARACTERSITICS
OF HIGH VERSUS LOW MACHIAVELLIANS:
THE COOL SYNDROME AND THE SOFT TOUCH

In this section we will use experimental results to indicate refinements in the original, somewhat global conception of the manipulative person. This is a rather unorthodox procedure. Often when scales are constructed as the Mach scales were (measures of internal consistency, etc.), some studies are conducted to test the construct validity of the scale. We have gone beyond this stage, however, and have used the behavior of high- and low-Mach experimental subjects to delineate more clearly their characteristics as persons.

We think the construct validity of the Mach scale is well supported. In situations meeting the three criteria described above high Machs do manipulate more, or more successfully. The evidence for this argument is summarized in Table XV-1. Next, we examine the behavior of high and low Machs which can account for their difference as manipulators in situations meeting the criteria above.

In laboratory studies the hallmark of the high Mach has become what we term the cool syndrome. This has gone beyond the original concept. Not only do high Machs remain relatively unmoved by emotional involvement with others; they also appear equally unaffected by their own beliefs and even their own behavior.

In the Exline *et al.* study (Chapter IV) the high Machs were capable of looking an interrogator in the eye while lying to a greater extent than lows. They were also rated by judges as less anxious than lows during both the base line and interrogation periods. Although high and low Machs did not differ in self-reported involvement in the Con Game tournament (Chapter VII), it was our subjective impression that the highs were task involved in winning while the lows had become ego involved with details (loyalty of partners, breaches of reciprocity, fairness and justice in dividing the prize) which arose in the bargaining process.

These impressions suggested that one reason for lows losing to highs was that the lows were distracted from effective bargaining by emotional involvements irrelevant to winning. A new study (Legislature, Chapter XI) was designed to vary the potential for affective involvement. As predicted, high and low Machs did not differ in success in lobbying on prosaic issues, but the highs won when the bargaining discussions revolved around such sensitive and affect-arousing issues as abolishing the Peace Corps, universal military conscription, etc. In this study the emotional detachment that led to the highs' winning was not coolness toward other people but detachment from their own ideological positions.

However, the high Machs' coolness may not be more than skin deep (Oksenberg, 1964†). Subjects spent a minute writing down words beginning with a letter (A, B, C, D, or F) selected at random and not known to the experimenter. The subject was then connected to a PGR recorder and instructed to say "no" to all of the letters, each repeated six times in random order on a tape recording. Highs were caught by a visual inspection of the PGR record as often as lows, and the magnitude of their deflections to the crucial letter were not significantly smaller than the lows'. In this situation the highs were not more cool, autonomically at least, than the lows.

RESISTANCE VERSUS SUSCEPTIBILITY TO SOCIAL INFLUENCE

High Machs do appear cool, however, in the face of social influence. They will change their opinions or comply with requests if given sufficient justification; otherwise they remain unmoved. Low Machs are soft touches. They are more likely to do or accept what another wants simply because he wants it. In one of the first laboratory studies involving Machiavellianism (Jones *et al.*, 1962†), college girls were given negative feedback about themselves allegedly based on their self-descriptions. The prediction was that high Machs would attempt to ingratiate themselves with the next interviewer by changing their self-descriptions for him. At that time, of course, there were few previous data relating to the overt behavior of high and low Machs. The experimenters were consequently surprised but faithfully reported the significant disconfirmation of their hypothesis. It was the low-Mach girls who tried harder to make a favorable impression.

Exline *et al.* (Chapter IV) noted that their high Machs

...first put up a stronger resistance to a confederate's attempt to implicate them [in cheating], continued to resist the confederate more strongly as they worked through the critical tasks, then after the die was cast in spite of their efforts, more strongly resisted the interrogator's attempts to elicit a confession from them.

Durkin's encounter study (Chapter XIV) provided a somewhat different perspective on high Machs' emotional detachment, and probably pushed the social influence idea the furthest. Here there were no opinions, discussions, or issues on which subjects were trying to influence each other. He used a team action task — jointly rolling a ball up a spiral path — and the interaction term in a subjects-by-subjects design to measure susceptibility to personal influence. In this situation, the high Machs' individual skill levels accounted for their team performances. They remained uninfluenced by the particular other person who was serving as their partner. Low Machs, however, responded differently, depending on who their partner was. Their team performances could not be accounted for by the individual skill levels of the partners involved. This suggested that low Machs become engrossed in the interaction process and follow in whatever direction the other is going.

This general interpretation can account for all of the persuasibility results in which influence was attempted in a live, ongoing interaction. For example, in three different group discussion studies (Geis, Krupat, & Berger, 1965†; Rim, 1966†; Harris, 1966†) low Machs privately reported opinion change after face-to-face discussion, whether fellow discussants were high or low Mach, while highs showed no change at all. In a followup to the face-to-face condition, Harris (1966†) used written persuasive communications presented as either scientific information or polled opinions of young adults. Both highs and lows shifted in the direction of the factual arguments but only lows changed in the direction of the more socially oriented poll data. This pattern has turned up consistently in several independent investigations:

1. Highs and lows are equally persuaded by factual information or rational arguments.

2. Lows but not highs are also moved by sheer social pressure.

3. Although lows seem to be more susceptible in live face-to-face interaction, they are also moved by written communications representing beliefs or wishes of others.

This pattern was illustrated in the Bogart *et al.* dissonance studies (Chapter XIII). Subjects were urged by a supposed partner to join him in cheating on the experimental task. Justification for complying was varied by describing the partner as a Phi Beta Kappa graduate law student or as an unstable and not particularly bright undergraduate. High Machs complied more with more justification, but lows did not discriminate. (The partner's urging was identical in both description conditions.) In Bogart's replication (Chapter XIII) the same paradigm was used, but the partner's suggestion came in a written note and contained some rational arguments in support of cheating. In this case high Machs complied more than lows, but still preferred the attractive partner.

These studies also provided data on cognitive changes following cheating. The dissonance theory prediction that later beliefs will be changed toward consonance with former "unjustified" behavior was supported by low Machs but not by highs. Just as high Machs go along less with what others believe or what others want them to do, they also appear less influenced by what they themselves have just said or done. This was true in the two studies just mentioned and also in two other studies using different dissonance situations.

Both Epstein (1969†) and Feiler (1967†) induced college men to give "voluntary" arguments contrary to their private conviction. In both studies only the low Machs changed their opinion on the posttest to agree with their arguments. In these situations the low Machs literally talked themselves into opinion change. They got carried away with going along with what another person wanted — in these cases, the experimenter. In Epstein's control condition subjects silently read a prepared, rational argument contrary to their convictions and then took a postmeasure. In this situation, with little social pressure but substantial rational justification, high Machs changed slightly more than lows in the direction advocated. Feiler ran a "consonant" control condition in which subjects publicly defended a position they also privately endorsed. Since there was no dissonance in this condition, attitude change could not be attributed to dissonance reduction. However, the subject could get carried away with his own arguments. Again, highs showed no attitude change (no new, rational arguments were introduced), but lows did, endorsing the position they had defended more strongly than before.

In none of these four dissonance studies did high Machs change their opinions to agree with their "inconsistent" behavior in the high-dissonance conditions. In every case lows did. The only condition among the four studies in which high Machs changed their cognitions from before to after an experimental treatment was Epstein's control condition, the only one in which attitude change was urged with rational, informative arguments.

These findings suggest that high Machs might be more successful in bargaining because they do not give in to sheer social pressure as readily as lows. They may be more successful manipulators in mixed-Mach groups because their detachment enables them to resist both explicit and implicit social demands and simply wait until the lows fall in with their suggestions. This is essentially Durkin's argument in Chapter XIV. However, lack of persuasibility alone cannot explain the results of the Legislature study in which the high Machs were presumably equally unpersuadable in both conditions but won only when important issues were discussed.

High Machs' resistance to social influence in general has two specific consequences on which data are available: (a) high Machs resist "unjustified" inducements to lie or cheat; (b) highs are suspicious of experimenters' and others' explanations.

LYING AND CHEATING. One of the four initial characterizations of high Machs was that they would show little concern for conventional morality. This is almost definitional, as indicated by their responses to some items on the Mach scale. Such attitudes can be seen as a consequence of affective detachment. High Machs are less likely to accept others' wishes or beliefs without justification, and similarly, they remain unconvinced by the larger social consensus of conventional moral standards. However, private approval or disapproval of lying in general does not automatically differentiate lying in specific situations. Interesting as these behaviors may be because of their illicit nature, they can be seen as instances of the general class of compliance or persuasibility, at least in the laboratory situations studied.

Exline *et al.* (Chapter IV) found that lows were equally prone to accede to a confederate's cheating (two highs and two lows out of 42 subjects refused to continue) but that highs were more resistant to confession and were also rated by judges as lying more plausibly during the interrogation.

Deception of others was permitted, encouraged, or explicitly requested by the experimenter in nine subsequent studies: the Machiavel study (Chapter V), Braginsky (Chapter XVI), Epstein (1969†), Feiler (1967†), Novielli (1968†), Nachamie (Chapter XVI), Edelstein (1966†), Geis and Leventhal (1966†), and Oksenberg (1964†). In none of these studies did more low Machs refuse to deceive than highs; in one of the nine (Edelstein's) highs told more lies (bluffs in a game) than lows, and in the Machiavel study they told larger lies.

Further evidence suggests that high Machs will lie or cheat more when given more rational justification while lows will go along more when given more personal persuasion. This explanation brings the lying and cheating data into line with the general social influence pattern.

In the Bogart *et al.* dissonance study (as in the one by Exline *et al.)* subjects had to decide whether or not to cheat without knowing of the experimenter's complicity in the situation. As noted above, high Machs cheated more when urged by a (purported) Phi Beta Kappa graduate law student and less when their partner was described as an undergraduate undistinguished academically or otherwise. Low Machs cheated equally often with the partner under both labels.

The one study in which highs cheated more than lows (other than in accord with game rules) was Bogart's followup (Chapter XIII). Consistently, changes in the inducement to cheat fit the persuasion conditions outlined above under which high Machs are more likely to be persuaded and lows less likely.

1. The inducement in the follow up study was written rather than face to face.

2. The subject received a single message rather than a series of increasingly stronger urgings.

3. After receiving the written message the subject had time to weigh the pros and cons, and come to his own private decision.

4. Some rational reasons for cheating were given in the written message.

5. Cheating in the second study was made to appear virtually undetectable, while in the original situation the cheating would have been obvious had the experimenter returned.

Low Machs, though opposed to dishonesty in principle, can be persuaded to cheat or lie given a strong, personal, and repeated inducement, especially in a face-to-face situation in which they have little time to reflect, but must act, either accepting the other's wishes or rejecting them; in these situations external "rational" justifications had little effect on their decisions. In contrast, high Machs, although not opposed to dishonesty in principle, will cheat less if the "rational" incentives are low or the costs (such as the probability of getting caught) are high.

Evidence on the question of success in deceiving others is less clear. Measures of effectiveness or success were taken in seven of the studies mentioned above (Exline *et al.*, Braginsky, Epstein, Novielli, Nachamie, Geis & Leventhal, Oksenberg). High Machs were clearly more successful as liers in only two of these. In the Exline *et al.* study highs were rated as lying more plausibly while denying cheating, and in Nachamie's (Chapter XVI) dice bluffing game high-Mach children's bluffs were less often challenged than those of lows. Braginsky's (Chapter XVI) high-Mach children were more successful in getting a peer to eat more bitter crackers, but it is not clear whether this was accomplished through lies or by other tactics.

It is possible that high Machs may be more effective when *subjects* have to decide when and what to lie about versus being assigned specific lies by the experimenter. (This is similar to the latitude for improvisation variable discussed above.) The subjects of Exline *et al.* were entirely on their own. Nachamie's children knew from the game rules that successful bluffs constituted "winning," but were free to decide on each trial whether to bluff or not. In contrast, Epstein, Novielli, Geis and Leventhal, and Oksenberg assigned subjects specific lies with no choice of content or occasion.

There is an ironic footnote to this discussion of lying and cheating. It is beginning to appear that low Machs who are telling the truth may be "successful deceivers" inadvertantly. This phenomenon first appeared in the Legislature study (Chapter XI). Each subject had to seek voting support from others in the group for some issues he privately endorsed and some he privately opposed, and low Machs lost primarily on those they genuinely believed in. Then in the Geis and Leventhal deception study each subject was given the task of convincing two others of his beliefs on two issues, his actual belief on one and the opposite of his belief on another. Low Machs telling the truth were believed significantly less often than similarly truthful highs.

It appeared that the low Mach's affective involvement with his own beliefs might hinder him in making an effective argument for them. This idea was tested by Novielli (1968†) using debates left unstructured except for a time limit. Two subjects debated while two others served as judges. Each pair debated twice. In one debate each defended the position he also privately endorsed; in the other the position contrary to his own belief. High Machs did no better than lows when both were defending "insincere" positions, but lows lost to their high Mach opponents (22 out of 32 decisions) when both were defending their actual convictions.

Although the low Machs' relative inability to tell the truth credibly is theoretically consistent, the implications for social life outside of the laboratory bear reflection.

SUSPICIOUS HIGH MACHS. Our earliest contact with high Machs in the laboratory — running pilot subjects for the Machiavel study — impressed us sufficiently with their suspiciousness of experimental procedures to lead us to include a question on the topic in the final design. We now see the highs' suspiciousness as another example of their lack of susceptibility to social influence, in contrast to the lows' tendency to accept others' (in this case the experimenter's) definition of the situation.

Specifically, high Machs appear to be suspicious of people — experimenters, other subjects, fellow students, etc. — not of events, objects, or ideas. An example illustrates the point. In working out the dice game for Nachamie's study the thought of using loaded dice occurred. Inquiries at dice manufacturing companies revealed that professionally loaded dice were not sufficiently biased for our purposes. We therefore loaded our own so that a pair would come up .68 "the same" or "different," depending on the sides loaded. Much to our surprise none of the 16 subjects playing two series of 50 trials with these dice caught on. One high-Mach math major who had just expressed suspicion (justified) about the results of a Prisoners Dilemma game showed no suspiciousness when rolling runs far beyond the .001 probability level with the loaded dice. This was especially surprising since players had to record the outcome of every roll. He was so busy eyeing his opponent that he failed to notice his own written evidence of the significantly biased outcomes.

The difference in high Machs' attitudes between the Bogart *et al.* dissonance study and the followup (Chapter XIII) also suggests that highs are suspicious primarily of people. When the deceptively described confederate was physically present, 7 out of 33 highs and only 1 out of 28 lows were suspicious of the person or the procedure. In the followup when the subject was in a booth so that neither experimenter nor confederate was exposed, none of the 48 highs expressed suspicion. In the Penny–Dollar Caper (Chapter X) high Machs rated their supposed fellow player as significantly less "trustworthy" than the lows did when all they knew was his pattern of choices (identical for all subjects) and assumed him to be one of the other subjects in the room. However, only 2 of the 21 highs as opposed to 5 of the 19 lows were suspicious of the situation.

Paradoxically, in the deception study (Geis & Leventhal, 1966†) it was the low Machs who guessed accurately whether a speaker was lying or telling them the truth, not the highs. Perhaps highs are suspicious *because* they aren't sure. Their probing for clues could easily be interpreted by wary experimenters as "suspicion." Lows may fail to detect experimenter's deceptions (a) because experimenters do not usually ask subjects to focus on the question, and (b) because lows get carried away in the process of doing what the experimenter asks — and "forget" their suspicions.

In summary, high Machs resist sheer social pressure. They can be persuaded to change their beliefs or comply with requests when given rational justification, and will be persuaded less as costs or risks increase. For low Machs costs and risks are less decisive, especially when the social pressure occurs in a face-to-face interaction in which the low cannot deliberate in private but must act, either accepting or rejecting the other's wishes. High and low Machs' decisions about whether to lie or cheat are seen as following the same pattern, but highs may be more successful liars, possibly when they can choose the occasion and content. Similarly, high Machs are suspicious in experiments to the extent that experimenters' explanations qualify as "sheer social pressure."

COGNITIVE VERSUS PERSONAL ORIENTATIONS

What do high Machs do while the lows are busy going along with others' wishes in social interactions? A possible answer is that they are processing information about the situation. Zajonc (1965) resolved the contradictory findings generated by research on "social facilitation" — effects of the presence of others on behavior. He argued that the presence of others triggers arousal and that arousal facilitates the performance of already well-learned behavior while inhibiting the acquisition of new information. Although we have not tested the formulation directly, our analyses suggest that both of these general arousal effects are due largely to low Machs. If this is true, the high Mach's success in bargaining and persuasion situations can be seen as a result of a lack of arousal or the ability to control it in social situations in which information processing pays off. In every laboratory study in which implicit assumptions concerning human relations, social values, or ethical considerations could have interfered with task achievement, the high Mach appeared to ignore them and operate instead according to the explicit, cognitive definition of the situation.

An important distinction should be clarified before proceeding further. High Machs do not *appear* unconcerned. On the contrary, they often express more interest and concern than lows. The important difference is that the highs are not personally or emotionally involved in the concerns. They do not assume that partners *should* be loyal, so are not upset when loyalty is betrayed.

Examples of low Machs' being influenced by implicit assumptions to which they are emotionally committed compared to highs' attending to explicit definitions, rules, and overt actions abound in the data.

Low Machs accept the implicit "ought" in the cognitive consistency formula. Although they can be induced into overt actions which are unjustified by their cognitions (a point we will return to in a moment), they subsequently change their cognitions to agree. Privately, in reporting cognitions, they accept the implicit assumption that one ought to do what he believes in and believe in what he does. As noted above, high Machs show little evidence of such constraints.

The assumption of similarity, the assumption that another holds the same beliefs, attitudes, or standards of conduct as oneself, can also operate implicitly. In the Eye of the Beholder (Chapter XII) low Machs guessed their target person as closer to themselves in Mach score than he was. Although we have no data, the interesting question is whether the lows' assumption that others were similar was specific to the response-guessing task used in the study, or whether it might be characteristic of them in interpersonal situations generally, since this would result in the lows' attributing non-Machiavellian motives to the highs' Machiavellian behaviors. High Machs did not assume similarity. They were consistently more accurate than lows in picking out exactly how their target person differed from themselves.

A favorite implicit assumption of low Machs concerns interpersonal relations. This is the assumption of reciprocity. In the Con Game (Chapter VIII) 11 cases were noted in which a high- or low-Mach subject made a coalition with a partner on condition that the partner give his promise not to break it. The four low Machs evidently took their partner's promise as their own and did not break the coalition; all seven highs did subsequently break the coalition they had required their partner to promise not to break. On the other hand, no high Mach ever broke a (recorded) promise *he* had given explicitly.

The tendency of low Machs to invest affect in implicit assumptions irrelevant to "winning" accounts for the highs' advantage in situations characterized by the potential for "irrelevant affect."

A different kind of involvement on the part of low Machs, also irrelevant to winning, accounts for the highs' advantage when subjects have to improvise to win. It was noted above that low Machs can be led into activities which violate their beliefs. For example, they disavow dishonesty on the Mach scale, but are as likely as highs (who do not disavow it) to lie or cheat when urged, in person, by a partner or experimenter. Specifically in the process of ongoing, face-to-face interaction in which participants must follow the action and improvise responses in context, without time for private reflection, low Machs can get "carried away" in going along with others. Durkin (Chapter XIV) termed this process "encountering," and described it as operating on a noncognitive, action (or emotional) feedback principle. In the process of such immediate, mutual responding, low Machs can "forget" not only general beliefs or principles, but also individual strategies for winning.

In contrast, again, high Machs concentrate on what is explicit, and how to exploit it. They appear to aim at achieving the possible and adapt their tactics to the specific conditions of the situation at hand. This general orientation is usually called "opportunistic" by those who deplore it, and "realistic" by more admiring observers. For example, high Machs have manipulated obviously (i.e., significantly more than lows) when the manipulator was not dependent upon the victim's cooperation. This was true in the Machiavel study (Chapter V), in the group discussion study (Geis *et al.*, 1965†), and in the "interrogator" role in the deception study (Geis & Leventhal, 1966†). In contrast, high Machs did not use any of the recorded tactics more frequently than lows in the Con Game (Chapter VIII) in which potential victims could retaliate, nor did they play the exploitive strategy more than lows in the Penny–Dollar Caper (Chapter X) in which a supposed opponent could also presumably retaliate. In Nachamie's dice bluffing game a child who consistently bluffed or challenged would have been an easy mark for his opponent. High-Mach children bluffed and challenged more successfully, but not more frequently than lows. It was proposed previously (Chapter VIII) that high Machs are attuned to some psychological equivalent of the .05 probability level, that they know how to push the limits of the possible without breaking them. No evidence to date contradicts that proposition.

High Machs adjust the amount of manipulation, and also change their strategy in more subtle ways when the situation changes. In the Con Game both high and low Machs made coalition agreements reflecting their power position in the groups when power positions were public but highs (unlike lows) ignored concealed power positions. When the Penny–Dollar Caper (Chapter X) was changed from points to money, high Machs changed their strategy to more cooperative (resulting in higher joint winning for the pair), but lows did not. In the Ten Dollar Game (Chapter IX) there were no differential power positions that could be used to suggest unequal divisions of the money. In this situation the highs won by getting into the coalition (100% of them did), but were more willing to divide the money equally (five of seven agreed to 50–50 splits). When success depended upon partners' cooperation high Machs offered "realistic" incentives — greater cooperation (with their also-cooperative partner) in the Penny–Dollar Caper, and even-money splits in the Ten Dollar Game. In the Con Game highs tended to offer slightly more points to partners than lows did, at least in the initial stages of bargaining.

High Machs are politic, not personal. We have no evidence as to whether successful politicians outside of the laboratory "tell 'em what they wanna hear," but our high Machs did just that in the Legislature game (Chapter XI). When the issue content was emotionally loaded, highs made speeches in the introductory period in which they mentioned popular issues, did not mention unpopular issues, and ignored the distinction between issues with high and low payoff for them personally. In the crucial bargaining and voting periods however, highs attended strictly to their high-payoff issues. In contrast, lows mentioned their own high-payoff issues in the preliminary period, ignored the popularity distinction, and lost in the voting period. Similarly, in the Con Game high Machs were able to make and break coalitions strategically. They ended up with more points in the game after breaking a coalition than if they had kept it to the end. Lows also broke coalitions, but ended up with fewer points after breaking one than they would have made if they (and their partner) had kept it.

One consequence of the high Machs' cool, cognitive, situation-specific strategy is that they never appear to be "obviously manipulating" — when being obvious would be a disadvantage. (In fact, lows are more apt to *appear* unreasonable.) A second consequence is that the highs generally end up with more than others of what everyone was vying for. The high Mach is the one who gets others to help him win in such a way that, in the process, they thank him for the opportunity.

Low Machs have not suffered from a lack of enthusiasm, motivation, or effort in the situations studied. They also appeared to be trying to win. However, they appear less politic in dealing with others. They become so engrossed with the particular person or content they are dealing with that they get carried away and neglect to manipulate, implicitly assuming that fair play will prevail. This appears to be a losing tactic.

That the lows' disability in interpersonal competition is due to the distraction of getting carried away is illustrated by their ability to process cognitions in privacy, undistracted by having to improvise strategy and repartee at the same time. In the deception study (Geis & Leventhal, 1966†) judges were given a moment to reflect, and the judgment measure itself did not require improvising. The judge had only to decide whether the witness had been telling "truth" or "lie," and lows were significantly more accurate than highs. The Miss Rheingold study (Chapter VI) and the Penny–Dollar Caper (Chapter X) also presented subjects with a choice in privacy among fixed alternatives, and lows guessed as many Miss Rheingold winners in one case, and won as many dollars in the other as highs. Similarly, when rewards are tied to objective, predefined criteria, as in making high scores on IQ tests, lows process cognitions as effectively as highs. The high Mach's advantage is specifically in interpersonal situations — in getting others to recognize his claims over those of competing low Machs.

Low Machs lose by opening themselves emotionally to others, by taking others' needs and concerns as their own. Highs win by being politic. Although they are aware of what the other wants, they do not take his needs personally, but rather use them impersonally, for example, to strike a bargain to their own advantage.

As might be inferred from the preceding discussion, both high and low Machs are "sensitive to others" — but in quite different ways. High Machs appear sensitive to information *about* the other person. They respond to cognitive, discriminative labels and explicit cues, particularly those that are relevant to planning strategy in the situation. Low Machs appear more sensitive to the other person as a person, from his point of view, and in terms of his feelings, wishes, and expectations.

For example, when different subjects were given different descriptions of a partner who later urged them to cheat in the dissonance studies (Bogart *et al.*, Chapter XIII) the high Machs complied differentially, according to the labels even though both "partners" were played by the same person. When given no cues high Machs did not discriminate — in playing ball and spiral (Chapter XIV), in choosing coalition partners in the Con Game, in guessing Mach scale answers for others (Chapter XII). In the two latter situations the highs' "averaging over partners" strategy was successful. In the Con Game they won; in the Eye of the Beholder the statistical nature of their view of others was evidenced by their lack of accuracy on particular items which produced overall accuracy when averaged out.

In contrast, low Machs appear to attend more to the particular person confronting them. Low Machs complied with the stooge under one label as often as the other in the cheating studies, but: preferred high Machs as a partner in the Con Game, discriminated accurately between high- and low-Mach target persons in the Eye of the Beholder, discriminated accurately whether others were lying or telling the truth in the deception study, and did better or worse with partners than skill could account for in playing ball and spiral.

When low Machs get carried away in interactions with others, the answer to where they "go" seems to be "to wherever the other 'is' as a person." Highs fail to discriminate between others because they do not go to the other, but stay within their own cognitive frame of reference, maintaining perspective on the situation as a whole.

For example, high Machs were more accurate in guessing how others had differed from themselves in answering the Mach scale, without discriminating (as lows did) whether their target person was higher or lower in Machiavellianism. One way to have accomplished this would be for the high Mach to have established a definition of where *he* stood vis-a-vis others in the preceding interaction. Not moving emotionally to where others "were" would account for failing to discriminate between high- and low-Mach target persons, while maintaining a self-definition as a fixed reference point would account for accuracy later in inferring how another differed from oneself. Low Machs could infer later where the other must "be" on the Mach scale, because they had moved to where others were in the preceding interaction, but because they had moved, they had no fixed reference point of "self vis-a-vis others" from which to infer how the other differed from themselves — and in fact, called him "closer" than his (previously given) responses actually were.

Low Machs were called "soft touches" partly to reflect their susceptibility to social influence, discussed above, but also to convey the flavor of their style in dealing with others. The low Mach comes to direct contact with another by moving to where he is, and touches others softly in the sense that his contact with another does not violate the position or intentions of the other person. In contrast, the high Mach remains unmoved himself in his transactions with others. Rather, he uses the transaction to move the others away from their intentions to where he wants them for his own purposes.

An implicit distinction should be made explicit. It should be clear from the discussion above that our characterization of high Machs as more "cognitive" is not intended to imply that cognitions are experienced as more important by high Machs than by lows. On the contrary, it is low Machs for whom cognitions are more "important" (i.e., invested with affect). Highs process and exploit cognitions more effectively in situations in which lows become distracted precisely because the highs' cognitions are unencumbered with emotional commitment.

It is not that lows fail to attend to cognitive cues or fail to learn them; rather, as Durkin's encounter analysis (Chapter XIV) indicates, lows get caught up in the ongoing interaction with others. Although they perceive the cues, they get carried away unintentionally in a direction which has nothing to do with the cues. One consequence is losing in affect-laden bargaining contests; another is the ability to discriminate accurately between other persons who differ, regardless of whatever true or false labels may have preceded the interaction. In contrast, high Machs keep their eye on the cognitive definitions. They do not become involved in going along with others, nor do they become involved with implicit assumptions about themselves, others, or interpersonal relations; rather they process information about the situation, including their own position vis-a-vis others. Thus, they concentrate on strategies for winning, and disregard individual differences between others unless given cues specifying discriminations which are strategic.

HIGH MACHS ARE EXPLOITIVE, NOT VICIOUS OR VINDICTIVE. It is true, we think, that given appropriate incentive, high Machs will exploit whatever resources the situation affords in pursuit of their goal. If the situation provides cooperative, yielding, or distractible low Machs, the lows will be exploited. However, high Machs select exploitable resources relevant to the situation. In the Penny–Dollar Caper (Chapter X) the experimenters were giving away money in sizable quantities, and subjects believed they were playing a Prisoners Dilemma-type game with a partner. As noted above, attempts to exploit the partner might reasonably have been assumed to provoke retaliation with a consequent loss of dollars to both players. In this situation the high Machs cooperated with their supposed partner in an apparent attempt to exploit the experimenter's urge to distribute money.

In no instance that we can recall have high Machs appeared behaviorally hostile, vicious, or punitive toward others. In the Machiavel study (Chapter V) subjects were given an ambiguous instruction to "confuse or distract" a supposed other subject to whom they were administering a test. Although highs did falsify their subject's scores to a greater extent than lows, they did not lower them significantly more often. In a study by Blumstein and Weinstein (1969†) a stooge invited hostility by demanding much payoff for little work or asking little payoff for much work. (In a control condition stooges also did more and less than their share of work, but claimed corresponding shares of the credit.) Low Machs pressed to right the wrong in both directions, while highs permitted the low claims and compromized with the high claims of both fair and unfair partners. Wahlin (1967†) put subjects in the "bottom dog" position in a Prisoners Dilemma-type game, in which the subject could not win relative to the other player. High Machs did lose more, and significantly so, in this condition, but did not play more competitively after moving to a traditional Prisoners Dilemma matrix.

Wahlin's highs who fought back in the losing position might seem inconsistent with Blumstein and Weinstein's compromising highs and with the Penny—Dollar highs who cooperated for dollars, thus exposing themselves to the risk of being exploited by the other. However, in the Penny—Dollar Caper the "other" was 80% cooperative; Blumstein and Weinstein's subjects were presented with a *fait accompli* and had no means of influencing the other (as subjects believed they had in the Prisoners Dilemma-type games). It would be a cognitive strategy to resist exploitation when it actually occurs but before it has become a *fait accompli*. Consistently, high Machs appear less likely to be angry or hostile than lows upon learning, after the fact, that they have been deceived in an experiment.

However, Wrightsman and Cook (1965) found that high Machs scored higher on Siegel's (1956) scale of manifest hostility (see Chapter III). It is conceivable that high Machs are indeed more hostile, but that the range of situations in which we have observed them simply did not elicit evidence of it. Our hunch is that they would be more likely to use hostility instrumentally, to achieve some desired goal. In general, they are adept at getting what they want from others without overt hostility. They take what they get cooly and do not reciprocate the generosity, but usually they have not promised reciprocity.

PRIVATE VERSUS PUBLIC COGNITIONS. A more general consequence of high Machs' cognitive approach should be noted. The behavior of high and low Machs in live, action situations does not invariably reflect what their differences in questionnaire responses might lead one to expect, and often appears quite the opposite. We have just argued that although high Machs admit more hostility than lows on a questionnaire measure, they do not appear more hostile in behavioral situations. Similarly, the behavioral evidence shows low Machs as more apt to change their attitudes under social pressure and more apt to reduce dissonance by changing cognitions to agree with "inconsistent" behavior. Yet, after discussions with a partner who disagreed with them (Thornton, 1967†) high and low Machs did not differ in self-reported "compliance," and on a questionnaire measure, highs reported preferring cognitively balanced over unbalanced situations more than lows (see Chapter III). Again, high Machs disclaim conventional morality on the Mach scales more than lows, but do not invariably lie or cheat more in behavioral tests. Also, in the only laboratory study (Legislature, Chapter XI) in which the subject's commitment to ideological positions was relevant, the high Machs claimed commitments as strong as lows' on the presession questionnaire but, unlike lows, did not let their commitments interfere with bargaining in the action phase of the session. Similarly, the high Machs approximately doubled their winning margin over the lows in the ambiguous condition in the Con Game, but then did not report preferring these games more than lows (Chapter VII). Finally, although high Machs claim less control over their fate on questionnaire measures (see Chapter III), we shall argue below that they appear in fact to have more control.

In each of these cases the behavior of high and low Machs in live, action situations contradicts the inference that would be drawn from their questionnaire responses. We have argued that high Machs act, in general, according to cognitions, both in answering questionnaires and in live interaction with others. A preference for balance does not necessarily imply an inability to tolerate imbalance; preferences for ambiguity may be irrelevant to coping with it successfully, and disclaiming honesty as a general principle does not automatically imply endorsing dishonesty as a general principle. High Machs may be accurate in reporting that they are sometimes hostile and that their fate is sometimes influenced by forces beyond their control, and lows may have either less insight or less honesty in these matters. Our argument is that low Machs may be swayed from a detached cognitive analysis by one set of sources in the privacy of responding to questionnaires, and by a different set in interactions with others. In answering questionnaires low Machs may be influenced by implicit assumptions, or what they expect of themselves. Then, in action situations they can get carried away from these private (and sincere) assumptions in going along with particular others in the process of interaction.

In summary, when high Machs have a goal, they attend to their own cognitive analysis of the situation, including cognitions about others and their actions, specifically in terms of relevance to the goal. Lows are more influenced by private, implicit assumptions, but also get engrossed in the process of ongoing interaction in following the other to wherever *he* is going. In general, high Machs win when the criteria for distributing rewards are ambiguous, for example, when a larger payoff goes to the one who can talk others into giving him more. Thus, they are more likely to win when all contenders are operating face to face, and all must devise and implement strategies for winning in the course of ongoing and also-improvised interaction. They win by politic strategies without manipulating obviously when success depends upon the cooperation or recognition of others. While low Machs take others personally, highs take others as objects viewed in relation to themselves as a fixed reference point. Low Machs touch others softly; highs use others coolly.

The highs' cognitive approach makes them exploitive but not punitive in contrast to the lows' greater interest in justice and reciprocity. Finally, the lows' implicit assumptions in answering questionnaires combined with their ability to get carried away in irrelevant (or opposite) directions in behavioral interaction makes it hazardous to predict differences in high and low Machs' interpersonal behavior from a face-valid interpretation of their respective questionnaire responses.

INITIATION AND CONTROL OF GROUP STRUCTURE

High Machs take over the leadership in informal face-to-face groups. They initiate and control the structure of the group and thereby control the process and outcome. This hypothesis was proposed to account for the Con Game finding (Chapter VIII) that low and middle Machs made more coalition offers to the high than either made to the other, and although middle and low Machs broke coalitions with each other, they tended not to break them with highs. The notion of initiating and controlling structure seemed to account for this "attracting" power of high Machs, and also seemed to fit their behavior in two previous studies, their more frequent and innovative tactics in the Machiavel study (Chapter V), and their steady gaze and judged aplomb in the Exline *et al.* study (Chapter IV). Obviously, initiating and controlling structure depends upon latitude for improvisation.

In the first study with a clear hypothesis that highs would "take over" subjects rated each other on a number of dimensions after a leaderless group discussion (Geis *et al.*, 1965†), and highs were rated higher in leadership by both lows and fellow highs. An illustration of how decisively at least several high Machs took over in their groups was provided spontaneously by a member. At the end of the semester the experimenter explained the study in full detail to the classes from which volunteers had been solicited. After the explanation a student who had participated raised his hand. "One of those guys in the group was a stooge, wasn't he ... [because]... he was too confident; the way he just took over, he couldn't have been one of us." The experimenter's truthful denial (there was actually no confederate in any of the groups) was to no avail. The class members were finally convinced only by comparison of what "the guy who took over" looked like by students who had participated in different sessions.

Subsequently, Durkin's encounter analysis (Chapter XIV) suggested that what had been viewed as an active process on the part of high Machs might be interpreted more parsimoniously as a contrast effect — in comparison to low Machs' going along with whatever direction or structure others proposed. This would make the high Machs' "initiation and control of structure" a matter of the lows' default, and another example of the highs' tendency not to become affectively involved, and act instead on cognitive definitions and goal-oriented strategies. The evidence to date does not permit a clear choice between the active and default interpretations. Regardless of the exact interpretation, however, when high and low Machs are placed together in an open-ended situation, the highs end up "in control."

Persuasiveness could be interpreted as indicating an ability to control social structure, but persuasiveness in one party has been separated from persuasibility on the part of the other in relatively few of the studies. In Harris's (1966†) dyadic discussions high Machs were not more persuasive; lows were more persuasible. However, in Braginsky's study (Chapter XVI), in which high- and low-Mach children tried to persuade a middle-Mach target child to eat quinine soaked crackers, the highs were more successful in this behavioral test of persuasiveness. In Novielli's (1968†) debating study naive judges awarded more decisions to the high-Mach debater than his low opponent when both were defending private convictions but not when they were not. Although both high and low Machs received slightly higher ratings overall when debating against a low-Mach opponent, the high Machs received the highest ratings in the study when they debated each other and both judges were lows.

High Machs were once caught initiating structure in the real world, or at least the semireal world of the college classroom (Geis, 1968†). Since a quarter of the semester's grade was at stake, the subjects presumably had a more concrete and personal investment in the outcome of their behavior than is usually considered possible in laboratory studies. Students were assembled into four person groups, given 20 min to "get acquainted," and asked to choose a leader. Groups with a high Mach available picked their highest Mach member more often than chance. Each group's joint project report was evaluated anonymously by the class at the end of the semester. Groups with their highest Mach member as leader did better on their projects than members did individually on course examinations, compared to the other groups' doing worse. Groups with high-Mach leaders somehow got whatever resources they possessed organized and applied to the group task more effectively than other groups.

However, Oksenberg (1968†) investigated taking control in a more structured situation and got negative results. Five-man groups were run in a standard Leavitt-type common symbol identification task, and highs did not send more organizational messages between trials than middles or lows, but also never sent a single message suggesting someone else as a leader. Lows sent an average of 1.10, middles 1.45 of such suggestions over the 20 trials each group was run.

High Machs also reported less enjoyment, less liking for the group, and less interest in working with the same group in the future than lows. Hindsight suggests that the "common symbol" problem was not intrinsically motivating to the high Machs. Lows worked diligently at the task because the experimenter asked them to; the highs' behavior appeared to reflect unconcealed boredom.

High Machs appear to have greater ability to organize their own and others' resources to achieve task goals, but this ability is not elicited by demand or request, but only by situations which are intrinsically motivating. Consistently, high Machs have been visible to others in unstructured situations in which subjects had an opportunity to be more active and had to improvise more. Highs were identified in the Machiavel study (Chapter V); they were overchosen as coalition partners in the Con Game (Chapter VIII); they were identified as leaders in a group discussion (Geis *et al.*, 1965†); and they were selected as most predictable (but turned out to be less so) in the Eye of the Beholder (Chapter XII). The highs' salience in such situations suggests that they were actively doing something which made others notice them rather than simply remaining passively uninvolved in following what others were doing.

Before concluding, a question frequently posed after discussions of Machiavellianism might be noted: Can a low Mach learn to be a high Mach? Although we have no data, our hunch is that under certain circumstances a low Mach can learn to act like a high. Specifically, if the low can anticipate a precarious situation and can fix in his own mind, in advance and in privacy, those goals he is unwilling to relinquish, and prepare himself to assert and defend them under social pressure, he might be able to act as effectively on behalf of his own interests as a high Mach in the specific situation for which he has prepared. We must emphasize that this is pure speculation. It is possible that low Machs can never become or act like highs; it is also possible that increasing one's Mach may be simply a matter of practice, or even more simply a matter of deciding to do so. (Data on the development of Machiavellianism from childhood to maturity will be considered in Chapter XVI.)

The opposite question, can a high Mach ever become or behave or "feel" like a low Mach, is equally unanswerable. In spite of the considerable research attesting to the "cool" of the high Machs, we still have no evidence to determine whether highs are insensitive to emotional involvements or whether they can simply disregard them at will in favor of more strategic considerations. The polygraph study (Oksenberg, 1964†) would seem to indicate that high and low Machs do not differ in the physiological responses represented by PGR records. On the other hand, the study of deception (Geis & Leventhal, 1966†) showed highs as unable to discriminate whether others were lying or not, while low Machs, observing the same performances, did discriminate, whether by "involvement," "empathy," "intuition," or some other means.

SYNOPSIS

The primary difference between individuals who score higher and lower on the Mach scales is the high scorers' greater emotional detachment. The 38 experimental studies listed in Table XV-1 which have been done since the initial formulations have demonstrated that detachment does have observable and predictable consequences, have clarified the kinds of situations in which it makes a difference, and have defined the meaning of "detachment" and its consequences more precisely.

High Machs manipulate more, win more, are persuaded less, persuade others more, and otherwise differ significantly from low Machs as predicted in situations in which subjects interact face to face with others, when the situation provides latitude for improvisation and the subject must initiate responses as he can or will, and in situations in which affective involvement with details irrelevant to winning distracts low Machs.

The dispositional differences between high and low Machs which account for their difference in behavior and outcome when these situational characteristics are present are all seen as related consequences of the highs' cool detachment compared to the lows' openness to emotional involvement. The weight of the experimental evidence indicates that high Machs are markedly less likely to become emotionally involved with other people, with sensitive issues, or with saving face in embarrassing situations. Although their coolness may not be more than skin deep, they appear to be thick skinned enough to withstand the enticements or dangers of interpersonal involvements which might interfere with task achievement.

One consequence of the high Machs' lack of susceptibility to emotional involvements in general is a lack of susceptibility to sheer social pressure urging compliance, cooperation, or attitude change — a characteristic which in turn accounts for their being no more likely than low Machs to be swayed by inducements to lie or cheat in most experiments. A second example of high Machs' resistance to social influence is their skepticism of experimenters' explanations and procedures, compared to lows' acceptance of the ex-perimenter's definitions.

It was proposed that the basic process underlying the highs' cool is a tendency on their part to focus on explicit, cognitive definitions of the situation and concentrate on strategies for winning, while lows get carried away in the direction proposed or imposed by the highs. The highs' tendency to act by what they know makes them effective in exploiting whatever resources the situation provides (including distractible low Machs). Evidence to date suggests that they are not hostile, vicious, or vindictive compared to lows. The low Machs' more personal, open orientation makes them less effective as strategists in the course of interaction, but more sensitive to others as individual persons.

In general, high Machs appear to have as little defensive investment in their own self-image or their own beliefs as they have in others or in interpersonal relations. This argument was invoked to explain their lack of attitude change in dissonance experiments; it could also account for their willingness to claim socially undesirable characteristics such as hostility, lack of control over their own fate, or the assorted social foibles presented in social desirability scales.

High Machs initiate and control the social structure of mixed-Mach groups. They are preferred as partners, chosen and identified as leaders, judged as more persuasive, and appear to direct the tone and content of interaction — and usually also the outcome. This characterization appears more true in more open-ended situations in which subjects have greater choice of content and strategy, and true only when the high Machs are intrinsically motivated by the situation.

CHAPTER XVI   **SOCIAL CORRELATES
OF MACHIAVELLIANISM**

Richard Christie

In the preceding 12 chapters we have been concerned with individual differences in scores on Mach IV and Mach V of college students serving as experimental subjects in laboratory situations. Within these aggregates we have come to some conclusions about the kinds of interpersonal behavior engaged in by high and low scorers and have made some inferences about the situational parameters, under controlled conditions, which are related to whether or not these individuals behave as predicted by their scores.

College students do not represent a random or representative sample of the majority of mankind. Most of the samples that were used in experiments were relatively small and were obtained from schools with which we were associated and therefore could by no means be viewed as representative of American college students. Before engaging in speculations about the applicability of experimental findings based on the differential behavior of high and low Machs to situations in the outside world (Chapter XVII), it is appropriate to examine some of the factors affecting Mach scale scores in both college and noncollege samples.

At roughly the same time we were beginning laboratory studies, in the spring of 1963, we participated in the Amalgam Survey of the National Public Opinion Research Center. Ten questions were included from Mach IV and ten from Mach V. The 1482 respondents were a representative sample of non-institutionalized adults within the United States.

In the fall of 1964 we collected data on Mach IV and V on 1782 students in 14 different colleges as part of a study of the relationship between scale scores and political attitudes toward the Presidential election. The colleges were selected to give as wide a range of Presidential preferences as possible and are probably very close in student characteristics to a representative sample of colleges. The colleges come out very close to the mean (50.2 as against 50.0 on a scale with a standard deviation of about 10.0) on Astin's (1964) college selectivity index.

One thing is quite clear from the comparisons in Table XVI-1. Both the NORC and college samples are very similar in the proportion of males and females to the base populations, both slightly overrepresented the proportion of nonwhites, and there is, of course, an over 20-year difference in median age between college students and adults in the national sample. More relevant to our

TABLE XVI-1

Comparisons of Samples and Populations on Selected Variables

	% Male	% Nonwhite	Median age	Mach IV score	Mach V score
College sample					
(n = 1782)	48.3	8.5	19	90.65	97.24
18-19-year-olds					
in college (1967)					
(n = 871,000)[a]	48.0	6.2	19	—	—
NORC Sample 21					
and over					
(n = 1477)	47.4	13.8	42	84.52[b]	92.26[b]
21 and over (1967)[a]					
in U.S.					
(n = 117,503,000)	48.0	10.3	44	—	—

[a] Bureau of the Census, 1967.

[b] These are scores converted to be equivalent to the full length (20-item) Mach IV and Mach V scales by the method described in Chapter II. The NORC sample received only half the items on each scale on a five instead of seven-point scoring system.

concern is the fact that the differences in Mach IV and V scores between the students in the college sample and the adults in the NORC sample clearly indicate that students sampled in 1964 scored higher than the adult NORC sample. The standard deviation on Mach IV for the student sample was 14.33, on Mach V, 10.85. Estimates of what the standard deviations would have been for the NORC sample if they had taken the full scales are slightly higher, but cannot be precise enough to serve as a test of the differences. The data suggest that the then-current generation of persons attending college and about to attain majority in the United States were significantly more in agreement with Machiavelli, however measured, than were those who were a generation or more older.

ON AN INCREASE IN MACHIAVELLIAN ORIENTATIONS IN RECENT TIMES

It has previously been noted (Christie & Merton, 1958) that older persons who might be expected to be highly manipulative, such as Washington lobbyists or business executives, scored lower on Mach items than did college students. The material summarized in Table XVI-1 supports the notion that older persons in general score lower on Mach than do college students.

There are two possible explanations. One would be that young adults are typically cynical and opportunistic and that as they grow older they find that society is more benevolent than it appears when one is beginning to find one's way. In consequence, Mach scores should decrease with increasing experience. The opposite argument would be that each recent generation in the United States is socialized to become more Machiavellian and that lower mean scores among older adults reflect a clinging to values common when they were growing to maturity. Inferential evidence (Lazarsfeld, Berelson, & Gaudet, 1944) suggests that political preferences tend to be related to the time at which one first voted, and values over 25 years after graduation from college (Newcomb, 1963) remain remarkably stable. The present argument is that something of the same sort is probably true of the complex of attitudes and behaviors which has been labeled Machiavellian. In short, Mach scores of adults appear to be more closely related to preadult influences than to experiences after attaining maturity.

The only clean-cut way to resolve these alternative explanations would be to have longitudinal studies of the same individuals over their lifetime, so that Mach scores or their equivalents could be related to life experiences. Such a study is not available. However, data which support the notion that the higher Mach scores of young adults reflect social changes are available. A number of questions were included about background characteristics in the NORC Amalgam Survey. It was possible to classify respondents on a host of variables, including: age, sex, race, religion, years of education, occupation, father's education, father's occupation, region and population of place of residence, political preference, number of older and younger brothers and sisters, birth order, income, marital status, previous military service, etc. Given this array of information, it was possible to construct a variety of indices. Hundreds and hundreds of pages of computer printout based upon cross tabulations, correlational analyses, and analyses of variance of the data were scrutinized. Contrary to initial expectations, there were few confirmations of such expected findings as positive correlations between upward social mobility and Mach scores, city dwellers scoring higher than their country cousins, etc.

One explanation for this might be that respondents gave such misleading information about themselves that this concealed any true relationships between their demographic characteristics and Mach-scale scores. This possibility seems unlikely. Checks on a variety of variables indicate that the NORC sample was representative of data collected in the 1960 census. Analyses of scores on Mach IV and V (see Appendix A) indicate that the answers to the questions on the part of the NORC and college sample were internally consistent and similarly structured.

It is therefore possible to have some confidence in the fact that the minimal relationships between demographic variables and Mach scores in the NORC sample reflect reality.

A possible explanation for higher scores in the college sample than in the national sample is that Mach scores are related to education. However, the data do not support this interpretation. An initially surprising finding was that there was a negative correlation of $-.26$ between respondent's years of education and scores on Mach IV (in pilot work no correlation was found). However, there was also a negative correlation between the derived measure of social desirability on Mach V and Mach IV scores of $-.30$ and between years of education and social desirability of $-.26$. A partial correlation of $+.02$ between years of education and Mach IV scores was found when social desirability as measured by the buffer items in Mach V was held constant. This would indicate that the higher Mach IV scores of those with less education was a function of their greater willingness to admit socially undesirable things about themselves than the more highly educated sample members. The correlation between Mach V, in which social desirability was controlled at least in part by the forced-choice technique, and years of education was $+.10$. Although a correlation of such magnitude would be expected by chance fewer than one time in a thousand in a sample of this size, the relationship accounts for only 1% of the common variance and it appears highly unlikely that the higher scores on both Mach IV and Mach V on the part of the college sample can be attributed to greater education. A further check compared the college sample with those adult members of the NORC sample claiming some college education, and it was found that college students' scores on both Mach IV and Mach V were higher than the scores made by adults with equivalent education, when the latter's scores were converted as described in Chapter II. Female respondents in the NORC sample also scored significantly lower than male respondents on both Mach IV and Mach V, although the level of significance was not as great as was true of college respondents.

In summary, these college respondents were more Machiavellian in scale scores than adults in a representative national sample who had some college education as well as those who had none. In addition, within the adult sample, there was a negative relationship (significant beyond the .01 level by analysis of variance) between age and Mach scores (Christie & Geis, 1968).

Lacking longitudinal data on the same individuals over time, another way of checking for trends would be to compare similar cohorts, e.g., college freshmen, at the same schools from year to year, where it might be expected that patterns of recruitment does not change markedly from year to year. This has not been done systematically for the Mach scales, since most of our samples were targets of opportunity. It is worth noting that of the three college samples collected in the fall of 1955, two had lower scores on Mach IV than *any* of the 14 collected nine years later in the fall of 1964. The school with the highest mean score in 1955 had a higher score than only one school in 1964, being lower than the other 13. Because of the haphazard selection processes involved, it is impossible to be precise. In the one university at which data were collected at both times, the 1964 group was significantly higher, but is noncomparable in that the first class was in introductory sociology and the second in introductory psychology. Thus these data support the hypothesized increase in Mach, but are subject to unknown biases in selection, so they are only suggestive.

Inferential evidence on decrease in idealism is available in a study by Wrightsman and Baker (1969). Entering freshmen classes at George Peabody College were given Wrightsman's Philosophy of Human Nature scales in 1962, 1965, 1966, 1967, and 1968. Data for males and females were analyzed separately. There were significant decreases over time on the subscales measuring Trustworthiness, Strength of Will, Altruism, and Independence among members of these five classes of both sexes. As noted in Chapter III, these are among the few scales found to be significantly correlated (negatively) with Mach IV. Interestingly, the two subscales not correlated with Mach IV, Complexity of Human Nature and Variability of Human Nature. showed the lowest change among girls and did not differ significantly among the boys. Given the correlation between Mach and the four scales showing significant changes, it would appear a reasonable assumption that Mach IV scores would have shown a significant increase if they had been given, but, again, this is only an assumption and not hard data.

It is necessary to turn to other data to indicate why a negative relationship between age and Mach among adults in the United States might exist.

One possibility is that the interpersonal kinds of manipulations associated with Machiavellianism are more typical of urban than rural life, so that there would be a positive relationship between Mach scores and population of place of residence within the NORC sample. Although the trends were in this direction, they did not reach acceptable levels of significance. There is a possible explanation related to the geographic mobility of modern Americans. The mechanization of farms has driven many of the less sophisticated to the inner cities and a reverse migration from cities to suburbs has been characteristic of many of the more successful urbanites. In consequence, very few Americans live in the places where they were reared.

Three bits of information suggest that Machiavellianism is associated with the size of the locale in which people were raised. Milburn (1966, personal communication) found a correlation of +.29 between size of home town and Mach V among a group of 66 female summer school students in China Lake, California. Since China Lake is a Naval Ordnance station in the desolate space between Bakersfield and Death Valley, it is highly unlikely that any of Milburn's respondents were born there or in the immediate vicinity.

A situation in which there was a lack of geographic mobility was true of students in Spain. de Miguel (1964) administered a Spanish translation of Mach V to 425 *Preuniversitario* male students, 16−18 years of age, who were attending 15 different *Colegios* and *Institutos* in nine different provinces of

Spain. There was a rank order correlation of .89 between the industrialization of the provinces and Mach V scores. Almost all of these students still resided in the province in which they were born, so that the effects of past and present residence in a given locale were combined.

TABLE XVI-2

Mach V Score by Industrialization in Spanish Provinces

Province	% Literacy	Mach V score	No. of respondents
High industrialization			
Barcelona	97	97.48	43
Guipuzcoa	97	92.32	25
Madrid	97	92.02	86
Submean	97.0	93.59	154
Medium industrialization			
Zaragoza	93	91.06	47
Valencia	92	91.00	34
Ponteverda	93	87.94	73
Submean	92.7	89.57	154
Low industrialization			
C. Real	89	87.88	53
Cadiz	84	84.38	33
Sevilla	84	82.90	20
Submean	83.7	85.85	106
Mean	91.1	90.11	414

The only known instance in which data were collected on both the size of the place of residence during adolescence and that of present locale was done by Guterman (1967). He collected questionnaires from 483 white collar and managerial employees in 26 hotels of two eastern chains with locations varying from Bangor, Maine, to Washington, D.C. He discarded hotels in which the refusal rate was over 30% in filling out the forms and the effects of this as a possible source of bias are indeterminant.

Approximately two-thirds of the respondents who volunteered to fill out the scale were male. Twelve Mach statements were given in a dyadic forced-choice format in which the keyed items were paired with the matched items from Mach V.

Guterman used metropolitan areas as a classificatory variable. He found that the population of the area in which the respondent spent most of his adolescence was more closely related to being a high Mach on his adaptation of the scale than was the population of the area in which he worked at the time of the study, as indicated in Table XVI-3. In retrospect, it seems incredibly naive not to have asked a question about where the respondents in the NORC study spent most of their early life so that the possibility that formative years are of crucial importance in the development of manipulative orientations was not explored among members of the representative NORC sample.

TABLE XVI-3

Percent High Mach by Place of Residence [a]

		Population of adolescent place of residence				
		Under 50,000	50,000 -999,999	Over 1,000,000	Mean	N
Population of present place of residence	Under 1,000,000	27	26	45	30	129
	Over 1,000,000	33	23	52	37	161
	Mean	29	24	50	34	290
	N	140	74	76		

[a] Based on Guterman (1967, Table 4.15, p. 119).

Urbanization is also related to cosmopolitanism. However, within cities some persons are more attuned to the blend and clash of cultures than others. Therefore, it might reasonably be expected that those involved in two or more cultures would be more "modern," e.g., high Mach, than those whose background is more traditional.

The hypothesis that differences in Mach scores are related to a traditional versus more cosmopolitan orientation was tested among secondary school students in Hong Kong by Lois Oksenberg (1967). Mach IV was translated into Chinese and given to 67 students in a school which taught a traditional curriculum upholding Confucian values and the language of instruction was the Cantonese dialect. They were compared with other 17-year-old Chinese students attending a school with Western sponsorship, many Western teachers, a "Western" curriculum, and where the language of instruction was English. Roughly half of the latter (72) took the scale in Chinese and 74 took it in English. The mean scores on the two versions were almost identical for the Westernized students; 100.70 and 101.93 for the Chinese and English versions, respectively, among males, 95.31 and 97.64 among females. Despite the difficulties of translation, the reliability of the scales was higher in the Chinese than the English version: .79 vs. .72 for males, .57 vs. .39 for girls. Male students in the traditional Chinese school had a mean score of 91.88, girls one of 88.96. The reliabilities were .74 and .61 respectively.

The crucial comparison is between the traditional Chinese students and those who were Westernized. The higher Mach scores of the Westernized students were significant beyond the .005 level by analysis of variance, lending strong support to the hypothesized relationship between traditionalism and low Mach scores.

FAMILY DEMOGRAPHIC CHARACTERISTICS AND MACH SCORES

Respondents in both the NORC and college samples were asked about the occupation and education of their fathers. The correlations with Mach IV and Mach V are indicated in Table XVI-4. As can be ascertained at a glance. the relationships are as null as possible. The respondents in the NORC sample, who were 21 or older, were asked about their father's occupation and education when the respondent was "about 16," which could have been from 5 to 75 years or more prior to the interview. The college samples reported contemporaneous data on their fathers. In neither case were there any significant relationships between the father's reported occupational status or education and the respondent's Mach scores.

TABLE XVI-4

Correlations between Reported Fathers' Education and Occupational Status by Mach Scale Scores

| | | | Scale | |
Sample	N	Fathers'	Mach IV	Mach V
Representative national		Education	− .05	.00
sample (NORC)	1482	Occupation	.00	− .06
White college males	764	Education	− .03	− .07
		Occupation	+ .04	+ .03
White college females	832	Education	+ .01	− .02
		Occupation	− .02	− .03

The only known evidence indicating a possibly significant relationship between parental social class status and Mach scores of children comes from a study by Braginsky (1966). Her sample was restricted to children in the fifth grade in two small cities in eastern mid-Connecticut, so that their parents were both younger and less representative than the populations of parents in the preceding comparisons. In addition, the dependent variable was a shortened version of the Mach scale edited for this particular age group. She found a correlation of $-.23$ (p < .05) between the children's scores on the modified Mach scale and family SES (computed according to the Hollingshead scoring technique) among the 102 girls in the sample and one of $-.08$ (n.s.) for the 70 boys.

It appears prudent to assume that if there is any relationship between parental status in the social order and the scores on Mach scales or derivatives, it is so slight as to elude detection with the measures of status and Machiavellianism used to date.

OTHER DEMOGRAPHIC VARIABLES. Table II-5 indicates that non-white male college students made higher scores on Mach IV than did their white counterparts, but that the pattern was reversed on Mach V. Nonwhite females scored lower than white females on both Mach IV and V. In any event, none of these findings was beyond chance expectations. In the NORC national sample as well, no significant differences between white and nonwhite respondents' scores on Mach IV and V were found. Because of the small numbers of respondents who could be matched, it was virtually impossible to control for other variables in making these comparisons. In a sample of sixth-grade students in one class in a ghetto area school in which almost all the children came from impoverished families, Nachamie found no differences on a children's Mach scale among respondents of Chinese, Negro, or Puerto Rican families. [There were not enough students of European descent ("others" in this school) for comparative purposes.]

In the NORC survey a question was asked which had the adult respondents identify themselves in general terms as Protestant, Catholic, Jewish, or other. No significant relationship with Mach scores was found. Such a question does not, of course, get at the variations within these faiths. Among college students it is those respondents with more orthodox or fundamentalist religious identifications within the broad categories who are the least Machiavellian and those with no claimed religious affiliation who score hghest. Strickland (1963, personal communication) indicated that when a host of other variables were matched among over 2500 male medical college students in eight medical schools, there was a significant tendency for those identifying themselves as Jewish to score higher on Mach IV than those identifying themselves as Protestant who in turn scored higher than Catholics. It seems most probable, in light of examination of background data on some thousands of college students, that this might be attributable to the higher proportion of nonpracticing Jews than Protestants or Catholics in these samples.

THE STAGES OF MAN AND MACHIAVELLIANISM

Despite the fact that gross demographic variables are not particularly predictive of scores on Mach IV and V, adult respondents do differ significantly on the scales and measures of internal consistency and retest reliabilities suggest these differences in responses are not random. Somehow, college students have been socialized to produce responses on paper-and-pencil tests that are significantly related to a variety of different behaviors in controlled laboratory situations.

An obvious question is at how early an age do such individual differences manifest themselves? There is a lower age limit at which persons can read, let alone answer, inventory questions. Before presenting data indicating that high- and low-Mach elementary school children behave differently, let us examine the evidence that children become more Machiavellian as they progress from the fifth or sixth grade through high school. The entire student body of a preparatory school near New York City was given Mach IV. As indicated elsewhere (Christie & Geis, 1968) there was reason to believe that these young males might have high scores. Figure XVI-1 indicates the increase in scores as the students shifted from what is the equivalent of junior high school to high school. This sharp increase between the eight grade and the first year of high school is partial documentation of the impressions of the faculty in this school. [Their observations of the changes in behavior of young males becoming more manipulative at this age prompted permission to give the scale. This is one case in which psychometrics affirmed folk (or faculty) wisdom.] The reason for the decline between students in the 11th and 12th grades is somewhat puzzling. Since these high school students as a whole made higher scores on Mach IV than college males (Table II-5), regression toward the mean might be suspected. There are other more probable explanations. A number of members of the then senior class had been expelled for violations of regulations shortly before the scales were given. Since Mach IV is subject to the influence of socially desirable responses, it might be hypothesized that the survivors presented a picture of themselves more in accord with expectations on a scale sponsored by the school administration than would otherwise be true. The opposite alternative is that it was the high Machs who transgressed (probably true), but they were so transparently guilty that they were booted out.

The increase in Mach scores with increasing age during adolescence was in accord with common sense expectations and it was not documented in detail by collecting other samples. However, one further sample was tested during the fall semester and again six months later in the spring to see if the hypothesized increase with age during adolescence in Mach scores was tenable when the same individuals were involved. These young gentlemen were in the second form (or eighth grade) of a prep school in New York City which had extremely high academic standards and whose students were the scions of professional and other high-status families. As with students in the other prep school, their mean scores on Mach IV were even higher than those of the mean of representative college students, although not quite as high as some in elite colleges (this point will be discussed later). More relevant to the point about the increase in Mach IV scores during adolescence is the fact that of the 87 boys taking the test in the fall and spring, the increase in mean scores from 95.13 to 98.74 was significant at the .01 level.

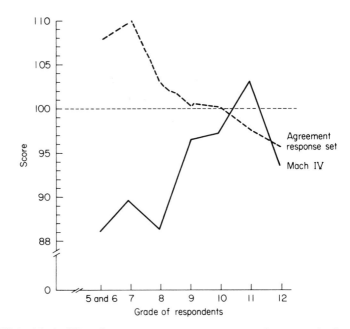

FIG. XVI-1. Mach IV and agreement response set scores for prep school students.

Moving from comparisons of prep school samples on Mach IV to Braginsky's (1966) study of fifth graders in small towns in Connecticut and Nachamie's (1969) study of sixth graders in a ghetto area in a large city, it is relevant to note that although direct comparisons are impossible, it is possible to make rough transformations. In both cases the calculated scores on Mach IV are below the mean prep school scores and the scores for both adult men and women in the NORC national sample.

Up to this point, it has been noted that Mach scores (at least on Mach IV) increase from the age of 10 or so through the age of 16 or 17 and that there is a gradual decrease of scores after the age of 40 (Christie & Geis, 1968). Lacking a longitudinal study in which systematic data were collected on the same individuals over 50 years or so of time, it is only pssible to speculate. Change scores on Mach IV and V were computed on students in their early 1920's in medical schools over a year's time. Unlike the scores in the prep school, from which some had graduated, no significant changes within a year's time were observed. Comparisons of the four classes in ten medical schools on Mach IV were analyzed. No significant differences were found among any of the classes in this sample. Agreement with Mach statements apparently increases through adolescence, peaks around 20 or so, and is lower among older respondents.

DIFFERENTIALS IN MACH SCORES

Although Mach scores are not related to years of education or IQ, they do seem to be related to certain characteristics of schools. This was first noticed in comparing mean scores on Mach IV of the senior classes of 12 medical schools in 1957–1958. The range in scores varied from 84.80 in one related to a fundamentalist church to 92.60 in one affiliated with an Ivy League university. There is a high degree of concensus among medical educators as to the relative eliteness of medical schools. Five were judged as elite, seven as nonelite. A Mann–Whitney U test of the ranked means indicated that the elite schools had significantly higher-Mach students ($p < .01$, two tailed). Scores of first-year students were available at ten of these schools and the mean differences between the first- and fourth-year students were negligible. This suggests that high-Mach students are more likely to apply to and be accepted by high-status medical schools.

An examination of Peace Corps trainees' Mach IV and V scores attending a special training program at Teachers College at Columbia University prepatory to going to Nigeria to teach in secondary schools was made. They were all college graduates and had attended a diverse group of colleges. Each college which they had attended was classified on a "fat-cat" index composed of faculty/student ratio, annual operating budget/number of students, number of books in the library/number of students, and number of students on scholarship/number of students. This is very similar to the "affluence" index devised by Astin (1962) on the basis of a factor analysis of college characteristics. There was a correlation of .33 ($p < .05$) between the index score of the college a particular trainee attended and high Mach IV score. This finding can only be viewed as suggestive, since in most cases there was only one graduate from a given college and he or she could by no means be viewed as representative of the student body. It was also clear from a scatter plot that the relatively small number of graduates of highly affluent colleges accounted for the correlation.

Examination of the colleges in which various samples have been collected indicates that the mean scores on Mach IV and V tend to be lowest among respondents in church-related schools (especially fundamentalist), in teachers colleges, in rural areas, and in schools with low prestige. Since none of these samples is representative of the total student body in these schools, it is impossible to make precise comparisons. In most cases, however, there is a common bias in that most of the respondents were taking undergraduate courses in psychology. High scorers tend to be found in schools where the student body is more cosmopolitan and/or the school is elite.

One exception has been found to the above generalization. A check was made on the college subsequently attended by the boys in the graduating senior class in the prep school alluded to earlier. There was no correlation between the "fat cattedness" of the college to which they went and their Mach IV scores. In this case, however, the school counselors made strenuous efforts to get the boys into the best college for which they were qualified (every graduate was placed in some college) so that the college to which they went was determined largely by their SAT scores and grades as evaluated by the counselors and college admissions officers. (There was no correlation between Mach scores and grades holding IQ constant among these students.)

All in all, the relationships between Mach scores and social factors are not overwhelming in their magnitude. The data are consistent, however, in indicating a relationship with factors associated with an urban rather than rural background and a cosmopolitan rather than a traditionalist way of life. The evidence suggesting a rise in Mach scores over time in the United States can be interpreted as a reflection of increasing urbanization and cosmopolitanism.

THE DEVELOPMENT OF INDIVIDUAL DIFFERENCES IN MACHIAVELLIANISM: SOME QUESTIONS AND SPECULATIONS

It is clear that the range of individual differences in Mach scores is much greater than can be explained by differences in such broad social categories as degree of traditionalism or cosmpolitanism. The evidence suggests that Machiavellian tendencies develop before adulthood, but what variables in the developmental history of the individual account for these differences?

An initial attempt at studying Machiavellianism in children was made by Susan Nachamie (1969). She noted that the fifth- and sixth-grade students in the prep school showed a noticeable agreement response set (see Fig. XVI-1) and an item analysis of the responses indicated that some of the items showed little discriminatory power among the younger students. This left the question as to whether the vocabulary and wording of the statements had been too complex for students of this younger age group or whether Machiavellianism was not measurable in a meaningful way among these preadolescents.

In an attempt to clarify this problem, Nachamie edited the items with a view toward using them on sixth-grade students. Special attention was focused on items with the poorest discriminatory power. Mach statements were revised and simplified to accord with the vocabulary, sentence construction and grammatical style of a fourth-grade reader used in the New York City public school system. The revisions varied from leaving one item alone to a substitution for the euthanasia item, since the original was deemed inapporpriate for this age level. The items were edited for "flavor" and congruence with the original items by a number of people who were familiar with Mach IV. They were also edited for comprehensibility and appropriateness for the age level of the potential respondents by the public school guidance counselor, reading coordinator and principal of the school in which the scales were administered. The final version of the scale (referred to as "Kiddie Mach") is shown in Table XVI-5.

TABLE XVI-5

Kiddie Mach Test

+	1.	Never tell anyone why you did something unless it will help you.
−	2.	Most people are good and kind.
+	3.	The best way to get along with people is to tell them things that make them happy.
−	4.	You should do something only when you are sure it is right.
+	5.	It is smartest to believe that all people will be mean if they have a chance.
−	6.	You should always be honest, no matter what.
+	7.	Sometimes you have to hurt other people to get what you want.
+	8.	Most people won't work hard unless you make them do it.
−	9.	It is better to be ordinary and honest than famous and dishonest.
−	10.	It's better to tell someone why you want him to help you than to make up a good story to get him to do it.
−	11.	Successful people are mostly honest and good.
+	12.	Anyone who completely trusts anyone else is asking for trouble.
+	13.	A criminal is just like other people except that he is stupid enough to get caught.
−	14.	Most people are brave.
+	15.	It is smart to be nice to important people even if you don't really like them.
−	16.	It is possible to be good in every way.
−	17.	Most people can not be easily fooled.
+	18.	Sometimes you have to cheat a little to get what you want.
−	19.	It is never right to tell a lie.
+	20.	It hurts more to lose money than to lose a friend.

Both the Kiddie Mach and Mach IV were administered to all four sixth-grade classes in a school located in a low-income area of a large city. The classes had been evaluated for the school's administrative purposes from bright to dull. The classes rated as brightest and dullest were given the Kiddie Mach first and several days later a different female graduate student administered the Mach IV. This procedure was reversed for the two classes rated as intermediate in brightness.

The items were read aloud by the tester and the subjects were asked to read along silently and then circle the response category that best described the way they felt about each item. For purposes of simplification, a five-point scale was used instead of a seven-point scale. A constant of 60 was added to raw scores so the possible range was from 60 to 140. All respondents were also requested to underline words or phrases which they did not understand.

It was necessary to delete the protocols of those students of Chinese and Puerto Rican descent who did not understand English well enough to follow instructions. This left an overall N of 91. Correlations between Mach IV and Kiddie Mach ranged from $+.37$ in the two dullest classes to $+.55$ for the two brightest classes. One class had a nonsignificant split-half reliability on both scales for reasons which we have not been able to explain. In the other three classes reliabilities were in the .50's for both scales, although they were slightly higher for the Kiddie Mach. There were, however, significantly more ($p < .001$) words and phrases underlined as not understood on Mach IV than on the Kiddie Mach.

Although these reliabilities fell short of those obtained among college students, it must be borne in mind that response set probably plays a greater part among younger respondents and that counterbalanced scales generally tend to decrease reliability. Further, this particular population, composed as it was of children in a deprived neighborhood, was not one in which paper-and-pencil tests might be expected to work particularly well. Apologies aside, the results were viewed as encouraging enough to suggest that the Kiddie Mach scale was differentiating among respondents and the next problem was to see if it related to behavior differences.

GAME PLAYING AND MACHIAVELLIANISM AMONG CHILDREN

One of the problems in studying game playing strategies and Machiavellianism among children is that many of the game situations used with college students had fairly complicated instructions. A survey of children's games indicated that many of them involved sheer luck in winning (like the Parcheesi-type games in which throws of dice or flips of spinners determine the pace of advancing along a path beset with unavoidable perils such as "Go back to Start" or "Return to the nearest Bramble Patch.") Given equal ability in counting from one to six, about the only advantage a juvenile con artist could have would be in saying that the point of the spinner on a line between two numbers was on six instead of one and carrying his point. In an attempt to get around these problems, we used a modification of a game which we had piloted with college subjects.

In this game each player was given two opaque plastic dice which were devoid of spots, numbers, or other material identifying any single face in a unique manner. However, three sides were painted black and three were painted white. The probability that the upper surfaces of both dice after being rolled would be the "same" (both black or both white) or being "different" (one white and one black) were both .50. The two players were seated at opposite sides of a felt-covered table which had low divider in the middle. They alternated in shaking their own two dice in a cup and banking them against the felt-covered divider. The divider was high enough so that neither player could see the other player's dice after they had been thrown, but low enough so that the two players could see one another's face. Each player had 20 throws.

On each trial the player who threw the dice had the first option. He could tell the truth or lie. If the upper surfaces were the same color, he could tell the truth and call them "same" or bluff and call them "different." If they were different, he could bluff and call them as "same" or tell the truth and call them "different." Then the second player had an option. He could either accept the statement of the first player or he could challenge it.

If subjects called their rolls truthfully or untruthfully at random, and believed or challenged at random, neithr would win over a series of trails. A further feature, however, was added which was designed to encourage deception on the part of the roller and accuracy in challenging on the part of the caller.

TABLE XVI-6

Payoff Matrix in the Bluffing Game

Roller bluffs, Other player believes him
Roller *wins* 5, Other gets 0
Roller bluffs, Other player challenges
Roller gets 0, Other *wins* 5
Roller tells the truth, Other player believes him
Roller gets 0, Other *wins* 2
Roller tells the truth, Other player challenges
Roller *wins* 2, Other gets 0

A payoff matrix (see Table XVI-6) was constructed which put a premium on successful bluffing and challenging. When the roller successfully bluffed by telling a lie and the caller believed him, he won five points and the caller won nothing. If, however, the roller bluffed and the caller challenged, the latter received five points and the roller none. When the roller told the truth but in such a transparent fashion that the other player was correct in believing him, the roller received no points and the caller received two points. If the roller was successful in telling the truth so deceptively that the other player erroneously challenged, the roller received the two points and the challenger nothing.

After the experimenter explained the game to each pair of subjects, the first player shook his two dice in a plastic cup and rolled them against the divider. Then his and the other player's calls were made and the winner was paid off in M&M candies. These were placed in a glass jar which was at the side of the divider. Each player had his own jar and both jars were in full view so that it was possible for each to see the relative accumulations of candy. The players alternated in rolling dice for 20 turns apiece. The experimenter kept a running record of calls, replies, and payoffs. The actual number of M&M's at the end of the game provided a reliability check on the experimenter's tallies.

Thirty-six pairs of subjects were run. To reduce variance attributable to possible cross-sex or ethnic variables, the respondents were matched on these factors. There were 13 Puerto Rican pairs, 9 Negro, 7 Chinese, and 5 of European ancestry. Two mixed pairs were also run. Each pair consisted of one high and one low scorer as determined by a median split [88 or below (roughly equivalent to 82 on Mach IV) and 89 and above]. There were no significant differences in Kiddie Mach scores for boys or girls or for the different ethnic groups.

The prediction was that since high Machs are hypothesized as being more successful bluffers and challengers, they should win more M&M's. In the 36 pairs run, highs won in 26 cases, lost in 8, and were tied in 2, so the prediction was confirmed at the .002 level.

A further finding is relevant in the present context. Previous self-reports by college students (Chapter VII) indicated that high Machs were more likely to play card and dice games which presumably involve varying degrees of skills, bluffing, and betting on outcome. These children were asked an open-ended question about the types of games they played and table and board games (cards, checkers, dice, and somewhat suprisingly, Monopoly) were separated from games involving primarily physical physical skill and from solitary activities (baseball, hopscotch, playing with dolls, etc.). Unlike college students, there were no significant differences between high and low Machs. Table and board game playing was significantly related, however, to winning in the laboratory game ($\chi^2 = 6.76$, $p < .01$). There was no interaction in game scores between the Kiddie Mach scores and self-reports of game playing.

Only 14% — that is, 3 out of the 21 low-Mach subjects who did not play extracurricular games — were able to win in the bluffing game. At the other extreme, 17 out of the 19 high Mach game-playing children won. Non-game-playing high Machs won more frequently that game-playing lows although this difference was not significant.

MACHIAVELLIANISM AND MANIPULATIVE BEHAVIOR IN CHILDREN

While the analysis of the game playing study was underway, it was discovered that an independent investigation of manipulative behavior among children had been conducted as part of a doctoral dissertation by Dorothea Braginsky (1966). Braginsky's modification of Mach IV differed from Nachamie's in that she eliminated 4 items (leaving 16), the items seemed to follow more closely those of Mach IV in wording, and she had respondents answer on a "true—false" dichotomy rather than on a five-point agree—disagree continuum. She found a split-half reliability of +.43 and a test—retest correlation of +.87 when the scale was given two weeks later.

Braginsky's sample consisted of ten-year-old white children in the fifth grade in public schools in two small cities in eastern Connecticut. She classified them as low, middle, and high Machs (scores of four or less, five or six, and seven or higher). Forty-eight subjects were run. Each was paired with a middle-Mach target person and the high- or low-Mach subject had the task of persuading the target child to eat as many quinine flavored crackers as possible. The pairs were matched for sex, parental SES, age, and IQ. Sociometric choices previously made were used to control for friendship or antipathy among members of the dyads.

The experimenter introduced herself as a home economist working for a cracker company who was finding out about childrens' evaluations of new "health" crackers. After the subject had tasted one cracker strongly flavored with quinine and savored it for 10 sec to be sure its flavor had been fully appreciated, he was allowed to drink some water and have a piece of candy to counteract the taste of the cracker. He then filled out a questionnaire evaluating his degree of liking for the crackers. Three of 69 potential subjects said they liked the crackers and were eliminated from the study.

The experimenter then told the subject that it was important for evaluative purposes to have the reactions of children who ate as many crackers as possible. The subject was requested to ask a second child (the middle-Mach target person) to eat as many crackers as possible. The subject was promised 5 cents for every cracker he could persuade the second child to consume.

The juvenile high Machs persuaded the target person to eat an average of 6.46 quinine flavored crackers; the low Machs persuaded their target persons to eat an average of 2.79 (the difference was significant at the .003 level). Interestingly enough, there were no significant sex differences in this sample either as to mean Mach scores or persuasive effectiveness.

One of the most suggestive aspects of Braginsky's analysis was based upon a content analysis of tape recordings of the strategies used by high- and low-Mach boys and girls. Lies designed to increase the target person's cracker consumption were classified as commissive (distortion of information) or ommissive (with-holding of information). Although high-Mach children did not tell significantly more lies overall, high-Mach boys told more commissive lies than low-Mach boys, while high-Mach girls used more ommissive lies than low-Mach girls. The sex by Mach interaction was significant at the .001 level.

PREADOLESCENT MACHIAVELLIANISM

The similarities and differences between Nachamie's and Braginsky's findings may be briefly summarized:

1. The use of two different versions of a children's Mach scale yielded low reliabilities in two quite different samples of 10- and 11-year-old children.

2. In two different experimental settings, one involving success in bluffing and challenging in a dice game and the other, a more freely structured verbal manipulation, high-Mach subjects were significantly more successful as mani-pulators than low Machs.

3. In neither case were there significant sex differences in mean scores on a paper and pencil measure of Machiavellianism or mean sex differences in effective manipulation.

These findings lead to the conclusion, especially since they are the only two known laboratory studies on preadolescent Machiavellianism, that an inter-personal manipulative orientation exists in a sufficiently differentiated form to be measured among preadolescents and that it predicts at least certain forms of interpersonally directed manipulative behavior.

The evidence suggests that endorsement of Machiavellian items is less pronounced at this age level than among adolescent and adult respondents. A precise comparison is impossible because of the differences in the scales used and different scoring methods. These data are in accordance with the popular notion that attempts are made to inculcate children with the belief that lying and cheating are bad but that exposure to the world outside the home leads to the fabled loss of childhood innocence and higher scores on the Mach scale. Although there is little reason to doubt that something akin to this does occur, there are still marked individual differences reflected in the experiments that have been conducted. Some adults score much lower on the Mach scale than the average ten-year-old and by all known criteria have maintained a trusting faith in their fellow man. When placed in experimental situations in which deception of others was not only permitted but encouraged, these few have refused to engage in such practices. The average low scorer, however, is distinguished more by his *ineptness* in deception than in his refusal to participate on moral grounds. On the other hand, while we have no systematic data as yet on children younger than ten, there is anecdotal evidence which suggests that some cherubs are very facile con artists.

There is no hard evidence concerning the genesis of individual differences in manipulative orientations. However, there are bits and snips of material which suggest some hypotheses.

SOME POSSIBLE FACTORS IN THE GENESIS OF INDIVIDUAL DIFFERENCES IN MACHIAVILLIANISM

The finding that ten-year-olds display interpersonal gamesmanship which is consonant with their scores on children's versions of the Mach scales directs attention toward possible differences in their childhood environment. In particular, one wonders about their families and the possible differences among them which might be related to the finding that some children are more highly manipulative than their peers. It is safer to eliminate various possibilities than to come to hard and fast conclusions.

PARENTAL MACHIAVELLIANISM SCORES. The only information available comparing parents' and their childrens' Mach scores is reported by Braginsky on a portion of her sample. Mach IV and V parental scores were obtained for 64% of the children in one of the two small cities. There is no way of estimating what, if any, effects bias in filling out the forms might have had on her findings. Surprisingly enough, not only was there no significant relationship, but the slight one found tended to be negative in separate mother–daughter, mother–son, father–daughter, and father–son correlations.

MACHIAVELLIANISM AND PERCEPTION OF PARENTS. Most of the subjects on whom experimental data have been reported have been college students living away from home. In the few samples in which we have used children as subjects, it was difficult to obtain data about their parents. For example, although the director of counseling in the prep school could give us some information about the students who had been referred to him, the school records were not illuminating in giving any information about their family background or that of the less wayward students. It was therefore impossible to test hunches about the possibility that high Machs were more likely to come from families in which the parents were separated or divorced, were geographically mobile, etc. With the exception of Braginsky's study, we know of no study in which direct comparisons have been made between family characteristics and Mach scores of children. In those cases where parents filled out scales, Braginsky did not find any significant overall correlation between parent's Mach scores and those of their sons and daughters.

The use of subjects' reports of others present problems. It was noted in Chapter III that high Machs are more likely to say unpleasant things about themselves, people in general, and persons with whom they have just interacted than are low Machs. It should come as no surprise to find that high Machs present a less cheerful view of their parents than do low Machs.

De Miguel asked two questions of his Spanish respondents which had to do with their perception of their parents. As can be seen in Table XVI-7, those respondents who felt their parents did not understand them and/or did not wish to model themselves upon their parents had higher Mach scores. Whether their parents in fact did or did not understand them is a moot question. The responses to the question are much more interesting in regard to the socialization of the high Machs; they report themselves as less likely to accept their parents as role models. Most studies of children's attitudes and values report positive correlations between parental standards and those of their offspring. It may be a far leap from Braginsky's failure to find a relationship between parents' and children's Mach scores among fifth graders in Connecticut and the estrangement from parents noted among de Miguel's Spanish male adolescents, but it is provocative.

TABLE XVI-7

Machiavellianism and Estrangement from Parents among Spanish Students

Response endorsed	Mean Mach V score	N
My parents understand me very well.	86.1	81
My parents understand me well enough.	90.3	217
My parents don't understand me too well.	91.6	111
My parents don't understand me at all.	97.2	15
	Mean 90.08	Total 424
How often does it happen?: When I think of the future I believe I would like to act like my parents."		
very often	88.4	208
often	90.0	125
sometimes	92.2	55
seldom or never	98.2	32
	Mean 90.12	Total 420

Guterman, as well, included questions about relationships with parents although in his case he was asking adults (median age in the early 40's) about relationships which on the average had occurred 30 years earlier. In these retrospective evaluations high-Mach respondents reported less rapport with parents. The index used for this measure was composed of responses on: (a) participation in recreational activities with the respondent, (b) the amount of confiding in parents about troubles, and (c) how effective the parents were in guiding the respondent through emotional crises during his teens. A negative relationship was found between this index of rapport and the respondents' Mach scores.

Guterman's parental strictness index was composed of the answers to two questions. One had to do with parental strictness towards all the children in the nuclear family and the other with how "soft" parents were in disciplining them. The greater the reported strictness, the higher was the Mach score of the respondent. High-Mach respondents reported both less rapport with parents and greater strictness on the latters' part and the two appear to be additive. Such a finding, if indicative of the true state of affairs, might well explain the high Machs' negativism about others.

The slipperiness of interpreting retrospective accounts is pointed up by another of Guterman's findings. He asked the respondents to indicate on a four-point scale from "Strongly Disagree" to "Strongly Agree" how they thought their father and mother would respond to the following two Mach items:

1. It is safest to assume that all people have a vicious streak and it will come out when they are given a chance.
2. There is no excuse for lying to someone else.

The respondents also rated on a five-point scale from "highly true" to "highly false" the following two statements about each parent:

1. Was unsuspicious and trustful toward people.
2. Was willing to engage in deception when there was a good reason to do so.

Responses to each item were then converted to a four-point scale by procedures not specified with item scores ranging from zero for a low-Mach evaluation to three for a high-Mach appraisal. Of the roughly top third of the distribution of respondents he classified as high Machs, 18% defined their same-sex parents as low by the index, 32% appraised them as medium, and 40% perceived them as high. Such data, if accepted at face value, suggest that high-Mach parents do tend to produce high-Mach offspring.

Although such a conclusion would seem to be in line with a number of developmental theories predicting positive correlations between parents' and children's scores on a variety of measures, we question whether it applies to Machiavellianism. For one thing, Braginsky found no significant correlation between parents' and children's Mach scores in the only instance in which both were tested simultaneously. In addition, Guterman's median score for all respondents on perceived parents' Mach was very low, 4.15 on a $0-12$ index. This is .69 of the way from an absolute low of zero to a theoretical neutral point of six. The respondents themselves were .94 on this equalized continuum. Although it has been argued that succeeding generations make higher Mach scores, this difference seems much larger than could reasonably be expected of parental–respondent differences in a single generation.

There is, however, a plausible explanation for Guterman's finding that does not involve role-modeling of the parents' Machiavellianism by the respondent. All available information indicates that high Machs are hardnosed, if not negative, in their estimates of others. Part of the reason for the reported relationship might be that high Machs are more willing to say (truthfully) socially undesirable things about their parents. If we add to this the Geis and Levy finding that high Machs are more likely to be accurate at guessing the true Mach scores of those with whom they have interacted (Chapter XII), then the discrepancy between the respondents' Mach scores and their reported estimates of their parents' might well have been increased by the fact that the high-Mach respondents reported their parents' Mach values accurately, while the low-scoring respondents were underestimating them.

The most suggestive variable relating to children and parental Mach scores emerged from a further analysis by Braginsky. She divided mothers and fathers at the median on both Mach IV and Mach V and compared the parent's classification with the child's Mach score and his success in manipulation. Children of mothers scoring below the median on both Mach scales scored significantly higher ($p \leq .005$) on the children's scale than children of mothers scoring high on both or low on IV and high on V. A parallel analysis for fathers was not significant. However, parents low on both scales had children who were more successful in manipulation ($\leq .05$ and $\leq .025$, respectively).

This is a startling finding which runs counter to almost all contemporary theories on child developments. This emphasis has been upon role modeling and identification with the parents on the part of the child. However, if a few assumptions are made, there is a plausible, testable hypothesis which could account for a negative relationship.

Suppose the following points are assumed:

1. There is no known genetic basis for differential manipulative behavior.

2. All infants have certain basic needs for food, warmth, comfort, etc.

3. Infants make these wants known by crying or acting uncomfortable when these needs are aroused and make happy sounds, smile, and cuddle when satisfied.

4. Those responses which are reinforced become part of their behavioral repertoire.

5. Low-Mach adults are more easily conned in face-to-face situations, where there is latitude for improvisation, and emotional affect.

6. Parents are adults and child rearing has the above characteristics.

If all of these things are true, then we would expect low-Mach parents to be more responsive to infants' demands. They would reward more attempts of the infant to obtain satisfaction and the latter would soon learn to engage in the appropriate activities to have their wants satisfied.

One obvious problem with this paradigm is that it implies a perfect negative correlation between parents' and children's Mach scores so it is necessarily oversimplified. However, by definition, low Machs are more moralistic in terms of their agreements with verbal statements, philosophies of life, etc. An argument can be made that most parents do not expect children to be able to learn moral distinctions until after they have learned to talk and to comprehend such concepts as right and wrong. By the time they are capable of such abstract behavior, they have had long experience in attempting with varying degrees of success to manipulate adults. If children of low-Mach parents (especially mothers) have already learned successful techniques of manipulation, an overlay of moral teaching (espousing high ethical standards) might not extinguish successful manipulative behaviors learned earlier in childhood.

Other possible ramifications are plausible and not mutually exclusive. Aside from the posited differences of high- and low-Mach parents being conned by their children, their values could lead to further inconsistencies in child rearing. The presence of siblings and their relative birth order could have marked effects not only in the treatment by the parents, but also what is learned or not learned from brothers and sisters. There is growing evidence that peer models are of great importance in learned behavior. It appears highly probable that more young children today have more and earlier peer experiences than would have been true 40 or 50 years ago. Kindergarten attendance was not common in the United States until after World War I, and now many children attend nursery schools at an early age. The growth of population and of housing developments occupied en masse by families almost all with young children increases the probability of peer contact at early ages as contrasted with the more age-mixed families in neighborhoods in the traditional American small town. The use of television as a baby-sitting device produces behavior models for small children which differ markedly from the models supplied by families in relatively greater social isolation.

This blending of multivariate influences, all of which might be expected to have an impact on the age at which and the speed and efficiency of the learning of manipulative bahavior, makes it extremely difficult to isolate specific variables which are of paramount importance in the development of Machiavellianism. It has been argued that the total impact of modern American society has been to increase the level of interpersonal manipulation, but which combinations of influences account for the range of individual differences is as yet unanswered.

SUMMARY

Analyses of data on students from the fifth grade through professional school in the United States and abroad and in surveys and other field studies of adult respondents indicate that there is a striking lack of major relationships between Mach scores and many demographic variables. High Machs are as likely to be found among the underprivileged as among those with high social status.

One conclusion is that Mach scores increase from preadolescence to the onset of maturity and then appear relatively stabilized. The lower scores of older adults are hypothesized as representing a clinging to values incorporated at the time of maturity. Available evidence suggests that the younger generation has been subjected to social influences such as increasing urbanization and cosmopolitanism in American society which are conducive to the fostering of manipulative orientations.

Individual differences in Machiavellianism exist at least as low as ten years of age, and have been found to be significantly related to manipulative behavior in experimental situations at this age level. There are no hard data indicating the causes of individual differences, but they are clearly not related to the social status of the parents and the evidence strongly suggests that they do not arise from the role modeling of parental behavior. It is suggested that some manipulative behaviors are learned at an early age by being rewarded unintentionally by parents and by early exposure to nonfamilial socializing agents such as peers and mass media. The one safe conclusion is that the marked individual differnces in Machiavellianism are attributable to a very complex social learning process, and that the parameters have not yet been clearly identified.

CHAPTER XVII **IMPLICATIONS AND SPECULATIONS**

Richard Christie and Florence Geis

In the first chapter the beginnings of an interest in Machiavellianism as a hypothetical construct which was related to psychological and sociological variables were described. The intervening chapters have indicated some of the adventures and misadventures that followed. In this final chapter we return to the speculative theme underlying the initial interest in Machiavellianism. We believe that our conjectures are consistent with the data which have amassed over the years but repeat that our extrapolations are speculative.

ON BEING DETACHED ABOUT MACHIAVELLIANISM

It has been suggested that we not use the term "Machiavellianism" in referring to our research because of its pejorative connotations. It is our feeling that this would be a Machiavellian tactic. Since most of the scale items and some of our research notions came from *The Prince* and *The Discourses,* it seems only candid to give credit where credit is due. Perhaps this book can be viewed as a partial vindication of Machiavelli's astuteness.

We have been plagued, however, by the problem of objectivity in discussing our results so we can respect this point of view without yielding to it. Initially, our image of the high Mach was a negative one, associated with shadowy and unsavory manipulations. However, after watching subjects in laboratory experiments, we found ourselves having a perverse admiration for the high Machs' ability to outdo others in experimental situations. Their greater willingness to admit socially undesirable traits compared to low Machs hinted at a possibly greater insight into and honesty about themselves. We were probably also influenced by the fact that high Machs were easier to schedule for experiments, and were more likely to show up than low Machs. This does not mean that our admiration was unqualified; it might better be described as selective. Although we do not claim that we have reached a stage of complete objectivity, we certainly do not have the same visceral reactions to the term "Machiavellianism" that we had earlier.

In retrospect, we were somewhat naive in the beginning in not realizing how strong people's reactions to the label would be. Perhaps an anecdotal account will indicate the beginning of awareness. In the fall of 1957 Robert K. Merton read a paper (Christie & Merton, 1958) at the annual meeting of the American Association of Medical Colleges which outlined six different techniques for measuring the value climates of medical schools. We were rather proud of some indirect measures we had used. However, one of the simplest techniques was a comparison of the agreement of medical school students on four Mach statements which had also been given, with other items, to samples of college students, Washington lobbyists, and business executives. It so happened that medical students were more likely than the other groups to agree that complete trust in someone else is asking for trouble; it is wise to flatter important people, it is hard to get ahead without cutting corners, and never to tell the real reason for doing something unless it is useful. A slide containing these comparisons, the seventh of 21, was flashed on a screen early in a 90-min talk, the rest of which was devoted to subtler techniques.

At the end of the presentation, the floor was opened for discussion. The assembled deans did not respond to the major part of the paper or the other 20 slides, but immediately focused on the Mach comparisons. An elderly dean from a Midwestern school rose and asked why medical schools had failed by turning out products who were more Machiavellian than Washington lobbyists and said it was time to reexamine the whole philosophy of medical education. A young dean from an elite medical school in an urban area jumped up and said that it was a good thing that medical students were tough minded, considering the sorts of patients with whom they had to deal. The verbal battle was on and the paper was forgotten. It was impossible to escape the conclusion that one could do a good job of predicting the Mach scores of the speakers by the way they lined up in the argument.

In general, both high and low Machs feel strongly about the positions they hold. It is not too great an oversimplification to say that high Machs feel that people who score low on the Mach tests are naïve, not with it, and behave unrealistically in the real world. Low Machs, on the other hand, think agreement with Machiavelli reflects a deplorable lack of compassion and faith in others, and is immoral, if not inhuman.

It was noted in the first chapter that power theorists have been known in both Eastern and Western cultures for milenia and that what appear to be prototypes of high and low Machs may be found in folklore and myth. One way to ascertain the generality of this distinction in the way people are alleged to believe and behave is to test it in different cultural settings. If the message has any universality, it should come through loud and clear after being translated from Italian into English and then violated by being put into an item—scale format, utilizing words and phrases more colloquial than literary. If this bastardized version of Machiavelli's notions can then be translated into yet another language and be meaningful, the message must be powerful indeed.

Previously, we mentioned that Mach IV had been translated into Chinese and that among the bilingual Cantonese-dialect high school students in Hong Kong, the English and Chinese versions had almost identical means and, more crucially, the split-half reliabilities were comparable.

Although the scales have also been translated into Hungarian, Japanese, and Spanish, neither item nor scale reliabilities were given. However, Professor Peter Shonbach (1966, personal communication) translated Mach IV into German to give to classes at the *Institut für Sozialforschung* at Frankfort. He raised a question as to the identity of Barnum. The reply was that if the German students did not know who Barnum was, it would probably be possible to substitute the name of any historic figure with whose writings or epigrams the students could not be expected to be overly familiar, e.g., Ghenghis Khan or Charlegmagne, since it was the concept and not the source which seemed universal. As can be seen, Barnum's name was retained in the translation, *"Barnum hatte unrecht, als er sagte, dab in jeder Minute ein weiterer Dummkopf geboren wurde."* Despite the use of a presumably unfamiliar proper noun and the fact that sucker and *"Dummkopf"* have slightly different connotations, the item discriminated significantly between high and low German scorers on the total scale — as did all the other 19 items. The split-half reliability was .79 — a figure exactly the same as that averaged in American samples. Such translatability lends some confidence to the argument that the concept has a modicum, at least, of generality in other lands.

Further, we have argued on the basis of our data that American life seems to be becoming more manipulative and impersonal as reflected in generational differences in Mach scores. A number of commentators seem to hold a similar view. For example,

A generation is coming of age in America that doesn't take the utterances of public figures straight, that doesn't take social games straight. It suspects the whole range of modern experience. It sees giant con games everywhere. It sees "the system" itself as a con game (Brackman, 1967).

A less impressionistic summary was given by Lubell (1966) after interviewing students at 36 American colleges and universities.

Across the whole of their lives, college students have apparently *accepted as an established fact that ours is a managed and manipulated society.* In adjusting to this manipulated state of affairs they have developed a striking psychological sensitivity. Despite their attacks on "conformity," college boys and girls are not really individualists in the sense of wanting to stand alone. They can be described more accurately as "personalists" in that *so many define right and wrong by "what it means to me," with the emphasis on the "me"* [Italics added].

For better or worse, we seemingly have stumbled on an area of behavior which concerns many people today. It may be only a temporary ripple in the wave of the future, but it certainly fascinates the current generation. When giving colloquiums or discussing the research in debriefing undergraduate classes, students who doze absentmindedly during a discussion of attitude measurement, organization theory, or religious beliefs edge forward in their chairs and their eyes light up when the topic of interpersonal manipulation is discussed. Their elders also seem interested, although we have not had so much relevant contact with them. At least we are assuming that the popularity of such volumes as Stephen Potter's (1948) book on gamesmanship or *Games People Play* (Berne, 1964) is not restricted to college students.

THE INTERPLAY BETWEEN THE LABORATORY
AND THE OUTSIDE WORLD

The possibility of studying Machiavellianism as an individual difference variable originated in speculations about the characteristics of persons who manipulated in that portion of the world outside the walls of laboratories. However, most of the research we have reported has been conducted under controlled conditions. In part, this reflects our greater confidence in findings obtained in situations in which the possible effects of uncontrolled variables are minimized.

There are both advantages and disadvantages to such a strategy. The fact that the situations studied were brief in duration is a disadvantage. Typically, high Machs achieved their success in from 5 min to a few hours. Although their ability to adapt their tactics to the specific situation, demonstrated in laboratory studies, would suggest that they might be equally effective in dealing with others to promote their own interests in longer-term situations, this is more speculative. However, we are not convinced that behavior in the laboratory is any less "real" than behavior occurring in a free environment. In fact, a reading of the current experimental literature in social psychology might well leave one with the impression that there is as much stress, anxiety arousal, and conflict elicited in the laboratory, if not more, than is normally true of that portion of the middle-class, affluent American world from which most of our subjects came. The crucial question is one of relevance. Is there any correspondence between behaviors elicited in controlled laboratory settings and those occuring under the control of forces in the larger society? This is a difficult question to answer.

In taking certain observations based upon writings of power theorists, observations of and interviews with and about individuals reputed to be successful manipulators, as a starting point we were able to conduct laboratory studies which clarified the situational parameters in the restricted laboratory situation. In general the more tightly we restricted the laboratory situation, as in modified Prisoner's Dilemma games in which the subject was playing a nonexistent opponent, had little latitude for improvisation, and there was little opportunity for irrelevant affect, the less well the high Machs did in relation to the low Machs. The more similar to the nonlaboratory world the experimental situation was, e.g., face-to-face contact, greater latitude for improvising behaviors, and the more affectively complex the situation, the greater was the relative advantage of high Machs. This gives us some confidence that our findings might be of some relevance to what occurs in the real world.

It does not, however, make straightforward extrapolation of our findings to the world outside the laboratory justifiable. In the first chapter we mentioned the often observed contrast between those who control the behavior of others on the basis of conning or gamesmanship and those who use naked power. These presumably represent end points on a continuum of tactics. Many exercises of power in the real world represent a combination of psychological manipulative tactics and implicit threat of harm such as the control over hiring, promoting, or firing an employee or financial loss by strikes or riots. Others represent explicit threats of physical harm such as the use of "enforcers" by the Mafia to collect gambling debts. In many cases, such recourse to direct power is not actually employed, but the possibility of its use is present and enhances the advantage of the manipulator who is employing more subtle forms of influence.

There are obvious ethical restraints on the use or threatened use of physical harm in the laboratory which make it difficult to add such dimensions to experimental studies. The interaction between manipulation and force can only be conjectured. There is some reason to suspect that high Machs with their more cynical attitude towards others might be less likely to abhor the use of naked power to gain their ends as compared with the more humaritarian low Machs. This is speculative, however, and not demonstrated.

One other restriction should be noted. Machiavelli observed that the rise of men from low condition to high rank was usually the result of force or fraud. Yet, even Machiavelli recognized legitimate authority, although he implicitly minimized its importance. There are certain areas of social life in which the rules of interpersonal conduct are codified and in which those playing different social roles exercise differential authority by virtue of observance of these commonly understood rules. Some people appear to take to the role of authority with more zest than others. In some of our studies (e.g., the Machiavel study) when high Machs were placed in positions of power, they did, in fact, manipulate more than did low Machs. However, they also won in those bargaining games which satisfied our three conditions even when there was no built-in power advantage, e.g., the Ten Dollar and Legislature Games. Our general line of argument has been that the use of Machiavellian tactics enhances the exercise of legitimate power only if the rules of society are not so highly structured that there is little opportunity for innovative behavior.

A problem common to most, if not all, attempts at generalizing from the laboratory to the real world is that of defining variables common to both situations. In the laboratory we can define the variables which we manipulate and, by random assignment of subjects to conditions, minimize the effects of irrelevant subject variables. A basic premise underlying such research is that the particular variables we study are also relevant under conditions not subject to experimental control. In abstracting from the complex forces operating in free situations, there is the danger that we select those for more intensive study which are of minor relevance. This might be due to the fact that our professional training sensitizes us to them, or because they are relatively easy to study in the laboratory, or because we lack the discernment to isolate the most important influences in real world situations.

Optimistically, we believe that we have isolated crucial variables from the blooming, buzzing confusion of the real world and studied them under controlled conditions. However, the problem of generalizing from the laboratory findings *back* to the real world is by no means a simple one. First, other variables exist in natural settings and we do not know the relative importance of the interaction between known and unknown variables. Interaction effects are stronger than main effects in many experiments. The same is undoubtedly true in the real world, and the problem of interpretation is confounded when known variables interact with others of unknown nature and strength. In our judgement, the value of our laboratory findings lies primarily in sensitizing us to their possible applicability in the real world and in suggesting possible interpretations of relationships occurring in situations structured by society rather than an experimenter.

TRANSLATING LABORATORY VARIABLES INTO THE OUTSIDE WORLD

Among the problems faced in generalizing from a controlled laboratory situation into the outside world is the fact that variables can be much more precisely defined in the laboratory. In our analysis of face-to-face contact for example, a simple dichotomy was made between no face-to-face contact and the physical presence of others. To be sure, there are a few solitary occupations such as lighthouse keeper, sheep herder, prospector, hermit, meditative monk, and the like which come close to the laboratory paradigm of no face-to-face interaction, but they are increasingly rare in modern society. There are, however, other roles when contact with others occurs but in which manipulation of others can make no difference in getting rewards. For example, an airline ticket agent or a supermarket checkout clerk is in almost continuous interaction with a large number of people, yet has minimal social influence on them. The price of groceries and airline tickets is predetermined and in turn, salaries or other fringe benefits usually cannot be increased by securing customers' cooperation. We have proposed that Machiavellianism becomes relevant when rewards or outcomes are not tied to objectively defined performances but can be influenced by the way the situation is handled. First, in our laboratory situations the subjects were typically motivated to accomplish something. The various "goals" could all be conceptualized as achieving or maintaining self-esteem with success represented by some concrete symbol such as points in a game, dollars, M&M candies, etc. Such goals could be represented outside of the laboratory by promotions, raises, job offers, more advantageous assignments, or other outcomes that could be conceived of as rewarding. Second, in the situations in which high Machs won, the subjects were usually dependent on varying combinations of chance, skill, and others' cooperation in accomplishing their ends. The crucial point is that one subject's outcome depended upon another's recognizing his claims and cooperating voluntarily to help him achieve them. In short, they were in situations and role relationships in which neither an external authority nor the structure of the situation itself dictated exactly what others were obligated to do or required to refuse. The situation in which high Machs performed most differently from low Machs was loosely structured: face-to-face contact varied empirically with both latitude for improvisation and irrelevant affect. Although the manipulation or influencing of others via telephone or correspondance is entirely conceivable, the impact of the manipulator's physical presence in face-to-face interactions might add weight to his claims.

Our classification of latitude for improvisation was also dichotomous primarily for expositional simplicity. However, the laboratory situations actually varied in degree and type of restrictions. In examining extra-laboratory conditions, it would seem better to make a comparison as to the relative amount of freedom to improvise. This again is determined by the structure of the situation. Tightly structured situations permit relatively little freedom to improvise; loosely structured ones permit a great deal.

Our third laboratory parameter, the presence of irrelevant affect, is not so tightly bound to the structure of the situation. We varied it by introducing different amounts of money or by socially loaded content. One could argue that loosely structured situations in the real world with no explicit rules about the nature of face-to-face contact or prescriptions for correct behavior would tend to arouse more irrelevant affect than highly structured situations in which the role relationships and procedural rules were specific. The opportunity for irrelevant affect interferes sufficiently with the performance of low Machs to give the high Machs an edge. However, in the laboratory we were not manipulating *structure* as much as *content* when differences between the behavior of high and low Machs attributable to irrelevant affect emerged.

In translating the laboratory paradigm into the real world, then, we are primarily interested in classifying the structure of the situation in terms of whether or not manipulation can make a difference and then assessing the amount of face-to-face contact engendered, the degree of latitude for improvisation provided, and whether the interaction involves socially loaded content which might arouse irrelevant affect.

FIELD STUDIES FROM THE PERSPECTIVE
OF LABORATORY FINDINGS

The Mach scales have been used in a variety of survey studies. In some cases the comparisons being made yielded results which were congruent with expectations based upon laboratory studies; in some cases they might have been, but not enough was known about the actual situation, and in some it is clear that other unknown variables were operating.

An early unanticipated finding in a study of three medical schools was that students who indicated an interest in subsequent specialization in psychiatry had higher Mach scores than those who chose (in decending order) pediatrics, internal medicine, obstetrics−gynecology, and surgery (not enough prospective physicians were interested in other medical specialties for analysis). A. B. Silverstein (personal communication) found a similar pattern in another medical school as did Kurt Back (personal communication) in eight other medical schools. Invariably potential psychiatrists made the highest Mach scores; potential surgeons scored at or near the bottom of the distribution.

Such consistent findings called for interpretation. Some possible explanations were easily ruled out. The desire of high Machs for more money could not be a factor since the annual income of surgeons is greater than that of psychiatrists. A need for higher status seemed unlikely since psychiatry was ranked equally low by both medical students and their faculty. Helen Gee (1957, personal communication) indicated that of 12 specialties ranked by students and faculty in 15 medical schools, psychiatry had the lowest status of all except dermatology.

There are many points of difference in the practice of psychiatry and surgery. Psychiatrists are by definition attempting to change (manipulate) human behavior. Surgeons are operators only in the technical sense of the word; rather than attempting to change behavior by psychological techniques, they are professionally involved in attempts to change the patient's body by direct physical intervention. "Success" in psychiatry typically depends upon the patient's voluntary cooperation in the process of therapy, while success in surgery depends more upon the surgeon's individual skill, at least during the operation itself. Thus, psychiatry provides a situation in which manipulation of others can make a difference in the psychiatrist's success (and presumably the other rewards associated with success) while interpersonal manipulation would be of little relevance to a surgeon's success in performing an operation.

It is possible to examine the differences in the physician−patient relationship in psychiatry and surgery from the standpoint of the three variables that make a difference in the laboratory. It seems probable that psychiatrists have *more* face-to-face contact with their patients than do most surgeons. First, the practice of psychiatry usually involves a prolonged period of interaction between the physician and his patient. Therapeutic sessions of "fifty-minute hours" several times per week have been known to last over a period of years. Even the orthodox psychoanalyst who sits out of sight of the patient is physically present and in at least intermittent verbal communication with the patient during the sessions. In contrast, surgeons typically see a patient for an initial consultation, refer him to technicians for laboratory tests, see him again to arrange for treatment, have interns and residents prepare him for the operation, have an anesthesiologists put the patient under sedation, operate when the patient is unconscious, and have most of the postoperative care done by members of the hospital staff with occasional visits by the physician himself. All in all, even with the inevitable variations from this hypothesized general pattern, psychiatrists typically have more face-to-face interaction with their patients both in absolute and relative terms than surgeons.

Surgical practice permits little latitude for improvisation. Diagnoses are relatively standardized and most operative techniques are also standardized. What improvisation occurs is primarily that of surgical skill or differences in allaying patients' fears prior to or after the operation. Psychiatrists, on the other hand, lack a uniform system of diagnosis and are increasingly eclectic in the methods they use to effect change. Methods of treatment vary from physical to verbal and even within psychotherapy, for example, methods vary from followers of one school to the other. The actual treatment by a particular psychiatrist may vary from one patient to the next as he modifies procedures in accordance with his interpretation of the patient's behavior. The fact that criteria for success of treatment are more commonly agreed upon by surgeons than psychiatrists is probably related to the fact that the latter have to improvise more and that it is consequently harder to determine success.

The third criterion, the presence of irrelevant affect, is perhaps most clear-cut. Most psychiatric patients are patients precisely because of problems of irrelevant affect. Surgical patients more frequently than not have fears about the operation and its aftermath. In many cases these fears are justified but in others they are embellished by anxiety .unjustified by the objective situation. The crucial distinction is that psychiatrists choose a specialty which centers around the treatment of irrelevant affect, whereas a surgeon's choice is for a practice in which the patient's irrelevant affect has little chance of influencing the surgeon's professional behavior during the operation.

None of this should be taken to indicate that relative skill in the manipulation of patients is the sole or even the most important reason some medical students opt for psychiatry and others for surgery. We are simply saying that the practice of psychiatry as we interpret it resembles the experimental situations in which high Machs are more successful than does the practice of surgery.

Data from the other nonlaboratory studies suggest that they are more likely to fit the paradigm than not. For example, Weinstock (1964) studied the acculturation of 50 Hungarian refugees who came to the United States following the abortive Hungarian revolution of 1956. Nine of the Mach IV items were translated into Hungarian and given to his respondents in conjunction with material from other scales and a lengthy interview. Two different measures of acculturation were used as dependent variables: one was a modification of the Campisi Scale (Campisi, 1947) which dealt with the Americanization of preferences for food (American rather than Hungarian) and movies (again, American rather than Hungarian), etc.; the second was a scale of familiarity with peculiarly American information (How many men on a baseball team? Who is Bishop Sheen?, etc.). These two measures correlated $+.40$. The abbreviated Mach scale correlated $+.33$ with the combined scores on these two measures ($+.25$ and $+.27$ with each, respectively).

It is, of course, possible that the faster refugees acculturated to the United States the more they accepted a uniquely American Machiavellian orientation. This possibility seems unlikely since Mach correlated $-.05$ with the length of time the respondent had lived in the United States. Evidently the initially more Machiavellian of the refugees acculturated the more readily. Although we have no objective indicators, it seems plausible that those who are more facile in face-to-face contacts are able to improvise, and those who are less subject to the arousal of irrelevant affect would adapt more readily to a strange society.

It is equally hard to test the applicability of our model from the results of a study of Washington lobbyists by Milbrath (1963). Here there was no overall measure of effectiveness or success as a lobbyist. Most of his measures had to do with ideological matters and there was little relationship between tham and summed scores on positively worded Mach IV items that had been included in a questionnaire. Milbrath noted that high-Mach lobbyists spent more time on Capitol Hill and entertained their clients more than did their low-scoring counterparts, which suggests they were taking advantage of latitude for improvisation. Two hunches about the relationship of Mach item responses to other information were tested with data Milbrath made available. One involved the difference between lobbyists who had law degrees and those who did not. The rationale was that legal training emphasizes the dispassionate handling of interpersonal matters which quite frequently are characterized by irrelevant affect. Lobbyists with legal training were significantly more in agreement with Machiavelli than nonlawyers. A second hunch was prompted by the observation that some lobbyists represented a single client, and others two or more. It seemed plausible that those representing more clients would have the highest Mach scores. Serving many masters may be more likely to arouse irrelevant affect and could only be handled by persons with a minimal tendency in this direction. It may also require greater facility in improvising. The prediction was supported beyond the .05 level.

The preceding studies illustrate a problem in attempting to generalize from the laboratory paradigm to the real world. There was simply not enough detailed information about the relative degree and kind of face-to-face contact, latitude for improvisation, and arousal of irrelevant affect in these situations to be precise in analyzing their influence.

The importance of having more detailed information about the situation is indicated by comparing a finding of Singer (1964) with its attempted replication in the prep school discussed in Chapter XVI. Singer reports partial correlations (with ability scores held constant) of $+.23$ between Mach V and grade-point average in a preliminary sample of 79 college students, one of $+.39$ in a second study of 63 males, and ones of $+.17$ for 269 first-born males and $+.33$ for 256 later-born freshman males. These data were collected at Pennsylvania State University. Mach scores accounted for more variance in predicting grades than did any of four measures of ability, birth order, or family size.

Ability test scores were available at the prep school where Mach IV scores had been obtained and we paralleled that portion of Singer's analysis. With ability held constant, there were no significant correlations between Mach and grade-point average in any of the grades $7-12$ and the overall correlation was zero. However, ability test scores correlated $+.76$ with grade-point average.

This failure to find similar results was puzzling. Aside from the difference in the ages of the students, which we have no reason to believe is a major factor, there was an obvious difference in the size of the two settings. In the fall of 1962, Pennsylvania State University had an overall enrollment of 23,584, of whom about 4000 were freshmen who attended classes in sections with as many as 400 students. The total enrollment at the prep school was about 330 at the time of the study and the classes were, of course, much smaller. About half of the students lived on campus as did some of the faculty. Going back to the laboratory paradigm, several rough comparisons can be made. In the smaller prep school setting there was much more face-to-face contact between students and faculty; it was practically unavoidable. In contrast to this enforced intimacy, students at Penn State could go through a semester without ever being closer to an instructor than a back seat in a lecture hall. They could, however, bring themselves to the attention of a teacher by asking questions after class, dropping into his office during office hours, or otherwise making themselves visible. In short, as contrasted with the prep school. it was a situation in where there was much more latitude for improvisation in initiating face-to-face contact.

It would also appear reasonable that there would be much greater latitude for other kinds of improvisation on the part of students in a large impersonal university than in a small tightly run prep school. The high correlation between ability scores and grade-point average at the latter suggests that if the instructors did not know the actual test scores of a particular student, they did know his reputation as a student. In short, at the prep school rewards (grades in this case) were tied to objective performance — in classroom work, if not on achievement tests — and interpersonal manipulation was apparently not a possible means of raising them.

We have no way of ascertaining the comparability of the two situations as to the potentiality for arousing irrelevant affect.

The Mach scales have been given as part of other studies to many samples in nonlaboratory settings. In general, the findings can be interpreted as congruent with our laboratory paradigm about the importance of the amount of face-to-face contact, latitude for improvisation, and the presence of irrelevant affect as favoring the high Mach over the low Mach in manipulative behavior. Such an interpretation depends, however, upon assumptions about the nature of the situations, and the data to check these assumptions and alternative explanations rigorously do not exist in any studies with which we are familiar. We believe, however, that it is potentially fruitful for future investigators of manipulative behavior in natural settings to analyze them in these terms.

A GENERAL MODEL

When we turn from an examination of specific experiments or studies to a more general formulation, it is possible to put matters into perspective. Our research has been based on an interaction model in which individuals with differing predispositions whom we refer to as high or low Mach behave in predictably different or similar ways, depending on the constraints or lack of them in a particular situation. This interaction of individuals and situation leads to different coping behaviors or, as we have tended to call them, tactics.

A rough, idealized model is presented in Fig. XVII-1. The high Mach's salient characteristic is viewed as coolness and detachment. In pursuit of largely self-defined goals, he disregards both his own and others' affective states and therefore attacks the problem with all the logical ability that he possesses. He reads the situation in terms of perceived possibilities and then proceeds to act on the basis of what action will lead to what results.

The low Mach is hypothesized as being much more open to others and liable to becoming affectively involved with them or with his own concerns. He becomes more engrossed in the content of conversation rather than its ultimate purpose in terms of his individual goals. He is more likely to get carried away in the process of interacting with others and acting upon the basis of noncognitive reactions to the situation.

Again oversimplifying, situations can be ordered along a dimension of loosely to highly structured. In laboratory experiments the degree of structure is defined by the experimenter; in the real world it is defined by the norms and rules of the social system. In highly structured situations the roles of the participants are clear, the way in which goals are achieved is clear, the reward associated with each goal is defined, and there is little wiggle room or latitude for improvisation. Rules for behavior are reasonably explicit and variation from them is penalized.

Loosely structured situations, on the other hand, are characterized by ambiguity as to the role of the participants, the means to achieve goals, and their associated rewards. In the absence of formal rules, the situation permits a variety of ways of introducing structure and taking advantage of its absence.

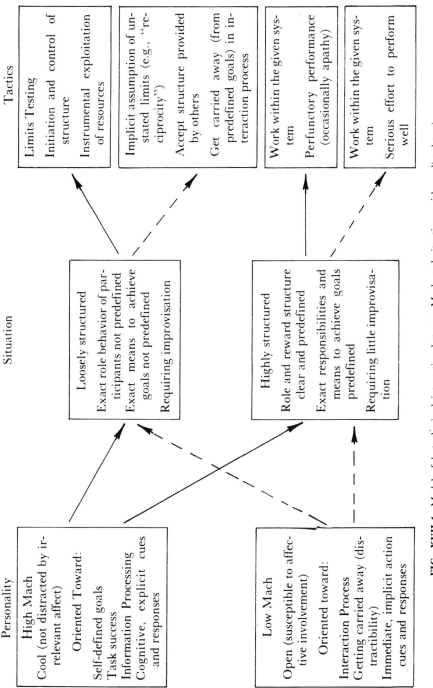

FIG. XVII-1. Model of hypothesized interaction between Mach and situations with predicted tactics.

As can be seen from Fig. XVII-1, this interaction model indicated that the greatest difference in the tactics used by high and low Machs occurs in loosely structured situations. We believe that this is supported by the experimental data summarized earlier and is consistent with results from field studies. A loosely structured situation puts the high Mach on his mettle. What are the limits? To what extent can the situation be exploited for one's own gain by imposing structure? The low Mach, rather than focusing on the structural aspects of the situation, is more likely to assume that a structure exists and is more amenable to others' (especially high Machs') interpretation of the structure. His susceptibility to affective involvement interferes with his ability to assay the situation in purely cognitive terms.

Our analysis suggests that in highly structured situations both high and low Machs tend to work within the given limits which are readily understood by both. If there is no challenge for the high Machs, they tend to perform in a perfunctory manner without any great enthusiasm. Lows, on the other hand, regard it as a moral obligation to do their duty and presumably would make a serious effort to perform well.

Such a model has implications for social change. It suggests that high Machs thrive in situations which are in flux. In their attempts to impose order on chaos they, if successful, establish a situation which by its very order does not give their manipulative tendencies full bent. It is somewhat provocative, in this respect, that Lord Shang, Kautilya, and Machiavelli all lived in times of considerable social disorder and all gave prescriptions, sometimes in great detail, as to how to establish order — one, to be sure, which was in their own or their protectors' self-interest.

One of the characteristics of the model as presented is that it implies a tendency toward a state of social balance. If by unspecified means a social system becomes disequilibrated, those most likely to analyze the situation and reimpose structure would be high Machs. With these built-in tendencies toward stability, how does an ongoing system become loosely structured? How does revolution occur?

One speculation in this regard is that when economic, political, or other social forces place a strain upon a social organization, high Machs attempt to modify and innovate within the existing structure. When the pressure becomes too great, such cognitively rational modifications do not work. Our suspicion is that revolutions are not initiated by high Machs but by a subset of low or middle Machs who are capable of great moral indignation at the failure of the existing system and who by virtue of their affective involvement with a potentially new order crystallize opposition to the existing one. Once the "revolution" has picked up enough steam to be a "movement," however, the situation changes. If the movement is loosely structured ("organizational chaos," as some observers have termed it), but nevertheless manages to disrupt the establishment to some extent, then high Machs might be attracted to either side to impose structure or take advantage of its absence to achieve other goals (e.g., positions of power or influence), regardless of the ideology being supported in the process.

Such a cosmic explanation has the dubious virtue of being as simplistic as those of Spengler or Toynbee but at least it is consistent with our data and observations.

Among the hundreds of high-Mach subjects we have observed, only a few were in leadership positions in radical groups and they articulated the moral indignation about abuses of "the establishment" which typically motivates such groups. The vast majority of high Machs, however, appear to despise inefficiency more than deplore injustice. Parenthetically, high Machs tend to savor the explanations of deceptions we have practiced upon them in experiments. Low-Mach subjects have not displayed openly an equal appreciation of the fine points of experimental manipulation. Some of the students tested in class on the Mach scales have been subjects in other experiments in which there was deception which was close to the borderline of accepted ethical standards. Among those subjected to such duplicity, only low-Mach students went so far as to complain to the Dean's office.

Mathematics Hall at Columbia University was one of the buildings "liberated" in the student rebellion in the spring of 1968 and the senior author was barred from his office and departmental laboratories. This seemed an appropriate time to examine the ideology of the liberators and their supporters. It appeared especially appropriate since the interest in political manipulation began with the role of extremists in political movements (see Chapter I) and it was possible to study them *in vivo* rather than through historical recreations.

Comparisons of (1) arrestees versus nonarrestees during the Columbia busts and (2) those entering freshmen scoring high and low on the New Left Scale (Christie, Friedman, & Ross, 1969) clarified some speculations. As was true of the comparisons in Chapter III, there was no overall difference in political attitudes or behavior and total Mach scores in any groups. The self-proclaimed student revolutionarys were not a subset of low Machs or high Machs. However, they did show, in both instances, a pattern of differential responses to Mach Tactics and Disbelief in People subscales (see Appendix A). Those arrested and those endorsing New Left ideology were low on the Machiavellian Tactics but high on the Distrust in People subscales.

Oversimplifying, it seems highly unlikely that someone who believes "The establishment unfairly controls every aspect of our lives; we can never be free until we are rid of it" (New Left agrees) would also agree as do low Machs that, "most people are basically good and kind." Or that one agreeing with the Mach Tactics statement, "It is wise to flatter important people" would hold a dean captive, occupy administration offices, or tell professors in a public meeting designed to cool the conflict that their efforts were "bullshit" (Avorn, 1968; Grant, 1969, p. 84).

Material is, at the time of writing, still being collected and analyzed on the revolutionaries of the New Left. The emerging pattern is complex but to date indicates agreement with an almost Rousseauian view of man, "Although men are intrinsically good, they have developed institutions which force them to act in opposition to this basic nature," while they disagree that, "most people can still be depended on to come through in a pinch."

It was noted in Chapter III that both a right-wing authoritarian, as measured by the F scale, and a nonideological high Mach are likely to agree that, "people are no damn good." According to available date young members of the New Left also share this premise. Instead of moralistically blaming the person for not overcoming his inherant weakness as do high authoritarians or dispassionately taking advantage of others' failings, these young rebels blame society for corrupting others. Translating this into political terms, it would seem that high authoritarians are politically counterrevolutionaires, the New Left is revolutionary, and high Machs coolly play both ends against the middle.

MACHIAVELLIANISM AND SOCIETY

One of the unexpected findings in the amalgam national sample was that when we factor analyzed Mach and anomia items, those items which fell on the factors labeled "Machiavellian Tactics" and "Honesty" had no appreciable correlation with occupational status or education (see Appendix A). When the latter were combined in a Hollingshead Index of Socio-Economic Status, there was not only no correlation with Mach but, contrary to our prediction, there was no relationship between upward social mobility (the change from father's SES to respondent's SES) and Mach. In the decades preceding the survey, apparently it was as likely for an honest man to get ahead in the world as a rogue. It is also possible that low Machs got ahead by hard work, while highs advanced by combining manipulative skills with less arduous labor.

In retrospect, this finding should not have been surprising. After all, we had earlier found that there was no correlation between Mach scores and IQ among student samples and education and IQ in the general population are highly correlated. We would argue, however, that there is a relationship between kinds of occupations and Mach scale scores. We do not have representative samples of occupations but in general those unsystematic aggregates who have taken the Mach scales have scores consistent with our interpretation of the degree of structure imposed by the occupation. Elementary and secondary school teachers who have been tested score considerably lower than most other occupational groups; professionals tend to score high.

It seems probable that the choice of occupations and professions is related to Mach scores as well as to relevant ability, training, knowledge of the field, and the possibility of access to it. One of the problems of testing these relationships is that functional job classifications are needed. To what extent does a particular occupational role involve control and manipulation of others for official or unofficial ends in situations in which success is related to keeping one's cool? The only person known to date making the highest possible score on Mach V was a gentleman in his late 30's with a Ph.D. in industrial social psychology from a relatively prestigious university who had founded a successful management consultant concern. The lowest score of a person identifiable by name in medical school samples was obtained by a young lady from a small midwestern town who was preparing to become a medical missionary. It appears probable that such simple dichotomies as blue collar or white collar, dealing primarily with persons or things, etc., are not of themselves any more related to tendencies toward manipulation than such variables as social status or father's occupation examined in the NORC representative sample. It is the *kind* of interpersonal roles associated with different occupations that are crucial and there is no known satisfactory occupational taxonomy which gets at this.

Since the research focus has been primarily on manipulative behavior in controlled laboratory situations, no systematic attempt has been made to discover how Mach scores are related to various occupational classifications which do not isolate the relevant role requirements. Bits of data made available by others suggest that Strong Vocational Inventory scores related to feminine occupations are negatively correlated with Mach scores; this is congruent with the sex difference typically found in Mach scores. In general, professionals tend to score higher than businessmen who have similar numbers of years of education. This is not surprising since it would appear probable that selection of, training for, and engaging in a professional career in contemporary American society is more likely to be related to a cosmopolitan than traditional orientation.

The complications involved may be illustrated by narrowing the focus to those involved in a single occupation which many persons believe to be highly Machiavellian, the salesman. The high-pressure salesman is enshrined in folk lore along with the carnival pitchman as the epitome of manipulation. For example, a coauthor of one of the experimental chapters was (and perhaps still is) convinced that salesmen for the *Encyclopedia Britannica* who prey upon professors with small children are highly Machiavellian. Interestingly enough, he did not fall for their blandisments, so it would seem that a disparity existed between his evaluation and their effectiveness.

Although this stereotype may be true, available data indicate that four nonrandom samples of salesmen who represented both institutional and door-to-door selling scored below the random sample of adults in the NORC sample on Mach V but were much higher on the built-in measure of social desirability. Although it is theoretically consistent that a high Mach would make a better salesman than a low Mach, there are good reasons why he might not enter the field or, if once in it, would leave. Very few people grow up with a burning desire to become salesmen, and entry into the field is frequently preceded by a failure to be successful at some other occupation. Given this assumed negative selection factor, even an individual who has the interpersonal skills to be an effective salesman and becomes one is quite unlikely to remain a salesman but is more likely to be promoted to a more responsible position or enter another occupation.

We have combined bits of data from a variety of contexts to argue that high Machs are more likely to be attracted to and come from nontraditional societies. In the national sample we found adult respondents under 40 to have higher scores than older respondents who were presumably reared under more traditional standards (Chapter II); de Miguel found a positive correlation between Mach V scores and the degree of industrialization of the province in which Spanish students lived and went to school (Chapter XVI); there is evidence that high Mach adults were more likely to come from urban rather than rural backgrounds (Chapter XVI); Oksenberg found that Chinese students in a transitional situation (attending a Western school) had higher scores than those attending a traditional Chinese school in Hong Kong (Chapter XVI).

MACHIAVELLIANISM
AND THE STRUCTURE OF AUTHORITY

We have proposed that loosely structured situations give high Machs more opportunity for manipulation and that they tend to initiate structure. What about their performance within a structure? Rather than ask whether or not high Machs make better leaders or administrators than low Machs, we will modify the question and ask what are the conditions under which we would predict superior or inferior performance?

In the first chapter some mildly disparaging remarks were made about a subset of administrators such as departmental chairmen, college deans, presidents, foundation executives, and the like. It might be questioned as to whether the academic arena is a good place to study Machiavellianism. Woodrow Wilson has been quoted as saying that power politics at the state and national level do not match in intensity experiences he had in university life. The only other person in recent American history known to have been both a university president and president of the United States viewed himself as above politics and is not known to have studied or compared the academic and political arenas in any analytic way. With all due respect to Wilson, we would hesitate to make a flat, overall comparison. Some colleges and universities are tightly structured; others almost approach Renaissance Italy with their warring factions. It is not entirely accidental that the term "empire building" is commonly used in reference to the activities of ambitious academicians. Political organizations also can vary widely in the tightness or looseness of their structure. The same is true of business, ecclesiastic, or fraternal organizations. The crucial point is the structure of the organization, not whether it is classified as educational or not.

In the years intervening since the senior author's sensitization to Machiavellian tendencies on the part of administrators in the academic and related fields, many additional observations have been made (including a few by the junior author) which have modified and augmented the initial reactions. Some people have a hobby of bird watching; his has become dean watching. (Once when mutually commiserating with another departmental chairman about the onerous duties involved, it was commented that the only saving feature of serving as a chairman was that it afforded a closer vantage point to observe the university administration in action and that some ideas for experiments in the study of manipulation resulted from watching deans in action. To which the colleague responded, "You're lucky. I'm studying creativity.")

In general, our observations and theoretical position suggest that anyone extremely low on Mach would make a poor administrator, He would be too likely to become affectively involved with those whom he was presumably supervising and lack the detachment necessary to depersonalize his relationships with them when a cognitive analysis of the situation was necessary. In almost any organization hard decisions have to be made which have negative consequences for some of its members — decisions such as not promoting or even firing an ineffective worker who is a nice guy, knowing when to tell people to shape up and being able to do so, and a host of other contingencies which demand taking a hard line for the benefit of the organization.

The problem with extremely high-Mach administrators is that their cool cognitive analysis of the needs of the organization coupled with a disregard for the individual needs of those within it could quite easily lead to disaffection and problems of morale which can cripple the organization.

The problem then becomes what the mission of the organization is and how its structure is related to its internal and external needs. In a rapidly expanding organization or in a fairly stable one that is changing its relationship to external organizations, relatively high-Mach executives should be more useful and successful. They would spend more time aggressively bargaining for funds or making arrangements for the organization's welfare with outside authorities. This would have two positive consequences: the resources gained for the organization would benefit its members and the administrator's insensitivity to the personal needs of others would be directed outside the organization. A low-Mach administrator in such a situation would (hypothetically, at least) not be nearly as adept in bargaining for the benefit of the organization in the outside world.

If we were dealing with a tightly structured system in which role relationships and administrative procedures were clearly laid out and the problem was the maintenance of the organization, a high-Mach administrator might well feel stifled. Lacking other outlets, he might start playing games with those people under his control which could lead to the morale problems alluded to previously. A moderately low Mach, e.g., one who is concerned with others but does not get too sucked into interpersonal involvements would probably be much better at keeping the system operative at the optimal level.

In summary, our speculations about the relative ability of high and low Machs to fit into administrative positions is that very low Machs are probably poor bets for any administrative position in a loosely structured organization; very high Machs are poor bets for most tightly structured organizations except when they are sent on what amounts to detached service in which there is freedom to wheel and deal to both their own and the organization's benefit.

SOME FINAL REFLECTIONS

If our speculations are correct, modern society is becoming increasingly more similar in structure to the kinds of laboratory situations in which high Machiavellians win. Available evidence also suggests that individual orientations toward manipulation are increasing. How long this process will continue and whether it is reversible or not are questions which we have no way of answering. We are social psychologists of the present, not predicters of the future.

One thing that has impressed us in the course of these researches is the fact that there are no marked differences in the ability of high Machs to score higher than low Machs on standardized tests of intelligence. In interpersonal situations which are fairly well structured, in which there is no face-to-face contact, and the affect involved is not irrelevant to task achievement, high Machs do *not* outcon and outbargain low Machs. The structure of intelligence tests is such that interpersonal conning or bargaining are not among the possible ways of getting higher scores. It is in interpersonal situations which are relatively unstructured, in which face-to-face interaction occurs in an affectively complex situation in which there is latitude for improvisation, that high Machs tend to win. Our interpretation is that high Machs tend to read the situation and remain detached from the affective distractions, among them other persons; although low Machs are equally capable of sizing up the situation, they get caught up in the interaction process with the other person(s), and this interferes with "rational" behavior. Sometimes it is not so much that high Machs win as that low Machs lose.

At the time of the initial interest in manipulation one plausible hypothesis was that those who manipulated others were able to do so because they were adept at sizing up other persons' weak points and then taking advantage of them. This may occur in certain cases. However, we have come to a different way of viewing our findings. We would argue that our manipulative high-Mach subjects have a singular disregard of others as individuals and tend to stereotype them as weak and subject to pressure. The advantage the high Machs have in manipulating others is that they seem more accurate in their views of others' weakness in general, and that the low Machs permit themselves to be run over and out maneuvered by the intransigent highs while clinging to their idealistic interpretation of how people should behave.

APPENDIX A

THE STRUCTURE OF MACHIAVELLIAN ORIENTATIONS

Richard Christie and Stanley Lehmann

Earlier (in Chapter II) it was noted that an impressionistic analysis of *The Prince* and *The Discourses* suggested three identifiable themes. The first was the advocacy of such manipulative tactics as the use of guile and deceit in interpersonal relations. The second was an unflattering view of the nature of man as being weak and cowardly and easily subject to pressure from others. The third, less-clearly demarcated theme dealt with what we called abstract morality or, more accurately, the lack of it.

In the original part−whole item analysis the items dealing with abstract morality failed to show high discriminatory power among aggregates of students at Iowa, North Carolina, and Hofstra. The 20 most discriminating items retained in Mach IV were almost equally divided between ones that had been *a priori* classified as dealing with interpersonal tactics and views of human nature. At that time we did not have the resources to do a factor analysis of a 71×71 matrix on 1196 respondents. We did examine the part−whole correlation between each item and the subscale to which it had been assigned. If the correlations between the individual items and the subscales to which they had been assigned had been higher than between the items and the total scale, this would have suggested the presence of the predicted discriminable dimensions. Upon inspection, no such marked relationship was apparent. It was therefore decided, since the scale reliability seemed reasonably high, that the best use of time and resources would be to see if the Mach IV scale had any relationship to outside criteria and not to pursue the question of structure further.

Most of the subsequent validation studies did in fact indicate that scores were related to various measures of interpersonal manipulative skill. In an experiment involving the largest number of subjects ($N = 66$) with a clear-cut definition and measure of success in manipulation, the Con Game (Chapter VIII), a correlation of $+.71$ was found between combined scores on Mach IV and V and the number of points won in bargaining in a triad. This is one of the highest correlations between a paper-and-pencil measure of an individual variable and an independent objective measure of individual behavior with which we are familiar. These results indicated only that individuals who endorsed statements that people are basically weak and that a lack of candor in handling them is an appropriate technique were able to manipulate others more successfully in laboratory situations. Whether this was related more to their endorsement of manipulative tactics than having a dim view of others, or both in equal combination, we could not say.

A FACTOR ANALYSIS OF MACHIAVELLIANISM
AND ANOMIA IN A REPRESENTATIVE NATIONAL SAMPLE

Seven years after doing the initial item analysis, the question of the structure of the Mach scales arose again. Over the intervening years, samples had been periodically collected for classroom training pruposes. Students were required to give Mach IV and V, a revision of the F scale (Christie *et al.,* 1958), and an exploratory, counterbalanced, local revision of Srole's Anomia scale. These were pickup samples in which students gave the scales to any respondents they could corner who had some college education, and to an equal number of people with a high school education or less. A negative relationship was uniformly found between education and scores on F and Anomia. These were consistent with other findings. Surprisingly, although no prediction had been made, there was no significant relationship between education and Mach. The patterns of correlation among the three scales also contained an anomaly. On theoretical grounds it had been predicted that there would be no significant relationships among the three scales. Gratifyingly enough, there were none between Mach IV and F or between F and Anomia. In two cases in which positive relationships had been found between the latter (Srole, 1956; Roberts & Rokeach, 1956), only positively worded items had been used in both scales and it was our contention that these findings were solely due to response set. We were somewhat surprised, however, to find positive relationships from .34 to .40 between Mach, which essentially seemed to tap a belligerently independent orientation toward others, and Anomia, which can best be described as a counsel of despair.

For these and other reasons, we became interested in whether or not the lack of relationship between Mach and education would hold in a national sample, and hoped to define more clearly the puzzling relationship between Mach and Anomia.

Early in 1963 it was possible to collect such data in the first National Opinion Research Center "Amalgam" survey. A number of social scientists bought into the survey with questions dealing with attitudes toward ability testing, death, and fallout shelters. (Fortunately, our items were asked prior to those about attitudes toward death or nuclear attack or we might have found greater Anomia than we did.)

Thirty of our items were included: 6 Mach originals and 4 reversals in a Likert format, the 10-item counterbalanced Anomia scale given in a modified Likert format, and the remaining 10 Mach items in the forced-choice format. All 20 Mach items were included in one format or the other. The allocation of items to either format was based upon the judgments of social desirability as described in Chapter II. The items in each form were equated for social desirability. This explains why we had 6 original and 4 reversed items from Mach IV rather than an even 5 and 5 split. On the basis of earlier research on response set we felt that this was not a great enough disproportion to seriously affect the results.

The instructions taken from the interview schedule follow:

> Next, I'm going to give you some cards on which statements are printed. While you read them from the card I will read them aloud, if you wish. These are matters of opinion on which people differ. We're interested in your honest answer so that we can find out what most people really think.
>
> Some of the statements may sound familiar to you, either because you have thought about them or because you've heard other people talk about them. Others may sound strange. We want your first reaction to them.
>
> Here's the first statement. *(Hand respondent green card A)* Do you agree or disagree that *(read statement A)?*
>
> *If Agree:* Do you agree a lot or a little? *(Code below)*
>
> *If Disagree:* Do you disagree a lot or a little? *(Code below)*
>
> *If no immediate answer:* (about 10 sec after reading): We want your first impressions of what you think about the statement. If you don't understand a statement, tell me. If you can't make up your mind — and some people can't — agree or disagree without thinking about it any further. In other words, do you feel like you would like to agree or disagree?

After the completion of these 20 items (10 Mach and 10 Anomia) the switch was made to the 10 forced-choice items from Mach IV. The instructions were:

> We've just asked whether you agree or disagree about some statements. Now we're going to ask a different type of question. I will give you a card with *three* statements on it. This time it won't matter how much you agree or disagree with them. We just want you to *compare* the statements with each other.
>
> I want you to tell me which one of them is closest to your own feelings, and which you think is the *most opposite* to what you really feel. Again, we're interested in your first impressions.
>
> (Hand respondent blue card A) Tell me which of these statements you *agree* with most. Then tell me which of them you *disagree* with most.
>
> Mark a + in front of the "most agree" item in Group A below. Mark an "0" in front of the "Most disagree" item.

In all, 1482 respondents were questioned. Available evidence indicated that this was a sample representative of all noninstitutionalized persons 21 years of age or over in the United States. We were somewhat concerned over obtaining responses to the forced-choice questions, fearing that they might be too difficult for respondents with little education. Actually, only 12 respondents failed to answer them and they were all interviewed by the same person in a Southern community so that the inference that the interviewer was at fault seemed tenable.

Originally it had been our intention to run the scales as straightforward measures of what they purported to measure while using Anomia as a control variable. Before doing so, however, we decided to avail ourselves of a factor analysis program and examine the relationship of the items with one another. The results were so compelling that we changed our strategy of analysis. The following data indicate why.

The 30 × 30 matrix of item intercorrelations was factored on the 7090 computer using the Harvard statistical laboratories factor analysis program. The principal components were subjected to a varimax rotation which yielded five relatively meaningful dimensions. As can be seen by following the item loadings on each factor in the upper left to lower right diagonal, each of the five appears relatively clear-cut. Reading scores across the rows, it can be seen that with minor exceptions most items load on only one factor. Three items did not belong to any factor: "It is possible to be good in all respects"; "The average man is probably better off today"; and "If you try hard enough, you can usually get what you want." They, therefore, do not appear in any of the national sample tables in this chapter.

It was apparent that we had five relatively independent factors but the problem of their interpretation was necessarily subjective.

TABLE A-1

The Factorial Structure of Mach and Anomia Items in a National Sample.[a]

Factor	Scale ident. [b]	Item number	Anomic Disen- chant ment	Machia- vellian Tactics	Polly- anna Syn- drome	Honesty	Machia- vellian Orien- tation
I	A+	14	-62c	-01	-08	-05	01
I	M+	11	-58	13	-14	-19	03
I	A+	8	-58	-09	12	-03	04
I	M+	15	-55	03	06	15	04
I	M+	16	-54	01	-30	-03	-10
I	A+	2	-54	17	01	16	06
I	M+	12	-53	-08	-12	-01	-14
I	A+	5	-51	16	13	-05	10
I	M+	9	-47	-20	09	-05	-30
I	A+	1	-41	07	-01	-19	-02
I	M+	20	-39	11	12	-11	30
II	MV	28	-09	63	00	16	-07
II	MV	30	-04	58	-12	-02	03
II	MV	22	00	53	-06	02	-03
II	MV	24	-12	48	-02	10	-28
II	MV	26	11	39	09	33	-23
III	M-	7	-09	05	71	03	-03
III	A-	13	-02	07	70	09	02
III	A-	3	-07	06	67	09	-08
IV	M-	4	04	02	-03	67	-15
IV	M-	18	11	15	01	58	-04

TABLE A-1 (continued)

Factor	Scale ident. [b]	Item number	Anomic Disen- chant ment	Machia- vellian Tactics	Polly- anna Syn- drome	Honesty	Machia- vellian Orien- tation
IV	A-	19	-03	20	-22	50	17
IV	M-	6	-01	-02	-24	45	05
V	MV	27	-12	09	-04	03	-68
V	MV	21	15	19	17	17	-41
V	MV	25	04	35	-09	-07	-41
V	MV	23	02	26	-14	-02	-36

[a] The residual items which did not cluster are not included in this and the following tables, except for Table A-13.

[b] A+, Anomia positively worded; A-, Anomia negatively worded; M+, Mach positively worded; M-, Mach negatively worded; MV, Mach forced-choice format.

[c] Decimal points omitted.

I. ANOMIC DISENCHANTMENT. Initially, the most striking thing about these items is that all 11 are keyed positively so that agreement with them means endorsement of Anomia and Mach IV items. In fact, this factor contains every agree item in the entire battery and not a single other one. The odds on this happening by chance are astronomical (1 in 54,627,300). The initial interpretation was that this might be exclusively the effect of agreement response set. If this were true, we would expect correlations approaching −1.00 with Factors III and IV which are composed of Mach IV and Anomia items in which agreement is scored in the reverse direction. The relationship hovered close to zero, however.

An examination of the content of the items (Table A-2) revealed a somewhat dismal view of the world and the nature of man. With the possible exception of items 15 and 20 these are not items indicating a manipulative approach. Rather, they reflect despair and a feeling of helplessness and apathy in a world of personal futility. Most of the studies on behavioral correlates of the tendency to agree on paper-and-pencil tests among college students indicate little relationship with conforming behavior. In some of these studies (reviewed by Christie & Lindauer, 1963) there is a strong suggestion that many of the subjects simply "don't give a damn" about anything and resort to a petulantly hostile approach to life. If this is so, the content of these items and a tendency to agree to almost any defeatist statement fit together. In any event, our tentative title of Anomic Disenchantment seems to fit this factor well.

TABLE A-2

Factor I: Anomic Disenchantment

Loading	Item number	Item
-.62	14	It's hardly fair to bring a child into the world with the way things look for the future.
-.58	11	It is safest to assume that all people have a vicious streak and it will come out when they are given a chance.
-.58	8	Nowadays a person has to live pretty much for today and let tomorrow take care of itself.
-.55	15	The best way to handle people is to tell them what they want to hear.
-.54	16	Anyone who completely trusts anyone else is asking for trouble.
-.54	2	Next to health money is the most important thing in life.
-.53	12	Generally speaking, men won't work hard unless they're forced to do so.
-.51	5	You sometimes can't help wondering whether anything is worthwhile anymore.
-.47	9	Most men forget more easily the death of their father than the loss of their property.
-.41	1	Most people in government are not really interested in the problems of the average man.
-.39	20	It is hard to get ahead without cutting corners here and there.

II. MACHIAVELLIAN TACTICS. This factor is also unique in that all of its items come from one format — in this case, the forced-choice one. An examination of the keyed items and their responses — "Honesty is the best policy in all cases" (disagreement); "Never tell anyone the real reason you did something unless it is useful to do so" (agreement); "It is wise to flatter important people" (agreement); "All in all, it is better to be humble and honest than to be important and dishonest" (disagreement) — indicates that all have clear implications for the way in which one conducts oneself with others. The only item which does not clearly fit into this interpretation is the one on Barnum (Item 30), which on the face of it, seems more related to views of human nature. An examination of Table A-3 indicates that this is not so. We have therefore bowed to the majority of the keyed items in naming this factor Machiavellian Tactics.

TABLE A-3

Factor II: Machiavellian Tactics

Loading	Item number	Item
.63	28	A. It is best to give others the impression that you can change your mind easily.
		B. It is a good working policy to keep on good terms with everyone.
		*C. Honesty is the best policy in all cases.
.58	30	*A. Barnum was probably right when he said that there's at least one sucker born every minute.
		B. Life is pretty dull unless one deliberately stirs up some excitement.
		C. Most people would be better off if they controlled their emotions.
.53	22	*A. Never tell anyone the real reason you did something unless it is useful to do so.
		B. The well-being of the individual is the goal that should be worked for before anything else.
		ªC. Once a truly intelligent person makes up his mind about the answer to a problem he rarely continues to think about it.
.48	24	A. The world would be a much better place to live in if people would let the future take care of itself and concern themselves only with enjoying the present.
		*B. It is wise to flatter important people.
		C. Once a decision had been made, it is best to keep changing it as new circumstances arise.
.39	26	*A. All in all, it is better to be humble and honest than to be important and dishonest.
		B. A man who is able and willing to work hard has a good chance of succeeding in whatever he wants to do.
		C. If a thing does not help us in our daily lives, it isn't very important.

* Keyed items.

ª The matched item C was changed for purposes of this study from the one in Mach V (see Table II-4, Item 3, alternative C).

III. POLLYANNA SYNDROME. This short and sweet factor seems very clear-cut. "Most people" seem to be pretty good folks. It is interesting to note again that this factor has a low positive correlation (+.16) with the misanthropism expressed in Factor I whose content seems to be the logical opposite. The Pollyanna items are all keyed negatively in contrast to those in Factor I and it is this contamination with response set which presumably washes out the native correlation which one would logically expect between the two.

TABLE A-4

Factor III: Pollyanna Syndrome

Loading	Item number	Item
.71	7	Most people are basically good and kind.
.70	13	Most people will go out of their way to help someone else.
.67	3	Most people can still be depended upon to come through in a pinch.

IV. HONESTY. Again, this is a factor in which all the items are keyed negatively, yet its items load only modestly on Factor III, which is scored in the same fashion. The high ethical standards underlying the endorsement of these items appear too obvious for expanded comment.

TABLE A-5

Factor IV: Honesty

Loading	Item number	Item
.67	4	There is no excuse for lying to someone else.
.58	18	One should take action only when sure it is morally right.
.50	19	Even today, the way that you make money is more important than how much you make.
.45	6	When you ask someone to do something for you, it is best to give the real reasons for wanting it rather than giving reasons which carry more weight.

V. MACHIAVELLIAN ORIENTATION. This, like the second factor, is composed exclusively of items taken from Mach V. It differs from Mach V in that most of the items refer to evaluations of others rather than to interpersonal tactics. The keyed items — "Most men are brave" (disagreement); "People suffering from incurable diseases should have the choice of being put painlessly to death" (agreement); "The biggest difference between criminals and most other people is that criminals are stupid enough to get caught" (agreement); and "Most people who get ahead in the world lead clean moral lives" (disagreement) — have a somewhat cynical cast. In content it seems the obverse of Factor III, the Pollyanna Syndrome, but those items were all asked in a Likert format.

TABLE A-6

Factor V: Machiavellian Orientation

Loading	Item number	Item
-.68	27	A. A man's first responsibility is to his wife, not his mother.
		*B. Most men are brave.
		C. It's best to pick friends that are intellectually stimulating rather than ones it is comfortable to be around.
-.41	21	A. Men are more concerned with the car they drive than with the clothes their wives wear.
		B. It is very important that imagination and creativity in children be cultivated.
		*C. People suffering from incurable diseases should have the choice of being put painlessly to death.
-.41	25	A. It is a good policy to act as if you are doing the things you do because you have no other choice.
		*B. The biggest difference between most criminals and other people is that criminals are stupid enough to get caught.
		C. Even the most hardened and vicious criminal has a spark of decency somewhere within him.
-.36	23	*A. Most people who get ahead in the world lead clean moral lives.
		B. Any man worth his salt shouldn't be blamed for putting his career above his family.
		C. People would be better off if they were concerned less with how to do things and more with what to do.

* Keyed items.

Two of the factors which we uncovered and named "Machiavellian Tactics" and "Honesty" were largely composed of items originally classified as belonging to the *a priori* identification of Tactics. Their appearance as two separate factors in the national sample seemed to be attributable to the fact that one was composed of items in a forced-choice format, the other of items in agree-disagree format. A third factor, also composed of forced-choice items and called "Machiavellian Orientation," contained mostly items earlier defined as "Views of Human Nature." One other Views item showed up in conjunction with two reversed Anomia items in a fourth factor dubbed the Pollyanna Syndrome, a trusting view of one's fellow man.

One of the frustrating things about interpreting these factors was that we had trimmed Mach IV and V in half for the national sample and had a restricted number of items with which to work. In the fall of 1964, the presidential election offered an opportunity to check several hypotheses about the relationship of Mach scale scores to presidential preference, and to assay the importance of the F-scale score in the decision to vote for Johnson or Goldwater. We also wanted to do a new factor analysis of a large population's responses to the complete Mach IV, Mach V, and Anomia scales in order to compare these results with those from the national sample. Since we were also using the F scale, we decided for reasons of curiosity to include it in the matrix as well.

Each respondent filled out the 20-item, counterbalanced Mach IV, the 20 item, counterbalanced revision of the F scale (Christie *et al.*, 1958), the 10-item counterbalanced Anomia scale, and the 20-item forced-choice Mach. This provided us with the basis for the item intercorrelations required for the analysis.

The population used for this study was selected by a deliberately nonrandom procedure. We wished to get a sample of college students as diverse as possible along the anticipated splits between preference for Johnson and Goldwater. Pilot results from other studies indicated that however vocal, Goldwater supporters were not numerous in the Ivy League schools or in the New York City colleges. It seemed desirable to search for schools in which a larger proportion of Goldwater partisans might be found. We used hunches about where such students might be and took advantage of the information supplied to us by friends and acquaintances at a number of colleges to make our selection of schools. Of the 11 faculty members at the various schools whom we approached for cooperation in obtaining student samples, all promised to do so, and surprisingly for a book in which there is an emphasis upon the believed untrustworthiness of human nature, all 11 did cooperate. In the end, we were able to collect material in 14 schools.

We obtained 1782 scorable protocols. They can in no way be viewed as representative of American college students since our primary purpose had been to get as wide a range of schools as possible in terms of the political preference of the respondents. There is no way of ascertaining what the actual range of proportion of political opinion in the college population was. The sample was limited in other ways as well. While in one school we used the entire freshman class, almost all of the respondents were students in education, psychology, or sociology classes. Since some of the people who helped us were reluctant to have their schools publicly named, the colleges will only be identified in the following way:

Three nonelite state-affiliated schools in New England.

A Mid-Atlantic municipal college in a large urban center.

A Mid-Atlantic Ivy League university.

A Mid-Atlantic church-affiliated private college.

A private college in a border state.

A border-state Negro public college.

A deep Southern state university located in a town best known in the Northern press for the number of Negro churches burned in the preceding few years.

A Southern urban state-affiliated university.

A Southwestern state-affiliated college.

A small Midwestern church-affiliated college.

A large Midwestern state-affiliated university.

A far-Western state-affiliated college located in a county reputed to be a stronghold of the John Birch society.

These colleges were located in towns or cities varying in population from 1170 to 7,781,984 (1960 Census figures). Enrollment varied from 823 to 30,922 (1962 figures from the American Council on Education). The schools were also checked against Astin's (1964) estimate of individual college selectivity which is based on the number of highly able students enrolled divided by the total student population. Two of the schools in the sample received the lowest possible rating. At the other extreme was one school which was two standard deviations above the national average. The overall mean for the colleges was .2 of a standard deviation above the estimated national average. Although the sample was not representative it certainly was heterogeneous.

The item matrix of the responses to the 1782 completed protocols was factor analyzed by the same procedure used on the national adult sample. Four factors emerged and are reported in Tables A-9–A-12.

A FACTOR ANALYSIS OF RESPONSES
AMONG COLLEGE STUDENTS

Before presenting and tentatively interpreting the four factors, one rather striking finding must be noted. Items were classifiable as Likert positively worded (disagreement scored high), Likert negatively worded (agreement scored high), and forced choice. Table A-7 presents the *format* distribution of items on the four factors.

TABLE A-7

Distribution of Items by Format on the Four Factors

Item format	Factor				Total
	I	II	III	IV	
Likert, positive	3	19	1	2	25
Likert, negative	6	0	10	9	25
Forced-choice	8	0	9	1	17
Total	17	19	19	12	67

The distribution of items across factors is clearly nonrandom. The chi square of 59.84 was highly significant (with $6df$, a value of 22.46 is significant at the .001 level). The first factor has the greatest balance across item format categories. The item composition of Factor II is the most lopsided since it consists only of items in which agreement is scored high. The third factor has the same number of forced-choice items as does the first one but is more heavily loaded with reversed items, both absolutely and proportionately. The fourth factor is most heavily loaded with items in which disagreement is scored high on the scales.

It would therefore seem prudent in interpreting the meaning of these factors to be cognizant of the fact that the way in which the item was presented made a difference in the way respondents reacted to it.

An alternate way of dissecting the item breakdown by factors is to look at the representation of the items from different scales that load on them. Table A-8 presents this scale content breakdown. A perusal of this table indicates that 15 of the 17 items on Factor I come from one of the two versions of the Mach scale. Factor II had roughly proportionate (35–40%) representation from the three Likert scales but has no forced-choice Mach V items at all. Factor III represents a composite of the two Mach scales and Anomia. Factor IV is based primarily on reversed *F*-scale items.

Summarizing the results of these two analyses, before looking at the actual items loading on the four factors, we can say the following:

Factor I is not strongly affected by the way in which items are presented but is heavily weighted by those coming from the scales based upon Machiavelli.

Factor II is composed only of items which are positively worded in the Likert format and seems to be equally representative of Anomia, *F*, and Machiavellian content.

Factor III is composed of mostly forced-choice and negatively worded items with Machiavellian and Anomia content.

Factor IV consists mostly of negatively stated items drawn from the *F* scale.

TABLE A-8

Items Loading on Factors as Classified by Scale Membership

Scale	Factor				Total
	I	II	III	IV	
Mach IV	7	7	5	1	20
Mach V	8	0	8	1	17
F Scale	0	8	2	10	20
Anomia	2	4	4	0	10
Total	17	19	19	12	67

I. DUPLICITY. The first factor consists almost entirely of items from Mach IV and V. Of interest is the fact that unlike the national sample of adults where forced-choice and agree-disagree items appeared on separate factors, in the college sample both forms of the same statement appear on the same factor. Those scoring high on this factor do *not* believe: (a) that there is no excuse for lying to someone else, (b) that honesty is the best policy in all cases, (c) that it is better to be honest and humble than to be important and dishonest, (d) in giving real reasons for wanting something rather than giving reasons which carry more weight, (e) that one should take action only when sure it is morally right, and (f) that the way you make money is more important than how much you make. They do believe: (a) that it is wise to flatter important people, (b) that the best way to handle people is to tell them what they want to hear, and (c) that next to health, wealth is the most important thing in life.

All of these items have to do with interpersonal candor or the lack of it except the two from the Anomia scale regarding wealth and how one makes money. We therefore named it "Duplicity."

TABLE A-9

Factor I: Duplicity

Scale classification	Item number	Item [a]	I	II	III	IV
			Factor loading [b]			
M–	20	There is no excuse for lying to someone else.	-517	-230	-241	164
M–	14	Honesty is the best policy in all cases.	-509	-169	-305	160
M(FC)	74	(Honesty is the best policy in all cases.)	507	084	186	-145
M–	27	All in all, it is better to be honest and humble than to be important and dishonest.	-470	-029	-199	068
M–	31	When you ask someone to do something for you, it is best to give the real reasons for wanting it rather than giving reasons which carry more weight.	-454	-027	-192	-021
M+	42	It is wise to flatter important people.)	451	-212	-085	080
M+	9	The best way to handle people is to tell them what they want to hear.	394	-246	-074	-036
M(FC)	62	(The best way to handle people is to tell them what they want to hear.)	362	020	-055	-037
M(FC)	70	(There is no excuse for lying to someone else.)	348	-030	162	-125
M(FC)	69	(All in all, it is better to be honest and humble than important, and dishonest.)	341	-056	006	-140
M(FC)	67	(It is wise to flatter important people).	328	-063	-035	214
A+	22	Next to health, wealth is the most important thing in life.	305	-260	-045	-073
M(FC)	66	(One should take action only when sure it is morally right.)	291	-012	063	-020

TABLE A-9 (continued)

Scale classification	Item number	Item [a]	Factor loading [b]			
			I	II	III	IV
M–	10	One should take action only when sure it is morally right.	–284	–220	–207	099
A–	50	Even today, the way that you make money is more important than how much you make.	–276	071	–138	–054
M(FC)	61	(Never tell anyone the real reason you did something unless it is useful to do so.)	267	–088	092	–013
M(FC)	65	(When you ask someone to do something for you, it is best go give the real reasons rather than giving reasons which carry more weight.)	–228	039	051	–133

[a] Items in parentheses were given in forced-choice format (Mach V).
[b] Decimal points omitted.

II. AFFIRMATIVE NEGATIVISM. The second factor is unique, as noted, in that it is scale format specific but not scale content specific. Twenty-five out of the original 70 items were in the format where agreement was given a high score. Nineteen out of these 25 emerge on this factor: 8 of the 10 F-positive items, 7 of the 10 Mach-positive items, and 4 of the 5 Anomia-positive items. Although clearly not tied to the content of the specific scales, examination of the items in Table A-10 indicates that the content is negative in reference to man and society. In general, persons who tend to agree with such statements have an ill-structured cognitive orientation toward social issues. Some interesting speculations about the personality of these "yea sayers" are proposed by Couch and Keniston (1960), who argue on the basis of test scores and clinical interviews that these are persons with weak ego controls who express impulses freely.

A number of possible labels for this factor were considered, including Embittered Suservience. Bearing in mind the agreement response set involved in these items and their social content, we finally decided to call this factor "Affirmative Negativism."

TABLE A-10

Factor II: Affirmative Negativism

Scale classification	Item number	Item	Factor loading[a]			
			I	II	III	IV
F +	36	Most of our social problems could be solved if we could somehow get rid of the immoral, crooked, and feeble-minded people.	012	–416	–145	069
M +	26	Generally speaking, most men won't work hard unless forced to do so.	039	–413	093	–085
M +	13	It is safest to assume that all people have a vicious streak and it will come out if they are given a chance.	166	–4.2	159	–069
A +	41	Most people in government are not really interested in the problems of the average man.	035	–392	175	–023
F +	17	Most people don't realize how much our lives are controlled by plots hatched in secret places.	043	–389	073	–002
M +	35	Anyone who completely trusts anyone else is asking for trouble.	161	–369	310	–121
M +	38	The biggest difference between most criminals and other people is that the criminals are stupid enough to get caught.	175	–364	090	–108
F +	45	Nowadays more and more people are prying into matters that should remain personal and private.	–049	–364	–051	016

TABLE A-10 (continued)

Scale classification	Item Number	Item	Factor loading[a]			
			I	II	III	IV
F +	57	Sex crimes, such as rape and attacks on children deserve more than mere imprisonment; such criminals ought to be publicly whipped or worse.	-018	-353	-087	033
F +	19	Human nature being what it is, there will always be war or conflict.	019	-351	043	-002
F +	15	It is essential for learning or effective work that our teachers or bosses outline in detail what is to be done and how to do it.	007	-345	-115	065
M +	6	Never tell anyone the real reason you did something unless it is useful to do so.	239	-344	046	016
F +	37	What the youth needs most is strict-discipline, rugged determination, and the will to work and fight for family and country.	-081	-340	-212	176
M +	49	It is hard to get ahead without cutting corners here and there.	285	-331	089	-106
F +	21	No weakness or difficulty can hold us back if we have enough will power.	-171	-316	-266	031
A +	34	It's hardly fair to bring a child into the world with the way things look for the future.	175	-364	090	-108

TABLE A-10 (continued)

Scale classification	Number	Item	I	II	III	IV
				Factor loading[a]		
M+	58	Most men forget more easily the death of their father than the loss of their property.	042	–262	164	–154
A+	29	You sometimes can't help wondering if anything is worthwhile anymore.	055	–241	060	–161
A+	25	Nowadays a person has to live pretty much for today and let tomorrow take care of itself.	–067	–237	046	–059

[a] Decimal points omitted.

III. DISTRUST IN PEOPLE. The third factor is composed of 8 forced-choice Mach V items, 5 reversed Mach IV items and 4 reversed Anomia items, with one positive and one reversed F-scale item. Our initial impulse was to call this the "Most People" factor since the first 8 items on the factor begin with this phrase. Those scoring high on this factor are rejecting items indicating that most people are good, kind, brave, altruistic, dependable, moral, etc. We have therefore named it "Distrust in People."

TABLE A-11

Factor III: Distrust in People

Scale classification	Item Number	Item [a]	I	II	III	IV
				Factor loading[b]		
A–	16	Most people will go out of their way to help someone else.	–010	091	–592	–062
M–	40	Most men are brave.	–027	006	–551	101
M–	12	Most people are basically good and kind.	–081	051	–480	–013
A–	8	Most people can still be depended upon to come through in a pinch.	–024	116	–450	–008
M(FC)	63	(Most people are basically good and kind).	151	–158	443	–121
M–	33	Most people who get ahead in the world lead clean, moral lives.	–112	060	–429	069

TABLE A-11 (continued)

Scale classification	Item Number	Item [a]	Factor loading [b]			
			I	II	III	IV
M(FC)	72	(Most men are brave).	-047	-020	375	-173
M(FC)	64	(Most people who get ahead in the world lead clean, moral lives).	138	-163	374	-049
F+	18	No sane, normal, decent person could even think of hurting a close friend or relative.	-110	-218	-301	105
A-	11	If you try hard enough, you can usually get what you want.	-046	-202	-294	-049
M-	43	It is possible to be good in all respects.	-118	-163	-269	129
M(FC)	78	(Anyone who completely trust anyone else is asking for trouble).	187	-122	259	-122
A-	48	The average man is probably better off today than he ever was.	-015	004	-228	-054
M(FC)	75	(It is possible to be good in all respects).	140	-099	206	-094
M(FC)	76	(Barnum was probably right when he said there's at least one sucker born every minute).	097	-024	204	-092
M(FC)	77	(It is safest to assume that all people have a vicious streak and it will come out when they are given a chance).	150	-131	172	-089
M-	44	Barnum was wrong when he said there's a sucker born every minute.	-123	099	-159	048
F-	28	It is highly unlikely that astrology will ever be able to explain anything.	012	068	133	-066
M(FC)	59	(Most men forget more easily the death of their father than the loss of their property).	-051	-091	128	-001

[a] Items in parentheses were given in forced-choice format (Mach V).

[b] Decimal points omitted.

IV. TRADITIONAL MORALISM. The fourth factor contains 9 of the 10 reversed *F*-scale items devised by Christie *et al.* (1958). The interesting addition is an item taken from Melvin (1955), designed to measure Toughmindedness, which we classified as positive Machiavellian; "People suffering from incurable diseases should have the choice of being put painlessly to death." This has the highest loading on this factor in both Likert and forced-choice format. A high score on this factor essentially comes from rejecting antiauthoritarian items. A low scorer might be characterized as having a rational, skeptical, and slightly rebellious orientation toward conventional societal norms. Since those who score high seem to be rejecting the values current among graduate students in the social sciences, for example, we named it "Traditional Moralism."

TABLE A-12
Factor IV: Traditional Moralism

Scale classification	Item number	Item [a]	Factor loading[b]			
			I	II	III	IV
M+	56	People suffering from incurable diseases should have the choice of being put painlessly to death.	191	–021	049	–626
M(FC)	60	(People suffering from incurable diseases should have the choice of being put painlessly to death).	149	038	–062	–526
F–	46	The findings of science may some day show that many of our most cherished beliefs are wrong.	145	–134	106	–370
F–	24	Books and movies ought to give a more realistic picture of life even if they show that evil sometimes triumphs over good.	022	–110	075	–320
F+	39	Every person should have complete faith in a supernatural power whose decisions he obeys without question.	–198	–264	–200	301
F–	30	Most honest people admit to themselves that they have sometimes hated their parents.	–054	–054	071	–286

TABLE A-12 (continued)

Scale classification	Number	Item [a]	Factor loadings [b]			
			I	II	III	IV
F–	5	People ought to pay more attention to new ideas even if they seem to go against the American way of life.	020	105	053	-277
F–	23	If it weren't for the rebellious ideas of youth there would be less progress in the world.	071	-115	009	-261
F–	55	In spite of what you read about the wild sex life of people in important places the real story is about the same in any group of people.	004	-121	-036	-189
F–	32	One of the most important things children should learn is when to disobey authorities.	114	-007	-110	-179
F–	32	The artist and professor are probably more important to society than the businessman and manufacturer.	-085	082	039	-151
F–	47	An urge to jump from high places is probably the result of unhappy personal experiences rather than anything inborn.	-041	-071	014	079

[a] Items in parentheses were given in forced-choice format (Mach V).
[b] Decimal points omitted.

A COMPARISON OF COLLEGE AND CROSS-SECTIONAL SAMPLES

Any factor analysis is a description of the relationships among responses to items in a particular sample. Items which were answered the same way by large groups of respondents appear together on the same factor. The same factorial structure may or may not emerge in different samples so that it is extremely hazardous to generalize from one particular sample to other populations. If, however, similar factors are found in different samples, some confidence may be entertained as to their generalizability.

A comparison of the factor analytic solutions to the nationwide sample and the later sample of the college student populations is therefore pertinent. Before presenting these results it is well to consider some of the differences in the two samples, the instruments used, and their administration. Any and all of these make any similarity found the more remarkable.

Data on the national sample were collected over a period of several weeks early in 1963. Those on college students were collected in the week preceding the 1964 presidential election. There is no apparent reason to suspect marked changes in responses to these particular items due to increases in Mach scores over such a short time, or to suspect that particular national or international events at the two times would make a marked difference. These are, however, possibilities.

Thirty items were common to the two administrations. Those in the national sample came after a series of background questions and a block of questions about mental testing. In the college sample they were mixed with other items from the same scales at the beginning of a questionnaire. The context in which they were asked thus differed markedly and this should decrease to an undeterminable extent the probability of obtaining similar factor structures.

In the national sample, an interviewer who was a stranger to the respondent asked the questions individually at the latter's home. A card with the question printed on it was presented to the respondent for examination while the interviewer read the question orally, and, after eliciting the response, recorded it. The college respondents were administered the scale by their instructor in a scheduled class period. There were two exceptions: in one case the entire freshman class was given a group administration and in the other the students took the questionnaires home to fill them out. All college respondents recorded their own answers on an answer sheet. These marked differences in administration could not be expected to enhance the similarity of factors in the two samples.

Finally, there were the dissimilarities to be found between a national sample of adults and a sample of college students. Respondents in the national sample closely match the 1960 Census figures on all demographic variables that can be checked. In our selection of student respondents we were concerned mainly with the possible range of political opinion and we had no way of knowing how closely our sample matched the college population or how well it paralleled the national sample. Some things we did know, however. Only a small percentage of these college respondents were 21 years of age or older: all respondents in the national sample were. By definition all the students had at least some college education; 24% of the adult sample claimed some.

We dwell on these differences to emphasize that they loaded the odds against finding similarity in the factors based upon the responses in the two samples.

Consequently, before collecting the material on the college sample we were pessimistic about the possibility of uncovering any great similarity in factor structure.

A comparison of the two factor analyses is contained in Table A-13. It has been prepared so that items which had originally been classified *a priori* as Tactics but which largely fell in Mach Tactics and Honesty in the adult sample and under Duplicity in the college sample are adjacent to one another. Similarly, Pollyanna and Mach Orientation are placed adjacent to one another. All 30 of the items used in the national survey are included in the format which was common to the two administrations.

Reading from the upper left corner and proceeding diagonally downward to the right, it can be seen that the items tend to group. First, it will be noted that eight of the nine items, falling under the rubrics of Mach Tactics and Honesty in the national sample, are common to the college factor of Duplicity. The exception, "Barnum," falls under Disbelief in People, where it was originally predicted to belong. Six of the 7 Mach items in this intersection were originally classified as Tactics items. The one exception is the item, "All in all, it is better to be honest and humble than to be important and dishonest." Originally, it had been classified with some misgivings as involving Abstract Morality rather than Tactics. Both the national and college samples clearly interpret it as a guide to one's own behavior.

Of the 11 items worded positively in the Likert format which fell on the factor called Anomic Disenchantment in the national sample, 9 fell under Affirmative Negativism in the college sample. The 2 that shift for the students both fall under Duplicity. The one Mach item shifting, "The best way to handle people is to tell them what they want to hear," was originally classified as a Tactics item. The other item shifting was from the Anomia scale. Response set seems a more potent factor in the adult than in the college sample. The former had 11 of 11 possible agree-response set items falling under Anomic Disenchantment whereas the college students had 19 of a possible 25 falling under Affirmative Negativism. These 2 items may have shifted because college students are slightly more discriminating about content.

Moving down and right again, it may be seen that all three Pollyanna items in the adult sample fit under Disbelief in People among college students. However, only two of the four Mach Orientation items are consistent. One that shifts, "People suffering from incurable diseases should have the choice of being put painlessly to death" was originally classified as Abstract Morality. In the college sample it fits tightly with the reversed *F*-scale items (in the factor Traditional Moralism) which were not asked in the national sample. In a sense, it did not have a factorial home to cluster in among the items asked of the adult sample. The most puzzling of all items in the comparison is the one, "The biggest

TABLE A-13

Comparison of College and Adult Samples on Factor Analyses[a]

Adults: / College Students: Duplicity	Affirmative Negativism	Disbelief in People	Traditional Morality	Other
Mach Tactics *Never tell real reason* T[b,c] *Flatter* T *Humble and honest* M *Honesty best policy* T	—	*Barnum* V	—	—
Honesty No excuse for lying T− Action morally right T− Way one makes money A− Give real reasons T−	—	—	—	—
Anomic Disenchantment Best way to handle people T+ Money next to health A+	Hardly fair to child A+ Vicious streak V+ Live for today A+ Never trust completely T+ Men won't work hard V+ Nothing worthwhile A+ Death of father V+ Gov't not interested A+ Cut corners V+	—	—	—

			People good and kind V- People go out of way A- People come through A- *Most men are brave V* *Clean moral lives V*	—	People good and kind V- People go out of way A-
Pollyanna	—	—		—	—
Machiavellian Orientation	—	—		*People put to death M*	*People put to death M*
Residual	—	—	*Good in all respects T* Average man is better A- Try hard enough A-	—	*Biggest difference criminals and others V* —

a Includes 3 residual items.
b Italicized items are from Mach V.
c The following indicates *a priori* classification: A = Anomia; T = Mach Tactics;
V = Mach Views; M = Mach Morality; + is positively keyed; - is negatively keyed.

difference between criminals and other people is that criminals are stupid enough to get caught." This item had initially been classified as a Views item and it fell appropriately under Machiavellian Orientation in the adult sample. We have absolutely no explanation as to why it ended up as a residual in the college sample.

The three residual items in the national sample all fell under the college factor of Disbelief in People. One, "It is possible to be good in all respects," had originally been classified as a Tactics item but clearly the college students did not interpret it as such. The other two are both reversed Anomia items which clearly reflect an optimistic view of life and their loading on Disbelief in People presents no major interpretive problem. Both are among the lower half in their loading on this factor and they probably were not strong enough to show up on the Pollyanna in the adult sample where there was not quite as much cognitive consistency.

In all, 22 of the 30 items fell on similar factors in the two samples. Four which shifted from one factor to another from the adult to college samples did so in a direction congruent with their content. The three items which were residual in the national sample emerge with low but appropriate loadings on the college factor Disbelief in People. The only item of the 30 which is completely baffling shifted from Machiavellian Orientations to being a residual in the college sample.

SOME QUESTIONS AND POSSIBLE ANSWERS

There is one nagging question. If clear-cut factors emerged in both the national and college samples and these were in large part congruent with one another and with the *a priori* classification of items, why didn't a similar pattern emerge in the original pool of items used for scale construction? Since the original data cards were long ago destroyed, it is impossible to reexamine them in search of a definitive answer. There are, however, a number of possibilities.

One possible explanation might be that the patterns of correlation between each item and the subscale to which it had been assigned and to the total scale did in fact support multidimensionality and that this pattern had been missed. I have been accused, occasionally justifiably, of sometimes reading too much into data, never the reverse. It seems unlikely, then, that I would have overlooked precisely the relationship that I was searching for.

Hindsight suggests a more probable reason. The 20 Mach items used in the factor analyses had been screened for their discriminatory power from a pool of 71 items. Yet 5 of the 10 positively keyed items from Mach IV ended up by falling in a response set factor in both the national and college student sample; 4 fell in the proper content domain on both, and 1 split between a response set and a content factor. In other words, half of these selected Mach items asked in a

Likert format were more influenced by a combination of response set and content than by content alone. The other 51 items in the original pool were not as specifically interpreted as the ones used in the factor analyses. In general, the more vague and ambiguous an item, the more subject it is to response set. At the time of the original items analysis the importance of counterbalancing items to minimize overall effects of response set was recognized but the strength of the tendency toward indiscriminate agreement to Likert items was seriously underestimated. The item versus subscale and whole-scale analysis was probably swamped by items responded to more in terms of agreement or disagreement than their content.

A second problem lay behind the collection of the data reported in this chapter — the relationship between Mach and Anomia, and their connection to education. Table A-14 shows the correlations among the factors in the national sample.

TABLE A-14

Correlations of Factor Scales and Social Desirability
on Nation-wide Sample of Adults

	Anomic Disenchantment	Mach Tactics	Pollyanna	Honesty	Mach Orientation	Social Desirability
Anomic Disenchantment	—	+ .01	+ .16	− .09	+ .11	− .35
Mach Tactics		—	− .16	− .34	+ .04	.00
Pollyanna			—	+ .19	− .11	+ .16
Honesty				—	− .18	+ .12
Mach Orientation					—	− .07
Social Desirability						—

Of perhaps the greatest relevance is that Mach Tactics and Honesty (which fell together under Duplicity in the college sample) correlate but +.01 and −.09 with Anomic Despair. Anomic Despair is composed of all the positively worded Likert-type Anomia and Mach items and also had the largest negative correlation with Social Desirability. Mach Tactics and Orientation, both composed of forced-choice items, have the lowest correlation with Social Desirability, .00 and −.07 respectively.

If the scales are scored as originally constructed, Anomia correlates +.51 with Mach IV, +.16 with Mach V, and −.37 with Social Desirability. Overall it seems that the correlation between Anomia and Mach IV which was puzzling at first is traceable to the following two reasons: (a) positively worded Anomia and Mach items have low Social Desirability in common, and (b) Anomia and Mach

IV have a pessimistic view of others in common. There appears to be little relationship with that component of Machiavellianism which relates to interpersonal tactics.

The other matter that originally stirred our curiosity was the lack of correlation between Mach scores and education in the pickup samples, whereas Anomia showed the expected negative relationship. Among the 1482 respondents in the representative national sample the correlations with years of education were − .32 with Anomia and − .25 with the abbreviated Mach IV. Clearly, the latter of these two relationships indicates the danger of extrapolating from casual samples. The correlation between Mach V and education was in the opposite direction, a trivial + .10, although with a sample of this size it is significant at the 01 level.

Given these relationships between education and the whole scales, the correlations of the factor scores with education should not be unexpected. Anomic Disenchantment correlates − .39 with education. This indicates a not surprising relationship between being among the "have nots" in American society and feelings of despair and diffuse hostility toward man and society.

Most of the interpersonal tactics items fell under the categories of Machiavellian Tactics and Honesty; here the correlations with education are + .15 and + .14, respectively. Since Honesty is scored in the reverse direction as a factor score, this means that these combined correlate approximately zero with education. The present interpretation is that the endorsement of duplicity in the personal relationships is not bound to the education of respondents. Or to put it another way, since the correlations with income parallel the preceding pair (+ .10 and + .09), it is as possible to find an honest rich man as a dishonest poor one or vice versa.

A final matter has to do with the items initially classified as Views of Man which fell under Pollyanna and Machiavellian Orientations in the national sample. These factors correlate − .05 and − .01 respectively with education. This is about as null a relationship as one is likely to find.

SUMMARY

A positive relationship between Anomia and Mach was found in a number of samples contrary to expectation. Factor analyses were performed on the items from the Anomia scale and half of those from Mach IV and Mach V in a representative national sample of 1482 adults. Five factors emerged, two of which dealt primarily with interpersonal tactics, one which was marked by agreement with items indicating a deplorable view of man, and two others which described human nature as essentially good or bad. One of the factors in both interpersonal Tactics and Views of Human Nature was composed exclusively of items from the forced-choice Mach V; the remaining two factors were composed exclusively of items keyed in the opposite direction in a Likert format.

A second factor analysis was performed of the response of 1782 students in 14 widely assorted colleges who had taken the full Anomia, Mach IV, Mach V, and counterbalanced F scales. Four factors emerged. One based primarily on interpersonal tactics items from Mach IV and Mach V was dubbed Duplicity. A second consisted of positively keyed items from Anomia, Mach IV and Mach V and was named Affirmative Negativism. The third factor consisted primarily of items dealing with the nature of man which came from Mach V, and negatively keyed items from Mach IV and Anomia. It was named Disbelief in People. The final one was composed almost entirely of negatively keyed F-scale items and was interpreted as Traditional Moralism.

A comparison of the items common to both samples indicated a high degree of congruence between their factorial membership. In general, college students' responses were more clear-cut than those from the nationwide sample since they were not as subject to the influence of response set and item format.

It is tentatively concluded that there are three identifiable factors in Mach IV, Mach V, and Anomia. One is characterized by a tendency to agree with positively keyed items from Mach IV and Anomia which have a diffuse negativistic content about society and has been named Anomic Disenchantment in the national sample and Affirmative Negativism in the college sample. A second factor is based upon items from Mach IV and Mach V dealing with ways of interpersonal manipulation. These items loaded on Machiavellian Tactics and Honesty in the national sample and Duplicity in the college sample. The third factor contains items from Mach V and negatively keyed items from Mach IV and Anomia. They deal essentially with the goodness or badness of man and fall under the factors of the Pollyanna Syndrome and Machiavellian Orientation in the adult sample and under Disbelief in People among college students.

An examination of the relationships of these factors with education in the representative nationwide sample indicated that the first factor of Embittered Subservience was significantly negatively related to education. Items reflecting Machiavellian tactics or orientation show no or a negligible relationship to years of formal education.

ANNOTATED BIBLIOGRAPHY OF STUDIES REFERRED TO IN TABLE XV-1

James Macperson

In some of these studies the use of the Mach scales was not the primary concern of the investigators. In such cases, the description of the studies is restricted to those manipulations which were relevant. In other instances the use of the scales was built into the experimental design, often along with other variables. Consequently, we have pared down descriptions of some highly complicated experiments. In general, only variables for which differences were predicted or discovered are mentioned.

Blumstein, P.W., & Weinstein, E.A. The redress of distributive injustice. *American Journal of Sociology*, 1969, 74, 408 – 418.

Thirty-two subjects were selected from an introductory sociology course at Vanderbilt University on the basis of Mach IV scores. The 8 highest- and 8 lowest-scoring males, and 8 highest- and 8 lowest-scoring females were used. Each subject participated in four 10-min work sessions making up attitude survey items for a campus questionnaire with a stooge (introduced as a partner from another section of the course) as a course assignment. At the end of each 10-min session each participant was instructed to record what percentage of the team's joint project he had contributed. Teams were informed that individual grades for the project would be determined by averaging the student's claim for himself with the percentage allocated to him by his partner's claim. Both members' claims were read aloud to the team at the end of each session.

Each subject worked with two different stooges, one for sessions one and two, the other for sessions three and four. Half of the subjects in each sex and Mach group had the control ("justice") condition. They worked with one stooge who did a third of the work and claimed a third of the credit for himself in both of their sessions together, and another stooge who consistently did two-thirds of the work and claimed two-thirds of the credit (counterbalanced for sequence). In the "injustice" conditions one partner did one-third of the work but claimed two-thirds of the credit for himself consistently (victimized the subject); the other partner did two-thirds of the work but claimed only one third of the credit, making the subject an undeserving beneficiary (also counterbalanced for order within Mach and sex groups).

The dependent measure was the percentage of points the subject claimed for himself in the second session with each stooge (sessions two and four). The overall mean was for subjects to claim 61% of the credit for themselves. High and low Machs did not differ; highs claimed 62% over all conditions; lows claimed 60%.

The low Machs attempted to redress injustices in both directions; high Machs did not redress either type of injustice. When their partner did more work and claimed fewer points for himself low Machs claimed 44 points (giving him 54); highs claimed 54 for themselves. When their partner did little of the work but victimized them by claiming two-thirds of the credit, the lows retaliated in their second session with him by claiming 76% of the credit for themselves; highs claimed 63%.

Averaging across justice and injustice conditions, low Machs appeared to be giving credit where credit was due: they claimed 47% of the credit in the second session with the hard-working partner, 72% when paired with the slacker. Highs paid less attention to the actual difference in partner performance; they claimed 55 and 68% of the credit in the two partner-performance conditions, respectively.

The highs attended to the stooge's claim more than lows: when their partner claimed only a third of the credit, they took advantage of his generosity and claimed 64% (averaged across the two actual-performance conditions); when he claimed more (again averaged across stooge-performance conditions), they claimed less (60%). For the low Machs these means were, respectively, 56 and 63% ($p < .001$).

Danielian, J. Analysis of person perception, physical perceptual style, and selected personality variables. Unpublished doctoral dissertation, Columbia University, 1964.

The subjects were 105 summer school students of both sexes at Brooklyn College. They observed five filmed interviews that Cline and Richards (1960) had collected in Salt Lake City. Subjects' perceptual accuracy scores were determined by comparing their estimates with ratings made by the filmed target person's friends. The analysis followed Cronbach's (1955) procedure.

In this situation there was a marked discrepancy between the subjects and the filmed targets and friends on such variables as region of the country, ethnic background, student versus nonstudent status, etc.

There was a $-.22$ correlation ($p < .05$) between Mach IV scores and stereotype accuracy. Correlations of Mach with differential accuracy and interpersonal accuracy were negative but insignificant.

Daniels, V. Communication, incentive, and structural variables in interpersonal exchange and negotiation. *Journal of Experimental Social Psychology*, 1967, 3, 47–74.

Dyads of male undergraduates (160 Ss) played 40 trials of one of four versions of a bargaining game. In all versions Ss sat at opposite sides of a table separated by a 6-ft screen; no talking or verbalizations of any sort were permitted during the session. The game consisted of exchanging one chip each (by mechanical device) at each trial. Each S had chips of seven colors, representing different costs to him to give one up. The seven different colors of his partner's chips represented seven different values when received by him. S knew only the cost of each color of his own chips and the value to him (*not* the cost to his partner) of his partner's chips. Variations ranged from complete independence (S selected one of his chips, passed it to his partner, and received the chip his partner sent in return) to "bargaining" (S passed a chip to his partner as an "offer"; the partner did likewise; if the counteroffer suited the first S, he released his offered chip to the partner, and the partner's counteroffer was automatically released to him. Alternatively, the first S could withdraw his initially offered chip, and substitute another, and so on.)

Prior to participating, Ss completed the Mach scale (version unspecified) and Seeman's (1963) powerlessness scale. Although one partner consistently did better than the other in the dyads, Machiavellianism was unrelated to any of the outcome or process measures examined. However, Machiavellianism was negatively related to self reports of internal power ("internal locus of control," $p < .01$).

Edelstein, Rivcka. Risk-taking, age, sex, and Machiavellianism. Unpublished manuscript, New York University, 1966.

The subject played six rounds of a dominoes game against an opponent. Each player was given ten poker chips (to keep score) and a hand of nine dominoes placed face toward him, back toward his opponent (so players could not see the number faces of opponents' pieces). To begin play the experimenter placed an extra domino on the table face down, announcing the value of one of its faces, e.g., "five." Thereafter, players alternated, each playing a domino from his hand, face down, announcing that the domino played had a face matching the one played previously. If a player did not have a matching domino he could "confess," pay the experimenter a chip, and change the face number being played, or he could "bluff," and play a nonmatching domino, claiming that it was a match. After each play the opponent could challenge if he wished. Upon a challenge, the domino in question was turned face up. If the challenger was correct (the player had actually bluffed on that move), the unsuccessful bluffer payed the challenger a chip. If the challenger was wrong (the domino had the announced number of spots at one end), he paid the truthful player a chip. The player's score at the end of the round was the difference between the number of chips he had and the number his opponent had. (Thus, "confessing" was a conservative strategy, since the subject lost one chip, but his opponent did not gain one, while bluffing and challenging were riskier strategies since failing in either case meant that the player lost a chip *and* his opponent gained one.

"Risk" was further varied by making the "penalty" (for confessing, detected bluffing, and false challenging) one chip in the first two rounds, two in the second two, and four in the last two.

Since incentives to bluff might be greater with an opponent who challenged less, and incentives to challenge greater with an opponent who bluffed more over the six rounds, a stooge was used as opponent for all Ss. (The study was designed to investigate tactics, not outcomes.) The stooge was instructed to play to win with the restriction that he was to bluff three times and challenge three times, no more or less, in each round. The particular dominoes given the subject and stooge for each round were preselected and painted in code so that the experimenter could record bluffing.

One hundred forty-nine subjects participated: 104 college-age adults (all were college students or college graduates), 73 males and 31 females, and 45 children from middle-class neighborhoods from 10 to 14 years of age, 34 boys and 11 girls. (The stooge was always the same age and sex as the subject.) The young adults completed Mach IV and V, and were divided by median split of combined scores (103.5 for males, 98.0 for females). The children took Nachamie's (1966) Kiddie Mach, and boys were divided by median split (83.50); data from the 11 girls (median = 84.00) were not analyzed by Mach classification due to the small sample.

The high Machs "confessed" less than lows (men, $p = .05$; women, $p < .005$; boys, $p < .05$), and bluffed more (men, $p < .001$; women, $p < .005$; boys, $p < .10$). High-Mach men challenged the stooge more than low-Mach men ($p < .001$), but there was no difference in challenging for the younger boys (low-Mach boys challenged as often as high-Mach boys, and also as often as high-Mach men), or for the college age women. In general, the Mach differences that were significant were significantly stronger at the higher "risk" levels (number of chips paid as penalties). On a questionnaire after the games high-Mach men reported more suspicion (guessed their opponent had bluffed more often) than low-Mach men.

This study was replicated by the author, with further refinements and controls, as a master's thesis at the State University of New York at Stony Brook, 1969, but details of the replication were not available at the time of going to press.

Epstein, Gilda F. Machiavelli and the devil's advocate. *Journal of Personality and Social Psychology,* 1969, 11, 38–41.

The subjects were 80 male undergraduates at Columbia University who were under 30 years of age and were American. Half were classified as high Mach who had scores on the combined Mach IV and V forms above the median (116) and low Machs as those below the median. The subjects had also been selected on a pretest as being strongly in favor of fluoridation and no significant differences between high- and low-Mach subjects were found.

The cover story was that the experimenter was working on a tape-recorded discussion series about water fluoridation which would be used by college radio stations. All subjects read one of two booklets, one with a positive "sponsor" and one with a negative "sponsor" giving identical arguments against fluoridation. Half the subjects in this $2 \times 2 \times 2$ design were then placed in a role-playing situation in which they were asked to improvise talks against fluoridation for possible use on radio programs.

There were no significant main effects for the sponsorship variable or other main effects. The predicted interaction effect between Mach and the role-playing variable was found. Low Machs shifted on a posttest measure toward antifluoridation attitudes after role playing more than after silent reading only. High Machs showed the opposite pattern by becoming more antifluoridation when presented with factual arguments than in the role playing condition.

Feiler, J. Machiavellianism, dissonance, and attitude change. Unpublished manuscript, New York University, 1967.

Fifty-eight undergraduate males from the introductory psychology subject pool at New York University participated in groups of four. Subjects were classified as scoring above or below the median of averaged Mach IV and V scores (103.50) of samples obtained from the same pool in the previous summer and spring semesters ($N = 240$ males). Two subjects debated each other twice (in alternate rounds) and served as cojudges of the two debates of the other pair. A "free-choice" dissonance manipulation was used to induce each subject to defend a counterattitudinal position in one of his two debates. (For his other debate he was simply assigned a position he privately endorsed.) Opinions on the issues debated were measured before and after the debating sessions.

The dissonance prediction (attitude change in the direction of public, counterattitudinal advocacy) was supported for low Machs ($p < .025$) but not for highs. The effect for lows occurred (as predicted) when the debater believed he had won ($p < .005$), but not when he guessed he had lost. However, low Machs also changed their attitudes after consonant debates ($p < .05$), endorsing the position they had held previously more strongly than before. High Machs showed no significant attitude change in any condition, and regardless of guessing they had won or lost.

Geis, Florence. Machiavellianism in a semireal world. *Proceedings of the 76th Annual Convention of the American Psychological Association,* 1968, 3, 407–408.

Students in two introductory personality courses at the University of Delaware were assigned to four-person groups on the basis of Mach scores. Medians on averaged Mach IV and V were 106.50 for 152 males, 96.50 for 146 females. Groups were composed of all highs, all lows, or two of each. The study was designed to: (1) find out if high Machs would take control in groups when members had a more "real" stake in group outcome than can usually be provided in laboratory studies, and (2) to determine whether high Machs' ability to organize resources, exploit and focus them on winning, which had appeared in studies of individual competition, would also appear in the cooperative situation within the groups (as measured by competition between groups).

At the first meeting of the group members knew they would work together all semester on a laboratory project which would count one-fourth of their final course grade. They were given 20 min to "get acquainted and begin discussing project ideas," and then asked to choose a group leader. In 19 of the 44 groups (43%) with a high Mach available, the highest scorer in the group became leader more frequently than any of the three lower-scoring members, compared to the 20 all-low-Mach groups ($\chi^2 = 8.18, p < .05$).

In one of the initial classes group efficiency was examined. The final report of each group was read by 24 other members of the class, each of whom compared it against the report of another, different group in the class. The reader's task after each comparison was to call one paper "superior" to the other on each of three grading criteria ("idea," "procedure," "report clarity"). Each group's final project grade was determined by the percentage of "superior's" received across the 72 comparisons. The 14 groups in which the highest Mach available was leader made higher grades on their joint project than the members individually made on course exams, compared to 17 groups with lower-Mach leaders which made lower project grades ($t = 2.14, p < .025$).

Geis, Florence, Krupat, E., & Berger, D. Taking over in group discussion. Unpublished manuscript, New York University, 1965.

Male undergraduate volunteers ($N = 41$) were classified as above or below the median on average Mach IV and V scores (103.50). Thirty-two (17 highs, 15 lows) subsequently participated in groups of four or five, selected to represent the range of scores in the sample tested. Two highs and two lows in each group were further selected for disagreeing with each other on the Mach IV item, "The best way to handle people is to tell them what they want to hear." (Thus, in each group one high and one low agreed with each other, and mutually opposed another high–low pair.) Each group was asked to discuss a revised version of the item (" . . . tell them what they want to hear, rather than telling the truth," for half the groups, " . . . tell them the truth rather than telling what they want to hear," for the other half) for 10 min. After collecting private opinions on the version to be discussed, the experimenter urged the group to try to reach consensus and left the room.

After the discussion each subject privately completed a questionnaire giving his current opinion on the item, and also rating each of the others on: (1) effectiveness in presenting ideas; (2) listening to others; (3) quality of ideas; (4) amount of leadership displayed; (5) overall contribution to group's progress; and (6) a sociometric question.

Low Machs changed their opinion on the issue from before to after discussion ($p < .025$); highs did not change at all ($p > .05$).

High Machs were rated significantly higher than lows on all of the task performances (1–5, above) by low Mach members separately as well as by other highs in the group, but were not preferred to lows on the sociometric (" . . . how much you think you would like him personally, as a friend") by either highs or lows.

Geis, Florence L. & Leventhal, Ellen. Attempting to deceive and detecting deception. Unpublished manuscript, New York University, 1966.

Sixty-two male undergraduates, 35 from the New York University Introductory Psychology subject pool (median averaged Mach IV and V scores = 103.50) and 27 from an introductory psychology course for nonmajors at Queens College, New York (median combined score = 100.50 participated in groups of three or four. Subjects were told the veridical purpose of the study — "to find out whether people can tell when another is lying to them, or not." Three subjects took turns serving as "witness" until each had served twice. The witness's task was to convince the others that he sincerely endorsed the position designated by the experimenter on an opinion statement taken from a questionnaire he had completed 5 min previously. At one turn each subject was assigned his true (private) opinion; at his other turn he was assigned the position opposite his private belief. The other two active subjects served as interrogators during the 4-min defense. Their task was to ascertain whether the witness was lying or telling the truth. When a fourth subject was present, he was assigned the role of "impartial judge." He simply listened passively to each of the interrogations and recorded his "lie" or "truth" guess afterwards. The data from interrogator judges and passive judges were combined.

As predicted from the Eye of the Beholder (Chapter XII), low Machs were superior at discriminating truth from lies in others. The lows were accurate in 67% of all guesses, compared to 50% for highs ($t = 2.70, p < .005$). High and low Machs were compared as judges of: high Machs telling the truth, lows telling the truth, highs lying, lows lying, all high-Mach witnesses (combined across truth and lies), all low-Mach witnesses, all witnesses telling the truth (combining high and low Machs) and all witnesses lying. The low's mean accuracy scores ranged from 66 (detecting other lows lying) to 71% (believing highs who were telling the truth). The high's accuracy scores ranged from 41 (detecting low Machs lying) to 57% (believing other highs telling the truth).

Contrary to prediction, high Machs were not more successful deceivers. Their lies were detected by 56% of their judges, and so were those of lows. The biggest difference between high- and low-Machs as witness was in credibility as truth tellers. Highs were believed 69% of the time, lows 57% ($t = 1.81, p < .05$).

Harris, T. M. Machiavellianism, judgment independence and attitudes toward teammate in a cooperative judgment task. Unpublished doctoral dissertation, Columbia University, 1966.

Thirty-eight high-scoring male undergraduates (94 or above on Mach IV and 100 or above on Mach V) were selected, as were 38 low scorers (scores of 93 or lower on Mach IV and 99 or lower on Mach V). They were students in a small, coeducational church affiliated college in a mid-Atlantic suburb. Most of the students lived at home.

Subjects were required to read excerpts from Beckett's *Waiting for Godot* (1954) and to individually rate one of the two major characters, ("Pete" and "Tom" in this study) on a deliberately esoteric rating form of 16 traits on a 10-point scale. Half the subjects rated one of the two characters first with either a high- or low-Mach partner, then discussed their individual ratings before coming to a joint rating. The design was counterbalanced so that they were with a different partner the second time and were evaluating the different protagonist in a different excerpt from the play. High scorers changed their judgments significantly less than low scorers when working with both high-scoring and low-scoring teammates. Low scorers modified their ratings significantly whether paired with either a high or low Mach.

The finding that high Machs were not influenced in this face-to-face interaction and held to their own ratings and that low Machs shifted to agree more with their partner led to a followup study more typical of attitude change research.

McGuire's (1960) truisms were given to a sample of 36 males in summer school at Teachers College and Columbia University. The respondents were older (29 years median) and more highly educated (17 years median) than normal college samples. The mean combined Mach score was 101. Two counterattitudinal refutational messages were given. One was factual and the other was presented to obtain a bandwagon effect using fake "public opinion poll" data showing public support on the part of social elites for the refutation. It was found that low Machs changed significantly in the bandwagon situation, high Machs did not. Under factual refutations the high Machs changed slightly but not significantly more than the lows.

Jones, E. E., & Daugherty, B. N. Political orientation and the perceptual effects of an anticipated interaction. *Journal of Abnormal and Social Psychology,* 1959, 59, 340–349.

Eighty-three male undergraduate volunteers in groups of one to seven listened to a tape recording of E interviewing first one and then another stimulus person (played by two stooges reading prepared scripts). The "political stimulus person" claimed to like being a leader and making decisions, and expressed admiration for "people who handle themselves well with others . . . who know how to get things done without getting others angry." The "esthetic stimulus person" disparaged the "all-American boy," claimed to like reading, religion, and philosophy, and admired Freud and Schweitzer. (The political and esthetic interviewee roles were counterbalanced between stooges and for the order in which Ss heard them.) After the interviews, S described each stimulus person by sorting 30 trait descriptions (15 favorable and 15 unflattering) into a seven-category forced, normal distribution (from most to least characteristic of the interviewee). A "flattery score" was derived from these sorts (the extent to which S sorted favorable traits as "characteristic" and unfavorable ones as "uncharacteristic").

In the experimental condition, S believed that he was hearing the interviews live (via intercom), that the interviewees were two of the subjects present in the group, and that after the interviews he would interact with one of the two interviewees (a cooperative interaction was promised for half of these Ss, a competitive interaction for the other half). In the control condition Ss were told the interviews had been tape recorded with Psychology 1 students in the preceding year, and no interaction was promised.

Prior to participating Ss had completed Mach IV and the AVL political scale. The correlation between these two measures was .30 in a "large undergraduate sample" (n not specified). The only significant Mach finding was a negative partial correlation ($-.667$, $p < .001$, with AVL political score held constant) with flattering the political stimulus person when anticipating a cooperative interaction with one of the interviewees later. The corresponding partial correlation between AVL political score and flattery (with Mach constant) was $+.576$ ($p < .01$). Although none of the zero-order correlations between Mach and flattering the stimulus person was significantly different from zero, all six of them (political and esthetic interviewees, each described in control, interact competitively, and interact cooperatively conditions) were negative in sign. Apparently, low Machs tended to attribute the favorable trait descriptions to the interviewee somewhat more than highs did.

Jones, E. E., Davis, K. E., & Gergen, K. J. Role playing variations and their informational value for person perception. *Journal of Abnormal and Social Psychology,* 1961, 63, 302–310.

Male undergraduates ($n = 134$, participating in groups of $5 - 20$) listened to a tape recording of a "student role playing a job interviewee." The recording began with the "psychologist" instructing the role player to present himself in the interview in such a way as to impress the interviewer that he was ideally suited for a particular job. This was followed by a description of the job for which he would be interviewed, either that of "submariner" (described as requiring social, other-directed traits) or "astronaut" (requiring independence, and inner-directed traits). In the following job interview the "student role player" took either a clearly inner- or other-directed stance. (The "student role player" was in all cases the same person, a trained stooge.) Thus, there were four conditions, two in which the interviewee gave job role-consistent answers (other directed for the submariner job, inner directed for the astronaut job), and two in which he gave role-inconsistent responses (inner directed for submariner, and other directed for astronaut). After listening to one of the four versions of the tape recording, Ss completed a number of paper and pencil measures giving their impressions of the interviewee. All Ss had taken the Mach IV scale in class prior to participating. High Machs rated the role-consistent interviewees as more intelligent than they rated those giving role-inconsistent responses, while low Machs showed the reverse pattern ($t = 2.15, p \leqq .05$).

Jones, E.E., Gergen, K.J. & Davis, K.E. Some determinants of reactions to being approved or disapproved as a person. *Psychological Monographs,* 1962, 76 (No. 2, Whole No. 521).

Forty female students in the upper third of the distribution of scores on Mach IV (94 and above) and 40 in the lower third (82 and below) volunteered as subjects. The scale was given in an introductory psychology course several months before the experiment (probably at Duke).

The 80 subjects were divided into 8 groups of 10 each. Each subject was given an initial interview by one of 10 male graduate student interviewers. The interviews were conducted in a "neutral" manner and covered five simple questions about the self-perceived personality of the subject. Included was a 16-item set of triads on each of which the subject could give a favorable, neutral, or negative impression of herself. The subjects were told that the results would be used for a graduate course in personality in which the interest was in the impressions interviewees had of interviewers and vice versa. Half the subjects were told to give as honest as possible a portrayal of themselves. The other half were given a hypocrisy set in which they were supposed to con the interviewer into thinking that they were somewhat nicer than they were.

After finishing the interview the interviewer disappeared to study the interview results and write an evaluation. During this period the subjects filled out their impressions of the interviewer. They were then given either positive or negative feedback as to their personality and then rerated the interviewer.

All subjects were then interviewed by a different interviewer with the same procedure being followed as before except that the second interviewer gave an opposite evaluation from the first one.

In this 2 × 2 × 2 design only the main effect of set (hypocrisy versus accuracy in self report) on the questionnaire was significant. Jones, Gergen, and Davis report surprise at finding a significant interaction between Mach scores and changes in self-reports after initial negative feedback. High-Mach subjects were relatively unaffected, lows changed significantly more in the direction of giving positive self-descriptions after having had a negative evaluation of their personality.

Lake, D. L. Impression formation, Machiavellianism, and interpersonal bargaining. Unpublished doctoral dissertation, Teachers College, Columbia University, 1967.

Eighty male subjects (average age, 29) were collected from a variety of settings varying from a vocational high school through three undergraduate colleges, two graduate schools, and a professional organization.

They were split at the median (100 and below, 101 and above) on combined Mach IV and Mach V scores. Each of these groups was split into two groups, one of which was led to expect a cooperative Other, the second a competitive Other. They then played 35 trials in Hornstein and Deutsch's Products Game (1967) in which the programmed "other" played either in such a way as to confirm the initial impression or disconfirm it. They then played another 35 trials.

In this particular game, low Machs actually won more pennies ($1.18) over the 35 rounds than high Machs ($1.02), n.s.

There were a variety of observed behavioral differences in the game playing behavior of high and low Machs in this particular experimental situation. One of the more interesting was that highs were more aggressive in game strategy when anticipating a competitive Other and lows more defensive (p. 128).

Metze, R. Unpublished manuscript. 1967.

Students, primarily enrolled in education courses at the 1966 summer session at the University of Oklahoma, were given Mach IV and V. Thirty males, half above and half below the median on the combined scales, were paired as were 30 females.

The 30 paired same sex subjects then played the same dice-bluffing game that Nachamie used with children. The dice were the same and the procedural payoff matrix was the same. The only difference was that the payoff was in pennies instead of M&M's.

Only 9 of 15 high Mach males won more pennies than their low-scoring fellow-players, 8 of the 15 high Mach females won more. It is impossible to determine if this failure to replicate Nachamie's results is attributable to differences in:

1. the age of the two samples,

2. the different incentive value of pennies for these late adolescents as compared with M&M's for preadolescents, or,

3. other unknown differences in the experimental situations.

Novielli, J. Who persuades whom. Unpublished master's thesis, University of Delaware, 1968.

Sixty-four male and 64 female Delaware undergraduates participated in like-sex groups of four. In each session two subjects debated each other on alternate trials, and served as cojudges of the two debates between the other two. In one of each pair's debates both defended a privately endorsed position; in the other, a position contrary to private opinion. Subjects were classified by median split on the Mach IV and V scales (95.84 and 102.98, respectively, for males; 89.31 and 100.61 for females). In half of the sessions (16 tetrads, 8 male, 8 female) a high Mach debated with a low (and the two "judges" were also a high and a low). In the other half of the groups debates were between like-Mach opponents and were judged either by two highs or two lows (counterbalanced).

After each debate the two judges privately rated each of the debaters, and the winner was determined by combining their ratings (not revealed to subjects until the conclusion of the session). High Machs received higher ratings, overall, than lows ($F = 4.66, p < .05$). However, this was due entirely to the low-Mach judges' significant preference for high- over low-Mach debaters. High-Mach judges did not discriminate. In the opposite-Mach debates, high Machs won when both debaters were defending private convictions (22 of 32 decisions), but not when both were defending counterattitudinal positions (17 of 32 decisions). Results for males and females did not differ.

Oksenberg, Lois. Machiavellianism and emotionality. Unpublished master's essay, Columbia University, 1964.

Subjects were recruited from introductory classes in psychology and sociology at the 1964 summer session. The study was on 20 high-scoring males (means 99 and above on Mach IV and 111 and above on Mach V) and 15 low-scoring males (98 and below on Mach IV and 110 and below on Mach V); comparable cutting points on the 15 female high-Mach and 11 female low-Mach subjects were 90 and 108, respectively.

Each subject, when brought into the experimental room, was requested to pick one of five cards laying face down on a table. He was asked to turn the card over and look at the letter on the other side and memorize it. He then put it into a Manila envelope and was requested to spend 2 min writing down every word he could think of beginning with the letter chosen. This list was also put into the envelope by the subject. This was to insure that the subject had actually noticed the one letter of the five he had chosen and to increase the likelihood that he remembered it (he did not know what letters were on the other four cards and the experimenters did not know until after the experimental session which letter he had seen). This procedure is a modification of one used by Gustafson and Orne (1963).

The next procedure was to have the subject lie on a cot and be connected with an apparatus recording GSR, respiration, and blood pressure. In actual fact, the last two measures were not used because the apparatus was a surplus Corps of Engineers polygraph (Lafayette Model No. 603s) which required an undue amount of care to keep the GSR recordings accurate — and this, of course, was the prime interest given Gustafson and Orne's findings.

The five letters had been recorded on tape. Each was repeated six times in random order at 20-sec intervals. Subjects were told to "beat the machine" by responding "No" to every letter including the one that they had seen so that the experimenters could not determine which letter they had seen.

It had been anticipated that the rate of correct guessing would be somewhat below that of Gustafson and Orne because neither the experimenter nor the graduate student assistants had previous experience in obtaining and evaluating GSR records and the instrumentation was on an antique (relatively speaking) piece of equipment which had to be teased into working. It was therefore a cause for wonder when on the spot visual inspection of the GSR recordings by the experimenters correctly identified the letter seen by 56 of the 61 subjects (91.8% accuracy). Such a high rate of correct identification vitiated any comparison of high and low Machs under the assumption that the highs' coolness might be more than skin deep. Almost everyone, high or low, was caught when telling a relatively trivial lie.

It might be expected that since most of the subjects did react with a perceptible GSR response when lying, that the magnitude of the "guilty" response might differentiate between high and low Machs. A ratio score [magnitude of deflection on critical (seen-letter) trials/magnitude of deflection scores on noncritical trials] did indicate that high Machs showed less arousal as measured by GSR than low Machs. The amount of individual variance in responses was so great that the relatively minor differences among high and low Mach males was not significant, nor was the trend for females where the high and low scorers showed greater mean differences.

Oksenberg, Lois. Machiavellianism and organization in five-man task-oriented groups. Unpublished doctoral dissertation, Columbia University, 1968.

One hundred and twenty male undergraduates at the University of California, Santa Cruz, were recruited in dormitories. They were divided into 12 homogeneous and 12 heterogeneous groups on the basis of combined Mach IV and V scores. The distribution was divided into sextiles. There were six homogeneous groupings from each of which two work groups were composed and the 12 heterogeneous groups were composed of members drawn from five different sextiles.

The task was a group problem-solving task used by Shure *et al.* (1962). The five members sat around a table. They could not see or talk to one another but could communicate by passing coded IBM cards through a central core. In one condition (unambiguous) any member could send or receive messages from any other person. In a second condition (ambiguous) one incoming and one outgoing channel was blocked.

The problem task was for all members of the group to find what symbol they all held in common. The most efficient and fastest way to solve the problem is to establish a communication net so that all information is sent to one person (Keyman), who then sends the relevant information back to the members. Messages can be passed among participants during the 19 2-min intertrial intervals and these messages can then be coded for types of organizational proposals, and a complete record of all messages sent permitted analysis of group organization. There was no individual competition, but subjects were told their group would be compared with others in problem-solving effectiveness.

The heterogeneous groups did not, as expected, develop an organized pattern sooner than the homogeneous groups. Further, in the heterogeneous groups the high Machs did not become keyman and made significantly fewer organizational suggestions. Analysis of postexperimental questionnaires indicated that high Machs found the group task significantly less enjoyable than the low Machs.

Rim, Y. Machiavellianism and decisions involving risks. *British Journal of Social and Clinical Psychology*, 1966, 5, 30–36.

Fourteen groups of 5 male subjects each filled out their responses to six of Kogan and Wallach's (1964) risk-taking problems as well as Mach IV and other scales. They then engaged in group discussion. These subjects were older (30) than most college samples, and were students of architecture, industrial engineering and management, teachers and school principals.

It was found that "subjects scoring high on the Mach scale tend to be the influencers in the group discussion, leading to a shift of the whole group in the risky direction [p. 35]." High-Mach subjects tended to be high on risk-taking initially and showed scores both before and after the group discussion which were closer to the second group risk-taking mean.

Thornton, C. C. The resolution of disagreements in dyads. Unpublished doctoral dissertation, University of Delaware, 1967.

Twelve male and 12 female dyads discussed 4 issues (5 min each) on which members privately disagreed. Members of each dyad were matched for Mach (above or below the median) and College Board verbal scores. Three dyads of each type (e.g., male, low Mach, high IQ) were run. After each issue discussion members privately reported (on questionnaires) how much they had complied with the other's position and how much he had complied with theirs. High and low Machs did not differ on either measure, nor did Machiavellianism figure in any significant interactions. After all four discussions, subjects privately completed forms giving (evaluative) impressions of their partner and estimates of importance of each of the issues discussed. Machiavellianism provided no significant effects on these measures either.

Vejio, C.K., & Wrightsman, L.S., Jr. Ethnic-group differences in the relationship of trusting attitudes to cooperative behavior. *Psychological Reports,* 1967, 20, 563 – 571.

Eighty female students at the University of Hawaii, half of whom were Caucasian and half of whom were Japanese American, played in a standard Prisoner's Dilemma game. The "other player" was identified as a fellow student of either Caucasian or Japanese ancestry. The actual program was a random 76% cooperative response over 50 trials.

Mach IV was among other personality tests given the subjects a month before the experiment. There was a nonsignificant correlation of − .10 between Mach and cooperative behavior over all subjects playing all opponents. One of the subcomparisons, that of Caucasian females purportedly playing another (cooperative) Caucasian female did yield a correlation between Mach IV and cooperation scores of − .53 (significance < .01), however.

Wahlin, W. S. Machiavellianism and winning or losing mathematical games. Unpublished doctoral dissertation, Columbia University, 1967.

Thirty-four males who scored low on combined Mach IV and V scores (102 or lower) and 35 high scorers (103 and above) were tested individually in a game-playing situation. They were from the River Campus at the University of Rochester.

Roughly half of the subjects were row player's, "bottom dogs" in Table XV-1, and half "top dogs" or column players. This determination was made in the first of two games which had the following matrix:

	White	Red
White	15, 25	0, 15
Red	25, 5	− 25, 10

In this asymmetric matrix a column player who consistently played Red couldn't possibly lose, absolutely or relatively. A column player who played predominantly White could lose only if he played very passively and the other player was very aggressive, e.g., predominantly played red.

In this matrix a row player could accumulate points if he had a cooperative (consistent white) fellow player. If the row player opted for the aggressive red choice he could either win against a passive player, but could only lose against a random or aggressive (red-playing) opponent.

The other "player" presumably interacting in this situation was not physically present. "He" was a contingently programmed other. As long as the row player chose white, the programmed opponent played white. Whenever the row player chose red the "other player" played vindictively by switching to red on the next trial and continuing to play Red for a randomly preprogrammed series of trials. If on the last sequence of these trials — no matter what the subject did earlier in the series — the subject chose white, the mythical opponent went back to a white choice and continued this until the subject made a red choice. This triggered off another sequence of red choices as before.

In this game, which was played for points, it is interesting to note that the high Mach subjects in the row or "bottom-dog" position lost significantly more than low Mach subjects. Of the 50 experiments reviewed in Table XV-1 this is the only instance in which highs did less well than lows, contrary to prediction. It should be noted that the fictional "other" in this situation behaved *in response* to the more aggressive behavior of the high Machs in a noninterpersonal game-playing experiment.

There were no significant differences between high and low Machs in the column or "top-dog" position in game-playing against an unknown and not seen other.

Wahlin was interested in testing a revenge hypothesis. The high-Mach row playing subjects did not, after (self-induced) drubbing, perform more competitively on a standard Prisoner's Dilemma Matrix game than their low-scoring counterparts. This was true whether or not they had played in row conditions in which they aggressively lost more or in the column position in which they did not take advantage of their position.

Weinstein, E. A., Beckhouse, L. S., Blumstein, P. W., & Stein, R. B. Interpersonal strategies under conditions of gain or loss. *Journal of Personality,* 1968, 36, 616–634.

Forty-eight subjects were drawn from an introductory sociology course at Vanderbilt University on the basis of sex, Mach IV scores, and Kogan and Wallach's (1964) "Chance Bets Instrument," a measure of risk-taking (six subjects per cell — e.g., male, high Mach, low risk taker, etc.)

Subjects were assigned to role play the interviewee in three job interviews of 7–10 min each. (Interviewers were played by three trained graduate students). Each interview situation was structured by instructions given the subject just before the interview. In one interview (gain potential) the subject was a $7500 employee and had a chance of promotion and raise to $13,000 at stake in the interview; in another (loss potential) he was a $13,000 employee with a chance for demotion and salary cut to $7500; in a third (equal alternative) he was a college graduate with a job offer from one company at $10,000, interviewing for a similar job at $10,000 with a second company. Sequences were counterbalanced.

Each interview was taped and all were rated in randomized order by trained judges naive to the Mach and risk-taking scores of subjects for three dimensions of *altercasting* (role or identity projected on to the other — in this case the interviewer — by the subject), including (a) degree of freedom given the other in defining the situation, directing the content and tone of the interview, and (b) status superiority imputed to the other (deference shown by subject, ingratiation).

On the ingratiation measure, low Machs (both sexes) did not differentiate among the three situation-outcome structures. High Machs (both sexes) did: high-Mach males ingratiated most in the loss potential condition; high females in the equal alternative condition (the interaction between sex and situation structure was significant at the .01 level within the group of high Machs).

On the measure of "freedom accorded the interviewer," females, regardless of Machiavellianism, failed to differentiate, except that high-Machs females exercised the least interpersonal control (accorded the interviewer most freedom) in the equal alternative condition. Among males, regardless of situation structure, high Machs were more controlling and exercised heavier constraints (i.e., gave the interviewer less freedom) than lows ($p < .05$). High males did not vary the amount of constraint across situations; lows attempted to control the interviewer in the loss-potential situation more than in either of the other two ($p < .01$).

Wrightsman, L. S., Jr. Personality and attitudinal correlates of trusting and trustworthy behaviors in a two-person game. *Journal of Personality and Social Psychology,* 1966, 4, 328–332.

In the second of two experiments reported, Mach IV was used. Subjects (56 George Peabody female undergraduates) were run in a variant of a Prisoner's Dilemma game, but one in which on one of the first two choices the subject was told that the other player would know her choice after it was made. Before the second choice, she was not informed as to the choice made by the second player. Payoffs in real or imaginary dollars were randomized for the two choices.

The respondents were classified as Trusting ($n = 22$), Distrusting ($n = 14$), and Other ($n = 30$), on the basis of their sequence of choices. No significant relationship with Mach IV was found.

REFERENCES

Adorno, T. W., Frenkel-Brunswick, E., Levinson, D. J., & Sanford, R. N. *The authoritarian personality.* New York: Harper, 1950.

Allinsmith, W. Moral standards: II. Learning of moral standards. In D. R. Miller & G. E. Swanson (Eds.), *Inner conflict and defense.* New York: Holt, 1960.

Allport, G. W., & Vernon, P. E. *A study of values.* Boston: Houghton, 1931.

Almond, G. A. *The appeals of communism.* Princeton, N. J.: Princeton University Press, 1954.

Astin, A. W. An empirical characterization of higher educational institutions. *Journal of Educational Psychology,* 1962, 53, 224–235.

Astin, A.W. Unpublished manuscript, ADI Document No. 7262, 1962.

Astin, A.W. *Who goes where to college?* Chicago: Science Research Associates, 1964.

Avorn, J. L. *Up against the ivy wall.* New York: Atheneum, 1968.

Back, K. W. Influence through social communication. *Journal of Abnormal and Social Psychology,* 1951, 46, 9–23.

Beckett, S. *Waiting for Godot.* New York: Grove Press, 1954.

Berne, E. *Games people play; the psychology of human relations.* New York: Grove Press, 1964.

Blake, R. R., & Mouton, Jane S. Personality. *Annual Review of Psychology,* 1959, 10, 203–232.

Block, J. *The Q-Sort-Method in personality assessment and psychiatric research.* Springfield, Ill.: Thomas, 1961.

Blumstein, P. W., & Weinstein, E. A. The redress of distributive injustice. *American Journal of Sociology,* 1969, 74, 408–418.

Bogart, Karen. Machiavellianism and individual differences in response to cognitive dissonance. Unpublished doctoral dissertation, New York University, 1968.

Bond, J. R., & Vinacke, W. E. Coalitions in mixed-sex triads. *Sociometry,* 1961, 24, 61–75.

Borgatta, E. F., Couch, A. S., & Bales, R. F. Some findings relevant to the great man theory of leadership. *American Sociological Review,* 1954, 19, 755–759.

Brackman, J. The put-on. *The New Yorker,* June 24, 1967, 34–73.

Braginsky, Dorothea D. Machiavellianism and manipulative interpersonal behavior in children: Two explorative studies. Unpublished doctoral dissertation, University of Connecticut, 1966.

Brehm, J. W., & Cohen, A. R. *Explorations in cognitive dissonance.* New York: Wiley, 1962.

Brown, D. M. *The white umbrella.* Berkeley: University of California Press, 1953.

Buber, M. *I and thou.* New York: Scribners, 1958.

Budner, S. Intolerance of ambiguity as a personality variable. *Journal of Personality,* 1962, 30, 29–50.

Campisi, P. J. A scale for the measurement of acculturation. Unpublished doctoral dissertation, University of Chicago, 1947.

Caplow, T. A theory of coalitions in the triad. *American Sociological Review,* 1956, 21, 489–493.

Caplow, T. Further developments of a theory of coalitions in the triad. *American Journal of Sociology,* 1959, 64, 488–493.

Caplow, T. *Two against one: Coalitions in triads.* Englewood Cliffs, N.J.: Prentice-Hall, 1968.

Cartwright, D., & Zander, A. (Eds.) *Group dynamics,* (2nd ed.) Evanston, Ill.: Row, Peterson, 1960.

Cattell, R.B. On the theory of group learning. *Psychological Bulletin,* 1953, 50, 27–52.

Chaney, Marilyn V., & Vinacke, W. E. Achievement and nurturance in triads varying in power distribution. *Journal of Abnormal and Social Psychology,* 1960, 60, 175–181.

Christie, R. Review of H. J. Eysenck, *The psychology of politics. American Journal of Psychology*, 1955, 68, 702–704.

Christie, R. Eysenck's treatment of the personality of communists. *Psychological Bulletin*, 1956, 53, 411–430. (a)

Christie, R. Some abuses of psychology. *Psychological Bulletin*, 1956, 53, 439–451. (b)

Christie, R., & Budnitzky, S. A short forced-choice anxiety scale. *Journal of Consulting Psychology*, 1957, 21, 501.

Christie, R., Friedman, Lucy, & Ross, Alice. The new left and its ideology: An exploratory study. *Proceedings of the 77th Convention of the American Psychological Association*, 1969, 4, 299–300.

Christie, R., & Geis, Florence. Some consequences of taking Machiavelli seriously. In E. F. Borgotta & W. W. Lambert (Eds.), *Handbook of personality theory and research*. Chicago: Rand McNally, 1968.

Christie, R., Havel, Joan, & Seidenberg, B. Is the F-scale irreversible? *Journal of Abnormal and Social Psychology*, 1958, 56, 143–159.

Christie, R., & Jahoda, Marie. *Studies in the scope and method of "the Authoritarian Personality."* Glencoe, Ill.: Free Press, 1954.

Christie, R., & Lindauer, Florence. Personality structure. *Annual Review of Psychology*. 1963, 14, 201–230.

Christie, R., & Merton, R. K. Procedures for the sociological study of the values climate of medical schools. In Helen H. Gee & R. J. Glaser (Eds.), *The ecology of the medical student*. Evanston, Ill.: American Association of Medical Colleges, 1958.

Church, J. *Language and the discovery of reality*. New York: Vintage, 1966.

Cline, V. B., & Richards, J. M. Accuracy of interpersonal perception—a general trait? *Journal of Abnormal and Social Psychology*, 1960, 60, 1–7.

Comrey, A. L. Group performance in a manual dexterity task. *Journal of Applied Psychology*, 1953, 37, 207–210.

Couch, A. S., & Keniston, K. Yeasayers and naysayers: Agreeing response set as a personality variable. *Journal of Abnormal and Social Psychology*, 1960, 60. 151–174.

Cronbach, L. J. Response sets and test validity. *Educational and Psychological Measurement*. 1946, 6, 475–494.

Cronbach, L. J. Further evidence on response sets and test design. *Educational and Psychological Measurement*, 1950, 10, 3–31.

Cronbach, L. J. Processes affecting scores on "understanding of others" and "assumed similarity." *Psychological Bulletin*, 1955, 52, 177–193.

Crowne, D. P., & Marlowe, D. A new scale of social desirability independent of psychopathology. *Journal of Consulting Psychology*, 1960, 24, 349–354.

Crowne, D. P., & Strickland, Bonnie R. The conditioning of verbal behavior as a function of the need for social approval. *Journal of Abnormal and Social Psychology*, 1961, 63, 395–401.

Danielian, J. Analysis of person perception, physical perceptual style, and selected personality variables. Unpublished doctoral dissertation, Columbia University, 1964.

Daniels, V. Communication, incentive, and structural variables in interpersonal exchange and negotiation. *Journal of Experimental Social Psychology*, 1967, 3, 47–74.

de Miguel, A. Social correlates of Machiavellianism: The Spanish students. Mimeographed paper, 1964.

Draguns, J. G. Connotations of several levels of stimulus ambiguity: A study by means of the semantic differential. Paper presented at the annual meeting of the Eastern Psychological Association, New York, April 1966. (Duplicated, Research Institute of Life Sciences, Worcester State Hospital, Worcester, Massachusetts, 1966.)

Duncan, D. B. Multiple range and multiple F tests. *Biometrics*, 1955, 11, 1–42.

Durkin, J.E. Groups in loops: a study of social behavior process in team performance tasks. Unpublished doctoral dissertation. Rutgers — the State University, 1966.

Durkin, J. E. Empathic orientation in physical encounters. Paper presented at the annual meeting of the Eastern Psychological Association, Boston, April 1967. (a)

Durkin, J. E. Moment of truth encounters in prisoners' dilemma. Paper presented at the meeting of the American Psychological Association, Washington, D. C., September 1967. (b)

Durkin, J. E. Dyadic permeability in a non-cognitive interpersonal reaction time task. Paper presented at the meeting of the American Psychological Association, San Francisco, September 1968.

Duyvendak, J. J. L. (Transl.) *Kung-san Yang. The book of Lord Shang.* Chicago: University of Chicago Press, 1928.

Edelstein, Rivcka. Risk-taking, age, sex, and Machiavellianism. Unpublished manuscript, New York University, 1966.

Edwards, A. L. *The social desirability variable in personality assessment and research.* New York: Dryden Press, 1957.

Epstein, Gilda F. Machiavelli and the devil's advocate. *Journal of Personality and Social Psychology,* 1969, 11, 38–41.

Etzioni, A. *A comparative analysis of complex organizations,* New York: Free Press of Glencoe, 1961.

Evans, G. Effect of unilateral promise and value of rewards upon cooperation and trust. *Journal of Abnormal and Social Psychology,* 1964. 69, 587 – 590.

Exline, R. V. Explorations in the process of person perception: Visual interaction in relation to competition, sex and need for affiliation. *Journal of Personality,* 1963, 31, 1–20.

Exline, R.V. & Eldridge, C. Effects of two patterns of a speaker's visual behavior upon the perception of the authenticity of his verbal message. Paper read at Eastern Psychological Association Meetings, Boston, Mass., April 6-8, 1967.

Exline, R.V., Gray, D., & Schuette, Dorothy. Visual behavior in a dyad as affected by interview content and sex of respondent. *Journal of Personality and Social Psychology,* 1965, 1, 201-209.

Exline, R. V., & Winters, L. Affective relations and mutual glances in dyads. In S. Tomkins & C. Izzard (Eds.), *Affect, cognition and personality.* New York: Springer, 1965. Pp. 319–350.

Eysenck, H. J. *The psychology of politics.* London: Routledge & Kegan Paul, 1954.

Feiler, J. Machiavellianism, dissonance, and attitude change. Unpublished manuscript, New York University, 1967.

Festinger, L. *A theory of cognitive dissonance.* Evanston, Ill.: Row, Peterson, 1957.

French, J. R. P., & Raven, B. The bases of social power. In D. Cartwright and A. Zander (Eds.), *Group dynamics,* (2nd Ed.) New York: Harper & Row, 1960, Pp. 607 – 623.

Gallo, P. S., & McClintock, C. G. Cooperative and competitive behavior in a mixed motive game. *Journal of Conflict Resolution,* 1965, 9, 68–78.

Gamson, W. A. A theory of coalition formation. *American Sociological Review,* 1961, 26, 373–382. (a)

Gamson, W. A. An experimental test of a theory of coalition formation. *American Sociological Review,* 1961, 26, 565–573. (b)

Geis, Florence L. Machiavellianism and success in a three-person game. Unpublished doctoral dissertation, Columbia University, 1964. (a)

Geis, Florence L. Machiavellian and the manipulation of one's fellow man. Symposium presented at the annual meeting of the American Psychological Association, Los Angeles, September 1964. (b)

Geis, Florence L. Machiavellianism in a semireal world. *Proceedings of the 76th Annual Convention of the American Psychological Association,* 1968, 3, 407–408.

Geis, Florence L. Two ways of being with others—cognitive vs. empathic relations. Round table discussion presented at the annual meeting of the American Psychological Association, Washington, September, 1969.

Geis, Florence, L., Bogart, Karen, & Levy, Marguerite. No dissonance for Machiavellians? Paper presented at the annual meeting of the Eastern Psychological Association, Boston, April, 1967.

Geis, Florence L., & Christie, R. Machiavellianism and tactics of manipulation. Symposium address at the annual meeting of the American Psychological Association, Chicago, September, 1965.

Geis, Florence L., Krupat, E., & Berger, D. Taking over in group discussion. Unpublished manuscript, New York University, 1965.

Geis, Florence L., & Leventhal, Ellen. Attempting to deceive and detecting deception. Unpublished manuscript, New York University, 1966.

Geis, Florence L., Levy, Marguerite, & Weinheimer, S. The eye of the beholder. Paper presented at the annual meeting of the Eastern Psychological Association, New York, April, 1966.

Geis, Florence L., Weinheimer, S., & Berger, D. Playing legislature: Machiavellianism in log-rolling. Paper presented at the annual meeting of the American Psychological Association, New York, September, 1966.

Goffman, E. *The presentation of self in everyday life.* Garden City, N. Y.: Doubleday, 1959.

Goffman, E. Fun in Games. *Encounters: Two studies in the sociology of interaction.* Indianapolis, Ind.: Bobbs-Merrill, 1961. Pp. 17–81.

Grant, Joanne. *Confrontation on campus.* New York: New Directions, 1969.

Guilford, J. P. Intelligence: 1965 model. *American Psychologist,* 1966, 21, 11–20.

Gustafson, L.A., & Orne, M.T. Effects of heightened motivation on the detection of deception. *Journal of Applied Psychology,* 1963, 47, 408–411.

Guterman, S.S. Moral character and social milieu: A social psychological study. Unpublished doctoral dissertation, Columbia University, 1967.

Harris, T.M. Machiavellianism, judgement, independence and attitudes toward teammate in a cooperative judgement task. Unpublished doctoral dissertation, Columbia University, 1966.

Hartshorne, H., & May, M.A. *Studies on the nature of character.* New York: Macmillan, 1928–1930, 3 vols.

Hastorf, A.H., Richardson, S.A., & Dornbusch, S.M. The problem of relevance in the study of person perception. In R. Tagiuri & L. Petrullo (Eds.) *Person perception and interpersonal behavior.* Stanford, Calif.: Stanford University Press, 1958.

Heineman, C. E. A forced-choice form of the Taylor Anxiety Scale. *Journal of Consulting Psychology,* 1953, 17, 447–454.

Hoffer, E. *The true believer.* New York: Harper & Row, 1951.

Hornstein, H. A., & Deutsch, M. Tendencies to compete and to attack as a function of inspection, incentive, and available alternatives. *Journal of Personality and Social Psychology,* 1967, 5, 311–318.

Janis, I., & Gilmore, J. The influence of incentive conditions on the success of role playing in modifying attitudes. *Journal of Personality and Social Psychology,* 1965, 1, 17–27.

Jensen, D. L. (Ed.) *Machiavelli: Cynic, patriot, or political scientist?* Boston: Heath, 1960.

Jones, E. E. *Ingratiation.* New York: Appleton-Century Crofts, 1964.

Jones, E. E., & Daugherty, B. N. Political orientation and the perceptual effects of an anticipated interaction. *Journal of Abnormal and Social Psychology,* 1959, 59, 340–349.

Jones, E. E., Davis, K. E., & Gergen, K. J. Role playing variations and their informational value for person perception. *Journal of Abnormal and Social Psychology,* 1961, 63, 302–310.

Jones, E. E., Gergen, K. J., & Davis, K. E. Some determinants of reactions to being approved or disapproved as a person. *Psychological Monographs,* 1962, 76, (No. 2, Whole No. 521).

Jordan, N. Behavioral forces that are a function of attitudes and cognitive organization. *Human Relations,* 1953, 6, 273–287.

Kelley, H. H., & Arrowood, A. J. Coalitions in the triad: Critique and experiment. *Sociometry,* 1960, 23, 231–244.

Kelman, H. C. Processes of opinion change. *Public Opinion Quarterly,* 1961, 25, 57–78.

Klinger, E. Fantasy need achievement motivation as a motivational construct. *Psychological Bulletin,* 1966, 66, 291–308.

Kogan, N., & Wallach, M. A. *Risk taking: A study in cognition and personality.* New York: Holt, 1964.

Kosa, J. The role of some personality factors in the selection of field in medicine: A study in the F and M scales. Mimeographed, University of North Carolina, 1961.

Lake, D. L. Impression formation, Machiavellianism, and interpersonal bargaining. Unpublished doctoral dissertation, Teachers College, Columbia University, 1967.

Langmuir, I. Science, common sense and decency. *Science,* 1943, 97, 1–7.

Lasswell, H. The selective effect of personality on political participation. In R. Christie & Marie Jahoda (Eds.), *Studies in the scope and method of "The authoritarian personality,"* New York: Free Press, 1954.

Lazarsfeld, P. F., Berelson, B., & Gaudet, Hazel. *The people's choice.* New York: Duell, Sloan, & Pearce, 1944.

Lazarsfeld, P. F., & Thielens, W., Jr. *The academic mind: Social scientists in a time of crisis.* Glencoe, Ill.: Free Press, 1958.

Lerner, D. The Nazi elite. *Hoover Institute Studies. Series B: Elite Studies,* 1951, No. 3.

Lowe, P.M. Some social determinants of two-person non-zero-sum games. Unpublished honors thesis, Harvard University, 1966.

Lubell, S. *Today's college student is a credit to American life.* New York: United Feature Syndicate, April, 1966.

Luce, R. D., & Raiffa, H. *Games and decisions: Introduction and critical survey.* New York: Wiley, 1957.

Machiavelli, N. *The prince. The discourses.* New York: Modern Library, 1940.

Magorah, M. The second cybernetics: Deviation-amplifying mutual causal systems. *American Scientist,* 1963, 51, 164–180.

Marks, E., & Lindsay, C. A. Machiavellian attitudes: Some measurement and behavioral considerations. *Sociometry,* 1966, 29, 228–236.

Marlowe, D. Need for social approval and the operant conditioning of meaningful verbal behavior. *Journal of Consulting Psychology,* 1962, 26, 79–83.

Marlowe, D., & Crowne, D. P. Social desirability and response to perceived situational demands. *Journal of Consulting Psychology,* 1961, 25, 109–115.

Marlowe, D., Gergen, K. J., & Doob, A. N. Opponent's personality, expectation of social interaction and interpersonal bargaining. *Journal of Personality and Social Psychology,* 1966, 3, 206–213.

Marwell, G., & Schmitt, D. R. , Dimensions of compliance gaining behavior: An empirical test. Mimeographed, University of Wisconsin, 1966.

McClelland, D. C., Clark, R. A., Roby, T. B., & Atkinson, J. W. The projective expression of needs. IV: The effect of the need for achievement on thematic apperception. *Journal of Experimental Psychology,* 1949, 39, 242–255.

McGuire, W. J. Cognitive consistency and attitude change. *Journal of Abnormal and Social Psychology,* 1960, 60, 345–353.

Mead, G. H. *Mind, self, and society.* Chicago: University of Chicago Press, 1934.

Melvin, D. An experimental and statistical study of two primary social attitudes. Unpublished doctoral dissertation, University of London, 1955.

Metze, R. Unpublished manuscript, 1967.

Milbrath, L.W. *The Washington lobbyist.* Chicago: Rand McNally, 1963.

Minas, J. S., Scodel, A., Marlowe, D., & Rawson, H. Some descriptive aspects of two-person non-zero-sum games. II. *Journal of Conflict Resolution,* 1960, 4, 193–197.

Nachamie, Susan. Machiavellianism in children: The children's Mach scale and the bluffing game. Unpublished doctoral dissertation, Columbia University, 1969.

Newcomb, T. M. Persistence and regression of changed attitudes: Long-range studies. *Journal of Social Issues,* 1963, 19, 3–14.

North, R. C. Kuomintang and Chinese communist elites. *Hoover Institute Studies. Series B: Elite Studies,* 1952, No. 8.

Novielli, J. Who persuades whom. Unpublished master's thesis, University of Delaware, 1968.

Oksenberg, Lois. Machiavellianism and emotionality. Unpublished master's essay, Columbia University, 1964.

Oksenberg, Lois. Machiavellianism in traditional and westernized Chinese students. Unpublished manuscript, Columbia University, 1967.

Oksenberg, Lois. Machiavellianism and organization in five-man task-oriented groups. Unpublished doctoral dissertation, Columbia University, 1968.

Orne, M. T. On the social psychology of the psychological experiment: With particular reference to demand characteristics and their implications. *American Psychologist,* 1962, 17, 776–783.

Parsons, T. On the concept of influence. *Public Opinion Quarterly,* 1963, 27, 37–62.

Potter, S. *The theory and practice of gamesmanship: Or the art of winning games without actually cheating.* New York: Holt, 1948.

Ranson, J. C. Survey of literature. *Two gentlemen in bonds.* New York: Knopf, 1927.

Rapoport, A. *Fights, games, and debates.* Ann Arbor, Mich.: University of Michigan Press, 1960.

Rapoport, A., & Orwant, C. Experimental games: A review. *Behavioral Science,* 1962, 7, 1–37.

Richardson, L. F. *Arms and insecurity; mathematical study of the causes and origins of war.* Pittsburgh: Boxwood Press, 1960.

Rim, Y. Machiavellianism and decisions involving risks. *British Journal of Social and Clinical Psychology,* 1966, 5, 50–36.

Roberts, A., & Rokeach, M. Anomie, authoritarianism and prejudice: A replication. *American Journal of Sociology,* 1956, 61, 355–358.

Roby, T. B., & Lanzetta, J. A study of an "assembly" effect in small group task performance. *Journal of Social Psychology,* 1961, 53, 53 – 68.

Rosenberg, S., Erlick, D., & Berkowitz, L. Some effects of varying combinations of group members on group performance measures and leadership behaviors. *Journal of Abnormal and Social Psychology,* 1955, 51, 227–236.

Rosenthal, R. Experimenter outcome-orientation of the results of the psychological experiment. *Psychological Bulletin,* 1964, 61, 405–412.

Rotter, J. B. Generalized expectancies for internal versus external control of reinforcement. *Psychological Monographs,* 1966, 80 (No. 1, Whole No. 609), 1–28.

Runkel, P., Keith-Smith, J., & Newcomb, T. A. Estimating interaction effects among overlapping pairs. *Psychological Bulletin,* 1957, 54, 152 – 159.

Schueller, G. E. The Politburo. *Hoover Institute Studies. Series B: Elite Studies,* 1951, No. 2.

Schutz, W. C. *Joy.* New York: Grove Press, 1967.

Scodel, A., Minas, J. S., Ratoosh, P., & Lipetz, M. Some descriptive aspects of two-person, non-zero-sum games. *Journal of Conflict Resolution,* 1959, 3, 114–119.

Seeman, M. Social learning theory and the theory of mass society. Paper read at the annual meetings of the American Sociological Society, Los Angeles, 1963.

Shamasastry, R. (Transl.) Kautilya's *Arthaśastra.* Mysore: Wesleyan Mission Press, 1909.

Shears, Loyda M. The effect of variation in power pattern on alliance formation in male tetrads. *American Psychologist,* 1962, 17, 335. (Abstract)

Shils, E. A. Authoritarianism: "Right" and "Left." In R. Christie & Marie Jahoda (Eds.), *Studies in the scope and method of "The authoritarian personality."* Glencoe, Ill.: Free Press, 1954.

Shure, G.H., Rogers, M.S., Larsen, I.M., & Tassone, J. Group planning and task effectiveness. *Sociometry,* 1962, 25, 263–282.

Siegel, Saul. The relationship of hostility to authoritarianism. *Journal of Abnormal and Social Psychology,* 1956, 52, 368–372.

Siegel, Sidney. *Nonparametric statistics for the behavioral sciences.* New York: McGraw Hill, 1956.

Simmel, G. Sociology of the senses: Visual interaction. In R. E. Park & E. W. Burgess (Eds.), *Introduction to the science of sociology.* Chicago: University of Chicago Press, 1921.

Simmel, G. *The sociology of George Simmel.* (Translated and edited by K. H. Wolff.) Glencoe, Ill.: Free Press, 1950.

Singer, J. E. The use of manipulative strategies: Machiavellianism and attractiveness. *Sociometry,* 1964, 27, 128–150.

Skinner, B. F. *Science and human behavior.* New York: Macmillan, 1953.

Smith, E. E. The power of dissonance techniques to change attitudes. *Public Opinion Quarterly,* 1961, 25, 626–639.

Spranger, E. *Types of men; the psychology and ethics of personality.* (Authorized translation of the fifth German edition by P. J. Pigors.) Halle (Saale): M. Niemeyer, 1928.

Srole, L. Social integration and certain corollaries: An exploratory study. *American Sociological Review,* 1956, 21, 709–716.

Stagner, R. Fascist attitudes: An exploratory study. *Journal of Social Psychology,* 1936, 7, 309–319.

Steiner, I. D., & Spaulding, Jaqueline. Preference for balanced situations. Report No. 1, Department of Psychology, University of Illinois, 1966.

Stewart, Naomi. Methodological investigation of the forced-choice technique, utilizing the officer description and the officer evaluation blanks. AGO, Personnel Research Section, Report No. 701, July, 1945.

Strodtbeck, F. S. Family interaction, values, and achievement. In D. C. McClelland, A. L. Baldwin, U. Bronfenbrenner, & F. L. Strodtbeck (Eds.), *Talent and society.* New York: Van Nostrand, 1958.

Stryker, S., & Psathas, G. Research on coalitions in the triad; findings, problems and strategy. *Sociometry,* 1960, 23, 217–230.

Taft, R. The ability to judge people. *Psychological Bulletin,* 1955, 52, 1–21.

Taylor, Janet A. The relationship of anxiety to conditioned eyelid response. *Journal of Experimental Psychology,* 1951, 41, 81–92.

Thibaut, J. W., & Kelley, H. H. *The social psychology of groups.* New York: Wiley, 1959.

Thornton, C. C. The resolution of disagreements in dyads. Unpublished doctoral dissertation, University of Delaware, 1967.

Tomkins, S. *Affect, imagery, consciousness.* Vol. II. New York: Springer, 1963.

Vejio, C. K., & Wrightsman, L. S., Jr. Ethnic-group differences in the relationship of trusting attitudes to cooperative behavior. *Psychological Reports,* 1967, 20, 563–571.

Vinacke, W. E., & Arkoff, A. An experimental study of coalitions in the triad. *American Sociological Review,* 1957, 22, 406–414.

Wahlin, W. S. Machiavellianism and winning or losing mathematical games. Unpublished doctoral dissertation, Columbia University, 1967.

Wallach, M.A., & Kogan, N. Sex differences and judgment processes. *Journal of Personality,* 1959, 27, 555–564.

Webster, J. The white devil. 1612. In F. L. Lucas (Ed.), *The complete works of John Webster.* London: Chatto & Windus, 1927.

Weinberg, C. The growth of conscience. In I. Iscoe & H. Stevenson (Eds.), *Personality development in children*. Austin, Texas: University of Texas Press, 1960.

Weinstein, E. A., & Deutschberger, P. Some dimensions of altercasting. *Sociometry*, 1963, 26, 454–466.

Weinstein, E. A. Identities and interpersonal control. Symposium address presented at the annual meeting of the American Psychological Association, Chicago, September, 1965. Mimeographed, State University of New York at Stony Brook, 1965.

Weinstein, E. A., Beckhouse, L. S., Blumstein, P. W., & Stein, R. B. Interpersonal strategies under conditions of gain or loss. *Journal of Personality*, 1968, 36, 616–634.

Weinstock S. A. Some factors that retard or accelerate the rate of acculturation—with specific reference to Hungarian immigrants. *Human Relations*, 1964, 17, 312–340.

Werner, H. *The comparative psychology of mental development*. (rev. ed.) Chicago: Follet, 1948.

Wert, J. E., Neidt, C. O., & Ahmann, J. S. *Statistical methods in educational and psychological research*. New York: Appleton-Century-Crofts, 1954.

Whyte, W. J. *The organization man*. New York: Simon & Schuster, 1956.

Witkin, H. A. Individual differences in ease of perception of embedded figures. *Journal of Personality*, 1950, 19, 1–15.

Wrightsman, L. S., Jr. Measurement of philosophies of human nature. *Psychological Reports*, 1964, 14, 743–751.

Wrightsman, L. S., Jr. Personality and attitudinal correlates of trusting and trustworthy behaviors in a two-person game. *Journal of Personality and Social Psychology*, 1966, 4, 328–332.

Wrightsman, L. S., Jr., & Baker, Norma J. Where have all the idealistic imperturbable freshmen gone? *Proceedings of the 77th Convention of the American Psychological Association*, 1969, 4, 293–294.

Wrightsman, L. S., Jr. & Cook, S. W. Factor analysis and attitude change. *Peabody Papers in Human Development*, 1965, 3, No. 2.

Wrightsman, L. S., Jr., Radloff, R. W., Horton, D. L., & Mecherikoff, M. Authoritarian attitudes and presidential voting preferences. *Psychological Reports*, 1961, 8, 43–46.

Zajonc, R. B. Social facilitation. *Science*, 1965. 149, 269–274.

Zimbardo, P. G. Involvement and communication discrepancy as determinants of opinion conformity. *Journal of Abnormal and Social Psychology*, 1960, 60, 86–94.

Zimbardo, P. G. (Ed.) *The cognitive control of motivation*. Chicago: Scott, Foresman, 1969.

Zimbardo, P. G., Weisenberg, M., Firestone, I., & Levy, B. Communicator effectiveness in producing public conformity and private attitude change. In P. G. Zimbardo (Ed.), *The cognitive control of motivation*. Chicago: Scott, Foresman, 1969.

AUTHOR INDEX

Numbers in italics show the page on which the complete reference is listed.

SUBJECT INDEX